International commissions and the power of ideas

International commissions and the power of ideas

Edited by Ramesh Thakur, Andrew F. Cooper and John English

United Nations University Press
TOKYO • NEW YORK • PARIS

Academic Foundation
New Delhi

This edition is published in India in 2006

by : ACADEMIC FOUNDATION
4772-73 / 23 Bharat Ram Road, (23 Ansari Road),
Darya Ganj, New Delhi - 110 002 (India).
Phones : 23245001 / 02 / 03 / 04.
Fax : +91-11-23245005.
E-mail : academic@vsnl.com
www.academicfoundation.com

First published in 2005 by the United Nations University Press,
The United Nations University, 53-70 Jingumae 5-chome, Shibuya-ku,
Tokyo 150-8925.
(ISBN 92-808-1110-X)

International Commissions and the Power of Ideas
Edited by Ramesh Thakur, Andrew F. Cooper and John English

ISBN 81-7188-499-7
(South Asian Edition)

Printed and bound in India.

Contents

Abbreviations vii

Foreword by Gareth Evans x

Acknowledgements xiii

1 International commissions and the mind of global governance 1
Andrew F. Cooper and John English

2 The Brandt Commission: The end of an era in North–South politics 27
Jean-Phillipe Thérien

3 The Palme Commission: New thinking about security 46
Geoffrey Wiseman

4 The World Commission on Environment and Development: Ideas and institutions intersect 76
Heather A. Smith

5 Equivocating on the future of world order: The Commission on Global Governance 99
W. Andy Knight

6 Regulating the possession and use of nuclear weapons: Ideas, commissions, and agency in international security politics – the case of the Canberra Commission 123
Marianne Hanson

7 Beyond temples and tombs: Towards effective governance for sustainable development through the World Commission on Dams 142
Sanjeev Khagram

8 Fair assessment: The Independent International Commission on Kosovo 167
Richard J. Goldstone and Nicole Fritz

9 Intervention, sovereignty, and the responsibility to protect 180
Ramesh Thakur

10 The responsibility to protect: Assessing the report of the International Commission on Intervention and State Sovereignty 198
Jennifer Welsh, Carolin J. Thielking, and S. Neil MacFarlane

11 The responsibility to protect: Humanitarian intervention and the principle of non-intervention in the Americas 221
Jorge Heine

12 Ideas, institutions, and the evolution of women's human rights 246
Elizabeth Riddell-Dixon

13 Ideas, think-tanks, commissions, and global politics 266
Jon Pedersen

14 UN Reform Commissions: Is anyone listening? 277
Edward C. Luck

Appendix: International Commission on Weapons of Mass Destruction 288
Ambassador Jayantha Dhanapala

Contributors 295

Index 300

Abbreviations

ARF	ASEAN Regional Forum
ASEAN	Association of Southeast Asian Nations
ASEAN+3	ASEAN plus Three (China, Japan and South Korea)
AusAID	Australian Agency for International Development
BCR	Brandt Commission Research agency
BWC	Biological Weapons Convention
CBMs	confidence-building measures
CD	Conference on Disarmament
CFE	Conventional Forces in Europe
COPRI	Copenhagen Peace Research Institute (formerly Copenhagen Centre for Peace and Conflict Research)
CSCAP	Council for Security and Cooperation in the Asia-Pacific
CTBT	Comprehensive Test Ban Treaty
CTBTO	Comprehensive Nuclear-Test Ban Treaty Organization (PrepCom – Preparatory Committee)
CWC	Chemical Weapons Convention
DID	Development International Desjardins (Canada)
DSM	Dispute Settlement Mechanism
EAC	Economic Commission for Africa
ECOSOC	Economic and Social Council (of the UN)
ENGOs	environmental non-governmental organizations
ESCAP	Economic and Social Commission for the Asia–Pacific Region
EU	European Union
Fafo	Institute for Applied Social Science (Norway)
G-77	Group of Seventy-Seven (developing countries)

GATT	General Agreement on Tariffs and Trade
GIC	good international citizenship
GLCs	government-linked companies
GNP	gross national product
HEU	highly enriched uranium
HI	Humanitarian Intervention
IAEA	International Atomic Energy Agency
ICC	International Chamber of Commerce
ICISS	International Commission on Intervention and State Sovereignty
ICOLD	International Commission on Large Dams
ICRC	International Committee of the Red Cross
IDPs	Internally Displaced Persons
IGOs	International government organizations/Intergovernmental organizations
ILO	International Labour Organization (of the UN)
IMEMO	Institute of the World Economy and International Relations (Russia)
IMF	International Monetary Fund
INF	intermediate-range nuclear forces
INGOs	international non-governmental organizations
INTERFET	International Force for East Timor
IOs	international organizations
IUCN	International Union for the Conservation of Nature
NAFTA	North American Free Trade Agreement
NAM	Non-Aligned Movement
NATO	North Atlantic Treaty Organization
NGOs	non-governmental organizations
NICs	newly industrializing countries
NPT	Non Proliferation Treaty
NPTREC	Nuclear Non-Proliferation Treaty Review and Extension Conference
NSAs	non-state actors
NTB	non-tariff barriers
NWFZs	nuclear-weapon-free zones
NWS	nuclear weapon states
OAS	Organization of American States
OAU	Organization of African Unity
OECD	Organisation for Economic Co-operation and Development
OPCW	Organisation for the Prohibition of Chemical Weapons
OSCE	Organization for Security and Cooperation in Europe
PMEAs	"People of Middle Eastern Aspect"
PRIO	Peace Research Institute of Oslo
R&D	research and development
SAARC	South Asian Association for Regional Cooperation
SADC	Southern African Development Community
SAL	structural adjustment loan

SAP	social action programme
SDI	Strategic Defence Initiative (US)
SIPRI	Stockholm International Peace Research Institute
SPD	Social Democratic Party (Germany)
START	Strategic Arms Reduction Treaty
TINGOs	temporary international non-governmental organizations
UNA-USA	United Nations Association of the USA
UNCED	United Nations Conference on Environment and Development (1992)
UNCHE	United Nations Conference on the Human Environment
UNCTAD	United Nations Conference on Trade and Development
UNDP	United Nations Development Programme
UNEP	United Nations Environment Programme
UNGA	United Nations General Assembly
UNHCR	United Nations High Commissioner for Refugees
UNICEF	United Nations Children's Fund
UNSSOD	United Nations Special Session on Disarmament
UNWSSD	United Nations World Summit for Sustainable Development
WB	World Bank
WCD	World Conference on Dams/World Commission on Dams
IUCN	World Conservation Union
WCED	World Commission on Environment and Development
WHO	World Health Organization
WMD	weapons of mass destruction
WPI	wholesale price index
WSSD	World Summit on Social Development
WTO	World Trade Organization
WWF	World Wildlife Fund

Foreword

The role that international or independent commissions have played in linking ideas and institutions has not received the attention it merits. The names of many of the key commissions, often best remembered by the individuals who headed them – Brandt, Palme, Brundtland, Carlsson/Ramphal, for example – continue to be recognized. But the impact of commissions – what they have achieved, and how they have done it, both individually and collectively – has been too often neglected.

My own experience has convinced me that commissions have legacies that can influence debate and events long after the commissioners have dispersed and their report has been published. That seems to me the case with the Canberra Commission on the Elimination of Nuclear Weapons, which I had a role in creating when I was Australian Foreign Minister. The centrepiece of its findings, the simple mantra that "so long as other countries have nuclear weapons others will want them; so long as anyone has them they are bound one day to be used, by accident or design; and that any such use will be catastrophic" is one that is still quoted, and richly deserves to be internationally embraced. It was certainly the case with the Carnegie Commission on Preventing Deadly Conflict, chaired by David Hamburg and Cyrus Vance, of which I was a member, and which perhaps did more than anyone else to create among government policy makers and international organizations what we now acknowledge to be (at least when it comes to lip-service: substance always takes longer!) a "culture of conflict prevention".

And I hope it is the case with the International Commission on Intervention and State Sovereignty (ICISS), which I co-chaired with Mohamed Sahnoun, which – in the context of the "humanitarian intervention" debates that coursed throughout the 1990s, and are with us now again – sought to find common ground between antagonists by reconceptualizing "the right to intervene" in altogether different, and potentially more acceptable, terms as "the responsibility to protect". Our hope was that this would prove to be the most useful such exercise since the Brundtland Commission, with its introduction of the idea of "sustainable development", gave environmentalists and developers not only a new vocabulary but, more importantly, a common new meeting ground.

History teaches us that ideas are the seeds of controversy. What are principled beliefs for some are self-interest or unacceptable agendas for others. Careless or oversimplified blending of religious or cultural values with political ideas and actions can create a dangerous brew, one that poisons relations between states and peoples: Huntington's "clash of civilizations" has, sadly, become much more than an interesting academic theory. But, employed constructively, ideas can and do act as beacons for shaping the world and its governance in better ways. And institutions in turn can be both the passageway and the testing ground for putting the mind of global governance into practice.

The institutions that continue to matter most, not necessarily in directly generating ideas, but in encouraging others to do so, recognizing their salience and translating them into action, are national governments. Middle powers – Australia, Canada, the Scandinavians – have been particularly important players in this respect: perhaps on the principle that relative lack of military and economic clout can be made up for by real competitiveness in the ideas market, where what matters most are imagination, creativity and energy. The Canberra Commission initiative, for example, as Marianne Hanson rightly suggests, belongs in the context of a broader set of ideas prevailing in Australia (at least at the time: all these things are subject to the vagaries of domestic politics!) around the theme of good international citizenship. The Cambodian peace initiative, the agreement on mining in the Antarctic which we campaigned for, and the Chemical Weapons Convention which we brought to conclusion were all cross-fertilizing reflections of that broader perspective.

All that said, ideas – and commissions to produce them – are not always there when they are needed. In his fine essay, UN Under-Secretary-General for Disarmament Affairs Jayantha Dhanapala calls for an international commission to consider the problem of weapons of mass destruction. How helpful such a commission report would have been in picking up where the Canberra Commission left off, and cutting across some of the extraordinarily confused debate of recent times on that subject. And of course ideas and commission reports don't always get the attention they deserve from those who should most be paying that attention.

But one of the great values of this book, deriving from a conference sponsored by the United Nations University and the University of Waterloo in Canada that brought together scholars and practitioners from all continents and with diverse backgrounds, is that it is an argument against pessimism. Like John Maynard Keynes' "defunct economist", a commission's influence and imprint long survives its formal death. Ideas at the wayside can be rediscovered and take their place at the centre of political debate.

The essays here clearly map what is needed for lasting effect. A commission is most effective when its work reflects a distribution of labour among representatives from different quadrants of the world: a major criticism of many commissions (well avoided in the case of ICISS) has been their Northern or Western-centric membership and orientation. There must be outreach to governments and, increasingly, non-governmental organizations. Commissions cannot succeed unless they draw upon the rich body of research and literature that exists today. And their job is not done when the report is written. There must be renewal of commitment by those who first committed, continued demonstration of the intellectual integrity of the commission's work, and a willingness to apply the energy to see the task through.

Commissions and commissioners may sketch the road ahead in each case, but it is for states and intergovernmental organizations and their leaders to travel it. Getting them moving – showing them why and how they have to act, and stimulating and exciting and encouraging them to do so – is what commissions are all about. And it's a continuing responsibility of members of commissions who have had something to say and believe passionately in its continuing relevance, to stay the course – guiding them through the forks and diversions, and doing everything possible to stimulate them when they lag. It may take a long time to reach journey's end, but if the goal is worth it the fatigue and the frustration are eminently bearable. That is perhaps one of the underlying messages of this book, and it's a very important one.

Gareth Evans
President and CEO, International Crisis Group

Acknowledgements

This edited collection is a testament to the power of ideas in reshaping global governance. However, it also underpins the salience of institutions as conduits or receptors for ideas. This is certainly true in the international arena where a wide variety of organizational structures act to stimulate the agency of new ways of thinking and operating in the global arena. But such a nexus between ideas and institutions is equally relevant – and commendable – in terms of academic or research facilities.

In the case of this book a number of organizations deserve recognition for their support of this project. In doing so they have demonstrated that they take International Commissions – and the ideas promoted through them – seriously on an individual and collective basis. And that they had faith that the cast of talented contributors to this volume could capture the essence of those Commissions in a sophisticated and reflective, albeit not uncritical fashion.

As on other projects the editors wish to acknowledge the United Nations University – and especially The Rector, Professor Hans Van Ginkel – for its generous support of this research programme. The Canadian Department of Foreign Affairs and International Trade (DFAIT) provided additional support for the conference in Waterloo, Ontario, where many of the contributions were originally rehearsed. At that conference we were privileged furthermore to hear presentations by a number of other prominent individuals. These included: Paul Heinbecker, the former Canadian Ambassador to the United Nations (and now a Senior

Fellow at the Centre of International Governance Innovation); Eduardo Stein Barillas, the former Guatemalan Foreign Minister (and current Vice-President of Guatemala); Thomas Weiss, the Director of the Ralph Bunche Institute for International Studies and one of the major contributors to the United Nations Intellectual History Project; Don Hubert, a policy analyst at DFAIT and, with Professor Weiss, a key contributor to the research for the International Commission on Intervention and State Sovereignty; Ernie Regehr, the Executive Director for Project Ploughshares in Waterloo; Elizabeth Dowdeswell, a Visiting Professor at the University of Toronto and the former Executive Director of the United Nations Environment Program (UNEP); Susanne Soederberg, then a Professor of Political Science at the University of Alberta; and Professor Brian Orend, from the Department of Philosophy, at the University of Waterloo.

The editors wish to thank *Security Dialogue*, vol. 33 no. 3 (September 2002) for granting permission to reprint in slightly modified form the chapter by Ramesh Thakur. We also wish to express our appreciation to the Social Sciences and Humanities Research Council of Canada for providing financial support for several of the individual contributors.

In Waterloo we wish to thank our staff both at the Centre for Foreign Policy and Federalism and our new research institution, the Centre for International Governance Innovation: Lena Yost, Jen Beckermann, Matthew Bunch, Jason Churchill, and Ryan Touhey. Andrew Schrumm provided a first-rate job of research assistance. Andrew Thompson deserves much of the credit for getting the manuscript ready for publication, as he managed the process with great acumen and resolution throughout its many stages.

The University of Waterloo helped this project in a number of ways. We are grateful in particular to President David Johnston, Dean of Arts Robert Kerton, and colleagues in the Departments of Political Science and History.

The final thanks – once again – are to the people associated with the United Nations University Press. This includes the reviewers, the Publication Officer, Scott McQuade, the editor, Gareth Johnston, and the copy-editor, Mary Warren.

1

International commissions and the mind of global governance

Andrew F. Cooper and John English

The structure – or body – of world politics has become an established object of close scrutiny. This is especially true with respect to the pillars of global governance, involving both the current ordering and a possible reform of the architectural composition and procedural makeup. As one recent book notes: "In nearly every study of global governance, international organizations loom large in the analysis and are often characterized as the building blocks for establishing a new global system".[1]

What may be termed the mind of global governance by contrast has suffered from comparative neglect. Only recently have the power of ideas been taken seriously as a form of agency in international relations. And even amidst this marked shift to embrace the "ideational turn"[2] there is still much analytical ground to catch up on so as to be able to capture this dynamic more accurately as it has been played out in specific domains of activity.

This book explores the power of ideas, as transmitted via the mind of global governance, through the focused lens of international or independent commissions. An awareness of the salience of commissions on a selective or one-off basis has long existed among both global policy makers and attentive publics. Indeed the names of these commissions – Brandt, Palme, Brundtland, the Commission on Global Governance, and the International Commission on Intervention and State Sovereignty (ICISS), to list just the best known ones – have taken on an enormous recognition factor around the world. Yet, as both an interconnected process shaping global governance and/or as a component of the wider ideational turn – the nature of international commissions remains under-analysed. The specific character – and level of impact – of each of the commissions merits study of their own, as witnessed by the pivotal position individual case studies of key selected commissions are placed in this collection. To understand the phenomenon of international commissions more completely, however, not only their content, track records, and controversies on an individual basis but their generalized context must be explored and appreciated. Before moving into what makes each of these commissions unique, therefore, a more systematic treatment is attempted with a focus on how this collective set of instruments fits into the larger ideational turn and what repertoire range can be found among them.

Setting the boundaries

What stands out about the role of ideas through the entire span of post-1945 international relations is their bounded condition. Ideas were given some ample legitimacy to operate in terms of shaping or re-shaping the national mind especially within the industrialized countries. As rehearsed in an influential article by Anthony King in the early 1970s – which highlighted the need to view ideas as "a necessary condition" for explaining public policy[3] – an awareness of the importance of ideas as a determinant of national political and policy cultures became a strong theme in the academic literature.

This is not to suggest that under rare and compelling exigencies "national" ideas could escape from under these disciplines. The transnational flow and influence of Keynesian economics stands out as the obvious illustration (as does the backlash to this current of thought via monetarism).[4] These escapes were the exceptions, nevertheless, that proved the rule. As captured well by John Ruggie – notwithstanding the dominance of the United States (US) – the structure of "embedded liberalism" emergent in the post-1945 world order was not crafted according to one universal script.[5] National cultures and modes of policy-making remained crucial in differentiating this pattern along differentiated country-specific lines concerning approaches to the welfare state, industrial strategy and a wide variety of other policy issue areas.

The hegemony of realist thinking in the academic culture of international relations reinforced these well-defined parameters. What mattered under this mantra was positioning in the global hierarchy and structural power. As underscored by Ngaire Woods, ideational factors – or indeed other considerations that deviated from an understanding of world politics based firmly on power relations and interests of state – were simply "left out".[6]

When directly challenged this realist establishment (either in its classic or neo-formulations) marginalized or rebuffed alternative belief systems or world-views. Intellectually, practitioners/scholars such as Robert Cox could voice different opinions, to the effect that "In the final analysis, our world is ruled by ideas – rational and ethical – and not by vested interests".[7] But this perspective remained at the edges of scholarly discourse through the 1980s.

From a policy perspective the reaction was even harsher. The prime illustration of this disciplinary impulse in action came with the mobilization of the South through the creation of a New World Order. Instead of situating the debate on normative grounds, as suggested by Cox, this challenge was countered by an exclusive focus on the interest-based nature of these claims that the South was acting as a trade union of developing countries directed towards a redistribution of power within the global hierarchy. The wealth of ideas emanating from the South could thus be dismissed as ideological gloss or self-help advocacy.[8]

Breaking out ideas

The movement towards an ideational turn in international relations went hand in hand with the erosion of discipline associated with the end of the Cold War and the accelerated forces of globalization not only in the sphere of markets but of principles, communication, and information, together with the flow of people and culture.

Some of the best-known intellectual entrepreneurs have cloaked this process of novel and unanticipated change in structuralized baggage; most notably Fukuyama's thesis about the convergence of values.[9] For most observers, though, the hallmark of this new era has been the privileging of fragmentation and competition whereby space for thinking as well as action has been created and struggled over.

The difficulties of achieving consensus on the rules and form of global governance in this environment should not be downplayed. Escape from control in ideational terms has brought with it abundant concerns, and even fears, about emergent and acrimonious global divides and disorders centred around the putative clash of civilization, tensions between a sense of resurgent ultra-nationalism or tribalism and transnationalism, and the shape and merits of democratic practices.

Still the unevenness and dichotomies located in this trajectory should not be used to hide the advantages of possessing these opened global windows for the promotion of innovative projects with respect to the architecture of global governance. If ideas popped up and grappled with through often jagged and contradictory manifestations, this process offered important insights about the importance of agency. How actors think across the terrain of international relations – as much as what they do – mattered with the rupture of the tightly disciplined world featured with bipolarity and the Cold War.

Academic currents were swept along by the impetus of these changes. The interdependence school moved some way to embrace the ideational factor. Joseph Nye popularized the concept of "soft power" as a reaction to the limitations of the "hard" security agenda of structural realism.[10] Robert Keohane co-edited an influential book on ideas and foreign policy.[11] Both works opened the way forward by adding ideas to the mix of analytical models for the study of mainstream international relations. The first balanced the traditional emphasis on power – even for the US hegemon – with a regard for normative values. The latter provided an elaborate mapping exercise with respect to how ideas affected policy outcomes within a variety of discrete cases.

If deserving credit for bending the hold of the dominant academic model, nonetheless, this approach did not break the structuralist grip. The bias remained fixed on a rationalistic take on international relations, where actors took positions because of calculations vis-à-vis their own self-interest. Ideas were explicitly linked to instrumental gains – the reduction of transaction costs and other material benefits – as opposed to the assumption that ideas reflect expressions of social forces or pressures to think – as one sophisticated collection puts it – "ahead of the curve".[12]

The decisive push towards the ideational turn came with the challenge of the constructivist school. In its thickest versions this literature – while abundant in theory about the import of ideas in the social construction of identity and interest formation and pointing towards a future "where things do not have to be done as they have in the past"[13] – is pitched at too abstract a level to allow it to be of much use in the way of practical applicability for empirically driven research. The outstanding exception to this criticism has been the contribution of John Ruggie. Conceptually, Ruggie's embrace of ideational factors – not only ideas per se but cultural and normative influences more generally – provided this interpretation of international relations with enormous credibility. After he stated that he endorsed the view that the "building blocks of international reality are ideational as well as material; that they express not only individual but also collective intentionality ... and that the meaning and significance of ideational factors are not independent of time and place",[14] the traditional bias towards structure could no longer completely trump an allowance for agency.

Moreover, the temporal conditions of this endorsement – as Ruggie took on the role of Assistant Secretary-General of the United Nations – forged the crucial link between the swirl of intellectual currents and the pursuit of practical policies directed towards reshaping global governance. As Ruggie relates this experience: "it quickly became apparent that creative leadership in international organizations is social constructivism in action ... [the] project of international organization is all about how to stretch states' interests and preferences ... so as to produce in greater quantities the collective goods that the political marketplace of interstate behaviour otherwise under-produces. Ideational factors are an absolutely critical means by which this stretching is achieved".[15]

The channelling and the purpose of ideas

In trying to map out more carefully the interaction between ideas as intellectual constructs and as sources of inspiration for the application of policy prescriptions, the location of this process along two axes serves as a valuable starting point. One axis of this framework projects the means by which ideas – reflective of the mind of global governance – are channelled or circulated. The major formal component of this activity hinges on diplomatic mechanisms. This view of diplomacy as transmission belt or switchboard for the ideational turn, it must be stated, goes against the commonplace assumption that diplomacy acts as the defender of the status quo, warding off the influence of any new thinking that would shake things up in global affairs. As one critic has stigmatized this response: "Most diplomatic services have responded to the changing international context by burying their heads in the sand".[16]

Yet as more nuanced observers detect, diplomatic method has demonstrated some enormous capacity for facilitating as well as resisting change. As the critics infer, this adaptive quality is not necessarily driven by an espousal of novel ideas for their own sake. Rather this response may be animated more often than not for organizational advantage and/or the demands of situational exigencies. As Kal Holsti persuasively suggests, contemporary diplomacy in a variety of negotiating arenas puts a tremendous onus not only on "persuasion, but with creating and systematizing new knowledge, enunciating general principles, and 'educating' those who do not have all the relevant knowledge surrounding a problem".[17]

The evolving complexity in the sites and actorness of diplomacy also drives this component of the ideational turn. New ideas could quite easily have been ignored or blocked by foreign ministry officials when they possessed a near monopoly over the diplomatic process. In an age of blurring responsibilities among different government departments, and between state and societal actors, this avoidance approach was much more difficult.

One fascinating feature of the International Commissions under review is how often and through such diverse means diplomacy makes an appearance. Jean-Philippe Thérien, in examining the Independent Commission on International Development Issues (or Brandt Commission), talks of "development diplomacy" in the context of North–South relations. Geoffrey Wiseman, in his chapter on the Independent Commission on Disarmament and Security Issues (or Palme Commission), refers to "multipolar two-track diplomacy". With regard to her exploration of the World Commission on Environment and Development (or Brundtland Commission), Heather Smith details the technical aspects of "environmental diplomacy". In each case, although much of the diplomatic dynamic is state-oriented, there is increased space available for non-state actors to influence the stretching of the mind of global governance. Other contributors reinforce this image. Andy Knight embellishes the notion of commissions – in his case the Commission on Global Governance – as being on the intersect between old and new multilateral diplomacy.

Other contributors, while cognizant of the potential diplomacy possesses as a motor for the ideational turn, are also fully aware of the many obstacles and pitfalls putting a brake on this dynamic. Marianne Hanson puts some considerable emphasis on not only the opportunities but the operational problems placed in the way of "the search for diplomatic influence" as exemplified in the case of the Canberra Commission on the Elimination of Nuclear Weapons. Sanjeev Khagram highlights the split between the state-centrism of established practices and the expression of the "maverick" international experiment as promoted through the World Commission on Dams. The entire project of the Commission on Kosovo, as laid out by Richard Goldstone and Nicole Fritz, was underpinned by the failures of traditional modes of diplomacy in the prevention of severe violations of international human rights or the substantial suffering of civilian society. As well rehearsed by Ramesh Thakur, the report of the International Commission on Intervention and State Sovereignty was designed to reconcile a push for a new diplomacy – grounded on the concept of the responsibility to protect – with a full appreciation of the exigencies of "political realism". In their parallel examination of the ICISS, Jennifer Welsh, Carolin Thielking, and Neil MacFarlane focus, among other themes, on the question of finding the "right authority" for international activity and the constraints on diplomatic practice – including its vocabulary. Jorge Heine is careful to add history as a limitation, with the legacy of "gunboat diplomacy" shaping the Latin American regional view on any form of intervention.

The other axis animates the purpose for which ideas are promoted. At one end of the scale lay projects with a high degree of ambition with regard to good international citizenship, punctuated by a desire to stretch the mind of global governance as far as the diplomatic processes will allow. The emphasis is on a transformative ethos with ideas in the service of a normative design, usually through an expanded form of international architecture. At the other end, an onus is placed not on an overarching vision but on problem-solving in particular issue areas. Ideas through this lens have less of a heroic bias – with big ideas capturing attention in an immediate and robust fashion through high profile and diplomatically risky gestures. Rather the best ideas – and the means to sell them – are taken to be incremental and routine in nature, whereby they are applied in a low-key de-politicized and incremental fashion.

It is tempting to use this dichotomous approach to position the different commissions in either one category or the other. Hewson and Sinclair, most notably, divide some selected projects along these lines: "there is one striking difference in tone between the earlier global reform reports and the global governance report. The earlier reports had focused on solving a particular problem facing the world. The global governance report is more concerned with conveying the argument that pervasive global changes have altered the terrain on which global problem solving was to take place".[18]

On the basis of scope – and intensity – there is a good deal of validity to this form of labelling. Among other things, it brings out the degree to which a mesh exists between means and ends when located in these terms. Given the diffuse pattern found in formal diplomacy, the definition of actorness is usefully supplemented by the inclusion of informal networks. Some of these networks showcase problem-solving techniques, as illustrated by what are commonly called epistemic communities[19] or knowledge-oriented communities of experts.[20] Others, by way of contrast, exist as transnational advocacy networks operating with both a will (and often a capacity) to shape-shift existing ways of thinking and doing things.[21]

Yet, even with these merits, these divisions should not be drawn too starkly. The typology of networks often becomes blurred when scrutinized closely. Some of the best-known transnational advocacy networks have taken on the attributes of problem-solvers, as witnessed most explicitly through the actions of the anti-apartheid movement.[22] Nor – as Anne-Marie Slaughter illustrates clearly in the case of legal experts – can networks dominated by professional specialists be disassociated from normative considerations attached to a redesign of global governance.[23]

This complexity in the pattern of networks is confirmed in a number of thematic chapters added to this collection. Elizabeth Riddell-Dixon not only denotes the extensive campaign pursued by women's rights advocates through vast networks, she showcases the manner by which this network gained input into the negotiating process through the UN system. Jon Pedersen suggests specific ways that networks of researchers can have an impact on policy decisions and outcomes, as demonstrated by the activities of Fafo, a Norwegian think tank on the Middle East peace process in the early 1990s. Although much of this effort was directed at technical problem solving on specific projects on the ground, a distinctive advocacy component is retained as well. Edward Luck, in his excellent (if sobering) review of the workings UN Reform Commissions, hones in the need to address – or straddle – both sides of the problem-solving/advocacy divide, with equal attention devoted to both vision and practical proposals. In his call for an International Commission on Weapons of Mass Destruction – a call which in retrospect proved a harbinger for the recently announced initiative by Sweden for a Commission on Weapons of Mass Destruction chaired by Hans Blix – Jayantha Dhanapala insists on the need for a focused diplomatic effort that taps into the on-going efforts of a variety of actors with established reputations.

Timing and individual/collective source of agency

Delving deeper into the questions of how international commissions can contribute to the stretching of the mind of global governance, two additional themes require some elaboration. The first privileges the importance of timing. As in any other ideational manifestation, one basic ingredient for success of international commissions was simply the availability (or not) of an opportunity in terms of temporal conditions – or put another way, the degree of ripeness by which these projects were met. The reports of some commissions – regardless of the value of the ideas contained in them – simply ran up against closed inhospitable conditions. As Thérien details, it would be hard to imagine a more hostile ideological/political environment for the 1980 Brandt report to navigate for its notions of a grand social pact between North and South, with the end of détente and ascendancy of the new vigorous wave of neo-conservatism. The ideas flowing from this commission could be portrayed by its supporters as both attractive and necessary for the international community. But the immediate policy impact fell flat because of the poor timing of its initial release. When it was released in 1982, amidst the so-called second Cold War, the Palme report appeared to suffer a similar fate. In an atmosphere of renewed confrontation and arms-racing between the superpowers, its call for security – with, not against, the adversary – received little in the way of instant traction.

Other commissions were the recipients not of blockage but a boost because of the system-change produced with the collapse of the Soviet Union and bipolarity. As stressed by Smith, the 1987 Brundtland Commission constituted a classic case where "timing matters" in a positive sense. Instead of being stymied because of the tight grip of the Cold War this Commission had the good fortune of catching the wave when the disciples of that old order were crumbling. The 1996 Canberra Commission could exploit the same systemic opening in terms of the end of the Cold War bilateral paradigm. Both of these Commissions enjoyed as well a number of additional situational windows of opportunity for the pursuit of their agenda, whether in the case of the Brundtland Commission because of changing attitudes to the environment and the redefinition of security or in the case of the Canberra Commission, a programme based on complete nuclear disarmament.

Notwithstanding these supportive cases, it is misleading to put all of the commissions in such a temporal straightjacket. The context of the report of the Commission on Global Governance in 1995 reflected a much greater tendency towards ambiguity. As pointed out by Andy Knight in *Our Global Neighbourhood*, could still take advantage of the thawing of the Cold War. But these opportunities were countered by a range of competing tendencies which accented new forms of vulnerability, most notably the forces of accelerated globalization and the rise of different types of security threats. Even in cases such as the Canberra Commission openings at both the international and domestic levels could be contested and faced with closure.

Equally, however, the fate of some of the best-known Commissions could take U-turns in the other more positive direction. The most tangible case of this sort – as comprehensively portrayed by Wiseman – centres on the delayed impact of the Palme Commission. Despite directly hitting the wall of Cold War politics on its publication, after some period of mutation and re-channelling the core ideas of the Commission have been embraced in various influential strains of discourse and some areas of policy-making about security both at the multilateral and regional levels.

This fragility in terms of the receptive conditions and fortunes for International Commissions was, if anything, even more exaggerated in recent cases. As acknowledged by Goldstone and Fritz, a major contextual danger in the aftermath of the release of the Kosovo Commission report was the manner by which the formulating of its principles risked being distorted to justify the interventions in Afghanistan and Iraq. Consistent with their wider argument, such logic was unjustified as it confused humanitarian intervention with self-defence. The ICISS faced a similar challenge head-on subsequent to the release of its report shortly after September 11th, 2001. To the credit of the Commission the report resisted shifting its mandate – making explicit in Thakur's words that "self-defence is conceptually and operationally distinct from the protection of at-risk foreign populations". As in the case of the Palme Commission (albeit with a much shorter time-line), there appears to be opportunities as well as vulnerabilities positioned in these situational circumstances. If critical about some of the arguments and implications of the ICISS, the chapter by Welsh and her co-authors remains open about the constructive impact of the Commission. While acknowledging the very different – and far more intense – challenge that the ICISS report faces because of the reassertion of a hard security agenda in this post-post Cold War era, they also posit the claim that "an alternative reading … suggests a greater relevance for the ICISS and its view of sovereignty in a post-September 11 world".

The second prominent theme concerns the relationship between individual and collective agency as the platform for ideas. Some of the best-known commissions do bear the imprint of key personalities. This individualistic bias goes back to the origin of international commissions – with the branding of the Commission on International Development in 1969 as the "Pearson" report.[24] On the foundational "big three" commissions – Brandt, Palme, and Brundtland – a tendency exists whereby each is labelled via the name of their Chair. All of the commissions under review constituted impressive exercises where moral authority or normative leadership was exerted on an individual basis in world politics.

Yet this type of personal identification contributes to some misleading stereotypes about the commissions. Arguably the most ingrained of these inaccurate images is that of commissions as an exclusive home for retired and/or defeated politicians. Although it is true that some of the best-known commissioners fall into this category (starting with Lester Pearson, the former Prime Minister of Canada and Willy Brandt, the ex-Chancellor of West Germany), others belie this depiction. The example that stands out is that of Dr. Gro Harlem Brundtland, who was the Prime Minister of Norway when she agreed to take on the chair of the World Commission on Environment and Development. But a much longer list may be accumulated when smaller and lesser-known commissions largely outside of the purview of this book are added to the mix. These include in 2002 the "Globalization Debate of Prime Minister Guy Verhofstadt – the Belgian Initiative"; and The World Commission on the Social Dimension of Globalization (ILO Commission) co-chaired by the Presidents of Finland and Tanzania.[25]

Nor, it should be added, is personal identification – or the lending of a prized reputation – a requisite for a well-known image. Commissions such as the Commission on Global Governance, Kosovo, ICISS, or even Big Dams have established a strong and sustained mental brand without becoming attached to one individual in the manner of the earlier wave of commissions. From this perspective the instinct to simply portray commissions as objects promoted and controlled by one pivotal actor needs to be severely modified. A more accurate understanding of the role and salience of international commissions is only possible when this activity is analysed in a wider context. Consistent with their own belief systems and will, individuals retain the capacity to act as high profile and significant carriers of ideas through their work as commissioners. A full awareness of the impressive design of these projects shines through, however, only when they are treated as illustrations of a form of collective agency able to pursue a shared sense of the mental map or common vision concerning the shape of global governance.

Casting commissions as an expression of a social dynamic or force has, it must be stated, risks imparting some negative connotations. As opposed to being viewed as ad hoc exercises, international commissions become tagged as series of exercises driven by a global managerial class. Alternatively, though, a shift to appreciate this process of reproduction is far more cognizant of both collective memory and the capacity for the passage of knowledge as well as innovation through the entire life cycle of Commissions. If fitting into what both Andy Knight and Ed Luck term "blue ribbon panels", the commissions deserve recognition for their talent to think and propel action "ahead of the curve", encompassing ideas that were both unorthodox and transformative.

In individual terms, the myriad of connections between the commissions is striking. Robert McNamara not only took the lead in initiating the Pearson and the Brandt Commissions but served as a member of the Canberra Commission. Willy Brandt, a decade after chairing the Independent Commission on International Development Issues, convened a meeting with Ingvar Carlsson (the former Prime Minister of Sweden) and Shridath Ramphal (the then Commonwealth Secretary-General, later, in turn, a member of the Brundtland Commission) which led to the creation of the Commission on Global Governance. Olof Palme took an active role on the Brandt Commission before chairing the Independent Commission on Disarmament and Security Issues. Dr. Brundtland served as a Commissioner on the Palme Commission before moving to chair the World Commission on Environment and Development. Gareth Evans, the former Australian foreign minister, was a member of the Canberra Commission before becoming the co-chair of ICISS. Wiseman adds the important point that Evans remained influenced through this process by the ideas of the Palme Commission. Moreover, as demonstrated by the appointment of Jayantha Dhanapala – a member of the Canberra Commission – to the newly formed Blix Commission on Weapons of Mass Destruction, this pattern has continued up to the present.[26]

In thematic terms, the links between many of the commissions are just as strong. A flavour of this common narrative and/or substantive cross-fertilization may be made by reference to the shared emphasis between the Pearson, Brandt and Palme Commissions on the "mutual interests" argument in the push for a restructuring of the international order. The idea for the allocation of 0.7 per cent of a developed country's GNP for development assistance passed from the Pearson to the Brandt Commission. Dr. Brundtland viewed her Commission as the third pillar after the Brandt and Palme Commissions. And, as elaborated by Khagram on the case of the World Commission on Dams, the thinking of the Brundtland Commission has continued to radiate out. The Commission on Global Governance pushed in a similar fashion to the Canberra Commission for the elimination of nuclear weapons. It also introduced the concept of "security of people" that later informed the Kosovo Commission and the ICISS in so rich a fashion.

Debating the "ownership" of commissions

Tilting the analysis to affirm the value of collective as well as individual agency rehearses a much larger debate about international commissions. For the question of "whose ideas" are dominant on an individual basis conflates into the more general question of systemic "ownership". In addressing this question, three distinctive lenses stand out as serviceable devices. The first lens surveys ownership through an institutional prism. One possible candidate for this type of ownership is the International Financial Institutions, especially the Bank for Reconstruction and Development or World Bank. Institutional support for International Commissions runs through the ambit of these projects. McNamara initiated both the Pearson and the Brandt Commissions during the time he was President of the World Bank from 1968 to 1981. Although without a personal imprint of this nature, funding from the World Bank was crucial for the establishment of the World Conference on Dams (WCD).

Where the connection between the commissions and the "Bretton Woods" establishment must be refined is in terms of impact. The construct of ownership lends itself to an image of control imposed through structural adjustment and other forms of discipline.[27] Yet, in the case of the International Commissions sponsored by the World Bank, little evidence can be found of support for such a restrictive agenda. The Brandt Commission explicitly flew in the face of the ascendant forces of neo-conservatism in the early 1980s with its emphasis on poverty reduction through a global Keynesian "new deal". In terms of process, as Khagram notes, one of the great concerns of the WCD was to maintain an autonomous stance with respect to the World Bank. And at least from the perspective of many critical observers within civil society, the recommendations of the WCD in specific areas such as water directly contravene the strategy favoured by the World Bank.[28]

The alternative choice for ownership is through the United Nations (UN) system. A wide variety of commissions tapped into the resources and possessed strong personal/ideational links with the UN. The Brandt report, *North–South: A Program for Survival*, was submitted to the UN's Secretary-General and, as Thérien stresses at the outset of his chapter, associated strongly with the "UN paradigm". The Palme Commission's report, *Common Security*, was presented both to the United Nations Special Session on Disarmament and the UN Conference on Disarmament. Raising the notch even further, the World Commission on Environment and Development had much of its membership appointed via the UN system. The Co-Chairs of the Commission on Global Governance met with the UN Secretary General to explain its objectives. As referred to by both Thakur and Welsh and her colleagues, Secretary-General Kofi Annan strongly supported the ideas promoted through the ICISS report.

As in the case of the Bretton Woods institutions, however, the influence sought or imposed by the UN system on international commissions should not be exaggerated. None of the commissions under review can be considered "in house" projects channelled through the UN system (as manifested, for example, by the Brahimi Report on UN Peace Operations). Even when the UN acted as a catalyst the commissions – and the commissioners – still enjoyed a high level of autonomy. As Smith denotes, arguably the most telling case in point was the manner Dr. Brundtland steered the World Commission on Environment and Development in a new and creative direction.

Nor did the high degree of generalized encouragement and legitimacy accorded international commissions through the UN translate into uniform measures of support for their recommendations on an individual basis. As Wiseman concludes, the Palme Commission received little in the way of follow-up through the UN system. In sharper fashion, the Goldstone and Fritz chapter signals the degree by which the Kosovo Commission sought to distance itself from the UN.

A second lens scrutinizes ownership through an ideological lens. The common assumption of the bulk of the academic literature on international commissions is that some of the most prominent of these projects fit comfortably into a liberal reformist framework. This view is especially pronounced in the Report of the Commission on Global Governance.

Knight takes this approach in his chapter, with eloquent backing from Richard Falk.[29] Higgott embellishes this point of view in saying that *Our Global Neighbourhood* offers "somewhat grander, although still essentially liberal [vision] of a rejuvenated system exhibited in the Commission on Global Governance's publication".[30]

As advanced through the ideas of other cases besides the Commission on Global Governance, there is much of a liberal flavour that shines through the entire range of these projects. Nonetheless, there is a compelling hybrid aspect that should not be ignored. With the liberal component can be detected as well a potent social democratic touch. This pedigree obviously goes hand in hand with the political credentials built up by the key figures chairing a good number of the commissions, Brandt, Palme, Brundtland, Ingvar Carlsson, and Gareth Evans. But it is also a reflection of the support given to these commissions by a host of other individuals and governments located on the social democratic side of West European politics, extending from the early support of Chancellor Bruno Kreisky of Austria by both the promotion of Brandt and Palme up to the initiation by the Social Democratic Prime Minister Goran Persson on the Kosovo Commission.

The dominance of and between these political strands can be contrasted, furthermore, with the exclusionary tendencies found in the international commissions towards both the far left and more conservative elements. The Palme Commission stands out as the exception tilting on one side as it included not only some prominent leftists but Georgi Arbatov from the Soviet Union. Edward Heath, the former Prime Minister of the United Kingdom, was a member of the Brandt Commission; he was on the short-list to be the chair of the World Commission on Environment and Development; and, with some other moderate conservatives, was involved at the start-up phase of the Commission on Global Governance. Beyond these intrusions, though, some strict ideological barriers took shape. There was no Soviet representation, for example, on the Brandt Commission. And there was a noticeable absence of any individual with neo-conservative credentials through the run of commissions. Consensus inside the commissions was often vividly contrasted, therefore, with strong and protracted criticism outside from both categories of outsiders.

The third and final lens examines ownership through a national prism. At first glance it is tempting to couple the project of international commissions with the prime role of the United States as international agenda-setter through the entire post-1945 era.[31] Yet, at odds with the notion of "soft power" tightening this grip via the globalization of rhetorical principles and policy networks, the US did not have an unchallenged hold on the workings of the commissions. Some US institutions, copying the vision of the McNamara-led World Bank, did push hard for a leadership role in these activities. The most significant of these initiatives was the Carnegie Commission on Preventing Deadly Conflict, led by Dr. David Hamburg and Cyrus Vance, Jimmy Carter's first Secretary of State. Rather than providing strength, however, this US-base appears to have become a liability.[32] It did not safeguard the Report from partisan criticism from conservative forces within the United States. Certainly, it did not guarantee international exposure on a global scale.

For the most part the United States – both in terms of state officials and American intellectuals – played below their policy weight on the International Commissions. Outside of McNamara no prominent American stood out in the workings of the Brandt Commission, a feature repeated in the context of the World Commission on Environment and Development. Cyrus Vance presaged his chairmanship of the Carnegie Commission by sitting on the Palme Commission, but as Wiseman convincingly demonstrates the main effect of the Common Security Report in the United States was felt well below the political surface. As Hanson relates, the Canberra Commission stands out as the anomaly with not only McNamara but a former Commander in Chief of US Strategic Command acting as Commissioners. The Kosovo Commission stretched out the mind of global governance with the inclusion of Richard Falk, and the political weight of the ICISS was buttressed by the presence of Lee Hamilton. Still, if valuable contributors, these latter choices confirm the outlier status of these Commissions in conservative American circles, a point that Luck reiterates in his conclusion.

The far more robust national ownership of the International Commissions belonged to the so-called middle powers. This mode of possession of course coincided with the support afforded a good many of these projects by Social Democratic politicians and political parties. In specific policy areas the cross-cutting nature of this backing comes out most forcefully in the case of the Brandt, Palme, and Brundtland Commissions that in effect extended the concept of the welfare state from the domestic to the international arena. Still, other commissions revealed distinctive characteristics that have become associated with middle powers whatever the political persuasion of its government. The activist middle power diplomacy – with its profession of good international citizenship – targeted at the Canberra Commission by Gareth Evans went well beyond the traditional style of Australian Labor governments. The Canadian contribution to commissions – showcased by Thakur and Welsh et al. in the case of the ICISS – was an extension of Liberal international going back to Lester Pearson and extending through to Lloyd Axworthy and his embrace of the concept of human security.

To parade this middle power effort is not to minimize the difficulties associated with it. The most obvious constraint remained the discrepancy between the profile of these countries on military/security and economic/social agenda items. There was also the problem that in some cases national ownership took on either a parochial/political dimension and/or showcased status-seeking attributes. The first made a difference when an initiative took on a partisan hue, as in the case of the Canberra Commission. With the Keating/Evans Australian Labor Party acting as the motor for the initiative, the incoming Howard Liberal government applied the brake. The latter dilemma became magnified by tensions on two distinctive fronts. The first centred on the contrasting styles among established middle powers.[33] The second encompassed the divergence between what may be called the "old" middle powers clustered almost exclusively in the North and "new" emerging powers located in the South.[34]

A more exclusive form of ownership for these emerging powers was championed in particular by the Prime Minister of Malaysia, Dr. Mahathir Bin Mohamad, leading to the establishment of the South Commission (1987–1990). Consistent with the overall pattern of participation this Commission contained a mix of high-profile elder statesman and up and coming policy/political actors. Julius Nyerere, the former President of Tanzania, served as the Commission's Chair. At the core of the staff as Secretary-General was Manmohan Singh, a well-respected professional economist, who much later in 2004 became Prime Minister of India. In its stylistic expression this Commission contained many attractive features, not only in terms of its attention to technical detail but its willingness to open up the process to a wider debate through an ancillary volume of commentaries. In substance, the Commission offered a sophisticated approach with a strong emphasis on both an integrated and people-centred development strategy.[35] But in terms of practical – and arguably even intellectual – bite, however, the Commission proved a disappointment. Although the release of the report, *Facing the Challenge*, was paralleled by a generally positive burst of publicity, the Commission had little staying power in the world of ideas and (particularly when set against the popular image retained by the Brandt Commission) is rarely cited. The core demands of the report – the need for an opening up of global markets to the products of developing countries in the face of continued protectionist regimes in the North – remain unsatisfied up to the present amidst the debate over the Doha Development Round of the World Trade Organization.

Resilient to this challenge the embedded repertoire of middle power agency continued to shine through the Commissions. Unlike bigger powers – both in the North and South – the diplomacy of middle powers acknowledged the need for bargaining and compromise even on the most sensitive issues dealing with sovereignty. Unlike more formidable (and muscle-bound) states, middle powers – and a variety of individuals operating in the middle power context – were prepared to devote substantive resources, persistence, and diplomatic acumen to the promotion of these new ideas through sites such as international commissions. Ideational prowess was instinctively substituted for structural power in the international arena. Important principles and operational agendas were brought to life through a mix of technical and entrepreneurial or coalition-oriented activity. This variation of mission-oriented activity is well shown off in the case of the Palme, Canberra, and ICISS Reports – under Swedish, Australian, and Canadian leadership respectively. But this willingness and capacity of middle powers to run with good ideas goes beyond these primary examples. South Africa exhibited many of the same middle power attributes in its support for the WCD. Norway, as made clear in the Pedersen chapter, was able to tap into the intellectual infrastructure and good will in driving forward with the Middle East peace process in the early 1990s. In other cases individual middle power leadership morphed into collective effort. Most explicitly, Hanson and Dhanapala have pointed to the role of the Canberra Commission in the emergence of the "New Agenda Coalition", a geographically diverse group of countries (Brazil, Egypt, Ireland, Mexico, New Zealand, South Africa and Sweden) rallying support for a joint declaration on "The Need for a New Agenda".[36]

The content and delivery of international commissions

The concern of this collection extends well beyond the context of international commissions to a treatment of their substantive content. Indeed it is this focus that informs the line of analysis of the core chapters devoted to specific commissions. While not wanting to enter into a detailed discussion either of the narrative or of the conclusions made by individual contributors in their distinctive essays, it seems a useful exercise to provide some thematic snapshots not only about what content was contained but how it was delivered – or sold – throughout the entire collection of commissions.

The first thematic snapshot concentrates on the scope of these commissions. In stark dualistic terms, international commissions can be divided into two categories. The first features those commissions that have centred their activities in specific issue-areas. The second clusters those commissions that cover a far more extensive terrain across the security, economic and social domains. In Raimo Vayrynen's classification of commissions on the basis of their definitions of security the Palme Commission represents the best illustration of a commission that falls into the discrete category, with a selective focus and compression into one specific theme. The essence of the Palme Commission was found in the concept of common security, "a political and military concept". Although Vayrynen acknowledged that "the report of the Palme Commission contained a chapter on its economic aspects", even the addition of this component supported rather than detracted from the overall sense of concentration in the report in that it focused almost entirely on the material costs of the nuclear arms race.[37] By way of contrast, the Commission on Global Governance fits the model of diffuseness, with an extensive coverage of issues and volition to take "a long leap towards expanding the notion of security".[38]

This framework serves as a convenient short cut for ordering the entire span of commissions. Putting the emphasis on the dichotomous nature of commissions, however, covers up the ideational cross-linkages that from the start lay at the heart of so many of the commissions. The Brandt Commission focused on peace as well as development, making an explicit linkage between disarmament and development. Much of the genius of the Brundtland report was its explicit recognition between security and the environment.

Even among the more recent commissions that appear on the surface to be highly specialized there exists an appreciation of the need for linkage. Standing beyond the ambit of this collection, the 2000–2001 Commission on Macroeconomics and Health, established by the World Health Organization (under the leadership of Dr. Brundtland, from her position as Director General), and chaired by Jeffrey Sachs, falls into this category in that its underlying premise of its agenda was to make the connections between investments in health, economic growth, and poverty reduction.[39] The Commission on Human Security (2001–2002), which was funded primarily by the Japanese government, arose out of the UN Millennium Summit in September 2000, and took on a similar complexity with its mandate to explore the interface between poverty, human rights, violence, and security. Among the cases showcased in this book, both the Kosovo Commission and the ICISS demonstrate the manner by which targeted projects wedge out in a wide – and often controversial – number of directions both conceptually and operationally (into the domain of international law and the shifting terms of debate about humanitarian intervention).

As a starting point, therefore, a separation on the basis of range of activity still serves some purpose if only to differentiate a commission such as the highly targeted WCD from the far more extensive Commission on Global Governance. Sparseness of analysis, however, must be complemented by a more nuanced treatment.

A second thematic snapshot extends this coverage to include the style adopted by these commissions. One important variable from this perspective is the level of intensity adopted by the Commission. Some commissions have attempted to sell their ideas through a short burst – or sometime a series of bursts – of activity. The Brandt Commission can be viewed as the classic illustration of this mode of activity, in which the selling of the report was tied closely to the reputation of Willy Brandt as an individual and the credibility of each of its documents, initially in 1980 the *North-South: A Program for Survival* and three years later, *Common Crisis. North-South: Co-operation for World Recovery*. The WCD self-consciously imposed a limited time on its activities. Other commissions, through an alternative course, have either been designed or have taken on, through different circumstances, a longer life span. The Palme Commission demonstrates the salience of a time lag, as it gained a new bounce after its main ideas were picked up and utilized by Mikhail Gorbachev. The ICISS – in a more strategical vein – represents a very different model whereby a push for an immediate impact was supplemented by a longer eye to the prize where ongoing pressure was applied through the turmoil of September 11th and the Iraq war.

A second variable is the target of the commissions' proposals. As on scope there is a predisposition towards dividing the commissions up between those that use insider techniques targeting both national governments and international organizations and those that have adopted a more comprehensive approach. Still, looking more closely at this group of projects, what stands out is their hybrid nature. All of the commissions under review sought some degree of access to decision-makers. One of the major recommendations of the first Brandt report was the convening of a state-centric conference, an event that took place in Cancún, Mexico, in 1981. Brundtland, in the words of Smith, "travelled the world and met state leaders promoting the idea of sustainable development". The ICISS continued to attract support from Secretary-General Annan and both Prime Ministers Jean Chrétien and Paul Martin of Canada. This form of targeting did not preclude an expansion of networking of these same Commissions with members of civil society. The Brandt Commission's work not only gave rise to the Brandt 21 Forum, but because of its proposal for forgiveness of sovereign debt came to act as a harbinger for a newer generation of activists. Brundtland and her commissioners (including Maurice Strong) balanced their contacts with state officials with meetings with civil society representatives. Moving beyond this "ad hocery", the ICISS built a large civil society component within the ongoing structure of its activities.

Again, however, these sketches raise far more questions than they answer. One issue in terms of process that must be raised concerns the actual nature of the participation of civil society in the commissions' work; and one question that rises out of Riddell-Dixon's chapter is the role of women on the Commissions. Several prominent women played crucial roles in these projects, starting with Dr. Brundtland and extending to the role of Jane Holl as Executive Director for the Carnegie Commission and Sadako Ogata as co-chair (with Amartya Sen) of the Commission on Human Security established in early 2001. But in most cases women were either highly under-represented or completely missing. The exceptions that stand out have been the WCD and the Kosovo Commission, both of which included a number of high profile women.

Another issue that raises similar sort of questions relates to a comparative assessment of business interests versus civil society in the work of the commissions. Knight relates how the agenda on the Global Compact became a core ingredient of the Commission on Global Governance. Just as sensitively, Khagram notes the difficult search for balance between business and civil society on the WCD.

The issue that stands out concerns the recipe for success in terms of delivery. Extending the discussion between both style and targeting, commissions straddle the choice between aiming for a platform based on a sharp slogan that creates an immediate impact or buzz, or a more complex message which takes longer to draw results. On this continuum it seems clear that buzz wins out over complexity. The most successful commissions are the ones that have their key phrase catch-on both with policy makers and the general public. This conclusion comes out strongly from the Brundtland Commission's ability to popularize the term "sustainable development". Equally, the coining – and continuous promotion – by the ICISS Commissioners of the term "responsibility to protect" also helps reveal why that project has been able to ride out the trauma associated with September 11.[40]

On the negative side of things, neither the presence of prominent individuals nor good research guarantees success. In the former category falls the State of the World Forum: The Commission on Globalization which, notwithstanding its energetic leadership by Jim Garrison and a star-studded line-up of supporters (albeit without a single national champion and an extremely ambitious mandate), apparently has not been able to sustain itself as an ongoing site for a global leadership network. The indicative case in the latter category is the Carnegie Commission, which despite a wealth of analytical reports and edited volumes, failed to catch-on notwithstanding its apparent timeliness post-Rwanda and Bosnia. The message of prevention was not enough to overcome the opposition of conservative forces in the US about the value of the report. Nor was it enough to generate any excitement at the level of civil society. As the ICISS has shown, solid research – based on an efficient secretariat and with both a creative and accessible roster of background papers – has to be teamed with other ingredients for popular momentum to build.

Nor in some cases does even the possession of an attractive catch-phrase create an immediate buzz. It took five years before the Palme Commission's phrase "Common Security" – dismissed along with the Brandt report by a leading Nordic policy-maker as lacking the ingredients "to translate the studies into a practical strategy for change" – took on significant meaning in international relations.[41] The centrepiece of the Commission on Global Governance – the notion of a "Global Neighbourhood" – fell flat in that it was seen as overly simplistic or unbelievable as a policy-related concept in a world arguably dominated more by conflict than cooperation. As Falk punctuates it: "The modern world transmits other, far more sinister, conceptions of neighborhood-gang struggles for exclusive control, inter-ethnic hostility, and class differentiation. Some of the worst instances of genocidal violence have been between those intimately linked by bonds of proximity and shared traditions, including language".[42]

This discussion connects in turn with the ultimate set of outcomes generated through the commissions. The most direct form of delivery is captured through the connection of the ideas promoted by the commissions with institutional reform. This ideational–institutional nexus emerges most explicitly and comprehensively in the impact of the Brundtland Commission as appraised not only by Smith but by a number of other contributors in this collection. On a smaller scale, though, this link stands out in a number of other cases as well. The Commission on Global Governance, while failing to advance many of the ambitious proposals (including global taxation, an Economic Security Council, and an end to the veto for the P-5 in the Security Council), did create intellectual space for the initiative on the International Criminal Court by its call for a new Court of Criminal Justice. The Palme Commission – as elaborated by Wiseman – morphed into Gorbachev's different construct, the Common European House.

More frequently commissions have facilitated and legitimated the extension of soft law or norm creation.[43] The Brundtland Commission had the overall effect of embedding the norm of environmentally sustainable development. The Commission on Global Governance popularized the concepts not only of global governance and the Global Compact but the notion of civil society. Kosovo promoted the concept of fairness. The ICISS refined the concept of human security found in a number of other commissions through the powerful idea of responsibility to protect. If a catchy slogan, it was also a crucial substantive ingredient for norm creation.

Moving the normative dimension to the hub of the debate at the same time exposed commissions to different and acute controversies. These rotated especially around the North–South relationship. In contrast to the self-selected middle powers, the countries of the South retained a strong residue of suspicion concerning international commissions. In some cases – most notably in the case of the Brandt report – these initiatives were viewed as a means of suffocating even more ambitious schemes of global restructuring through the New International Economic Order – that is to say, as a tool for preventing the ideational turn from stretching the body of global governance too far. In other cases of norm development – alternatively – the criticism was the reverse. In other words, that the mind and body was being stretched too far. As Heine details in the case of Latin America, this sensitivity was especially acute on the entire set of questions concerning sovereignty and non-intervention. Indeed, the contestation of new norms as a challenge to the legitimacy and identity of actors in the South lies at the heart of the challenge for international commissions. In the words of Samuel Makinda, the aspirations of commissions such as the one on Kosovo come up against the reality that: "most developing states would not endorse 'a principled framework for humanitarian intervention' because they would regard it as a threat to their sovereignty".[44]

These debates could be tempered by the introduction of a better balance in the North–South participation on the commissions. Moving away from the asymmetry of most of the earlier commissions where individual commissioners from developing countries were badly outnumbered, recent commissions have been characterized by a much greater sense of equality. This shift from exclusion to inclusion is a feature found in the composition held by those projects featured in this collection. It is also a pattern located in a variety of commissions outside its domain, including the Commission on Human Security, The World Commission on the Social Dimension of Globalization (ILO Commission) co-chaired by the presidents of Finland and Tanzania, together with the UN Commission on Private Sector and Development co-chaired by former Mexican president Ernesto Zedillo and Canadian Prime Minister Paul Martin.

The authentic test for International Commissions remains, nonetheless, to replicate equality of representation with substantive equity.[45] The key to the Brundtland Commission's success lay in finding a sense of balance between North and South. But it is not a recipe that is easily replicated. These sensitivities permeate the debate about the Kosovo Commission as well as the ICISS.[46] They also have intruded quite seriously into the activities of other commissions. To give just one additional illustration, the Tokyo Forum (one successor to the Canberra Commission) met resistance not only from the US but India as a result of the changing strategic landscape in the sub-continent in the late 1990s. It was reported that Jasjit Singh of India "did not attend the last two meetings and ... made it known that he disagreed strongly with the contents and tone of the report".[47]

Bringing in the mind of global governance

From this overview it is clear that international commissions deserve concerted attention as part of a matching scholarly re-balancing exercise. To a hitherto unacknowledged extent international commissions have been central to international agenda setting. Although this minding of global governance often produces ambiguous and uneven results, the sheer staying power of these projects is impressive. At odds with the impression of Falk and other observers that they would fade away commissions have proliferated.

As attested to by all of the contributors – and above all by Luck in his concluding chapter – the role of these commissions is full of challenges and obstacles. They expose many of the raw divides and high degree of fragmentation that exist in international politics. They reveal how good ideas can be distorted out of their original intent even if they are not completely immobilized in their challenge to the existing architecture – or body – of global governance.

Still, if problematic, the promise of international commissions also says a good deal about the margins open for imagination and innovation as ideas are brought in and played out in world affairs. Although far from sanguine about the measure or the nature of the eventual or decisive impact of this mode of agency, each of the chapters in this collection looks seriously at the power of ideas. The wealth of diversity found amidst this form of idea-generating mechanisms allows a novel and salient take on the socially textured world of international politics.[48] As this introduction has attempted to show, however, international commissions deserve study not only on their individual merits and for their extensive range of activities but on the basis of their collective contribution with respect to the world polity whereby the mind of global governance is scrutinized and re-evaluated as part of a wider ideational turn in international relations.

Notes

1. James P. Muldoon, Jr. (2003) *The Architecture of Global Governance; An Introduction to the Study of International Organizations*, Boulder, Co: Westview, p. 12.
2. Mark M. Blyth (1997) "Any more bright ideas? The ideational turn of comparative political economy", *Comparative Politics* 29(2) (January): 229.
3. Anthony King (1973) "Ideas, institutions and the policies of governments: A comparative analysis", Part III, *British Journal of Political Science* 3(3) (October): 423. For a sample of recent work on variations of this theme, see Dietmar Braun and Andreas Busch (1999) *Public Policy and Political Ideas*, Cheltenham, UK: Edward Elgar; John L. Campbell (1998) "Institutional Analysis and the role of ideas in political economy", *Theory and Society* 27(3): 377–409.

4. On these themes, see Peter Hall (ed.) (1989) *The Political Power of Economic Ideas: Keynesianism Across Nations*, Princeton, NJ: Princeton University Press.
5. John Gerard Ruggie (1982) "International Regimes, Transactions and Change: Embedded Liberalism in a Post War Economic Order", *International Organization* 36(2) (Spring): 379–415.
6. Ngaire Woods (1995) "Economic Ideas and International Relations: Beyond Rational Neglect", *International Studies Quarterly* 39(June): 164.
7. Robert W. Cox (1979) "Ideologies and the New International Economic Order: Reflections on some recent literature", *International Organization* 33(2) (Spring): 279.
8. For the best-known treatment along these lines, see Stephen Krasner (1985) *Structural Conflict; The Third World Against Global Liberalism*, Berkeley: University of California Press. For a more sympathetic view, see Craig N. Murphy (1984) *The Emergence of NIEO Ideology*, Boulder, CO: Westview.
9. Francis Fukuyama (1992) *The End of History and the Last Man*, New York: Free Press.
10. Joseph S. Nye, Jr. (2002) *The Paradox of American Power: Why the World's Only Superpower Can't go it Alone*, Oxford: Oxford University Press.
11. Judith Goldstein and Robert O. Keohane (eds.) (1993) *Ideas and Foreign Policy*, Ithaca, NY: Cornell University Press.
12. Louis Emmerij, Richard Jolly, and Thomas G. Weiss (2001) *Ahead of the Curve? UN Ideas and Global Challenges*, Bloomington: Indiana University Press.
13. Alexander Wendt (2001) "Driving with the Rearview Mirror: On the Rational Science of Institutional Design", *International Organization* 55(4) (Autumn): 1049. See also his *Social Theory of International Politics* (1999) Cambridge: Cambridge University Press.
14. John Gerard Ruggie (1998) "Introduction: What makes the world hang together? Neo-utilitarianism and the social constructivist challenge", *Constructing the World Polity: Essays on International Institutionalization*, London: Routledge, p. 33. On Ruggie's role in "nudging the course of the mainstream in some new directions", see Iver B. Neumann (1997) "Conclusion", in Iver B. Neumann and Ole Wæver, *The Future of International Relations: Masters in the Making?*, London: Routledge, p. 365.
15. Ibid, Preface, p. xii.
16. Shaun Riordan (2003) *The New Diplomacy*, Cambridge: Polity, p. 9.
17. K.J. Holsti (1992) *International Politics: A Framework for Analysis*, 6th edn., Englewood Cliffs, NJ: Prentice Hall, p. 144. For a more detailed analysis of these trends, see Brian Hocking (1999) "Catalytic diplomacy: Beyond 'newness' and 'decline'", in Jan Melissen (ed.) *Innovation in Diplomatic Practice*, London: Macmillan, pp. 21–42.
18. Martin Hewson and Timothy J. Sinclair (1999) *Approaches to Global Governance Theory*, Albany: State University of New York Press, pp. 13–14.
19. P.M. Haas (1992) "Introduction: Epistemic Communities and International Policy Coordination", *International Organization* 46(1) (Winter): 1–35.
20. On "discourse coalitions", see Diane Stone (2002) "Knowledge Networks and Policy Expertise in the Global Polity", in Morten Ougaard and Richard Higgott (eds.), *Towards a Global Polity*, London: Routledge, pp. 125–144.
21. See for example, Margaret E. Keck and Kathryn Sikkink (1998) *Activists beyond Borders; Advocacy Networks in International Politics*, Ithaca, NY: Cornell University Press; Thomas Risse, Stephen C. Ropp, and Kathryn Sikkink (eds.) (1999) *The Power of Human Rights: International Norms and Domestic Change*, Cambridge: Cambridge University Press.
22. For an illuminating analysis of this case, see Audie Klotz (1995) *Norms in International Relations; The Struggle against Apartheid*, Ithaca: Cornell University Press.
23. Anne-Marie Slaughter (1997) "The Real New World Order", *Foreign Affairs* 76(5): 183–197; Anne-Marie Slaughter (2004) *A New World Order*, Princeton: Princeton Uni-

versity Press. See also Manuel Castells, "Politics and Power in the Network Society", LSE Miliband Public Lecture, London, 18 March 2004.

24. Commission on International Development (1969), *Partners in Development*, New York, Praeger.
25. For valuable reviews of this and other commissions, see Helsinki Process, A Survey of Global Commissions and Processes of Global Governance, Helsinki, Helsinki Process Secretariat, October 2003; Frédéric Lapeyre (2004) The outcome and impact of the main international commissions on development issues, Geneva, Policy Integration Department, World Commission on the Social Development of Globalization, International Labour Office, Working Paper No. 30, May.
26. ⟨http://www.dailymirror.lk/2003/12/17/news/7.asp⟩.
27. Thomas Biersteker (1995) "The Triumph of Liberal Economic Ideas in the Developing World", in Barbara Stallings (ed.) *Global Change, Regional Response; The New International Context of Development*, Cambridge: Cambridge University Press, pp. 174–196. See also Morten Bøås and Desmond McNeill (2003) *Multilateral Institutions: A Critical Introduction*, London: Pluto.
28. Patrick McCully, Campaigns Director, International Rivers Network, "World Bank seems keen to turn the tide on limits on environmentally damaging projects", Letter to *Financial Times*, 9 September 2003. The report of the World Commission on Dams is published as (2000) *Dams and Development: A New Framework for Decision-Making*, London: Earthscan.
29. Richard Falk (1995) "Liberalism at the Global Level: The Last of the Independent Commissions?", *Millennium: Journal of International Studies* 24: 563–576.
30. Richard Higgott (2001) "Economic globalization and global governance: Towards a post-Washington consensus?", in Volker Rittberger (eds.) *Global Governance and The United Nations System*, Tokyo: United Nations University Press, p. 136.
31. See for example, Stephen Gill (1991) *American Hegemony and the Trilateral Commission*, Cambridge: Cambridge University Press.
32. David Hamburg and Cyrus Vance (1997) *Preventing Deadly Conflict*, New York: Carnegie Corporation. On the response to these Commissions, see Edward C. Luck (2000) "Blue Ribbon Power: Independent Commissions and UN Reform", *International Studies Perspectives* 1(1) (April): 100–101.
33. Andrew F. Cooper, Richard A. Higgott, and Kim Richard Nossal (1993) *Relocating Middle Powers: Australia and Canada in a Changing World Order*, Vancouver: University of British Columbia Press/University of Melbourne Press; Andrew F. Cooper (2004) *Tests of Global Governance: Canadian Diplomacy and United Nations World Conferences*, Tokyo: United Nations University Press.
34. Andrew F. Cooper (ed.) (1997) *Niche Diplomacy: Middle Powers After the Cold War*, London: Macmillan; Andrew F. Cooper, John English, and Ramesh Thakur (eds.) (2002) *Enhancing Global Governance: Towards a New Diplomacy?*, Tokyo: United Nations University Press.
35. South Commission (1990) *The Challenge to the South*, Oxford: Oxford University Press; South Centre (1993) *Facing the Challenge: Responses to the Report of the South Commission*, London: Zed.
36. For more detail, see Jayantha Dhanapala, Under-Secretary-General for Disarmament Affairs, "The Canberra Commission; Lessons Learned for a Future Commission", Luncheon Keynote Address, The Ideas-Institutional Nexus, A Conference co-hosted by the University of Waterloo and the United Nations University, 18 May 2002.
37. Raimo Vayrynen (1999) "Multilateral Security: Common, Cooperative or Collective?", in Michael G. Schechter (ed.) *Future Multilateralism: The Political and Social Framework*, Tokyo: United Nations University Press, p. 56.

38. Ibid, p. 57.
39. ⟨www.cmhealth.org⟩.
40. See most notably, Gareth Evans and Mohamed Sahnoun (2002) "The Responsibility to Protect", *Foreign Affairs* 81(6) (November/December): 99–110.
41. Hans-Henrik Holm (1987) "Brandt, Palme and Thorsson: A Strategy That Does Not Work?", in Toivo Miljan (ed.) *The Political Economy of North–South Relations*, Peterborough, Ontario: Broadview, p. 141 (originally published in *IDS Bulletin* 16(4) 1985).
42. Falk, "Liberalism at the Global Level", p. 573. Held and his colleagues echo this criticism: "Many thinkers argue that accelerating globalization merely intensifies and generates conflicts as the nations of the world seek to secure their interests in the 'global neighbourhood'". Held and Anthony McGrew, David Goldblatt and Jonathan Perraton (1999) *Global Transformations: Politics, Economics and Culture*, Stanford: Stanford University Press, p. 451. The image of bad neighbourhoods, of course, has been reinforced by specific situations such as the Kosovo crisis. See for example, J.L. Holzgrefe and Robert O. Keohane (eds.) (2003) *Humanitarian Intervention; Ethical, Legal, and Political Dilemmas*, Cambridge: Cambridge University Press.
43. This theme remains at the core of some proposals for new International Commissions. Deborah Hurley, for example, has made the proposal that: "Similar to the Brundtland Commission of the 1980s, a World Commission on the Information Society should be formed to articulate and establish, based on human rights, the necessary norms and institutions for the information society" (Deborah Hurley (2003) *Pole Star: Human Rights in the Information Society*, Montreal: Rights and Democracy, p. 40).
44. Samuel M. Makinda (2001) "Human rights, humanitarianism, and transformation in the global community", *Global Governance* 7: 349. See also his (2000) "Recasting Global Governance", in Ramesh Thakur and Edward Newman (eds.) *New Millennium, New Perspectives: The United Nations, Security and Governance*, Tokyo: United Nations University Press, pp. 163–181.
45. The search for equality shaped the criticisms of International Commissions from the outset. See, for example, the critique of the Pearson Report by I.G. Patel that "the concept of genuine partnership in development ... lacks credibility" (I.G. Patel (1971)) "Aid Relationships for the Seventies", in Barbara Ward, Lenore D'Anjou, and J.D. Runnalls (eds.) *The Widening Gap: Development in the 1970s*, New York: Columbia University Press, pp. 295–311.
46. The influence of this model on the ICISS is made explicit by a report of one of its Roundtables: "The ICISS final Report will be succinct and accessible. It may draw on the Brundtland Commissions' approach to re-frame a concept in order to build consensus on a divisive issue. In that report the chasm between environmental concerns and mainstream theories of economic growth was bridged by inventing a new concept of sustainable development. Perhaps, the ICISS could achieve a similar objective" (Marketa Geislerova (2001)) "Report from the Ottawa Roundtable for the International commission on Intervention and State Sovereignty", Ottawa: Canadian Centre for Foreign Policy Development, 15 January, p. 3.
47. Patricia Lewis, Director of UNIDIR and a member of the Tokyo Forum (Patricia Lewis (2000)) "Facing Nuclear Dangers: An Action Plan for the 21st Century; The Report of the Tokyo Forum for Nuclear Non-Proliferation and Disarmament", in "What Next for the NPT?", *Disarmament Forum* 1: 51–55.
48. For the importance of this perspective, see John Gerard Ruggie (1998) "Introduction", *Constructing the World Polity*, London: Routledge, pp. 1–39.

2

The Brandt Commission: The end of an era in North–South politics

Jean-Philippe Thérien

On 12 February 1980, the Chairman of the Independent Commission on International Development Issues, Willy Brandt, officially presented his report, "North–South: A Program for Survival", to Kurt Waldheim, Secretary-General of the United Nations.[1] The presentation ceremony put an end, temporarily at least, to an enterprise that had begun almost three years earlier at the initiative of the president of the World Bank, Robert S. McNamara. Much like the report of the Commission on International Development chaired by Lester B. Pearson in the 1960s,[2] the Brandt Report – as it came to be known – proposed a major reform of the international economic order, with the aim of better addressing the needs of Third World countries. The political effect of the Brandt Report was "slow ... and limited in scope"[3] to such a degree that three years after its publication the members of the Commission felt it necessary to write a memorandum titled *Common Crisis. North-South: Co-operation for World Recovery*, sometimes referred to as the "second" Brandt Report. The lack of interest raised by this memorandum among world leaders marked the definite failure of the Brandt Commission.[4] The Commission had hoped to serve as a catalyst for a round of global negotiations on development issues; it turned out, in fact, to be the last grand manifestation of a particular vision of North–South relations.

Yet, in spite of the cool response it received from the international political elite, the Brandt Report had a significant influence on the history of development. Its reception within the development community and the general public was unprecedented for a document of this nature. Translated into more than twenty languages, the Report sold nearly one million copies.[5] Widely recognized for its high intellectual standards, the Brandt Commission became an inspiration and a model for subsequent international commissions of the 1980s and 1990s. In addition, since many of the problems tackled by the Commission are still on the international agenda two decades later, its Report remains an acknowledged reference in the development debate. As all this should make clear, studying the Brandt Report today is justified more by its impact on ideas than by the practical results of its recommendations.

From an analytical perspective, the work of the Brandt Commission must be examined within the broader context of the history of the global governance of development. For the last fifty years, that history has been dominated by a conflict between the "Bretton Woods paradigm", advocated by the International Monetary Fund (IMF), World Bank (WB), and General Agreement on Tariffs and Trade (GATT), World Trade Organization (WTO), and the "UN paradigm", put forward by UN agencies such as the Secretariat, Economic and Social Council (ECOSOC), United Nations Development Programme (UNDP), United Nations Conference on Trade and Development (UNCTAD), and International Labour Organization (ILO) among others.[6] Tightly controlled by the developed countries, the Bretton Woods institutions champion economic growth and the free functioning of markets – values traditionally associated with the Right. The UN agencies, more attuned to the developing countries' interests, tend to stress social justice and the need for political regulation – ideas generally associated with the Left. The (neo)liberalism of the Bretton Woods institutions has thus consistently opposed the more social-democratic views of the UN agencies.[7]

In the political struggle between the "Bretton Woods paradigm" and the "UN paradigm", the Brandt Report was plainly more aligned with the latter, an observation supported by a variety of elements. From an anecdotal point of view, it should be recalled that the Commission included a number of individuals who had been, or were to become, senior UN officials.[8] More importantly, however, the Commission's terms of reference contained an overt commitment to "pay careful attention to the UN resolutions on development problems".[9] Several of the Brandt Report's proposals were in fact a reformulation of ideas that had been discussed at the UN in the 1970s as part of the New International Economic Order (NIEO) debate; others were inspired by UN talks conducted in the 1940s and the 1950s.[10] Conversely, the Commission was very critical of IMF and World Bank policies. In the final analysis, the connection between the Brandt Commission and the "UN paradigm" was based on a shared ideology. In line with the UN tradition, the Brandt Report was social-democratic and openly promoted a form of global Keynesianism.[11] Hence, in the confrontation between the two visions of development traditionally offered by the "UN paradigm" and the "Bretton Woods paradigm", the position of the Brandt Report was never in any doubt.

This chapter divides the study of the Brandt Report into four parts. Section I explains the context in which the Brandt Commission was set up. Section II describes the content of the two Brandt reports. Section III summarizes the main reactions to the Commission's work. Section IV examines the political impact of that work. Finally, the conclusion assesses the overall contribution of the Brandt Commission to the global governance of development.

Setting the context

The international environment

The Brandt Commission was established at a time when the international community had never been so absorbed by issues of development and North–South relations. These concerns had gradually gained political salience for obvious reasons. At the turn of the 1980s, it was estimated that the North – 25 per cent of the world's population – received 80 per cent of the global income, while the South – 75 per cent of the world's population – lived on the remaining 20 per cent.[12]

It was in the 1960s, in the wake of decolonization, that North–South issues made their appearance on the international agenda. In 1964, the Secretary-General of the United Nations Conference on Trade and Development – an institution generally viewed as the "first major forum of North–South politics"[13] – articulated the structural change in international relations, asserting that "practical action in the field of trade and development is second to no other responsibility which the United Nations, established to maintain peace, must face in the 1960s".[14] Pope Paul VI aptly summarized the spirit of the times when he declared in 1967, "the new name for peace [is] development".[15]

Slowed by the heritage of colonialism and the lack of experience of newly sovereign states, development diplomacy received an unexpected boost from the oil crisis of 1973. By spotlighting the North's dependency on the South's raw materials, the OPEC decision compelled the rich countries to listen more seriously to the poor countries' demands for change. In this atmosphere of a somewhat forced compromise, the UN General Assembly unanimously adopted the "Declaration on the Establishment of a NIEO" in 1974. From 1975 to 1977, a group of 27 countries representing the developed and the developing countries met in Paris to translate the NIEO principles into concrete policies within the framework of the Conference on International Economic Cooperation. The failure of that conference prompted the UN to try to recover a leadership role in the North–South dialogue, and coincided with the creation of the Brandt Commission.

During the two years the Commission spent working on its Report, North–South diplomacy got bogged down in procedural questions. In 1979, based on a suggestion made by the Non-Aligned Movement, the UN General Assembly asked its committee of the whole to prepare a round of "global negotiations" on development in order to prod the debate out of its lethargy. The Brandt Report was completed in this climate of uncertainty, just a few months before the committee of the whole admitted it was unable to reach a consensus over "the agenda, the modalities and the timetable" of the global negotiations that were envisaged.[16]

As one author pointed out, the timing of the release of the Brandt Report was "highly unfortunate".[17] The developed countries' traditional lack of enthusiasm for the North–South dialogue only grew with the deterioration of the international economic environment that marked the beginning of the 1980s. Following the second oil shock of 1979, a sharp drop in output and exports slowed the world economy. Over the 1980–1982 period, international trade reached its lowest growth rate in 35 years.[18] Faced with persistent inflation and increasing levels of unemployment, the developed countries reacted with a set of protectionist and inward-looking policies. In his December 1979 draft introduction to the Report, Brandt himself seemed fully aware of the magnitude of the problems facing Northern governments, and recognized that the difficulties of the time were "more serious than those of past recessions and economic crises".[19] The election of Margaret Thatcher in the United Kingdom (1979) and of Ronald Reagan in the United States (1980), facilitated by the prevailing economic stagnation, also contributed greatly to the rejection of the development strategy put forward by the Brandt Commission.

In addition to being published under harsh economic conditions, the Brandt Report suffered from the consequences of rising geo-political tensions. In 1979, the Islamist revolution in Iran and the Sandinista revolution in Nicaragua had begun to upset the fragile East–West equilibrium. And in December of that same year, the spirit of détente collapsed completely when Soviet troops invaded Afghanistan. According to *The Economist*, the Brandt Report was "mauled on the road to Kabul".[20] The revival of the Cold War dramatically put into question everything in the Commission's work dealing with disarmament. More specifically, it belied the notion that significant financial resources can suddenly be diverted from defence to development. One could hardly imagine a more hostile economic and political environment for the Brandt Report to appear in.

The establishment of the Brandt Commission

As mentioned earlier, the initiative to establish "a private commission of experienced and distinguished individuals ... whose purpose would be to assess the critical development issues confronting the world," came from Robert S. McNamara, the president of the World Bank from 1968 to 1981.[21] McNamara made his idea public for the first time in January 1977 before the World Affairs Council of Boston, and he reiterated it a few months later at the IMF–World Bank Annual Meeting. While it may have contributed to reinforce the World Bank's reputation as the leading international think tank in the field of development, the Brandt Commission, it should be stressed, was not directly sponsored or funded by the Bank. In fact, Willy Brandt insisted on the Commission's "independence" being acknowledged even in its official designation. The Commission's expenditures were footed by a group of funders with a wide variety of interests. The Dutch government paid for about half of the costs linked to the production of the main report. The rest of the budget was provided by a number of other national governments (Denmark, Finland, India, Japan, Norway, Saudi Arabia, South Korea, Sweden, and the United Kingdom), the Commission of European Communities, OPEC, and various foundations and research centres.[22]

In September 1977, after some hesitation, Willy Brandt accepted McNamara's invitation to chair the Commission. As former Chancellor of the Federal Republic of Germany and Nobel Peace Prize winner, Brandt certainly had the prestige and skills to fill the post. McNamara's choice was nonetheless criticized in some circles, most notably in developing countries and in Germany. According to Brandt himself, his qualification to chair the Commission no doubt came mainly from the lessons he had learned with his *Ostpolitik*. This innovative foreign policy had convinced him that "areas of common interest" could arise in spite of "irreconcilable ideological controversies".[23]

The Commission was composed of 21 members (the president, 17 commissioners, and 3 ex-officio members), all recruited on an individual basis and not in their capacities as government officials. Despite the Commission's paying careful attention to the issue of representation, the degree to which it was actually representative of the international community was partial at best. First, all the commissioners were linked to the international political and economic establishment. The most prominent of them were three former heads of government: Eduardo Frei of Chile, Edward Heath of the United Kingdom, and Olof Palme of Sweden. In terms of geography, contrary to the Pearson Commission, the Brandt Commission's centre of gravity leaned towards the South, since a majority (11) of its members came from developing countries. One of its serious handicaps, however, was the absence of commissioners from the USSR, Eastern Europe, or China. In terms of gender, it nowadays appears deplorable that the Commission included only one woman. Finally, in terms of political orientation, scrupulous efforts were made to avoid "the extremes of left and right",[24] and to give the Commission a certain ideological homogeneity.

Between December 1977 and December 1979, the Brandt Commission held ten official meetings in different regions of the world to exchange views with political leaders and development experts. These meetings were supplemented by several less formal discussions. Given the lack of commissioners from Communist countries, as noted above, the informal talks between Willy Brandt and Leonid Brezhnev, the Secretary-General of the Soviet Communist Party and then the Chinese prime minister, Hua Guofeng, were of particular significance.[25] After the Report's publication the Commission ceased to exist formally, but in response to public invitations the commissioners met on five occasions between May 1980 and December 1982. On 15 December 1982, Willy Brandt announced in Ottawa that a Memorandum signed by the Commission would soon be published. This updated version of the emergency programme contained in the original report would, however, soon sink into oblivion.

The content of the report

The content of the Brandt Report reflects the broad mandate the Commission had given itself at its first meeting, in December 1977. This mandate consisted in studying "the grave global issues arising from the economic and social disparities of the world community" and in proposing "ways of promoting adequate solutions to the problems involved in development and in attacking absolute poverty".[26] To achieve these objectives, the Commission examined three main themes: the "record of development"; the "prospects for the world economy"; and the "roads to a new international economic order".[27] The last of these three themes was certainly the one presenting the greatest challenges. While constantly aware of the need to provide practical responses to North–South tensions, the Commission must "above all" seek "to carry conviction with decision makers and with public opinion that profound changes are required in ... international economic relations".[28] The failure of this "evangelical" mission is what best explains the Brandt Commission's limited influence.[29]

As its full title indicates, the Brandt Report is concerned with the survival of humankind, a vast concern determined by the belief that "the future of the world can rarely have seemed so endangered".[30] Consequently, peace stands out as a priority above all the others: "If reduced to a simple denominator, this Report deals with peace".[31] But although it does leave room for the traditional approach whereby security is understood in military terms, the Brandt Commission probes the question in more economic terms: "Much of the insecurity in the world is connected with the divisions between rich and poor countries".[32] The Report maintains, in sum, that North–South relations are sitting on a time bomb, which it is the international community's duty to defuse.

It has often been remarked that the Brandt Commission innovated in comparison with the Pearson Commission by introducing the "mutual interests" argument to convince the developed countries to accept a restructuring of the international economic system. Thus, the need to maintain international stability, expand markets, preserve the environment, and limit population growth represent material bases for the continued growth of North–South interdependence. Since the prosperity of the rich is linked to the progress of the poor, "the hard-headed self-interest" of the North should act as a powerful incentive for the strengthening of international cooperation.[33] Yet despite all the emphasis on interdependence and the need to go beyond a charity-based conception of development, the Brandt Report is ultimately anchored in "the great moral imperatives that ... are as valid internationally as they were and are nationally".[34] The Brandt Commission's message appeals, ultimately, to values more than to rational calculations, because "solidarity" is "something that goes beyond mutual interests".[35] Building on this world-view, the Report presents a list of recommendations to deal with the problem of world poverty. And while one of its characteristics is to take into account the particular responsibilities of Southern governments, its attention focuses essentially on the external constraints on development.

The analysis of development financing is generally considered "the crucial part" of the Brandt Report.[36] Favouring a large-scale transfer of resources to the Third World, the Report requests, first, that the developed countries live up to their commitment of allocating 0.7 per cent of their GNP to development assistance, and recommends that target be raised to 1 per cent before 2000. In order to help reach these goals, the Commission proposes the establishment of a mechanism of automatic taxation covering such things as arms exports or the exploration of seabed minerals. Resurrecting an old idea, the Report furthermore suggests a World Development Fund dedicated to programme lending be created and jointly managed by the countries of the North and the South. The Brandt Commission insists, finally, on the need to improve the basic structures of the international monetary system. To that end it proposes to use Special Drawing Rights to move towards a form of international currency, and to revise IMF decision-making procedures so as to give developing countries more power.

Another major concern of the Brandt Report is the expansion of world trade and the equitable sharing of its benefits. While seeing oil as a "worldwide concern"[37] that requires a distinct strategy, the Report calls for a new approach to strengthen the developing countries' commodity sector. Much in line with UNCTAD's work, it stresses the importance of stabilizing the prices of the raw materials exported by the South, and strongly supports the negotiation of international commodity agreements. With respect to the trade of manufactures, the Commission invites the developed countries to roll back protectionist policies, which are especially detrimental to Third World exports. The Commission also advocates the establishment of international codes of conduct to control the activities of transnational corporations, limit restrictive business practices, and regulate the sharing of technology. In short, the Brandt Report stands in favour of a trade regime based on rules rather than power relations.

The Brandt Report devotes particular attention to disarmament and development. Outraged by the fact that the international community at that time spent US$450 billion on defence and only US$20 billion on development assistance, the Commission adopts a resolutely pacifist position: "More arms do not make mankind safer, only poorer".[38] In order to contain the arms race generated by East–West tensions, the Commission pleads in favour of more confidence-building measures and the reinforcement of détente. It also severely condemns the commercial pressures placed on Northern governments to increase military exports to the Third World and supports the negotiation of international agreements to reduce the arms trade.

The Brandt Commission concluded its Report with a programme of priorities emphasizing the "alarming prospects" of the 1980–1985 period.[39] The program sets out a four-pronged solution: a large-scale transfer of resources to the South, a global energy policy, an international food initiative, and a start to the reform of international institutions.[40] This package, it is worth pointing out, relied on a delicate balance of interests. The main objective of its four components was of course to spur development throughout the Third World. Yet the food initiative was designed more specifically to respond to the needs of the poorest countries, whereas the energy policy was partly conceived as an answer to concerns in the North. The very last recommendation of the Report, aimed at generating political impetus for its various proposals, was the holding of a summit of selected world leaders.

The 1983 Memorandum proposed a programme of action intended to deal with the deterioration of the international economic environment that occurred after the publication of the 1980 Report. Centred on the analysis of the most recent trends in North–South politics, it does not articulate any fundamentally new ideas. "The second Brandt Report", one expert concluded, "shares much of the language and many of the recommendations of the first Report".[41] Rehashing the "mutual interests" argument, the document pleads for more coordination and interventionism in the management of the world economy. But in calling on the "imagination, intelligence and courage" of international leaders to implement these policy changes, Brandt II – just like Brandt I – was asking too much.[42]

A concert of discordant reactions

The Brandt Commission triggered all sorts of reactions. The attitude of the media and the public, albeit more favourable in Europe than in the United States, was generally positive. Governments, for their part, expressed much more contrasted views. Quite predictably, the countries of the North reacted to the Report with much less enthusiasm than those of the South. Yet their reservations were hardly uniform, those expressed by the Scandinavian countries or by powers such as France and Canada being much softer than the views of the United States and the United Kingdom. Frankly inflexible, the Anglo-American response to the Brandt Report stemmed from the conviction that "the greatest contribution" the North could make to development was "to restore a buoyant rate of growth in [the developed countries'] economies".[43] In the end, this was the world-view that prevailed.

Parallel to the debates in the media and foreign ministries, the Brandt Report also generated major controversies among development experts. But before turning to the content of these controversies, it is important to point out that the Brandt Commission prompted reactions from an impressive list of eminent scholars: Samir Amin, C. Fred Bergsten, Johan Galtung, André Gunder Frank, Michael Lipton, Cranford Pratt, Dudley Seers, Hans W. Singer, Frances Stewart, Susan Strange, Jan Tinbergen, Robert Tucker, Barbara Ward, and Immanuel Wallerstein, all figure among those who reviewed the Brandt Report. Few books throughout the history of the social sciences have attracted such a high level of attention, and few have generated such contradictory assessments.

To better understand the range of opinions expressed across the whole Right–Left spectrum it seems useful to identify two types of comments that went beyond the usual ideological divisions. First, observers from very different political allegiances noted that the Report was disconnected from the political realities of the day, sometimes "to the point of fantasy".[44] This evaluation has led more than one author to argue that the analysis of the Brandt Commission was superficial. The Report was most notably criticized for its binary, unsophisticated interpretation of the international system. Already in 1980, political geography was not as simple as the terms "North" and "South" might suggest. Second, a number of scholars deplored the fact that the Report lacked originality. As mentioned earlier, many of the recommendations made by the Brandt Commission were no more than an update of proposals that had been formulated elsewhere, at the United Nations in particular. That said, a telling illustration of the natural inclination of intellectuals toward disagreement came from the venerable Hans W. Singer, who, while recognizing the report's "lack of originality", suggested this "should be counted as an asset rather than a liability!"[45]

The harshest criticisms of the Brandt Report originated on the Right of the political spectrum. Bergsten, for instance, regarded the Report as little more than "an additional manifesto espousing the cause of the developing nations".[46] A populist-conservative current argued that the large-scale transfer of resources from North to South advocated by the Brandt Commission would be damaging for both the Western countries and the "ordinary people" in the South, and that it would serve only the interests of Third World rulers.[47] The Right unanimously rejected the "apocalyptic vision" of the international situation depicted by the Commission.[48] Things, according to that perspective, were after all not that bad. In particular, it was suggested that the IMF, the World Bank and the GATT had proved to be quite efficient in helping the countries of the South face the economic downturn of the 1970s, and that the debt problem was largely exaggerated. The Right also criticized the Brandt Commission for having neglected several important issues such as inflation, the role of the private sector, OPEC policies, and the lack of interest of the Communist countries in North–South affairs. Overall, the Right tended to view the Brandt Report as "counterproductive", basically because its moralizing tone was likely to engender a feeling of exasperation in Northern countries.[49]

The evaluation of the Left was barely less critical than that of the Right. Though it agreed with the Brandt Commission's goal of a redistribution of global wealth, the Left believed the reformist approach adopted in the Report could only lead to a dead end and "a strengthening of the unequal development".[50] Some authors stressed that the Report reflected "an ethnocentric form of cultural imperialism", and others that it did not deal with "the problem of political power".[51] But the vast majority concurred that the Brandt Commission had not investigated the root causes of poverty and that it had under-estimated the magnitude of capitalism's inherent contradictions. Gunder Frank argued that the Keynesianism advocated by Brandt would advantage the rich of the Third World much more than the poor, an idea that led Wallerstein to deride the title of the Report: "The Commission's 'programme for survival'", this author wrote, "may be that of the survival of the system".[52] In opposition to the Brandt Commission's strategy supporting a greater integration of the South into the world economy, Amin suggested the developing countries should follow a policy of "delinking" that would make them less dependent on external markets.[53] Finally, it would be an omission not to recall the sarcasm of the Left, which often asked why all the "good ideas" of the Brandt Commission had not been implemented while several of its members were political leaders in their respective countries.

The preceding summary is of course too brief to account for all the nuances of a complex debate. For, undeniably, the Right as well as the Left have occasionally supported specific elements of the Brandt Report, regarding energy or disarmament, for instance. The fact remains that the Commission's best allies were found at the social-democratic Centre.[54] Analysts of the Centre stressed, first, that producing a unanimous Report was in itself one of the Commission's most remarkable achievements.[55] Secondly, these analysts argued that the proposals of the Report were generally constructive because they opened "new vistas and new possibilities" in the management of North–South relations.[56] Accustomed to controversies among experts, Lipton founded his positive evaluation on common sense: "Academics can, and will, find many flaws in the Brandt Report. However, it is the best Brandt Report we have; and it has got the essentials right".[57] In the same vein, Ward supported the conclusions of the Commission by pointing out that there was no other alternative in sight: "Even if the Brandt proposals are no more than an insurance policy", she contended, "it is worth paying the premiums".[58] Yet it would be erroneous to claim that support from the Centre was unconditional. Singer, for instance, revealed that his reading of the Report had made him move "from praise to grumbling, and vice versa"; one of the major weaknesses of the Report, in his view, was that it evaded the whole question of the implementation of its recommendations.[59] Much more critical, Seers concluded that the publication of the Report had probably worsened the climate for North–South negotiations.[60]

This overview demonstrates that very few experts were entirely convinced of the Brandt Report's proposed method of reconciling solidarity and mutual interests or the relevance of its solutions. What is also clear is that since the Report was in the "centrist Fabian tradition",[61] it quite naturally received its warmest welcome within that tradition.

The impact of the Commission

The influence of the Brandt Commission can be examined by distinguishing its short-term from its long-term impact. In the short term, the Brandt Report served mainly as a catalyst for the organization of the Cancún Summit in October 2001. The scant results of that meeting of political leaders from North and South were to prefigure the unfolding of future events. Although the Report still remains an intellectual milestone for contemporary supporters of the "UN paradigm", the passage of time has largely marginalized the concept of development that it put forward.

The Cancún Summit

In order to follow up on the Report's very last recommendation, that of organizing a summit of selected world leaders devoted to development issues, Willy Brandt met with chancellor Bruno Kreisky of Austria in May 1980. It was in the wake of this initial contact that Mexico's president, José López Portillo, agreed to host a North–South summit. Sceptics feared a failure similar to what had happened at the 1975–1977 Paris Conference, and warned against excessive expectations. But the international community was generally supportive of the idea that a high-level meeting could impart symbolic and political impetus to a North–South dialogue that had become over-bureaucratized.

Among the great powers, the USSR refused to participate. China, for its part, seized upon the occasion to signal its renewed commitment towards development diplomacy. Concerned by the presidential campaign at home and the hostage crisis in Iran, the Americans were particularly reluctant to acknowledge the potential usefulness of such a summit. US hesitations were finally overcome in April 1981, after a meeting between presidents Reagan and López Portillo. In order to bring the United States on board, however, the Mexican president had to make a concession: Cuba – which was then Chair of the Non-Aligned Movement – would not be invited to Cancún.[62] In the end, 22 states – 8 from the North and 14 from the South – took part in the Summit, in addition to the UN Secretary-General.[63]

The planning of the Summit was organized at a series of preparatory sessions where the United States made it clear the meeting should not seek to come up with "binding resolutions and formal commitments".[64] Four general themes of discussion were put on the agenda: food, trade, energy, and finance. The developing countries were hoping that, due to its informal setting, the Summit could serve as a launching pad for global negotiations on international economic issues, within the UN framework. But just a few days before the opening of the meeting, President Reagan gave an important speech with a sobering message. Reagan argued that through its trade and aid policies the United States already contributed more than any other country to the development of the Third World, reaffirming his full confidence in the market economy and existing international economic institutions.[65] After this preamble, the Cancún Summit could hardly be expected to produce a programme of substantial reforms.

As is the custom in this kind of diplomatic gathering, the participants agreed that the very fact they had met to discuss global economic problems was in itself a success. But although there was some progress on agriculture and energy, most observers considered the results "insubstantial and disappointing".[66] No agreement was reached on the opening of global negotiations. Perhaps more tellingly, the participants rejected the idea of institutionalizing their forum. Even the most optimistic who, like Willy Brandt, maintained that Cancún had produced some new consensus, had to admit there was a "setback" in North–South relations after the Summit.[67] When the second Brandt Report was released in 1983, the "lost decade of development" was well under way. Its content looked too much like déjà vu to receive any serious attention.

North–South politics in stalemate

After 1983, the ideas of the Brandt Commission, as well as the whole NIEO project, were placed unequivocally at the bottom of the international agenda. More broadly, North–South politics lost the momentum it had gained in the 1960s and 1970s. Over the two "post-Brandt" decades, development has been marked by several changes, including the debt crisis, the end of the Cold War, and the rise of globalization. But beyond these structural transformations, two major ideological shifts best explain why the proposals of the Brandt Report were never able to take hold.

First, the very idea of a homogeneous South, sharing common interests, was increasingly criticized. The widening gulf between the high performance economies of East Asia and the stagnant economies of sub-Saharan Africa put into doubt the image of a Third World joined by the chains of underdevelopment. Because of this fragmentation, reflected in the "promotion" of some countries like Mexico and South Korea into Northern institutions, the North–South divide became blurred.[68] The second shift followed the rise of neo-liberalism. During the 1980s, a mixture of liberalization, deregulation and privatization came to be seen as the only economic policy alternative. Actively promoted by the Bretton Woods institutions, the new orthodoxy – dubbed the "Washington Consensus" – altered the very dynamics of North–South politics. Development was to a large extent redefined as a process aimed at increasing the role of the market and reducing that of the state.[69] In this shifting environment, the Keynesian social-democratic vision of the Brandt Report was considerably discredited.

In spite of these inauspicious conditions, the ideas of the Brandt Commission proved to be surprisingly resilient. Until 1987, for example, the Brandt Commission Research agency (BCR) continued to provide information to governments and the public about the Brandt reports and North–South issues. In 2001, the former BCR agency gave rise to the Brandt 21 Forum, an NGO mandated "to carry on the original work of the Brandt Commission".[70] In a detailed report published in 2002 to follow up on the Brandt Report's main recommendations, the Brandt 21 Forum firmly asserted, "the international community has not responded to [the Brandt Commission's] proposals in any meaningful way".[71] Eager to get development back on track, the Brandt 21 Forum put forward a global action programme centred on an emergency relief initiative and a worldwide referendum organized by the UN General Assembly.[72] Based to a great extent on a Brandtian approach, such ideas may sound idealistic to many, yet they find favour within a large segment of the development NGO community.

On a different level, the Brandt Commission affected other international commissions concerned with development issues. In 1987, Gro Harlem Brundtland, the Chairwoman of the World Commission on Environment and Development, explicitly presented her own report as a follow-up to both the Brandt Report and the report of the Independent Commission on Disarmament and Security Issues, chaired by Olof Palme.[73] A few years later, in 1990, Willy Brandt was the main initiator of the discussions that were to lead to the creation of the Commission on Global Governance. Shortly before he died in 1992, it was Brandt himself who approached Ingvar Carlsson, former prime minister of Sweden, and Shridath Ramphal, former Secretary-General of the Commonwealth and member of the Brandt Commission, to co-chair the new international commission. Predictably, several of the proposals contained in the report of the Commission on Global Governance, *Our Global Neighbourhood*, were similar to those formulated fifteen years earlier by the Brandt Commission.[74] Lastly, it is significant that as recently as 2002 the Party of European Socialists called for "an authoritative follow-up to the Brandt Report for the new century".[75] Whether or not this specific project goes ahead, it clearly shows that the Brandt Commission enjoys a legitimacy that has not faded away and that it still has the capacity to mobilize people.

That the ideas of the Brandt Commission are still alive is largely due, of course, to the persistence of many of the problems identified in 1980. At the beginning of the twenty-first century, global inequality is on the increase, as income disparities between and within countries widen. Fifteen percent of the world's population now controls 80 per cent of global wealth.[76] Despite a reduction of absolute poverty in relative terms, nearly 3 billion people live on less than $2 a day, and 800 million are undernourished.[77] Recognizing the alarming character of the situation, the 147 heads of state and government who gathered at the 2000 UN Millennium Summit agreed that the fight against poverty was the international community's highest priority and committed themselves to halve global poverty by 2015. As to whether this objective will be reached or not, the jury is still out. But for the purpose of this study, what should be highlighted first and foremost is that the Millennium Declaration and the Millennium Development Goals represent the world's first systematic response, twenty years later, to the challenges described in the Brandt Report.

Conclusion

The Brandt Commission had very little direct influence on the rules of the international economic order. At bottom, it was unable to convince the governments of the North to accept a set of reforms which, to a large extent, had already been rejected in various international forums. The reasons for this impasse, however, have never been totally elucidated. According to one observer from the South, the proposals of the Report fell "between two stools: ... they [were] too radical for the national establishments in most industrial and many developing countries but [were] not audacious enough to deal with the global problems of the 1980s".[78] Yet, as an analyst from the North has suggested, one cannot rule out the hypothesis that the Brandt Commission "no doubt knew full well that their recommendations would not likely be implemented".[79] The debate thus remains open: was the Brandt Commission naive or voluntarily idealist?

Although it produced few concrete results, the Brandt Commission stands nonetheless as a landmark in the evolution of global governance. From a general perspective, it certainly gave an intellectual push to the study of globalization. It also strongly contributed to institutionalizing and legitimizing the practice of international commissions, where elder statespersons are invited to share their visions of the world in order to move public opinion. That said, the field of development is, quite naturally, where the effect of the Brandt Commission has been the greatest. Even though many of the arguments expressed by the Commission had already been formulated within the UN system, it is fair to say that to date no UN report has been able to articulate such a sophisticated global Keynesian view. Because it was able to realize a high level of synthesis, intertwining development with security issues and philosophical notions with empirical facts, the Brandt Report became at once a best-seller and a monument of social-democratic thinking.

Additionally, the problems illuminated by the Brandt Commission remain, after two decades, extraordinarily current. The recent return of poverty to the international agenda has already been noted. The Brandt Report's approach to the relationship between security and development also appears altogether timely in the aftermath to 11 September 2001. When the president of the World Bank today declares, "without dealing with the question of poverty, no part of the world is going to be peaceful", he echoes the Brandt Commission's statement that "[h]e who wants to ban war must also ban mass poverty".[80] Finally, those fighting at the beginning of the twenty-first century for a more equal distribution of global wealth ground their action on the very principles defended by the Brandt Commission: interdependence and solidarity. Indeed, with the rise of globalization, the moral force of these two ideas has only grown stronger.

Thanks to the wisdom of hindsight, it is easy to point out the mistakes of the Brandt Commission. Locked into a conception of the Third World inherited from the post-war era, its Report put too much emphasis on the state, focused on helping poor countries instead of poor people, and failed to question a development model based on economic growth and consumerism. It is also true that the Brandt Report was somewhat simplistic – and perhaps hypocritical – in suggesting the cure to world poverty amounted to a magic wand called "political will".[81] But though it fell short of providing all the right answers, the Brandt Report succeeded in asking vital questions and in articulating unifying ideals. This was no small feat. And that is why, despite all its limitations, the Brandt Report is a document whose reformist thinking has to this day continued to inform the international debate between the "Bretton Woods paradigm" and the "UN paradigm", that is, between the liberal and the social-democratic visions of development.

Notes

I wish to thank Sylvie Thibault for her work as research assistant.

1. Independent Commission on International Development Issues (chaired by Willy Brandt) (1980) *North–South: A Program for Survival*, Cambridge, MA: MIT Press.
2. Commission on International Development (chaired by Lester B. Pearson) (1969) *Partners in Development*, New York: Praeger.
3. Independent Commission on International Development Issues (chaired by Willy Brandt) (1983) *Common Crisis. North–South: Co-operation for World Recovery*, Cambridge, MA: MIT Press, p. 164.

4. Frances Stewart (1983) "Brandt II – The Mirage of Collective Action in a Self-Serving World", *Third World Quarterly* 5(3) (July): 649.
5. See Independent Commission on International Development Issues, note 3 above, p. 3; and James B. Quilligan (2002) *The Brandt Equation: 21st Century Blueprint for the New Global Economy*, Philadephia, Brandt 21 Forum, p. 5.
6. Jean-Philippe Thérien (1999) "Beyond the North–South Divide: The Two Tales of World Poverty", *Third World Quarterly* 20(4) (August) 723–742.
7. A very similar view is presented in Bob Deacon (with Michelle Hulse and Paul Stubbs) (1997) *Global Social Policy: International Organizations and the Future of Welfare*, London: Sage, pp. 57–90.
8. Louis Emmerij, Richard Jolly, and Thomas G. Weiss (2001) *Ahead of the Curve?: UN Ideas and Global Challenges*, Bloomington: Indiana University Press, p. 101.
9. Independent Commission on International Development Issues, note 1 above, p. 296.
10. See Craig N. Murphy (1984) *The Emergence of the NIEO Ideology*, Boulder, CO: Westview Press, p. 135; Nassau A. Adams (1993) *Worlds Apart: The North–South Divide and the International System*, London: Zed Books, p. 175; and Emmerij, Jolly, and Weiss, note 8 above, p. 38.
11. See Cranford Pratt (1980) "From Pearson to Brandt: Evolving Perceptions Concerning International Development", *International Journal* 35(4) (Fall): 629; and Craig Murphy (1994) *International Organization and Industrial Change: Global Governance Since 1850*, New York: Oxford University Press, p. 5.
12. Independent Commission on International Development Issues, note 1 above, p. 32.
13. Robert A. Mortimer (1984) *The Third World Coalition in International Politics*, 2nd ed., Boulder, CO: Westview Press, p. 16.
14. UNCTAD (1964) "Toward a New Trade Policy for Development", Report by the Secretary-General of the Conference, in UNCTAD, *Proceedings of the United Nations Conference on Trade and Development*, vol. II, New York: United Nations, p. 4.
15. Pope Paul VI (1967) *On the Development of Peoples: Populorum Progressio*, Encyclical Letter of His Holiness Pope Paul VI, Vatican: Vatican Polyglot Press, p. 51.
16. Mohamed Bennouna (1983) *Droit international du développement. Tiers Monde et interpellation du droit international*, Paris: Berger-Levrault, p. 44.
17. Miguel S. Wionczek (1981) "The Brandt Report", *Third World Quarterly* 3(1) (January): 104.
18. GATT (1983) *Le commerce international en 1982–83*, Geneva, GATT, p. 4.
19. Independent Commission on International Development Issues, note 1 above, p. 12.
20. *Economist* (1980) "Sink or Swim Together", 16 February 1980, p. 12.
21. Robert S. McNamara (1981) "Foreword", in Friedrich Ebert Foundation (ed.) *Towards One World? International Responses to the Brandt Report*, London: Temple Smith, p. 21.
22. Independent Commission on International Development Issues, note 1 above, p. 304.
23. *Ibid.*, p. 9.
24. Susan Strange (1981) "Reactions to Brandt: Popular Acclaim and Academic Attack", *International Studies Quarterly* 25(2) (June): 330.
25. Independent Commission on International Development Issues, note 1 above, pp. 300–301.
26. *Ibid.*, p. 296.
27. *Ibid.*, pp. 296–297.
28. *Ibid.*, p. 297.
29. Dudley Seers (1980) "North–South: Muddling Morality and Mutuality", *Third World Quarterly* 2(4) (October): 682; Pratt, note 11 above, p. 627.
30. Independent Commission on International Development Issues, note 1 above, p. 12.
31. *Ibid.*, p. 13.

32. *Ibid.*, p. 124.
33. *Ibid.*, p. 77; see also p. 270.
34. *Ibid.*, p. 77. See also Robert H. Cassen (1981) "Mutual Interests", in Independent Bureau for International Development Issues, *The Brandt Commission Papers: Selected Background Papers for the Independent Commission on International Development Issues (1978–1979)*, Geneva-The Hague, Independent Bureau for International Development Issues, p. 395.
35. *Ibid.*, p. 64.
36. Wionczek, note 17 above, p. 113.
37. Independent Commission on International Development Issues, note 1 above, p. 160.
38. *Ibid.*, p. 117.
39. *Ibid.*, p. 269.
40. *Ibid.*, p. 276.
41. Stewart, note 4 above, p. 644.
42. Independent Commission on International Development Issues, note 3 above, p. 12.
43. Margaret Thatcher, in Friedrich Ebert Foundation (ed.), note 21 above, p. 106.
44. P.D. Henderson (1980) "Survival, Development and the Report of the Brandt Commission", *World Economy* 3(1) (June): 90.
45. Hans Wolfgang Singer (1980) "The Brandt Report: A 'Northwestern' Point of View", *Third World Quarterly* 2(4) (October): 698.
46. C. Fred Bergsten, in Friedrich Ebert Foundation (ed.), note 42 above, p. 127.
47. P.T. Bauer and B.S. Yamey (1980) "East–West/North–South: Peace and Prosperity?", *Commentary* 70(3) (September): 62.
48. Robert W. Tucker in Friedrich Ebert Foundation (ed.), note 21 above, p. 218.
49. See Graeme S. Dorrance (1980) "North–South: The Need for Discussion", *The Banker* 130(650–651) (April/May): 70; and C. Fred Bergsten, in Friedrich Ebert Foundation, ed., note 21 above, p. 126.
50. Vita Søgaard Pedersen and Peter Gebert (1985) "The Brandt Report as a Development Strategy", *Cooperation and Conflict*, 20(1) (March): 54.
51. Mahdi Elmandjra (1980) "Àpropos du Rapport de la Commission Brandt sur les problèmes de développement", *Futuribles* (34) (juin): 71; Pedersen and Gebert, note 50 above, p. 41.
52. André Gunder Frank (1980) "North–South and East–West Keynesian Paradoxes in the Brandt Report", *Third World Quarterly* 2(4) (October): 673; Immanuel Wallerstein, in Friedrich Ebert Foundation (ed.), note 21 above, p. 348.
53. Samir Amin, in Friedrich Ebert Foundation, ed., note 21 above, p. 350.
54. Left and Right, it should be recalled, are very much context-dependent. What looks on the "Centre" in academia is close to what looks on the 'Left' in the world of international institutions. In the development debate, most Centrist academics would support the "UN paradigm", which clearly stands on the Left of the views expressed through the "Bretton Woods paradigm".
55. Pratt, note 11 above, p. 629; Jan Tinbergen, in Friedrich Ebert Foundation, ed., note 21 above, p. 86.
56. Angelos Angelopoulos, in Friedrich Ebert Foundation, ed., note 21 above, p. 29.
57. Michael Lipton (1980) "Brandt: Whose Common Interest?", *International Affairs* 56(2) (Spring): 327.
58. Barbara Ward (1980–1981) "Another Chance for the North?", *Foreign Affairs* 59(2) (Winter): 396.
59. Singer, note 45 above, pp. 694.
60. Seers, note 29 above, pp. 692–693.
61. Stewart, note 4 above, p. 640.

62. Murphy, note 10 above, p. 136.
63. The countries of the North included Austria, Canada, the Federal Republic of Germany, France, Japan, the United Kingdom, the United States, and Sweden. The South was represented by Algeria, Bengladesh, Brazil, China, Guyana, India, Ivory Coast, Mexico, Nigeria, the Philippines, Saudi Arabia, Tanzania, Venezuela and Yugoslavia.
64. Carol Geldhart and Peter Lyon (1982) "North–South Monitor", *Third World Quarterly* 4(1) (January): 17.
65. See *Ibid.*; and Institut Français des Relations Internationales (IFRI) (1982) *Ramses 1982: Rapport annuel mondial sur le système économique et les stratégies*, Paris: Économica, p. 286.
66. Charles A. Jones (1983) *The North–South Dialogue: A Brief History*, New York: St. Martin's Press, p. 115.
67. Independent Commission on International Development Issues, note 3 above, p. 4.
68. Thérien, note 6 above, pp. 723–742.
69. Thomas J. Biersteker (1995) "The 'Triumph' of Liberal Economic Ideas in the Developing World", in Barbara Stallings (ed.), *Global Change, Regional Response: The New International Context of Development*, Cambridge: Cambridge University Press, pp. 174–196.
70. Quilligan, note 5 above, p. 58.
71. *Ibid.*, p. 1.
72. *Ibid.*, p. 47.
73. World Commission on Environment and Development (chaired by Gro Harlem Brundtland) (1987) *Our Common Future*, Oxford: Oxford University Press, p. x.
74. Commission on Global Governance (chaired by Ingvar Carlsson and Shridath Ramphal) (1995) *Our Global Neighbourhood: The Report of the Commission on Global Governance*, Oxford: Oxford University Press.
75. Party of European Socialists (2002) *Resolution from the Warsaw Council*, Warsaw, 14 November, p. 4.
76. World Bank (2003) "Poverty Reduction: The Future of Global Development and Peace", keynote address delivered by James D. Wolfensohn, President of the World Bank, Philadelphia, 27 March 2003, p. 1.
77. UNDP (2002) *Human Development Report 2002: Deepening Democracy in a Fragmented World*, New York: Oxford University Press, pp. 17 and 21.
78. Wionczek, note 17 above, p. 117.
79. Pratt, note 11 above, p. 638.
80. World Bank, note 76 above, p. 2; Independent Commission on International Development Issues, note 1 above, p. 16.
81. These criticisms were formulated by Strange, note 24 above, p. 341; Pratt, note 11 above, pp. 640–643; and Seers, note 29 above, p. 684.

3

The Palme Commission: New thinking about security

*Geoffrey Wiseman**

At the end of the 1970s and in the early 1980s, mutual hostility between East and West intensified, undoing years of détente and posing a sharply increased risk of nuclear confrontation between the Soviet Union (USSR) and the United States of America (US). In that atmosphere, the 1982 Report of the Independent Commission on Disarmament and Security Issues, under the chairmanship of the former Swedish Prime Minister Olof Palme, challenged the prevailing doctrine about nuclear deterrence by advancing the notion of "common security" – the idea that international security should be based not on mutual deterrence, but on mutual interests in avoiding nuclear war. Further, the Commission argued famously that security can best be achieved *with*, rather than *against*, the adversary, through UN-sponsored collective security and a wide range of disarmament, arms control, and confidence-building measures (CBMs), including the adoption of less threatening military policies. In the Commission's view, security is shared, not zero-sum.[1]

The Palme Commission, as it became known after Olof Palme's assassination in 1986, is generally credited with coining and popularizing the "common security" term.[2] Yet, two decades after the Palme Commission Report's release, it remains unclear whether common security is an idea, a theory, a principle, a policy, a strategic prescription, or a scheme for world order.[3] This chapter seeks to clarify this issue, but its primary task is to analyse the policy relevance and intellectual significance of the Palme Commission. It does so, first, by examining the Commission's origins, membership, and leadership. Secondly, the chapter considers the impact of the Palme Commission's Report and activities in the context of two key international debates: (a) the 1980s security controversies about NATO and Warsaw Pact military doctrine and (b) the 1990s (and ongoing) argument about why the Cold War came to an end. Finally, the chapter assesses the Palme Commission's record of success and failure, concluding with some general observations about its contribution to the "ideas" literature.

The Commission's origins, membership, leadership

The idea of an international commission devoted to security problems originated from a suggestion by Philip Noel-Baker, a leading British disarmament advocate since the 1920s. David Owen, the former British Labour Foreign Minister, claimed that both he and Palme "together ... set about establishing" the Commission modelled on Willy Brandt's Development Commission.[4] A secretariat was established in Vienna, with the support of Bruno Kreisky, then Prime Minister of Austria and Leader of the Austrian Social Democratic Party. The Palme Commission's goals, as described in its terms of reference, were threefold: (1) to chart a long-term course towards eventual disarmament; (2) to focus attention on short-term opportunities for arms control; and (3) to stimulate an informed public debate.[5]

In addition to Olof Palme, former Prime Minister of Sweden and chairman of the Swedish Social Democratic Party (then in opposition), there were sixteen members of differing national and political backgrounds from East and West, North and South. The Soviet Union, which did not have a member on the Brandt Commission, was represented. The Soviet Commissioner was Georgi Arbatov, the long-time director of the Institute for the United States and Canada, ISKAN. Cyrus Vance, President Carter's Secretary of State, agreed to join following his resignation over the disastrous US hostage-rescue mission in Iran. Western European membership looked, in Owen's description, "slightly like an offshoot of the Socialist International".[6] These Commissioners included Egon Bahr, the former West German politician and adviser to Chancellor Brandt; Gro Harlem Brundtland, the Norwegian Labour Party leader who became prime minister while serving on the Commission; and Joop den Uyl, the Dutch Labour Party leader who also became prime minister during the Commission's term – all were prominent members of the Socialist International. Commissioners from the "South" included Olusegun Obasanjo, the former Nigerian military head of state who became elected president in 1999; Shridath "Sonny" Ramphal, the charismatic former foreign minister of Guyana and long-serving Secretary-General of the Commonwealth; Salim Salim, foreign minister of Tanzania; Alfonso Garcia-Robles, a distinguished Mexican disarmament expert and diplomat (who in 1982 shared the Nobel Peace Prize with the Swedish disarmament advocate Alva Myrdal); and Soedjatmoko, the Indonesian leftist intellectual and former ambassador to the US during the Nixon administration.[7] Commission members served in a "private capacity" and "not under instruction from their respective governments".[8] Thus, the Commission was an example of what later became widely known as "second-track diplomacy".

Roughly speaking, a left/liberal internationalist worldview prevailed. In the more colourful words of an American journalist at the time, the Commission included "out-of-power Western liberals", "neutralists", "leftists", "communists", and a complement of "Third Worlders".[9] A left-liberal perspective was also generally reflected in the Commission's secretariat and small team of advisers.[10] As Commission chairman, Olof Palme – arguably Sweden's best-known international political figure of the twentieth century, second only to Dag Hammarskjöld – imposed a very strong personal imprint on its work.[11] In a sense, Swedish social democracy set the normative tone of the Commission, which was pragmatic yet progressivist. A role for small and medium-sized states was envisaged, and cooperative processes would involve non-state actors, social groups, as well as regional and international institutions.

The Commission was launched in Vienna in September 1980 and met – during its most important phase – twelve times in capitals around the world until April 1982. Governments of Commission members hosted and largely funded Commission meetings, with some private foundation support. Palme, as Commission Chairman, often met with heads of government during Commission meetings. In addition, individual commissioners met with other high-level senior government officials. In *Hard Choices*, Cyrus Vance later described meeting his former counterpart, Soviet Foreign Minister Andrei Gromyko, during a Commission meeting in Moscow in June 1981, but then as "a private citizen".[12] The Commission heard a range of opinion from government officials, diplomats, and experts. The Report's account of these views carefully presents a picture of balance between East and West, although internal tensions reflective of the times were conspicuous, as Gro Harlem Brundtland recounted in her 2002 memoir.[13]

The *Common Security* report was published in June 1982, in time to be presented to the (ad hoc) United Nations Special Session on Disarmament (UNSSOD) in New York and then in December to the (permanent) UN Conference on Disarmament in Geneva, where several countries submitted reservations.[14] The Palme Commission continued to meet throughout the 1980s, but it lost momentum after Olof Palme's death in 1986. In 1989, the Commission issued its Final Report, *A World at Peace*, in Stockholm.[15]

International policy context

The Palme Commission was established in the context of widespread international concern about growing East–West hostility and perceptions of an increased risk of nuclear war. There were reasons for this concern. As the 1970s ended, relations between the Soviet Union and the US deteriorated over armed conflicts in the Persian Gulf, the Horn of Africa, and, especially, Afghanistan. Simultaneously, Europe relapsed into a period of intense East–West hostility often described as the "Second Cold War".[16] This hostility arose primarily from NATO's 1979 decision to modernize its intermediate-range nuclear forces (INF) to match the Soviet deployment of SS-20 long-range theatre nuclear missiles in Eastern Europe. INF – Cruise and Pershing II – missile deployment, rooted in the NATO strategy of "flexible response", would maintain NATO's operational capacity at the intermediate level.[17]

The 1979 "dual-track" decision, as it was called, involved modernizing INF while at the same time pursuing negotiations with the USSR to reduce and balance these forces. The decision was widely interpreted as giving credibility to NATO's willingness to be the first to use nuclear weapons under flexible response to forestall a conventional Warsaw Pact attack. NATO's apparent growing reliance on "first use" of nuclear weapons was seen as increasing the likelihood of a nuclear confrontation in Western Europe. A further complication for NATO was that increased official speculation about fighting and winning nuclear confrontations accompanied the INF decision, stimulated in the late 1970s by the neutron bomb crisis and even more so by US plans to build a powerful, new offensive counter-force missile system – the MX – thought to be relatively invulnerable to a Soviet missile attack. Critics of this NATO trend towards nuclear dependency generally wanted to strengthen conventional defences and to raise the nuclear threshold by decreasing reliance on nuclear first use. But even NATO plans to improve its conventional strength envisaged interdicting and destroying Warsaw Pact "follow-on forces" deep in Pact territory and were thus seen as offensive and provocative. Additionally, the US arms build-up and the Reagan administration's sharp rhetoric on political and security issues caused further public concern in Europe.

Largely because of these developments in NATO policy, the peace movement in Europe and North America experienced a dramatic revival in the early 1980s. Demonstrations against NATO's planned deployment of the Cruise and Pershing missiles were most intense in the five Western European countries where the missiles were to be deployed. While focusing on INF modernization, activist peace groups and the revitalized peace research movement also addressed NATO's plans for strengthening its conventional forces.

Against this tense international background, the Commission's main objective was essentially "to bring new ideas and thoughts to the subject of disarmament".[18] The Commissioners expressed their concerns about the breakdown in superpower relations, focusing particularly on NATO's reliance on nuclear first use, and seeking to provide an intellectual basis to counter the perceived trend towards nuclear war-fighting.[19] However, they differed over precisely what to do with nuclear weapons in Western Europe, ultimately reaching a compromise proposal for a "battlefield-nuclear-weapon-free zone", a 150 km corridor on both sides of the East–West divide. This proposal was designed to reduce the concentration of forces required for surprise attack, lower the danger of nuclear escalation, and raise the nuclear threshold.[20]

The Commission's general view, which became a peace movement slogan, was twofold: nuclear weapons were militarily useless, and a nuclear war could never be won and must never be fought. The Commission's 180-page Report concluded with a long list of recommendations and proposals *inter alia* for drastic cuts in strategic and shorter-range nuclear arms, a comprehensive nuclear test ban, a global chemical weapons treaty, limits on conventional forces, nuclear non-proliferation, permanent UN stand-by forces, and regional conferences on security and cooperation.[21]

In some respects, the Commission was ahead of its time on many of these specific policy proposals. However, it was at the more general, conceptual (rather than specific policy) level that the Commission made its mark. In advancing the Commission's belief that real (i.e. common) security can be achieved only through mutual understanding between adversaries, the Report referred at several points to the need for countries to retain a restricted, non-permissive view of the self-defence norm and to develop "non-threatening strategies". After 1982, common security came to be seen by many as providing not only an alternative to nuclear deterrence but also an umbrella concept for the defensive complex of ideas variously known as *non-offensive defence, defensive defence, and non-provocative defence.*[22] The Report did not develop very sophisticated views on non-offensive defence. In fact, some of its supporters developed the defensive idea and gave it prominence. In this way, common security and non-offensive ideas became closely linked.

The Palme Commission and international security debate in the 1980s

In the years following the Palme Report's publication, the idea of common security and non-offensive defence "spread" via different channels and in different forms to several Western European countries, to the US, to regions such as the Asia-Pacific, and, as discussed separately in the following section, to the Soviet Union. There is much evidence to support this claim.

Reflecting the perceived "offensive" shifts in NATO doctrine described above and the peace movement's re-emergence, several West European opposition parties incorporated common security and non-offensive defence concepts into their party debates and policy platforms, following the release of the Palme Report. The most significant early case in this regard was West Germany. Drawing on the influence of common security advocates such as Brandt and Egon Bahr and the writings of German defensive theorists such as Horst Afheldt, the Social Democratic Party (SPD) considered a radical strategic departure from NATO doctrine. By 1986, the SPD adopted a new security platform, proposing a defensive strategy for both West Germany and NATO based on a "structural incapability of attack" and an East–West partnership in which both sides recognize each other's basic security needs.[23]

Unsurprisingly, the Palme Report attracted early interest in the Nordic countries, especially in Sweden. The major Stockholm newspapers carried reports on its release.[24] The Stockholm International Peace Research Institute (SIPRI), a leading institute funded by the Swedish Parliament, actively promoted the Report, and – with assistance from the Swedish Foreign Ministry – convened an international conference in September 1983 to develop common security policies.[25] In Norway, Johan Jørgen Holst, a Palme Commission consultant, supported his own cautious (minimalist) version of common security in which nuclear deterrence played a central role. However, Sverre Lodgaard, of the Peace Research Institute of Oslo (PRIO), promoted a maximalist version of common security and non-offensive defence ideas.[26] Johan Galtung, a prominent peace researcher for some 20 years, endorsed the common security idea and its defensive message (which he called *transarmament*); but he was scathing about what he regarded as the Report's cautious policy prescriptions.[27] In Denmark, the opposition Social Democratic Party adopted a 1986 security platform based on "defensive defence" ideas, although public controversy there focused on whether to allow port visits by nuclear-armed NATO warships. Even so, the Danish parliament continued to fund the Copenhagen Centre for Peace and Conflict Research (which became the Copenhagen Peace Research Institute, COPRI, in the 1990s), then a leading, independent European research centre advocating non-offensive defence ideas.[28]

In Britain, resistance to NATO nuclear weapons modernization, led by the opposition Labour Party and the Campaign for Nuclear Disarmament, emphasized unilateral nuclear disarmament rather than common security and defensively oriented doctrines. Nonetheless, the Labour Party formally supported common security and also the idea that – in the words of Labour's Foreign Affairs spokesman Denis Healey – the alliances should make "their defensive preparations less provocative and more transparent".[29] After the disastrous general elections of 1983 and 1987, at least partly attributable to its position on nuclear weapons, Labour abandoned unilateral nuclear disarmament in 1989. This lack of broad public support for nuclear disarmament notwithstanding, the peace movement in Britain did contribute to the Europe-wide atmosphere of protest against NATO policies. Alternative defence research activities and publications emerged, the best known being the first, and main, report of the Alternative Defence Commission.[30] Peace researchers such as Frank Barnaby and Robert Neild, both former directors of SIPRI in Sweden, wrote about common security and defensive ideas (although not President Reagan's Strategic Defence Initiative, SDI, about which they were highly critical).[31] So, too, did the small Foundation for International Security, which published a number of books advancing proposals for NATO under the common security and "defensive deterrence" rubrics.[32] Finally, several British International Relations scholars – such as Barry Buzan, Ken Booth, Adam Roberts and Peter Mangold – wrote about common security and defensive ideas from various perspectives.[33]

In Western Europe, therefore, a left-leaning critique of NATO policies emerged in the 1980s, one that was centrally informed by common security and non-offensive defence ideas. One of the ironies of this critique is that it appeared to have no direct influence whatsoever on official NATO policy.[34] The critics saw their ideas treated with much official public scepticism in the West, including in Washington, DC.

In the US, the Palme Commission's impact on security debates during the turbulent 1980s was, by most realist accounts, negligible. For example, a pro-NATO Swedish critic of common security, Ingemar Dörfer, pointed out that "The Report was never reviewed in *International Security*, or dedicated an article in *Foreign Affairs*. More problematically, the Harvard Nuclear Study Group's book [*Living with Nuclear Weapons*] ignored it, even though this became the standard book for the educated public".[35] While it is true that the Palme Report received little media and mainstream academic attention, and had less direct impact in the

US than in Western Europe, this view of the Commission and the manner in which it assessed the influence of ideas (short-term media coverage and citation and publication rates in established/establishment journals) is too narrow and underestimates other indirect forms of impact.

Common security and non-offensive defence ideas made their way into the American security *discourse*, rather than the *debate*, in several less obvious ways. First, the common security watchword was adopted by some leading American Nuclear Weapons Freeze Campaign activist-writers, of those, Randall Forsberg perhaps being the best-known. And the term appeared in the sub-title of a book – *From Protest to Policy: Beyond the Freeze to Common Security* – written by another key Freeze activist, Pam Solo.[36] However, as David Cortright and Ron Pagnucco have shown, the US peace movement never fully developed its transnational links with its Western European counterparts, thus common security did not catch on more widely within the Freeze movement.[37]

Secondly, there is some evidence that the Reagan administration may in fact have been aware of common security thinking, even accepting some of its ideas while refusing to acknowledge this fact. In a 1982 *Washington Post* article, Stephen S. Rosenfeld argued (after interviewing Cyrus Vance) that the European peace movement had "already had measurable impact on [President] Reagan, leading him to soften his statements on nuclear war and his policies on arms control". In Rosenfeld's view, the Palme Report invoked the peace movement constituency in the US as well as in Europe. Moreover, Rosenfeld argued, the Commission's proposal for a battlefield-nuclear-free zone reflected a long-held concern of some conservative American defence planners who feared that a crisis in Central Europe would force the President or a field commander to "go nuclear".[38] Some common security advocates later claimed that the conservatives actually *co-opted* Palme's ideas, albeit without acknowledgement. For instance, Palme Commission consultant Barry Blechman argued that statements by US and Soviet leaders on nuclear war in the late 1980s mirrored common security language.[39]

A third reason why common security's impact in the US is underestimated is that some well-placed members of the liberal policy-oriented, think-tank community in Washington, DC, undoubtedly aware of common security, chose to deal with it in a highly pragmatic way. These analysts dropped the term in favour of cooperative security and published a number of well-received works under this banner, a perfect example being a major volume edited by Janne E. Nolan, *Global Engagement: Cooperation and Security in the 21st Century*.[40] This tactic of rendering certain ideas more acceptable in a new political context can be described as ideas *re-labelling*.[41] Also worthy of mention in this regard is a 1991 book edited by Richard Smoke and a Russian counterpart

Andrei Kortunov. Their book, *Mutual Security: A New Approach to Soviet–American Relations*, was clearly influenced by the common security debate (they too preferred a different term). And, significantly in terms of my argument, the Prefaces to the book were written by Vance and Arbatov, both Palme Commissioners.[42]

Fourthly, some important theoretical International Relations scholarship in the US revealed an awareness of the European common security and defensive debate, but these scholars chose not to engage it in any systematic manner. Rather, the American theory debates about cooperative and defensive security approaches focused heavily on security dilemma theorizing and a rationalist social-scientific search for a predictive, rather than prescriptive, "offence-defence theory".[43]

Taking these four points into account, then, suggests that the Palme Commission's *direct* impact in the US was limited. However, this impact was not negligible as conservative critics claim, since its *indirect* influence was partially masked by a deliberate act of relabelling by pragmatic "ideas-brokers", a tactic designed to circumvent the country's relatively conservative political culture.

Palme Commission ideas surfaced elsewhere around the world, such as in the Asia-Pacific region. From the mid-1980s through the early 1990s in particular, several Palme Commission themes resonated in this large, unwieldy, and emerging "region". These themes included scepticism about the utility of nuclear weapons for the enhancement of regional security; the need for less-offensive conventional forces, especially air and maritime platforms; the role of economic prosperity as a basis for peace; and the belief that security and cooperation could be enhanced through regional organizations.

The main "ideas-carriers", however, were not regional members of the Palme Commission.[44] Ideas about common security and non-offensive defence travelled to the Asia-Pacific region via two main channels, influencing the security discourse there in limited yet subtle ways.[45] The first channel for these ideas was a loosely connected network of international social democratic political figures, peace activists, and peace research scholars based in, or linked to, Australia and New Zealand.[46] For example, the governing Australian Labor Party embraced the concept in its party platform under Foreign Minister Bill Hayden in the mid-1980s and, by the late 1980s, Foreign Minister Gareth Evans often referred it in speeches and policy statements. While still Foreign Minister in the 1990s, Evans co-wrote a book with Bruce Grant, a forıner Australian High Commissioner to India, in which the following appeared:

> [The end of the Cold War] represents the coming of age of a concept which seemed visionary, maybe even fantastical, when it was first articulated by a group

of statesmen from many different continents under the leadership of the late Swedish Prime Minister, Olof Palme, in 1982. This is the concept of "*common security*", sometimes also called "*co-operative security*".[47]

This quote clearly shows high-level governmental interest in common security as a basis for a new regionally oriented foreign policy. It also shows Evans's evolving interest in the cooperative security concept, one on which he eventually settled because, as he argued, it encapsulated common, comprehensive, and UN-style collective security.[48] Whereas Evans emphasized the common security side of the Palme Report, peace movement and academic critics published several works emphasizing the Report's defensive message. These critics argued that the Labor government was abandoning defensive self-reliance for a new version of forward defence – echoing left/peace movement criticisms of NATO in Europe. The critics urged the government to concentrate on continental defence.[49] Whereas the Australian debate was more concerned with common security's cooperative and defensive aspects, public debate in New Zealand focused on common security's anti-nuclear message at a time when the Lange Labor Government revoked visiting port rights to US nuclear warships. In sum, Palme Commission ideas – associated with Western European social democracy – found their way to, and an audience in, distant Australasia.

The second channel through which Western European common security thinking entered the Asia-Pacific security discourse was, perhaps even more oddly, via Soviet diplomacy. During the Cold War, there had been deep regional cynicism about proposals for region-wide, multilateral security mechanisms, such as one advanced by Soviet leader Brezhnev (at a time when the Soviet navy was expanding its presence in the strategically significant North Pacific). In the late 1980s, Gorbachev proposed new security- and confidence-building arrangements for the region, including the idea of "defensive" naval exercises in the North Pacific. Gorbachev's proposals (as will be argued in the next section) clearly reflected common security ideas, but were greeted with widespread official scepticism in the region and did not catch on. However, common security and non-offensive defence were applied with little fanfare to long-standing regional security problems such as Soviet/Russian border disputes with China and India, as well as to the fragile Korean peninsula.[50]

There is also some evidence that common/cooperative security advocates helped catalyse a host of regionally based ideas – initially emerging from "peripheral" Pacific states, Australia and Canada – for new, inclusive approaches to regional security dialogue.[51] Like their European counterparts, Australian and New Zealand common security advocates supported regional dialogue initiatives, partly because they were suspicious of US motives and actions and tended to be critical of post-war US dominance of regional security. These various proposals culminated in the 1993 establishment of the ASEAN Regional Forum (ARF), which by 2000 comprised the 10 ASEAN states and 13 other countries. ARF's significance to this discussion lies in its philosophy of inclusion, which is entirely consistent with common security. For example, one goal of this emerging multilateral process was to "socialize" countries such as Russia, China, Vietnam, and North Korea into improving defence transparency, raising trust levels, and reassuring neighbours about their intentions. The problem was that the region had a weak multilateral tradition, and ARF's initial contribution to regional security problems was modest. That said, the incipient security multilateralism of the 1990s provided a new, if narrow, channel for common security norms.[52]

In the conservative culture of Asian regional politics, and at a time when the "Asian values" debate was surfacing, common security advocates became wary about using Euro-centric terminology. Therefore, they downplayed the common security concept with its European social-democratic connotations, promoting instead the more neutral concepts of cooperative security and security cooperation. Similarly, the path to common security was to be via arms control, not disarmament, and limited confidence-building measures (CBMs), not radical defensive restructuring. Thus, if concepts needed to be pragmatically subsumed (relabelled) under some other rubric, such as cooperative security or CBMs, then so be it. In short, common security and defensive concepts, derived largely from the Palme Commission, found their way into a region-wide conversation about an inclusive dialogue process, but only as *disguised norms*.

This relabelling tactic was not only evident in the Asia-Pacific of the 1990s, but also in the Middle East and the Balkans.[53] Relabelling, however, makes it difficult for students of ideas to judge influence. This was far less of a problem in post-apartheid South Africa, where a lively and less restrained debate emerged about regional common security and the need for defensive reconfiguration of the South African Armed Forces.[54]

This review of the Palme Commission's role in international security debates during the 1980s (and the early 1990s) suggests that common security/non-offensive defence ideas spread in reaction to perceived offensive changes in Western security policies, achieving a degree of prominence in several West European centre-left opposition political parties and in established networks of peace researchers. In the US, however, common security did not become part of the mainstream security discourse, but had its effects, albeit limited, under another name. The same was generally true in the Asia-Pacific region. I now turn to common security's most stunning claim to success: its influence on Soviet security thinking and its possible contribution to the ending of the Cold War itself.

Palme Commission, Gorbachev and the debate about the Cold War's end

Did Palme Commission-inspired common security and non-offensive defence thinking, and the networks linked to this thinking, have any impact on Soviet policies under Gorbachev and the demise of the Cold War system? This question can be addressed in terms of three contending views which seek to explain the Cold War's end.[55]

A first, loosely realist, explanation focuses on Western *peace through strength* policies which changed the international balance of power in the West's favour, forcing the Soviet Union to adopt "new thinking" about foreign policy and associated concepts such as "reasonable sufficiency" in defence. In this view, Soviet setbacks in Afghanistan and Poland, and over the 1983 shooting down of the Korean civilian airliner, were largely due to Western resolve. In addition, the USSR exhausted itself trying to keep up with the West in high technology. Thus, INF deployment and the costly SDI programme demonstrated that the West effectively "won" the latest stage of the arms race. The Soviet Union was not undertaking fundamental change, but simply seeking to recover economically in order to achieve, over time, leaner and meaner armed forces. It therefore needed a "defensive breathing space" in its competition with the West. The shift in Soviet thinking was simply a Western-induced rational reassessment of the Soviet Union's (worsening) strategic situation. Reasonable sufficiency provided a new rationale that the military could accept, recognizing that nuclear dilemmas created common interests and, indeed, that the USSR had long exaggerated the likelihood of a NATO attack. Moreover, the military leadership began to understand how the West perceived the USSR as threatening. This included acknowledgement that deploying Soviet SS-20s actually produced the INF response from NATO, not least because Moscow had created an imbalance by failing to remove other missiles when it deployed the SS-20s. Hence, the West's peace-through-strength approach prevailed, partially resolving the security dilemma to its advantage by pressuring Gorbachev to accept new thinking, which included a shift to a defensive military posture, as a short-term expedient. Or, as Ingemar Dörfer starkly put it: "The Cold War is not over because the [Palme] Commission's recommendations were implemented, it is over because the USA won and the Soviet Union lost". In short, the West won because of its military and economic superiority.[56]

A second, loosely liberal, explanation emphasizes *domestic forces and changes* inside the Soviet Union and, more generally, Eastern Europe. This explanation highlights the paramount influence of Gorbachev as a unique, reforming leader open to ideas for modernizing his country. Gorbachev recognized the disastrous and potentially destabilizing state of the Soviet economy and devised a foreign and security policy that necessitated a retreat from competition with the West and even cooperation with it. This cooperation allowed Gorbachev to take drastic measures to open and restructure the Soviet economy. To do this, he co-opted the civilian defence specialists as an alternative to the military establishment, hoping to undermine its influence and be in a better position to implement reform. This interpretation is supported by Gorbachev's advocacy of conversion from military to civilian production. Belief in these ideas was seen as an important way to escape the shackles of inherited military policies and their dominance of Soviet life. Gorbachev, himself, has admitted that his new thinking was strongly influenced by such individuals as Aleksandr Yakovlev, a reform-minded former Soviet Ambassador to Canada who became head of the Institute of the World Economy and International Relations (IMEMO) in 1983. At that time, it was becoming clearer that the Soviet economy could no longer sustain the burden of high defence expenditure. Moreover, the Red Army could more easily pull back from the countries of Eastern Europe without exposing the USSR to new security risks if those countries could take care of themselves (albeit under communist rule).

A third, loosely constructivist, explanation – and one that heavily invokes the Palme Commission – is that new thinking emerged from a mix of international and domestic sources through the agency of *transnational actors, ideas, and dialogue*. As Jeffrey Checkel, Alan Collins, Robert English, Mathew Evangelista, Sarah Mendelson, Thomas Risse-Kappen, and others have argued, the shift in Soviet military doctrine resulted from Gorbachev's receptivity to ideas developed by, and transmitted among, transnational experts and activists. Significantly, the transnational interpretation emphasized the many unofficial or "second track" East–West contacts in the early-to-mid 1980s that promoted East–West cooperation, in general, and defensive restructuring, in particular. The evidence to support this interpretation, relating specifically to common security and non-provocative defence concepts, is extensive, and has been well documented elsewhere. A few examples illustrate the point.[57]

The Palme Commission played a key part in the early 1980s by facilitating informal exchanges between defensively oriented Western researchers and Warsaw Pact civilian analysts and military professionals. Willy Brandt noted Gorbachev's repeated references to the Commission. Also, Georgi Arbatov, the Soviet member of the Palme Commission, wrote in his fascinating 1992 memoir that the Commission played an important role in the evolution of his own strategic views and on new Soviet political leadership under Gorbachev. The Report – translated without any deletions – helped Gorbachev "introduce the idea of common security" to the Soviet public and thereby consolidate broad support for new thinking.[58] Moreover, Andrei Kokoshin, a deputy director of ISKAN who became Russian deputy defence minister in 1992 and was arguably the most influential Soviet defensive theorist of the Gorbachev era, also noted the significance of the Commission Report in the development of his ideas. Further evidence of transnational contacts can be found in Pugwash meetings, which involved scientific experts from the two blocs and which, as early as 1983, worked extensively on differentiating between forces with offensive and defensive potential.[59] Under Gorbachev, the Soviet Union actively promoted common security and non-offensive defence diplomatically at the UN and elsewhere. Also, when the Conventional Forces in Europe (CFE) talks opened in 1989, the Warsaw Pact's negotiating position reflected non-offensive defence ideas. Western common security advocates could claim with some justification that their ideas influenced Soviet decisions concerning the CFE negotiations. Yet the transnational argument – or at least my interpretation of it – does not rest there.

The public rejection of common security and defensive proposals by NATO and its member governments is one of the paradoxes of the 1980s security debate: even while NATO and its member governments continued to reject such ideas proposed by Western critics, they began adopting many of these ideas as they emerged from Soviet negotiators, and they even incorporated these ideas into the West's negotiating strategy at the CFE talks. The most successful act of communication by defensive advocates in the 1980s was not with Western publics or NATO member governments, but with counterparts in the Warsaw Pact countries. It was this particular aspect of the transnational common security discourse that had the most far-reaching consequences, helping to bring about a significant shift in Soviet thinking after 1986 and, perhaps, even the removal of the Iron Curtain itself. This is a potential case of Keck and Sikkink's "boomerang effect".[60] However, in contrast to the transnational literature's focus on the "low politics" issues of human rights and on repressive states as the point of origin of the boomerang effect, this case not only involved the "high politics" of security but also "boomerang throws" by groups in democratic states. Ironically, Western groups advocating common security influenced NATO via their influence on the Soviet Union.

Weighing the three explanations for the Cold War's end, it is unlikely that an international balance-of-power, domestic, or transnational explanation, on its own, can explain these momentous events.[61] A comprehensive explanation requires an understanding of all three levels and the complex pattern among them. Soviet reactions to developments in Western military thinking and activities – for example, SDI and INF deployment – implied, at least, that Western military activity and firmness vis-à-vis the USSR forced a change in Soviet thinking, even if it did not determine the direction of that change. This realist conclusion evokes the intriguing paradox that Western policies, perceived as thoroughly offensive, may have been what led the Soviets to emphasize defensiveness. If so, then the West broke out of its security dilemma with the USSR by "winning" the arms race and forcing its Cold War adversary to adopt defensive and cooperative policies – without going to war. However, for all the pressures generated by the West, it is difficult to imagine such dramatic change in the Soviet Union without Gorbachev, the individual leader, who was able to mobilize "liberal" supporters in favour of policy reform. The irony here is that Gorbachev got more than he bargained for. Ultimately, the events he facilitated evolved far beyond his control, to the long-term detriment of a coherent, defensive military doctrine. Even when taken together, the realist and domestic explanations seem inadequate without factoring in the transnational relationships that developed between common security proponents on both sides of the Iron Curtain.

The Cold War's end reinforced the (obvious) importance of ideas as catalysts for change in international relations. Arguments about which ideas were the most influential will continue. The different schools of thought – the realist peace through strength, the liberal domestic sources, and the constructivist transnational dialogue – all contributed to the retreat of the Soviet empire. But none should claim all the credit, as many realists tend to do. Common security adherents should not replicate that hubris, but they can certainly look back to the Gorbachev era with some satisfaction. Common security played a significant role in the transnational explanation, and to some extent its legacy is tied to constructivism's future. However, it also played some role in the domestic forces explanation, and even in the realist view. International relations now resembles a "three-level game": the international, the domestic, and the transnational.[62]

Assessing the Palme Commission's success and failure

Commissions are a distinctive type of international actor, deriving from their problem-solving purpose, investigative method, transnational character, and – critically – their intended impermanence. They can be described as temporary international non-governmental organizations, or

TINGOs, defined as ad hoc transnational investigative mechanisms, involving a range of government officials (present and former) and non-governmental representatives and other experts whose purpose is to conduct a systematic inquiry designed to bring new general ideas and specific proposals to a problem of international or global significance.[63] Given their transient nature, how can we consider the short-term and long-term success or failure of the Palme Commission? One method would be to compare the claims of the Commission's supporters with those of its critics. To some extent, I have already done this above. Another would be to consider whether the Commission succeeded in terms of achieving its own objectives. Elements of this approach have also appeared above.

Edward Luck's assessment of international "blue ribbon" commissions on UN reform provides a possible way through this analytical problem. Luck argues that successful commissions must satisfy at least five criteria. They should: (1) produce new ideas, concepts and proposals; (2) gain the attention of top – relevant – policymakers in the UN and in member-state governments; (3) acquire enough attention by the media, academia, NGOs, and the attentive public (so that their major ideas become part of the public policy agenda of civil society); (4) convince significant players in the official policymaking process to become advocates of the commission's conclusions or recommendations, and (5) demonstrate a shelf-life such that the principal concepts and recommendations remain part of the international dialogue for at least five years.[64] While the Palme Commission was not primarily addressing UN reform issues (although they were certainly addressed by it, often perceptively), Luck's success criteria represent a useful and systematic basis on which to judge the Palme Commission's record.

1. *Produce new ideas, concepts and proposals*. The Palme Commission coined and successfully popularized a new security concept along with a coherent set of proposals to implement it. One can hardly disagree with David Owen's 1989 comment that "the concept of common security had been the distinctive contribution of the Palme Commission".[65] The Commission's "primary focus" was indeed "conceptual".[66] I have argued that the common security concept has contributed to, and informed, several major international debates since the early 1980s. At the nuclear level, "common security" yielded a conceptual alternative to mutual nuclear deterrence (on which the West had become so dependent) and to its controversial limited war-fighting versions (towards which the US was shifting). At the conventional level, non-offensive defence offered a way out of the security dilemma's unwelcome embrace in a number of difficult security situations such as in Central Europe, on the Korean Peninsula, and along

the Russo-Chinese-Indian borders. Moreover, as argued, common security contributed to wider acceptance of an emerging view that security should not be limited to a traditional discussion about military threats to state security, even those as awesome as the possibility of nuclear war, but should include non-traditional threats. Evidence of the Palme Commission's contribution to broadening the security concept can be found in statements by Ramphal (already cited above), Obasanjo, Soedjatmoko, and Emma Rothschild, an adviser to both the Brandt and Palme Commissions. This wider view of security was advocated in the late 1970s by the *development*-oriented Brandt Commission, was taken up explicitly by the *security*-oriented Palme Commission in the early 1980s, and further developed by the *environment-* and *development*-oriented Brundtland Commission in the late 1980s. Taken together, the Brandt, Palme, and Brundtland Commissions consolidated acceptance of a broader approach to security and contributed to the emergence of the 1990s human security movement.

Many of the Palme Commission's proposals eventually became woven into Western policy, leading, for example, to major international agreements on intermediate and strategic nuclear weapons, conventional forces in Europe, chemical weapons, and a comprehensive nuclear test ban. Thus, the Palme Commission's record of being on the right side of history is quite impressive. The problem – and one for the ideas literature as a whole – is that it is almost impossible to establish a causal connection. But that is not the burden of this criterion. It is to produce new ideas, concepts, and proposals: a burden that the Palme Commission easily shoulders.

2. *Gain the attention of high-level policymakers (at the UN and within governments).* At the United Nations in the 1980s, the Palme Report won only limited rhetorical and expert-level support. For example, a 1986 UN Experts Report on *Concepts of Security* presented common security as one of several possible approaches for states to pursue. But this report did not have any discernible impact. It is noteworthy, though, that the ideas-carrier in this case was probably Anders Ferm, the executive secretary of the Palme Commission, who went on to become the Swedish Ambassador to the UN where he chaired the Experts Group.[67] This minor example aside, the Palme Commission was never the subject of a dedicated major UN-sponsored international conference (although the timing of the Palme Report was calculated to influence the 1982 UN special disarmament session, UNSSOD).

   Outside the UN system, as I argued, Western European opposition social democratic parties, especially the German SPD, drew heavily on common security and non-offensive defence thinking, providing a platform from which to challenge prevailing NATO military doctrine. In distant Australia, Foreign Minister Gareth Evans incorporated common security into his highly conceptualized foreign policy. And in neighbouring New Zealand, the Labor Government endorsed common security's anti-nuclear theme, although at great cost to its relations with Washington. However, the Palme Commission's greatest influence was on Gorbachev and the new thinkers in the Soviet Union. I have argued further that common security and non-offensive defence provided the conceptual pegs on which Gorbachev was able to reverse decades of security-dilemma Cold War thinking in a process that he could not control, thus bringing about the Cold War's end. While the Palme Commission is generally thought to have had negligible direct impact on the Reagan administration (a view vehemently argued by conservatives), some observers argued at the time that common security thinking contributed to the American anti-nuclear Freeze movement which, in turn, may have compelled Reagan to mollify his stance on nuclear war and arms control.

3. *Acquire enough attention by the media, academia, NGOs and the attentive public (so that their major ideas become part of the public policy agenda of civil society).*

The Palme Commission's success on this criterion is mixed and each sector – media, academia, NGOs – needs to be assessed in turn.

As conservative and radical critics alike have noted, the Western European and American media in general gave only limited attention to the Palme Commission Report following its publication, some of which have been cited above.

As for attention in academia, critics have also noted the almost complete absence of articles or reviews on the Palme Report in mainstream US journals. However, as I argued above, common security's fate in the US was more subtle than the realist dismissal suggests. In particular, liberal-minded strategists and policy analysts adapted common security in large part to avoid the liberal-social democratic baggage associated with the Report in America's generally conservative political culture and the specifically conservative political climate of the 1980s. Thus, liberal-minded American scholars interested in common security relabelled it in favour of the less incendiary term cooperative security.[68] And under this latter rubric, policy and academic works were published and had some influence during the Clinton years, a point oddly overlooked by conservative critics who tended to look for evidence of common security's influence under its original label – a serious oversight in what I would call the *ideas-tracing* process.[69]

Unlike the US, a good number of Western European scholars, especially peace researchers, embraced common security and non-offensive defence, producing extensive research and publications, with the most coherent programme being developed at COPRI by Danish peace researcher Bjørn Møller, a programme that continued throughout the 1990s.[70] European peace research journals (but not mainstream strategic studies) published extensively on common security and non-offensive defence. Moreover, Roy Allison, Nicholas Wheeler and Ken Booth, Barry Buzan, and others in the UK wrote on these ideas in the context of changes in the Soviet Union, NATO doctrinal reform, and theoretical puzzles such as the security dilemma to which common security combined with non-offensive defence offered a possible solution.[71] In 1997, Andrew Butfoy made a book-length case in Australia for recasting the common security concept. In fact, Butfoy developed the concept of "non-threatening defence", drawing directly on Palme Commission language, curiously ignored by others.[72] Finally, and this point is of special significance, constructivist end-of-Cold War scholars resurrected the Palme Commission to support their theoretical argument about the crucial role of transnational networks in bringing about change in the Soviet Union under Gorbachev.

As for the Palme Commission's success in attracting the attention of NGOs, there is little doubt that its key ideas drew significant interest from civil society actors such as peace movement groups and peace researchers linked to them in the 1980s.[73] This was true in Western Europe, Australia and New Zealand, and with the emerging "liberal", civil society actors of the declining Soviet Union. This influence dissipated dramatically everywhere in the 1990s, however, as "progressive" international opinion turned its attention to such new issues as civil war, ethnic conflict, and humanitarian intervention, the latter seeming to come into conflict with the prescriptions of non-offensive defence.

4. *Convince significant players in the official policymaking process to become advocates of the commission's conclusions or recommendations.* Clearly, Gorbachev was the Palme Commission's most historically important "success" under this criterion. In the US, where common security had no apparent active supporters in the Reagan administration, Cyrus Vance, as a former secretary of state, gave some respectability to the Palme Commission but did not campaign for it.[74] A problem with this criterion, as implied earlier, is that policymakers may be disinclined to acknowledge the source of their policies. Thus, even President Reagan appeared to adopt common security language in his second administration. Moreover, on a more permissive interpretation of this criterion – in which opposition democratic parties would be considered a part of the official policymaking process – the endorsement of common security by Western European social demo-

cratic parties was a success. That said, influencing government officials is clearly more significant as a success measure, although even here it should be noted that Brundtland and den Uyl became prime ministers during the Commission's term. As for the Third World, the Palme Commission's record of direct influence was minor, especially when compared, for example, with other Commission-generated concepts such as sustainable development. Common security never became a catch-cry of leading Third World countries or of the Non-Aligned Movement as a whole. Still, it is noteworthy that some of Palme's Third World Commissioners were clearly influenced by common security thinking and subsequently took up these themes in various ways.[75] On balance, common security attracted the support of sufficient influential political figures (only some of them actual Commissioners) to satisfy this criterion: Bahr and Brandt in Germany; Gorbachev and Arbatov in the Soviet Union; Brundtland and Holst in Norway; Gareth Evans in Australia; Palme, Theorin, Dahlgren in Sweden; David Owen in Britain; Cyrus Vance in the US; Obasanjo and Ramphal in the developing world.

5. *Sustain a shelf-life (so that principal concepts and recommendations remain part of the international dialogue on these issues for at least five years)*. In 1984, a critic (on the left) Johan Galtung argued that, except for the European battlefield-nuclear-weapon-free-zone proposal, the Palme Commission Report "passed by remarkably unnoticed. There has been almost no debate".[76] A decade later, in 1994, another critic (on the right), Ingemar Dörfer echoed this view.[77] These assessments overlooked the tendency of some ideas to have incremental, rather than immediate, influence. One way to test any commission's, or TINGO's, longevity is to assess the extent to which individual commissioners – as leading international opinion-formers or ideas-carriers – continue to make public statements, promoting the commission's concepts and proposals five years beyond, say, the Commission's main report.[78] In addition, it is important to note the post-Commission role of leading consultants, advisers, and the secretariat ("advisers").

Several genuine norm entrepreneurs (in the sense that they tried to move the general tone of the debate towards international cooperation) and policy entrepreneurs (in the sense that they advocated specific, short-term common security policy proposals) emerged from the Palme Commission.[79] Olof Palme as chairman stands out, but his tragic death in 1986 left a void for other commissioners to fill. Georgi Arbatov, as described above, accorded great weight to the Commission's influence on Gorbachev's new thinking, speaking about it in numerous forums.[80] Other Commissioners also pushed common security ideas years later, sometimes referring directly to the Palme Report and its recommendations (e.g. Brundtland's memoirs, Ramphal's speeches, and David Owen's opinion pieces).[81] Still others developed a regional common security philosophy clearly drawing on the Palme Commission, such as Olusegun Obasanjo's work on African common security in regional groupings like the Africa Leadership Forum.[82]

In the Palme Commission case, members of the Commission secretariat became important ideas-carriers beyond the five-year limit. For example, Barry Blechman became head of the Stimson Center, a leading Washington, DC think-tank, which in the 1990s developed major nuclear disarmament projects (see the chapter in this volume by Marianne Hanson). In Sweden, Hans Dahlgren wrote an assessment of the Commission published in 2002. Raimo Väyrynen became a prolific and respected writer in peace research. And Emma Rothschild established and ran the Common Security Forum, expressly linking common security to human security.[83] Finally, a small but well-organized transnational group of peace-oriented researchers continued to promote network-based research on common security and non-offensive defence throughout the 1990s, producing a body of publications on the Persian Gulf, the Middle East, East Asia, Latin America, and Southern Africa.[84]

Luck also suggested several other less explicit conditions in determining commission success: these concern organizational issues of leadership, funding, and membership. In his view, the absence of conservative voices from liberal commissions limits their appeal and makes them vulnerable to right-wing opposition.[85] In this regard, Swedish social democratic leadership of the Palme Commission was a mixed blessing. On the one hand, Sweden's long-standing foreign policy of small-power neutrality, Third World aid and solidarity, and anti-nuclearism enhanced the Commission's standing in the eyes of liberal internationalists and the Third World. On the other hand, conservatives saw the Commission as little more than an expression of the worst of Swedish foreign policy, characterized – especially in its historically dominant social democratic version – by self-righteous anti-Americanism (personified by Olof Palme himself, a vitriolic critic of the Vietnam War). Given the differences between the conservative Reagan–Thatcher policies and liberal/social democratic views in Western Europe and the US, it is hard to imagine a "balanced" Palme Commission emerging with challenging new ideas such as common security and non-threatening defence. In other words, while some commissions might aim for "bipartisanship", there will also be a time and a place for commissions to be partisan – both conservative and liberal – in order to push ideas beyond the constraints of the pragmatic middle ground. TINGOs should not always seek to occupy the centre in order to bring two competing views together: the truth does not necessarily lie between two extremes.

Another of Luck's concerns is that most blue-ribbon commissions are funded and run by organizations in Western, or Northern, developed countries, the result of which is a reduction in "their credibility and impact among the developing country majority at the UN". Despite its funding from predominantly Western countries, the Commission's membership was well-balanced regionally and geographically, although not politically.

Conclusions

In terms of Luck's five main criteria, there is sufficient – in fact an abundance – of evidence to conclude that the Palme Commission was a successful blue-ribbon commission. It developed the common security idea – a broad, prescriptive security concept that offered an alternative to nuclear deterrence (especially its nuclear war-fighting variant). It inspired the development of linked concepts such as non-offensive defence, concepts which challenged traditional ideas about offensive conventional military preparations based on threat and fatalistic security dilemma thinking. It won the attention of high-level policymakers, with Gorbachev and the Soviet new thinkers being its most dramatic success. Yet, the Commission had little impact on the UN and on the Western news media, wider publics, and mainstream academic institutions. However, it had significant influence on non-mainstream liberal/peace research and constructivist scholarship, and with activist elements of civil society in quite a few countries. It also clearly convinced a goodly number of significant players in the policymaking process – broadly defined – to become active advocates. Finally, as I argued, the Commission's main concepts and proposals have had a shelf-life of well in excess of five years.

Indeed, there are grounds for believing that this life may continue. In an important volume titled *Worlds in Collision* published in 2002 (20 years after the Palme Report), and in response to the terrorist attacks of September 11th, 2001, Ken Booth and Tim Dunne wondered:

> Can the community be protected by conceiving security as a condition to be achieved *against* others (national security) or can it only be ultimately achieved *with* others (a 'common security')?... The idea of security as a shared value has been dramatically highlighted by the direct attack on the US homeland. [However,] there has been an absence of defining statements of radical alternatives on the lines of common security.[86]

The issues may have shifted from the dangers of nuclear war-fighting between hostile, global superpowers, as in the early 1980s, but the deeper verities and rhetorical appeal of the Palme Commission remain relevant in an age of global terror and civil conflict. The common security principles still seem pertinent, moreover, in such intractable, hostile international relationships as between the Koreas, India and Pakistan, and Iran and Iraq. In fact, a re-reading of the Palme Report would direct our attention to the many dilemmas concerning weapons of mass destruction (WMD) that still haunt the global community today. These dilemmas include still excessive great-power nuclear stockpiles, the horizontal proliferation of mass destruction weapons to ever more states, and dangerous talk from George W. Bush's Washington, DC – eerily reminiscent of the Palme Commission period – about the need to develop a new generation of more usable nuclear weapons against WMD-capable terrorists and rogue states.[87] The Palme Commission retains its policy relevance.

As for its intellectual significance, the Palme Commission case raises issues of interest to the study of ideas in International Relations and I have commented on many throughout this chapter. Four are worthy of mention in conclusion. First, the Palme Commission reinforces the argument about the power of ideas in determining international outcomes. Governments understand this only too well, which helps explain why conservative Australian and Danish governments went to such lengths to dissolve peace research centres that *inter alia* had actively promoted common security ideas. The unique contribution of TINGOs, such as blue-ribbon commissions, is that while they develop, articulate, promote, and disseminate ideas, they do not – by definition – seek to embody them in the institution that actually developed them because that institution ceases to exist. In this limited and intriguing sense, commissions do allow ideas to float freely.

Secondly, ideas – such as common security and non-offensive defence – travelled vast distances (e.g. from the West to the Asia-Pacific) and via forbidding and circuitous routes (e.g. from behind the Iron Curtain back to the West). And they did so – over time – without the ultra-modern means of global communications that many now believe are an essential condition for the transnational flow of ideas.

Thirdly, network analysis – explaining how transnational groups are connected – and what I have called ideas-tracing – explaining how ideas spread – are complex processes indeed. They are compounded by some very real research difficulties and human instincts: sometimes an idea's detractor will refuse to recognize or acknowledge its merits, even when aspects of that very idea gain acceptance (hubris); sometimes advocates will downplay an idea's success so as not to humble an opponent (prudence) or in order to not attract unwanted attention to themselves (modesty); sometimes imitators will claim somebody else's idea as their own (plagiarism); sometimes memories will fade, or become embellished in memoirs, as participants think back on their roles (memory); sometimes supporters of an idea need to conceal its genesis or change its name for instrumental reasons (pragmatism and relabelling); and sometimes ideas need individuals, or groups, who are prepared to keep the flame alight during the bad times (as torch-bearers).

Finally, as an elite, second-track, international group, whose incremental success owed much to traditional liberal and social democratic political party leadership and connections, the Palme Commission stood uneasily between old-style international party politics and new-age transnational network politics. The Palme Commission was a product of a particularly virulent chapter in the Cold War and the evidence suggests that – in various ways – its ideas played no small part in helping find a way out of that lamentable period in international affairs.

Notes

* I wish to thank the United States Institute of Peace for a grant (#SG-86–99) on the diplomacy of non-state actors and the Center for International Studies at the University of Southern California for its support. I am also very grateful for research assistance and comments by Szilvia Musurlian.

1. The Report of the Independent Commission on Disarmament and Security Issues under the Chairmanship of Olof Palme (1982) *Common Security: A Programme for Disarmament*, London: Pan Books (hereafter Palme, *Common Security*).
2. Egon Bahr, a key Palme Commissioner and adviser to Willy Brandt, the former West German Chancellor, claimed credit for "inventing" the term. One observer has suggested that Johan Jørgen Holst and Barry Blechman were primarily responsible for formulating it; see Ingemar Dörfer, "A Comment on the Palme Commission Report", in Olav F. Knudsen (ed.) (1996) *Strategic Analysis and the Management of Power: Johan Jørgen Holst, the Cold War and the New Europe*, London: Macmillan, p. 109. Another observer noted the term's earlier roots in the German security debate; see Thomas Risse-Kappen (1995) "Ideas Do Not Float Freely: Transnational Coalitions, Domestic Structures, and the End of the Cold War", in Richard Ned Lebow and Thomas Risse-Kappen (eds.) *International Relations Theory and the End of the Cold War*, New York: Columbia University Press, p. 212, fn. 2.
3. Risse-Kappen, "Ideas Do Not Float Freely", p. 194; and Andrew Butfoy (1997) *Common Security and Strategic Reform*, London: Macmillan, p. 111.
4. David Owen (1991) *Time to Declare*, London: Michael Joseph, p. 443. Three members of the Palme Commission (Olof Palme, Haruki Mori, and Shridath Ramphal) served as Brandt commissioners. For Ramphal's view on the "inter-connectedness" of the two Commissions' themes, see his (1988) *Inseparable Humanity: An Anthology of Reflections of Shridath Ramphal*, introduced and edited by Ron Sanders, London: Hansib, p. 349.
5. Palme, *Common Security*, pp. 187–188.
6. Owen, *Time to Declare*, p. 443.
7. Other countries represented were Canada, France, India, Japan, and Poland. For a full list of commissioners and their background, see Palme, *Common Security*, pp. 184–185.
8. Palme, *Common Security*, p. 184.

9. Stephen S. Rosenfeld (1982) "Just Propaganda, or is It?", *Washington Post*, 4 June, p. A19.
10. Anders Ferm, the first executive secretary, and Hans Dahlgren, press officer and assistant to the chairman, were both Swedish social democrats close to Palme. Ferm later became the Swedish ambassador to the UN and Dahlgren an Under-Secretary of State in the Swedish Foreign Ministry. Commission experts included Barry Blechman, Emma Rothschild, and Raimo Väyrynen, whose writings are consistent with a left-liberal internationalist label. A scientific consultant to the Commission was Johan Jørgen Holst, a leading Norwegian defence intellectual and senior member of Labor governments; he was more centrist than the others. US ambassador James Leonard succeeded Leslie H. Gelb as a scientific adviser in May 1981. General Mikhail Milstein was a Soviet scientific adviser.
11. For two sympathetic Swedish assessments of Palme's role, written 20 years after the Palme Commission, see Hans Dahlgren (2002) "Olof Palme och Palmekommissionen" (Olof Palme and the Palme Commission), and Wilhelm Agrell (2002) "Gemensam säkerhet – en omläsning efter två decennier" (Common Security – a review after two decades), in Erik Åsard (ed.), *Politikern Olof Palme* (The Politician Olof Palme), Stockholm: Hjalmarson and Höberg (my translations).
12. Cyrus Vance (1983) *Hard Choices: Critical Years in America's Foreign Policy*, New York: Simon and Schuster, p. 17.
13. Brundtland also related her view that Arbatov and his number two, General Milstein, were there to "check one another". Gro Harlem Brundtland (2002) *Madam Prime Minister: A Life in Power and Politics*, New York: Farrar, Straus and Giroux, p. 161.
14. The US, France, the FRG, Turkey, India, and Japan; Dörfer, "A Comment", p. 111, fn. 6.
15. The Palme Commission on Disarmament and Security Issues, *A World at Peace: Common Security in the Twenty-first Century*, Stockholm, April 1989. By this time, notable new commissioners were Anders Ferm, the Commission's first executive secretary, and Brian Urquhart, former Under-Secretary-General of the United Nations.
16. For example, Fred Halliday (1983) *The Making of the Second Cold War*, London: Verso.
17. For a review of INF by a leading Swedish social democrat close to Palme, see Pierre Schori (1989) "INF and Common Security", in Radmila Nakarada and Jan Øberg (eds.) *Surviving Together: The Olof Palme Lectures on Common Security 1988*, Hampshire: Dartmouth Publishing.
18. Palme, *Common Security*, p. viii.
19. Palme, *Common Security*, p. vii. On the strength of Soviet concerns about limited nuclear war, as conveyed contemporaneously by Arbatov, see Georgi A. Arbatov and Willem Oltmans (1983) *The Soviet Viewpoint*, New York: Dodd, Mead, e.g. pp. 95–97.
20. For an account of the "contentious" nature of this issue within the Commission, see Blechman, "Common Security", pp. 96–97.
21. For full details, see Palme, *Common Security*, ch. 6 and Annexe 1.
22. Bjørn Møller (1992) *Common Security and Nonoffensive Defense: A Neorealist Perspective*, Boulder, Colorado: Lynne Rienner; and Geoffrey Wiseman (2002) *Concepts of Non-Provocative Defence: Ideas and Practices in International Security*, Basingstoke: Palgrave.
23. For a detailed, sympathetic account of the German "defensive" debate, see Bjørn Møller (1991) *Resolving the Security Dilemma in Europe: The German Debate on Non-Offensive Defence*, London: Brassey's. For an account deeply sceptical of the wisdom of these ideas, see David Gates (1991) *Non-Offensive Defence: An Alternative Strategy for NATO?*, London: Macmillan.

24. See, for example, "Palme-komissionen är enig: Kärnvapnen måste bort" (The Palme Commission is united: Nuclear weapons must go), and "Gemensam säkerhet" (Common security), both appeared in *Dagens Nyheter*, 2 June 1982.
25. See SIPRI (1985) *Policies for Common Security*, London: Taylor & Francis. This book is a major collection of chapters by international contributors and should be seen as a scholarly accompaniment to the Palme Report.
26. Lodgarrd, then at SIPRI, later became Director of the UN Institute for Disarmament Research (UNIDIR) in Geneva and continued to support these ideas in his subsequent writings. On the minimalist/maximalist distinction, see Bjørn Møller (1995) *Dictionary of Alternative Defense*, Boulder, Colorado: Lynne Rienner, p. 85. For differences between three strands of common security (Utopian, Palme-SIPRI, and Managerialist), see Butfoy, *Common Security*, pp. 17–18.
27. Johan Galtung (1984) *There are Alternatives! Four Roads to Peace and Security*, Nottingham: Spokesman, esp. pp. 138–145.
28. In January 2003, COPRI was disbanded and reorganized into the Danish Institute for International Studies, thus losing its distinctive brand name. See Stefano Guzzini and Dietrich Jung (eds.) (forthcoming) *Contemporary Security Analysis and Copenhagen Peace Research*, London: Routledge.
29. Denis Healey (1987) "Collective security after fifty years", *LSE Quarterly* 1(1) (March): 20.
30. The Commission, which made several references to various Palme Commission proposals, favoured a military posture of defensive deterrence and advocated a nuclear-disarmed Britain; see Alternative Defence Commission (1987) *The Politics of Alternative Defence: A Policy for a Non-Nuclear Britain*, London: Paladin.
31. Anders Boserup and Robert Neild (eds.) (1990) *The Foundations of Defensive Defence*, London: Macmillan; and Frank Barnaby (1986) *What on Earth is Star Wars?: A Guide to the Strategic Defense Initiative*, London: Fourth Estate.
32. See, for example, Stan Windass (ed.) (1985) *Avoiding Nuclear War: Common Security as a Strategy for the Defence of the West*, London: Brassey's.
33. Barry Buzan (1987) "Common security, non-provocative defence, and the future of Western Europe", *Review of International Studies* 13(4) (October): 265–279; Ken Booth, "Alternative Defence", in Ken Booth and John Baylis (1989) *Britain, NATO and Nuclear Weapons: Alternative Defence versus Alliance Reform*, London: Macmillan; Adam Roberts, "The Idea of 'Defensive Defence': Historical Aspects", paper delivered at British International Studies Association Annual Conference, University of Kent, Canterbury, 18–20 December 1989; and Peter Mangold (1990) *National Security and International Relations*, London: Routledge, esp. ch. 6.
34. For a full analysis of this critique, see Wiseman, *Concepts of Non-Provocative Defence*, ch. 4.
35. Dörfer, "A Comment", p. 109. See also Ingemar Dörfer (1991) *Nollpunkten: Sverige i det andra kalla kriget, 1979–1986* (Point Zero: Sweden in the Second Cold War, 1979–1986), Stockholm: Timbro, esp. ch. 8, "Gemensam säkerhet" (Common security).
36. Pam Solo (1988) *From Protest to Policy: Beyond the Freeze to Common Security*, Cambridge, Massachusetts: Ballinger, pp. 177–186.
37. David Cortright and Ron Pagnucco (1997) "Limits to Transnationalism: The 1980s Freeze Campaign", in Jackie Smith, Charles Chatfield and Ron Pagnucco (eds.) *Transnational Social Movements and Global Politics*, Syracuse: Syracuse University Press, pp. 165–169.
38. Rosenfeld, "Just Propaganda, or is It?". See also Cyrus Vance and Robert Hunter, "The Centrality of Arms Control", *New York Times*, 26 December 1982, an op-ed piece in which common security is heavily promoted. For a book-length argument about the

peace movement's impact, see Jeffrey Knopf (1998) *Domestic Society and International Cooperation: The Impact of Protest on US Arms Control Policy*, Cambridge: Cambridge University Press.

39. Blechman, "Common Security", pp. 95–96.
40. Janne E. Nolan (ed.) (1994) *Global Engagement: Cooperation and Security in the 21st Century*, Washington, DC: Brookings Institution. Note: Nolan, married to Barry Blechman, unquestionably knew about the Palme Commission and common security, a personal-links point that supports my general argument here and also suggests that marriage and family connections may well be underrated in the ideas-transmission literature. On cooperative security, see writings by John Steinbruner, Ashton Carter, and Ivo Daalder.
41. Yet another illustrative example of relabelling is that the US edition of the Palme Report substituted the British edition's use of the politically-loaded disarmament term in its sub-title, "A Programme for Disarmament", for the more ambiguous "A Blueprint for Survival". This relabelling has continued in the current decade; for example, Jeffrey A. Larsen (ed.) (2002) *Arms Control: Cooperative Security in a Changing Environment*, Boulder, Colorado: Lynne Rienner.
42. Richard Smoke and Andrei Kortunov (eds.) (1991) *Mutual Security: A New Approach to Soviet-American Relations*, New York: St Martin's Press. By this time, even Randall Forsberg was using the cooperative security label; see "After the Cold War: A Debate on Cooperative Security", *Boston Review*, November/December 1992.
43. For an excellent account of the US literature, including recognition of the European "defensive defence" debate, see Sean Lynn-Jones (1995) "Offense–Defense Theory and Its Critics", *Security Studies* 4(4) (Summer): 660–691.
44. On ideas and individuals, see Kathryn Sikkink (1991) *Ideas and Institutions: Developmentalism in Brazil and Argentina*, Ithaca, New York: Cornell University Press, 1991, e.g. pp. 244–247.
45. For an earlier explication of this argument, see Geoffrey Wiseman (1992) "Common Security in the Asia-Pacific Region", *Pacific Review* 5(1): 42–59. For a later discussion on how (English School) ideas travelled to China, see Yongzin Zhang (2003) "The 'English School' in China: A Travelogue of Ideas and their Diffusion", *European Journal of International Relations* 9(1) (March): 87–114.
46. Andrew Mack was a crucial ideas-carrier between European peace research and Australia in the 1980s; see, for instance, his (1985) *Peace Research in the 1980s*, Canberra: Strategic and Defence Studies Centre, Australian National University. Kevin Clements performed a similar ideas-envoy role in New Zealand; see his (1989) "Common Security in the Asia-Pacific Region: Problems and Prospects", *Alternatives* XIV(1) (January): 49–76. Both Mack and Clements became head of the Peace Research Centre at the Australian National University. For an example of the Centre's interest in this subject, see Geoffrey Wiseman (1989) *Common Security and Non-Provocative Defence: Alternative Approaches to the Security Dilemma*, Peace Research Centre Monograph, Research School of Pacific Studies, Australian National University.
47. Gareth Evans and Bruce Grant (1991) *Australia's Foreign Relations in the World of the 1990s*, Melbourne: Melbourne University Press, pp. 80–1. I worked for (then) Senator Evans as a private secretary from 1988–90, during which time I drafted several statements for him on common security. From memory, *he* invariably initiated discussion on the topic.
48. See Gareth Evans (1993) *Cooperating for Peace: The Global Agenda for the 1990s and Beyond*, St Leonards, NSW (Australia): Allen & Unwin, pp. 15–16. For helpful definitional distinctions, see David Dewitt (1994) "Common, Comprehensive, and Cooperative Security", *Pacific Review* 7(1): 1–15.

49. Graeme Cheeseman and St. John Kettle (eds.) (1990) *The New Australian Militarism*, Sydney: Pluto Press.
50. See, for example, Gary Klintworth, "The Practice of Common Security: China's Borders with Russia and India", Department of International Relations, Australian National University Working Paper (WP1993/1); Håkan Wiberg (1990) "Nonoffensive Defense and the Korean Peninsula", UNIDIR, *Nonoffensive Defense: A Global Perspective*, New York: Taylor and Francis; and Andrew Mack (1991) "The Theory of Non-provocative Defense: How Relevant for Korea?", *Korean Journal of Defense Analysis* III(1) (Summer). See also Bjørn Møller (1997) "A Common Security and NOD Regime for the Asia-Pacific?", *Pacifica Review* 9(1): 23–43; and Bjørn Møller (1998) *Security, Arms Control and Defence Restructuring in East Asia*, Aldershot: Ashgate.
51. Canada actively promoted the North Pacific Co-operative Security Dialogue. A good account of regional proposals and dialogue activities in the early 1990s is Paul M. Evans (1994) "The Dialogue Process on Asia Pacific Security Issues: Inventory and Analysis", in Paul M. Evans (ed.) *Studying Asia Pacific Security*, University of Toronto/York University Joint Center for Asia Pacific Studies.
52. For a supporting argument, see Blechman, "Common Security", p. 101.
53. See Kosta Tsipis (ed.), *Common Security Regimes in the Balkans*, (New York: Columbia University Press, 1996); and Bjørn Møller (1998) *Non-Offensive Defence in the Middle East?*, New York: UNIDIR.
54. Gavin Cawthra (1997) "Prospects for Common Security in Southern Africa", in Gavin Cawthra and Bjørn Møller (eds.) *Defensive Restructuring of the Armed Forces in Southern Africa*, Ashgate: Aldershot. Several other chapters in this volume refer to regional common security.
55. This framework is adapted from several important constructivist works cited in this section; e.g. Sarah E. Mendelson (1998) *Changing Course: Ideas, Politics, and the Soviet Withdrawal from Afghanistan*, Princeton: Princeton University Press, ch. 2. An extended version of my argument here is in Wiseman, *Concepts of Non-Provocative Defence*, esp. ch. 5. There is now a vast literature on the Cold War's ending. For a helpful review article, see Margarita H. Petrova (2003) "The End of the Cold War: A Battle or Bridging Ground Between Rationalist and Ideational Approaches in International Relations?", *European Journal of International Relations* 9(1) (March).
56. Dörfer, "A Comment", p. 110. Among the many realist accounts, see Stephen G. Brooks and William C. Wohlforth (2000/01) "Power, Globalization, and the End of the Cold War: Reevaluating a Landmark Case for Ideas", *International Security* 25(3) (Winter): 5–53. See also a subsequent exchange between Brooks and Wohlforth and Robert D. English in *International Security*, vol. 26, no. 4 (Spring 2002), pp. 93–111.
57. For detailed documentation, see Risse-Kappen, "Ideas Do Not Float Freely", passim; Jeffrey T. Checkel (1997) *Ideas and International Political Change: Soviet/Russian Behavior and the End of the Cold War*, New Haven, Connecticut: Yale University Press, e.g., pp. 82–4; Alan Collins (1997) *The Security Dilemma and the End of the Cold War*, New York: St Martin's Press, e.g. pp. 62–5; and Mathew Evangelista (1999) *Unarmed Forces: The Transnational Movement to End the Cold War*, Ithaca, New York: Cornell University Press, e.g. pp. 160–2, 184–92.
58. Georgi Arbatov (1992) *The System: An Insider's Life in Soviet Politics*, New York: Random House, pp. 311–312.
59. For interesting details, see Boserup and Neild, *The Foundations of Defensive Defence*, esp. ch. 1.
60. For more on the "boomerang effect" and the "boomerang throw", see Margaret E. Keck and Kathryn Sikkink (1998) *Activists beyond Borders: Advocacy Networks in In-*

ternational Politics, Ithaca, New York: Cornell University Press, for example, pp. 12–13; and Thomas Risse and Kathryn Sikkink (1999) "Introduction", in Thomas Risse, Stephen C. Ropp, and Kathryn Sikkink (eds.) *The Power of Human Rights: International Norms and Domestic Change*, Cambridge: Cambridge University Press, p. 18.

61. Daniel Deudney and G. John Ikenberry (1991) "Soviet reform and the end of the Cold War: Explaining large-scale historical change", *Review of International Studies* 17(3) (July): 225–250.
62. This point builds on Robert Putnam (1988) "Diplomacy and domestic politics: The logic of two-level games", *International Organization* 42(3) (Summer): 427–460.
63. Arbatov regarded the Palme Commission as an international non-governmental organization (INGO), a common acronym; see *The System*, p. 209.
64. Edward C. Luck (2000) "Blue Ribbon Power: Independent Commissions and UN Reform", *International Studies Perspectives* 1(1) (April): 98.
65. David Owen (1989) "Agenda: How to Grasp the Chance of Peace", *Guardian*, 17 April.
66. Blechman, "Common Security", p. 94.
67. Department for Disarmament Affairs Report of the Secretary-General (1986) *Concepts of Security*, New York: United Nations, see pp. v and 13–14.
68. An interesting exception here is Michael Mandelbaum, the Johns Hopkins University scholar, who, in 1996, made a fascinating case for a post-Cold War common security order, fully acknowledging the Palme Commission's earlier, Cold War role; see Michael Mandelbaum (1996) *The Dawn of Peace in Europe*, New York: Twentieth Century Fund Press, see ch. 6. Also in the 1990s, the small Project on Defense Alternatives in Cambridge, Mass. actively published prescriptive and critical defence-policy papers building explicitly on non-offensive defence concepts.
69. I have derived the notion of "ideas tracing" from "process tracing"; see Alexander L. George and Timothy J. McKeown (1985) "Case Studies and Theories of Organizational Decision Making", *Advances in Information Processing in Organizations* 2: 34–41.
70. Bjørn Møller has been a prolific writer. See his full publication record at www.copri.dk/.
71. Roy Allison (1991) "New thinking about defence in the Soviet Union", in Ken Booth (ed.) *New Thinking About Strategy and International Security*, London: HarperCollins; Nicholas J. Wheeler and Ken Booth (1992) "The Security Dilemma", in John Bayliss and N. J. Rengger, *Dilemmas of World Politics*, Oxford: Clarendon Press; and Buzan, "Common security".
72. Butfoy, *Common Security*, ch. 4.
73. The Commission's staff included an NGO co-ordinator.
74. For an explicit public statement referring to the Palme Commission, see Vance's Preface in Smoke and Kortunov, *Mutual Security*.
75. In addition to Ramphal, *Inseparable Humanity*, already cited, see Mansour Khalid (ed.) (2001) *Africa Through the Eyes of a Patriot: A Tribute to General Olusegun Obasanjo*, London: Kegan Paul, see for example, pp. 73, 78, 81, 83; and Kathleen Newland and Kamala Chandrakirana Soedjatmoko (eds.) (1994) *Transforming Humanity: The Visionary Writings of Soedjatmoko*, West Hartford, Connecticut: Kumarian Press, see for example, p. 110, pp. 130–33.
76. Galtung, *There are Alternatives!*, pp. 138–139.
77. Dörfer, "A Comment", p. 109.
78. This five-year limit could be taken to be five years beyond the 1982 publication of the Common Security Report (i.e. 1987), or five years beyond the formal closure of the Commission in 1989 (i.e. 1994). I have chosen 1987 because the 1982 Report is widely regarded as being the high point of the Palme Commission and because after Palme's 1986 death the Commission continued, in David Owen's phrase, in "a lower key" until 1989 (see *Time To Declare*, p. 444). This choice does not significantly affect the conclu-

sions reached. I started doing research on the Palme Commission in 1987, but this was not a factor here.

79. I have suggested elsewhere that "norm" and "policy" entrepreneurs could be more clearly distinguished, arguing that *norm* entrepreneurs be seen as "outsider proponents", and *policy* entrepreneurs as "insider proponents"; see Wiseman, *Concepts of Non-Provocative Defence*, p. 102. This distinction is in practice hard to maintain, but some unbundling of these two closely-related concepts seems in order. See Keck and Sikkink, *Activists Beyond Borders*, p. 2; and Martha Finnemore and Kathryn Sikkink (1999) "International Norm Dynamics and Political Change", in Peter J. Katzenstein, Robert O. Keohane, and Stephen D. Krasner (eds.) *Exploration and Contestation in the Study of World Politics*, Cambridge: MIT Press, see for example, pp. 256–259.
80. Arbatov also claimed that several leading international political figures "worked closely" with the Commission. He mentioned Rajiv Ghandi, Bruno Kreisky, Pierre Trudeau, Bettino Craxi, and (another Swedish Prime Minister) Ingvar Carlsson; see *The System*, p. 311.
81. David Owen (1989) "Agenda: How to Grasp the Chance of Peace", *Guardian*, 17 April.
82. See for example, Olusegun Obasanjo (1999) "Collective Security Is the Answer", *Africa Forum* 3(2 and 3) (October), see http://www.africaleadership.org/library/Africanleaders.htm.
83. See for example, Emma Rothschild (1995) "What is Security?", *Dædalus* 124(3) (Summer): 54. For details, see the Common Security Forum's web-site, www.kings.cam.ac.uk/histecon/csf/index/htm.
84. The network, whose publications have been cited above, was organized by Bjørn Møller at COPRI and partly funded by the Ford Foundation. As a program officer at the Ford Foundation, I recommended the first grant to COPRI for this project in the mid-1990s.
85. Luck, "Blue Ribbon Power", p. 89.
86. Ken Booth and Tim Dunne (eds.) (2002) *Worlds in Collision: Terror and the Future of Global Order*, Basingstoke: Palgrave/Macmillan, pp. 16–17 (emphasis in original). Palme Commissioner Obasanjo – as Nigeria's president – also referred to common security as a way to deal with the post-September 11 world; see "Nigeria: Obasanajo in Paris, Stresses Common World Security, Prosperity", *Africa News*, 10 February 2002. See also Obasanjo's comments at a NEPAD Paris meeting press conference, 8 February 2002; www.sarpn.org.za/NEPAD/PressConferenceFeb2002/page2.php.
87. William M. Arkin (2003) "New Nukes? No Way", *Los Angeles Times*, 17 August, p. M1.

4

The World Commission on Environment and Development: Ideas and institutions intersect

Heather A. Smith

The Brundtland Report incorporated concern for the environment into the concept of development by erecting "sustainable development" as the conceptual roof for both violating and healing the environment.[1]

Published in 1987, the World Commission on Environment and Development (WCED), or Brundtland Commission as it came to be known, popularized the phrase "sustainable development". Sustainable development was defined in the WCED as the ability to "meet the needs of the present without compromising the ability of future generations to meet their own needs".[2] This concept embedded at the core of Commission report, *Our Common Future*, has resonance to this day. Indeed, "sustainable development" has become a central tenet in the international environmental governance discourse and it is inextricably linked to and embedded in international environmental governance institutions.

From the outset the phrase "sustainable development", and by extension the work of the Commission, has been contested. What does it really mean? For whom is sustainable development? Was it a conceptual breakthrough that has since become an "inspirational norm", in the words of Peter Haas,[3] resulting in governments' addition of "ecological integrity to the traditional goals of wealth and power"? Or is it, as Wolfgang Sachs[4] and others[5] have suggested, an anthropocentric mantra designed to perpetuate Western ideals and values, reinforce degrading notions of progress and marginalize vulnerable peoples and nature. In terms of policy guidance, the value of the concept has also been questioned. How does one implement a sustainable development strategy, given the contested and imprecise nature of the idea?

Sustainable development remains contested and imprecise, but perhaps imprecision facilitated the diffusion across states and sectors and perhaps that same imprecision helps us to understand the sustainability of "sustainable development". The longevity of the concept of sustainable development cannot however be explained simply by its conceptual characteristics. It is essentially given that ideas and norms are contested. To understand the longevity and popularity, even power, of the concept of sustainable development we need to assess the convergence of forces that catapulted sustainable development onto the international environmental agenda. The work of the WCED could have been lost in the Cold War privileging of security, but it was not. Sustainable development continues into the twenty-first century to be a central concept in international environmental discourse. This longevity and popularity of the concept cannot be explained by simply saying the Brundtland Commission popularized the idea. Rather, sustainable development has been reinforced and legitimized by the very institutions, conferences, government agencies, and development initiatives that adopt it as a guiding principle. Ideas and institutions intersect and mutually reinforce each other.

This chapter begins with a brief examination of the conceptual origins of sustainable development and the political origins of the World Commission on Environment and Development. The subsequent popularization of the Commission's work is then explained by an examination of the confluence of ideas, exogenous forces, and key personalities. Simply put, timing mattered. We then turn our attention to the Commission report itself with the aim of describing its contents. The penultimate section of the chapter assesses the short- and long-term impact of the Commission's report with the intent of showing how ideas and institutions intersect over time to reinforce and legitimize the concept of sustainable development. It will be seen that there is little doubt that the work of the World Commission on Environment and Development has had a lasting influence on how we understand and define international environmental governance, but it is unclear as to whether or not it is more than an "inspirational norm". If, as Lorraine Elliott argues, "global environmental governance ... is a political practice which simultaneously reflects, constitutes *and masks* global relations of power and powerlessness"[6] we are beholden to inquire: for whom and what is sustainable development? Sustainable development, as an inspirational norm, has not inspired a global re-evaluation of our relationship with nature.

Origins of an idea and a commission

How did "environment" and "development" become linked under the aegis of sustainable development? What constellation of forces explains the formation of the WCED and how do we understand the attention sustainable development garnered in the late 1980s? As this section reveals, the idea of sustainable development evolved over time and by the late 1980s the public and governments alike, by virtue of a number of factors described below, were open to the views articulated in *Our Common Future*.

The starting point of the intellectual evolution of sustainable development as a concept which links environment and development is contested. Wolfgang Sachs dates variations of sustainable development back to forest management in Germany in the 1800s and the American Progressive movement after 1900,[7] while David Carruthers regards sustainable development as, originally, a radical concept associated with grassroots initiatives in the 1970s.[8] Peter Thacher argues that "the linked issues of environment and development were put together on the UN agenda by the 'Founex Report' early in 1971, which concluded that environmental problems result not only from the development process itself, but also from lack of development".[9] Maurice Strong, a key participant in the Founex meeting, describes the report as seminal and declares the meeting as having had a profound influence on the 1972 Stockholm UN Conference and on the "evolution of the concept of the environment–development relationship".[10] Thacher, consistent with Strong, argues that early iterations of the idea of sustainable development can be found in the declaration of the 1972 United Nations Conference on the Human Environment (UNCHE), or the Stockholm Conference. The United Nations Environment Programme (UNEP) formed as an institutional outcome of the UNCHE was seen as pivotal in the articulation of some variation of sustainable development. Strong went on to be the first Executive Director of UNEP.

While the genesis of sustainable development and by extension the WCED is often associated with the 1970s, more commonly, the development of the World Conservation Strategy in 1980 by the International Union for the Conservation of Nature (IUCN) with support from the World Wildlife Fund (WWF) and the UNEP, is regarded as the first policy statement to connect the environment and development. Again, according to Thacher, the World Conservation Strategy "was one of the first to stress sustainability, especially of natural life-support systems in the context of supporting human needs".[11] In 1982 the United Nations General Assembly (UNGA) produced the World Charter for Nature. In

1983 the UNGA established the World Commission on Environment and Development "to examine the condition of and prospects for the economy and the environment in the prospect of the year 2000 and beyond".[12] The WCED report was published in 1987 and subsequently became the impetus behind the UNGA resolution of December 1989 to convene a conference on environment and development on the twentieth anniversary of the Stockholm Conference. That conference, the United Nations Conference on Environment and Development (UNCED), was held in 1992 in Rio de Janeiro. But, one must ask – why the interest in the environment and development? Why did this Commission report become the catalyst for one of the most high profile world conferences in the 1990s?

To understand the attention garnered by the WCED and ultimately, the popularity of the concept of sustainable development we need to examine the confluence of ideas, exogenous forces, and personalities. In terms of ideas, it is important to recall sustainable development appealed, broadly, to both Northern and Southern elites, although in the case of the latter it took some persuasion by key personalities. Recall, the intellectual precursor of sustainable development was the "limits to growth" argument. In contrast to the "limits to growth" discourse of the late 1960s and early 1970s, which articulated an apocalyptic vision of the earth running out of resources and advocated proposals contrary to the interests of Western capitalism, sustainable development seemed both more hopeful and more pragmatic. "The maxim for sustainable development is not 'limits to growth'; it is 'the growth of limits'. Some limits are imposed by the impact of present technologies and social organization. But many present limits can be expanded, through changes in modes of decision-making, through changes in some domestic and international policies, and through massive investments in human and resource capital".[13] Sustainable development sought to combine environment and development in such a way that the interdependence of the economy and environment was recognized and allowed for both environmental protection and economic growth.[14] This combination met the requirement of the elites of developing states by ensuring their right to develop, while simultaneously ensuring the right to sustained growth by already developed states.

Sustainable development was also more than a recognition of the interdependence between the environment and development, for some, it was a holistic concept. Maurice Strong has identified a sense of holism offered by sustainable development when he defines sustainable development as linking the "economic, social, population, gender [and] human settlement dimensions of development".[15] Sustainable development was a flexible concept, subject to multiple interpretations. Sustainable development was the megafix – designed to unite all participants.[16] Indeed, sustainable development did offer something to everyone.

However, as argued above, it is not sufficient to assert that sustainable development was an imprecise or flexible concept and thus acceptable to many. System change is pivotal to our explanation of the "success" of the WCED. After all, the Commission was established in 1983 in a period, called by many, the New Cold War. The New Cold War corresponded to the early years of the administration of Ronald Reagan. It was in 1983 that the Reagan administration proposed the Strategic Defence Initiative and it was also in that same year that a Korean Airlines flight was shot down. The environment may have been important to the United Nations General Assembly, but it was not uppermost in the minds of many world leaders. When *Our Common Future* was published in 1987, tensions between the East and West remained, but there was new sense of hope with the changes taking place in the Soviet Union under Mikhail Gorbachev. With the fall of the Berlin Wall in November 1989 the world felt a heady optimism about the future, and thus perhaps it is no coincidence that the UNGA recommendation for the United Nations Conference on Environment and Development was proposed in December 1989. The high profile nature of UNCED can be explained, at least in part, by the structural changes that provided for a shift in the international agenda that allowed for more international attention to the environment. The concept, the Commission and the conference were all affected by the changing world order.

The appeal of sustainable development and the attention paid to the Commission's work also relates to public awareness of the environment. During the late 1970s and early 1980s there was heightened public concern about environmental problems. According to Lorraine Elliott, there were a series of disasters that captured the public's attention. These disasters ranged from the "1979 partial melt down at the Three Mile Island nuclear power plant" to the explosion at Chernobyl in 1986. "In 1984, the methyl isocyanate gas leak at Bhopal in India, . . . killed 2000 and injured 200,000, [and] in the same year, 30 tons of toxic chemicals were washed into the Rhine following a fire at a Sandoz warehouse in Switzerland".[17] Public concern about environmental problems was not only linked to disasters, by the mid-to-late 1980s, there was also a growing awareness of the connection between the local, regional, and global, and an increased awareness of the global nature of environmental issues.[18] The Social Learning Group's 2001 study *Learning to Manage Global Environmental Risks* includes analysis of the attention to global environmental atmospheric issues. In the cases of the United Kingdom, Germany, the Netherlands, Hungary and Japan, for example, attention to ozone depletion spiked in the mid-to-late 1980s although Germany spiked slightly earlier in the decade. On climate change, almost across the respective states, attention spiked in 1987–1988. Publics, at least in these developed states, became increasingly aware of the global atmospheric issues, thus contributing to the international greening.

One of the key causal factors in the increased public and elite awareness, aside from high profile environmental disasters, is science. We cannot underestimate the importance of the scientific community in shaping, identifying and framing global environmental issues. Typically, the scientific definition of the problem precedes the popular definition of the problem, and the scientists, sometimes functioning as an epistemic community, can function as a catalyst. For example, the work of Joseph Farman and his team that essentially identified the ozone hole in the Antarctic in 1985 is pivotal to our understanding of the global risk associated with ozone depletion.[19] Similarly, the science of climate change has a long history, but the combination of extreme events in 1987–1988, high profile American scientists making comments about the urgency of global warming, and an extremely well-managed international conference in Toronto in the summer of 1988 on the global atmosphere, propelled climate change onto the international political agenda. The work of the WCED occurred concurrently with the sense of urgency about ozone depletion and climate change. Thus, governments, grappling with these issues, sought appropriate management tools and the work of the WCED and the concept of sustainable development provided a foundation for attempts to manage the environment. The sense of urgency also contributed to the high profile nature of UNCED.

Two additional trends contributed to the opportunity window that opened in the late 1980s and early 1990s.[20] First, during the 1970s and 1980s environmental non-governmental organizations (ENGOs) multiplied, especially in developed states. The proliferation of ENGOs was an expression of popular awareness of environmental issues that also served to reinforce the growing sense of urgency about environmental degradation. Second, "the 1970s and 1980s also witnessed an immense growth in international environmental law, both 'hard' (treaties and conventions) and 'soft' (non-binding declarations of principle)".[21] One of the key accomplishments of international environmental law during this time was the 1987 negotiation of the Montreal Protocol on Substances That Deplete the Ozone Layer. The successful negotiation of the Montreal Protocol was regarded by Richard Benedick[22] as "a paradigm for new diplomatic approaches to new kinds of international challenges". The Montreal Protocol built on a trend toward the management of international environmental issues through diplomatic means and reinforced a faith in international environmental law thus providing the tools of statecraft, to be fused with the concept of sustainable development as guiding principle, for the management of issues such as climate change and biodiversity.

Finally, we can neither underestimate the role of the commissioners themselves nor the importance of political leaders who joined the sustainable development bandwagon. In 1982 Gro Harlem Brundtland was approached on behalf of Mostafa Tolba, then the Executive Director of the United Nations Environment Programme. Tolba, according to Brundtland's memoirs,[23] came to talk to her about a new commission, although he himself was sceptical about the idea. She was short-listed for the Commission along with former American President Jimmy Carter and former British Prime Minister Edward Heath. In spite of being Norwegian Prime Minister, she took the job when offered to her by Secretary-General Pérez de Cuéllar. They then began the task of putting together the Commission.

The commissioners were drawn from around the world and included many high profile individuals. Maurice Strong brought to the Commission his background as the first Executive Director of the United Nations Environment Programme and the Secretary-General of the UN Conference on the Human Environment. Another key member of the Commission was Shridath Ramphal, then Secretary-General of the Commonwealth of Nations. Although initially reluctant to join the Commission, Brundtland persuaded him to do so. Jim MacNeill joined the Commission as Secretary-General. He brought with him a wealth of experience including six years as the Director of Environment at the Organization for Economic Cooperation and Development.

The appointment of the Vice-Chair of the Commission was apparently a source of contention. According to Brundtland, the "Secretary General of the UN initially wanted to appoint President Senghor of Senegal ... but Tolba refused to cooperate further until his good friend and confidant Mansour Khalid was appointed instead. Khalid had previously been Foreign Minister in the Sudan and had good contacts in the African and Arab world".[24] While Brundtland ultimately regarded Khalid as a crucial member of the Commission, her autobiography strongly suggests that there was tension in the early period of the Commission when Khalid seemed to assume that he was co-chair rather than vice-chair. In Brundtland's words, "Mansour Khalid considered me a relatively young and inexperienced woman and clearly believed that it would be easy to wrest control from me. He would be disappointed".[25]

The Commissioners worked in various capacities to promote the Commission and its findings. The Commission held public hearings prior to the publication of *Our Common Future* and included a post-publication advocacy phase in its work plan. According to Jim MacNeill, Secretary

General of the WCED, "the proposal for an 'advocacy phase' arose from what I had learned about the fate of the recommendations of earlier commissions. The Brandt and Palme Commissions, for example, had simply published their reports, and governments felt quite free simply to table or ignore them".[26] The public hearings phase was not without its difficulties. The kinds of public hearings envisioned by the Commission were both unprecedented and unwelcome in some states. Brundtland recalls that public hearings in Indonesia, Brazil and the Soviet Union were not simple to arrange. "Elim Salim, Indonesian Minister of State for Population and the Environment, [and Commission member] was our liaison to the Indonesian government, which was decidedly opposed to the public forum".[27] Ultimately, the public hearing did take place but it was carefully "managed" by the Indonesian government. The Brazilian government feared that discussion of rainforests might infringe on domestic affairs thus threatening their sovereignty. In Russia, there was some doubt as to whether or not Brundtland would have access to Gorbachev. She also had to deal with sexism. Brundtland writes: "Those who had visited Moscow in advance to prepare the meeting were asked, 'Is she going to meet Raisa?' There were many who thought it natural for a Norwegian Prime Minister to meet the Soviet leader's wife. My colleagues gave an emphatic 'no.' This was as silly as asking if Gorbachev was going to meet Dennis Thatcher in London. After all, both of them were men. This was 1986, and still the Soviets as well as the Americans working on the commission considered it natural for me to meet Raisa".[28]

In spite of intra-commission tensions, state concerns about public meetings, and outmoded ideas about the role of women, Brundtland and the commissioners persevered. Brundtland travelled the world and met state leaders promoting the idea of sustainable development. Once published, and despite the end of the Commission's work, many WCED members remained active on the global stage promoting sustainable development. Gro Harlem Brundtland, for example, gave one of the keynote addresses at the Toronto Conference on the Changing Atmosphere – the same meeting that is typically associated with the arrival of climate change on the international agenda. Through articles appearing in academic journals to public speeches, Brundtland actively worked to promote the findings of the WCED. Maurice Strong went on to function as the Secretary-General of the United Nations Conference on Environment and Development in 1992 and he continues, to this day, to promote the concept of sustainable development. Jim MacNeill, Secretary-General of the WCED authored important books and articles on the state of the environment and the greening of international relations in the 1980s.[29]

The Commissioners were eventually joined by several world leaders who "greened" in the late 1980s. Among the leaders were Canadian Prime Minister Brian Mulroney and British Prime Minister Margaret Thatcher. As states and state leaders jumped on the sustainable development bandwagon they vied for recognition of their new-found commitment to environmental well-being. Canada, for example, became a declaratory leader in the fight against climate change, co-hosting the "Toronto Conference" otherwise known as "The Changing Atmosphere: Implications for Global Security" in 1988. Interestingly this conference originated in the desire to have something to showcase Canada's commitment to the environment when the Brundtland Commission came to Canada on its public meetings tour prior to the report's publication. The extent of the greening of leaders in developed states can be observed in at least the rhetorical commitment to sustainable development in the 1988 Toronto G7 Communiqué and the place of primacy accorded to the environment in the 1989 Paris G7 summit, regularly referred to as the "Green Summit".

Thus, the high profile accorded to the Commission's work is explained by several important variables. Ideas evolved over time. Sustainable development, perhaps a "megafix", also captured the attention of the public and world leaders, all increasingly aware of global environmental issues. Science contributed to the awareness and the end of the Cold War provided for the systemic shift that allowed for the environment to be propelled onto the international agenda. The hard work of the commissioners, complemented by successes in international environmental diplomacy, contributed to a broader "greening of international relations". Jim MacNeill, writing in 1989, reflected on the confluence of forces:

> *Our Common Future* was released in April 1987 and presented to the General Assembly six months later. It could not have come out at a better time. During the past few years environmental issues have become deadly serious. A sea change in public opinion has forced them to the top of the political agendas in the United Nations, in Washington, London, Moscow and other capitals around the globe, in some multinational banks, and in many of the board rooms of the Fortune 500. Momentous changes have also occurred in international relations which open the door to fresh thinking about environmental and other non-military security threats to global security.[30]

But what did the Commission say? Certainly the most important contribution of the WCED was and remains the popularization of sustainable development that is now central to the discourse of international environmental governance. Yet *Our Common Future* is more than the concept of sustainable development. The work of the Commission, as will be seen in the next section, attempted to capture several competing visions of our relationships with environment and hoped to reconcile the needs of the North and the South. And while it may be dominated by a Northern perspective, there is an embedded radicalism in the document that is frequently lost in analyses of the Brundtland Commission.

Our Common Future described and revisited

According to the foreword of *Our Common Future* written by the Chair of the Commission, Gro Harlem Brundtland, the work of the WCED was designed to be a "third and compelling call for political action: After Brandt's *Programme for Survival* and *Common Crisis*, and after Palme's *Common Security*, would come *Common Future*".[31] In this call to action, the report sought to promote a vision of possibility – a hope for the common future, but with the recognition that the realization of that future was dependent on political will to change. "The Commission's hope for the future is conditional on decisive political action now to begin managing environmental resources to ensure both sustainable human progress and human survival".[32]

Sustainable development was the cornerstone of the document. As noted earlier, the standard definition of sustainable development is "development that meets the needs of the present without compromising the ability of future generations to meet their own needs".[33] It was argued that sustainable development contained within it, two key concepts: "the concept of 'needs', in particular the essential needs of the world's poor, to which overriding priority should be given; and the idea of limitations imposed by the state of technology and social organization on the environment's ability to meet present and future needs".[34] Sustainable development, thus defined recognizes intergenerational equity and promotes a sense of a common interest. The common interest is a reflection of the ecological interdependence. The articulation of a common interest, consistent with the metaphor of "our common future", in the view of Lorraine Elliott is intended "to reflect our shared vulnerability to and responsibility for global insecurities".[35] This being the case, and in the words of the WCED, "it is not that there is one set of villains and another of victims".[36] At the same time, the WCED acknowledges inequity, and recognizes that there are "losers". " 'Losers' in environment/development conflicts include those who suffer more than their fair share of the health, property and ecosystem damage costs of pollution".[37] Villains denied and losers identified – the uneasy tension between the North's denial of its complicity in the environmental crisis and the South's need for recognition of the impacts of the global economy is expressed in sustainable development.

Beyond sustainable development the report identifies a set of strategic imperatives that follow from the concept of sustainable development. Those imperatives, or critical objectives include: "reviving growth; changing the quality of growth; meeting the needs for jobs, food, energy, water and sanitation; ensuring a sustainable level of population; conserving and enhancing the resource base; reorienting technology and managing risk; and merging environment and economics in decision making".[38]

Reviving growth responds to the poverty of developing states. Changing the quality of growth "requires a change in the content of growth, to make it less material- and energy-intensive and more equitable in its impact".[39] Meeting essential human needs is primarily focused again on developing state poverty but recognizes that "the demands of those not in poverty may have major environmental consequences".[40] Ensuring a sustainable level of population growth is self-explanatory. The conservation and enhancement of the resource base is linked to consumption patterns of the North, anticipated increases in consumption in the South and population growth.[41] In this regard, it is argued that the conservation of nature "is part of our moral obligation to other living beings and future generations".[42] The reorientation of technology is directed at the design of appropriate and efficient technology that meets sustainable development needs. The need to merge environment and economics is recognition of the interdependence of the two forces, in contrast to assumptions that environmental well-being and economic progress function in an oppositional manner.

After fleshing out the concept of sustainable development and identifying the strategic imperatives, *Our Common Future* details the challenges facing the quest for sustainability and describes several pressing issues facing humanity at the time of publication. Chapter three focuses on the role of the international political economy while chapters four to nine describe the "common challenges" of population and human resources, food security, species and ecosystems, energy, industry and urbanization. The report then proceeds to consider the management of the commons and the interconnections between peace, security, development and the environment in chapters ten and eleven, respectively. Finally, the report concludes with proposals for institutional and legal change. It is argued that there are six priority areas for change: "getting at the sources; dealing with the effects; assessing global risks; making informed choices; providing the legal means and investing in our future".[43]

"Getting at the sources" has a number of elements. First, there is a focus on national policies and institutions. The WCED recommends that sustainable development be incorporated into national policy making through vehicles such as annual environmental reporting and foreign policies for the environment.[44] Second, this priority area includes regional and interregional action. It is recommended that "the existing regional and subregional organizations within and outside the UN system need to be strengthened and made responsible and accountable for ensuring that their programmes and budgets encourage and support sustainable development policies and practices".[45] Global institutions and programmes are also included. In this section, a call for UN leadership in the transition to sustainable development is made. Greater UN agency accountability for sustainability is recommended as well as improved interagency coordination.

"Dealing with the effects" relates to the need for "governments [to] strengthen the role and capacity of existing environmental protection and resource management agencies".[46] Agencies falling under this recommendation include national environmental protection agencies and the United Nations Environment Programme. The prescriptions related to UNEP are extensive, ranging from the recommendation that the UNEP "provide leadership, advice, and guidance in the UN system on restoring, protecting, and improving the ecological basis for sustainable development", to enhanced capabilities in environmental assessment and reporting, to calls for increased UNEP funding by states.[47]

"Assessing global risks" relates to risk associated with new technologies. The recommendations under the assessment of global risks focus on capacity building in monitoring and risk assessment and, to that end, the WCED recommended the establishment of a "Global Risks Assessment Programme".[48]

The fourth priority area is "making informed choices". The prescriptions in this section relate to increasing public awareness and participation in the policy process. In addition, there is an explicit call for the increased participation of the scientific community and non-governmental organizations. The impact of industry on sustainable development is recognized in the call for increased cooperation with industry.[49]

The Commission makes a series of recommendations related to international law in the discussion of "providing legal means". In this section, four areas are targeted as urgent needs: "to recognize and respect reciprocal rights and responsibilities of individuals and states regarding sustainable development; to establish and apply norms for state and interstate behaviour to achieve sustainable development; to strengthen and extend the application of existing laws and international agreements in support of sustainable development; [and] to reinforce existing methods and develop new procedures for avoiding and resolving environmental disputes".[50]

Finally, the Commission addressed the issue of finance in their recommendations related to "investing in our future". The need for significant spending, at least in the short term, is recognized as is the need for significant assistance to developing states. States will be required to spend on national sustainable development and developed states will be required to increase their overseas development assistance, although no specific target is provided. The environment-related activities of the World Bank and International Monetary Fund are acknowledged. The efforts of the World Bank to include sustainable development in its mandate is greeted as promising, but it is also stated "but it will not be enough unless and until it is accomplished by a fundamental commitment to sustainable development by the World Bank, and by the transformation of its internal structure and processes so to ensure its capacity to carry this out".[51]

The Commission, in concluding its consensus-based report, states: "we are unanimous in our conviction that the security, well-being and very survival of the planet depend on such changes, now".[52]

The Commission report, as a consensus document, inevitably had to reconcile competing tensions and perhaps those tensions were clearly not reconciled to the liking of all the critics, as will be seen. However, we should not lose sight of the embedded radicalism in the document, nor should we completely disregard the efforts of the commissioners to promote an idea that in some small measure sought to cast some focus on the environment. Indeed, there are critical questions to be asked about the short- and long-term impact of the report and the concept of sustainable development, but is it all so hopeless? These questions will be raised in the next section.

The significance of the WCED considered

In our consideration of the significance of the WCED we begin with some of the critical analyses of the report and the concept of sustainable development. We then turn to the diffusion of the concept of sustainable development. It will be seen that the legacy of the Commission is apparent in the durability and the continued popularity of "sustainable development". But, durability and popularity do not necessarily translate into effective action, as will be seen in a discussion of world conferences. Finally, we turn our attention to the present state of the environment. For all the talk of sustainable development, have we witnessed the long-term change advocated by the Brundtland Commission?

Sustainable development, and the work of the Commission, has been roundly criticized. Tanvi Nagpal notes that the work of the Commission has been regarded as culturally bankrupt, dominated by Western values, and silent on human dignity. The silence on human dignity is related directly to indigenous perspectives on humanity's relationship with the environment. These perspectives are spiritual – "sustainability is not about prosperity but about living a life of dignity in harmony with nature".[53]

The Western individualist and technocratic values that inform the Commission and its emphasis on management are seen as silencing the voices of the margins while simultaneously privileging the voices of polluting elites.

David Carruthers considers sustainable development, originally, to be a genuinely radical idea. Elements of that radicalism can be seen in the Commission report. Embedded in the document are calls to action that challenge the nature of the status quo – then and now. There is an explicit recognition that change is required in consumption patterns in the North. "Sustainable development requires that those who are more affluent adopt life-styles consistent within the planet's ecological means".[54] Further, it is accepted that change will not be easy. "Painful choices have to be made ... sustainable development must rest on political will".[55] However, the radicalism was muted and bent to the will of the dominant pro-growth discourse resulting in what Carruthers calls a "defanged version of sustainable development".[56] Ultimately, by the time Agenda 21 was developed at UNCED the line between sustainable development and sustained economic growth was gone. "Once poised as polar opposites, these concepts were now practically synonymous. Liberated from the distasteful implications of scarcity and limits, sustainability had come full circle, back to an essential belief that open-ended growth will lift all boats".[57]

One of the most passionate critics of the Brundtland Commission and the concept of sustainable development is Wolfgang Sachs. He argues that development became the bandage for the problems of development and that sustainable development has little to do with the environment. "It is not the preservation of nature's dignity that is on the international agenda, but the extension of human-centred utilitarianism to posterity".[58] Sachs is also critical of the sense of management that pervades the sustainable development discourse and the general inability to look at the broader structural causes of environmental degradation. "Unwilling to reconsider the logic of competitive productivism that is at the root of the planet's ecological plight, it [the marriage of environment and development] reduces ecology to a set of managerial strategies aiming at resource efficiency and risk management".[59]

The concept that arguably was designed to reconcile competing perspectives and which was regarded as a "mega-fix" appears to have not appeased all observers. Yet, as noted earlier, the diffusion of the concept has been remarkable. In 1992 the world witnessed the United Nations Conference on Environment and Development. Out of UNCED came the UN Commission on Sustainable Development which was established in 1993,[60] in part, to monitor the implementation of Agenda 21, the massive blueprint for sustainable development that was one of the key documents produced at UNCED. Former Soviet leader Mikhail Gorbachev founded Green Cross International, an organization dedicated, in the spirit of the Rio Conference, to the creation of a sustainable future.[61] The World Bank includes a variation of sustainable development in its vision: "the World Bank's mission is to fight poverty through sustainable and equitable economic growth and social progress".[62] The United Nations Millennium Declaration identified "respect for nature" as one of the fundamental values for the twenty-first century and reaffirmed "support for the principles of sustainable development including those set out in Agenda 21, agreed upon at the United Nations Conference on Environment and Development".[63] In the fall of 2002, the World Summit on Sustainable Development was held in Johannesburg, South Africa.

Around the world, communities, often in partnership with environmental non-governmental organization and international institutions, actively pursue sustainable development as a reality and not simply a vision for the future. For example, the Southern Alliance for Indigenous Resources worked in Mozambican refugee camps in Zimbabwe to "combat deforestation around the camps and reduce firework consumption".[64] In another case, the municipality of Santos in Brazil, created a programme in the early 1990s that saw significant improvements in the water quality of local beaches.[65] Almost everyone is on the sustainable development bandwagon. World conferences envision it, international institutions monitor it, governments advocate it, ENGOs protect it, and communities and individuals try to implement it – or so it appears at first glance.

Business and industry related organizations have also jumped on the sustainable development bandwagon. A key example of business engagement is the activities of the International Chamber of Commerce (ICC). The ICC actively promotes its "Business Charter for Sustainable Development". "The Charter – which captures 16 key principles for environmental management – was developed by a group of business executives over a two-year period from 1989 to 1991. Launched prior to the watershed 1992 United Nations Earth Summit in Rio de Janeiro, the Charter is regarded by many as a visionary document that set the environmental agenda for business and industry during the 1990s".[66] Among other things, the Charter recognizes environmental management is a key determinant to sustainable development, calls for improved corporate policies where the environmental performance is concerned and advocates an openness to public and employee concerns.[67] Oddly, or perhaps not, the ICC Charter does not include a definition of sustainable development. Given two years of work to design the Charter, surely the omission is purposive. The Charter is vague enough that it is open to multiple interpretations, but what is less fuzzy is the position articulated by the Secretary-General of ICC India at the Eighth Conference of Parties to the United Nations Framework Convention on Climate Change in November 2002.

Dr. Amit Mitra, speaking on behalf of "businesses, big and small, in both developed and developing countries" stated that in terms of climate change "the business challenge is all about successfully internalizing the sustainable development costs in the face of brutal market realities and becom[ing] global corporate citizens".[68] To enable business to achieve this end, Dr. Mitra stated that enterprises needed to be able to meet emissions reductions at the least possible cost and called on the world community to "create incentive structures and market premiums for technologies and business processes that meet the climate change challenge through knowledge".[69]

Is this sustainable development or sustainable economic development? The vagueness of the Charter and the market-oriented language of the statement at the climate change negotiations support the criticisms raised by Nagpal, Carruthers and Sachs. A pro-growth and pro-market discourse dominates the language of the ICC as sustainable development becomes a "cost" as opposed to an imperative. Somehow, business becomes the good corporate citizen which must take on the cost of sustainable development. It is not in the interest of those represented above, which are in no way all businesses, to challenge the status quo because they are the status quo. This sustainable development, consistent with Sachs above, has little to do with the environment. It is "weak sustainability".[70] Weak sustainability assumes "that the current development trajectory can be maintained in an environmentally safe manner through relatively minor modifications. These models favour market-based approaches, private ownership of natural resources and technical solutions to environmental problems".[71]

If some business initiatives have not measured up, or at least confirmed the views of critics, what about the world conferences that followed the publication of the WCED? While Lorraine Elliott and Wolfgang Sachs are critical of international (or global) environmental diplomacy for its ineffectiveness and inability to translate into substantive improvement of the natural environment, Peter Haas is more optimistic. Haas argues "that many conferences provide direct effects that may be beneficial for inducing states to make more progressive steps toward governance and sustainable development".[72] The conferences, such as UNCED and the UN World Summit on Sustainable Development, "have promoted broader processes of social learning and the construction of new, more comprehensive conceptual frameworks for global environmental governance through issues clarification, popularization of issues, and the new introduction of new environmental policymaking approaches to governmental officials".[73] Rejecting the assumption that UN conferences should translate into lasting effects, Haas continues "it would be unreasonable to expect such conferences to yield lasting and clear effects on states and on the environment. It is equally unreasonable to assign blame to conferences for failing to reverse environmental decline".[74] Thus rather than look at the state of the environment as a marker of success, Haas focuses on a set of diplomatic functions and argues that there many activities undertaken by world environment conferences including: agenda setting, popularization of issues and raising consciousness, generating new information and identifying new challenges for governments, providing general alerts and early warning of new threats, galvanizing administrative reform, adopting new norms, and promoting mass involvement of new actors.[75] If we accept that world conferences are themselves an expression of norms such as sustainable development, then consistent with Haas we might argue that the long-term legacy of the Commission is reflected in the kinds of activities arising out of the UNCHE and UNWSSD, many of which are broadly valuable to states and non-state actors alike.

Yet, there is a lingering question: what of the environment? We can argue that the WCED functioned to set agendas, we can note that there have been financial commitments made around the world in pursuit of sustainable development, we can calculate the millions of dollars spent on commissions and summits, but so what? Why is it unreasonable to expect lasting and clear effects on states and on the environment? Is international environmental governance so slow or so incremental? Moreover, should not the environment and its well-being be the centre of our measure of our success or lack thereof? Or is it that when we look at statistics and data on environmental well-being that we become aware of the ineffectiveness of the millions of dollars spent on conferencing.

The outlook is not entirely promising. According to the United Nations Environment Programme "if present trends in population growth, economic growth and consumption patterns continue, the natural environment will be increasingly stressed. Distinct environmental gains and improvements will probably be offset by the pace and scale of global economic growth, increased global environmental pollution and accelerated degradation of the Earth's renewable resource base".[76] UNEP does hold out some hope for change, but that change requires action. It is noted "trends toward environmental degradation can be slowed, and economic activity can be shifted to more sustainable patterns. Choices for development, and levels and patterns of consumption, are shaped by human aspirations and values and these choices can be influenced by policy interventions".[77] UNEP, in the last sentence defaults again to "management" as critiqued by Sachs and thus, while calling for change, the call remains embedded in the dominant international environmental discourse. Without wanting to be too critical of UNEP because it has worked under difficult circumstances to promote the environment, one cannot wonder if the management twist in the last statement is a reflection of part of the problem. If institutions and conference and commissions are embedded in a discourse that privileges particular kinds of progress over others, a discourse that promotes Western values that make us stewards and managers of the environment, a discourse that continues to privilege state sovereignty and functions to support our denial of our impact on the earth on which we walk, why would we expect conferences and commissions to be effective?

The environment, or more appropriately, nature, should be part of the sustainable development equation. Sustainable development, as interpreted here, is not about sustained economic growth, nor does it equate progress with an increase in gross domestic product. Living in peace with nature is not the norm. We disrespect the sacred and deny our dependence on and vulnerability to natural forces. We are in the midst of a "worldwide crisis of nature"[78] that suggests that while sustainable development is a popular, diffuse and much parroted concept, there has been a failure of international environmental governance to translate ideas into action. Perhaps we should reject the concept of sustainable development. Perhaps we should redefine the undefinable. Perhaps we should accept the uncertainty and diversity of interpretations. Or perhaps we simply accept that sustainable development has been implemented, but not with nature in mind. While one may wish to advocate on behalf of the concept of sustainable development, while others may wish to dispense with it, the fact remains that there are challenges ahead – challenges that have been recognized by a former member of the World Commission on Environment and Development. Perhaps we should ponder the vision of Maurice Strong who observed that a sustainable future requires significant cultural change – "a reorientation of the ethical, moral and spiritual values which provide the primary motivations for human behavior. Concepts of caring, respect for, sharing and cooperation with others must be at the centre of the motivational system that undergirds the transition to sustainability."[79]

One way or another, we will need to find a new ethic for the earth. Time, however, is not necessarily on our side.

Concluding reflections

If we are still awaiting the transition to sustainability, contained in a new ethic for the earth, what does this say of the relevance of the World Commission on Environment and Development? How is it that 25 years after the publication of *Our Common Future* the Secretary-General of the United Nations, Kofi Annan, feels obliged to state: "Let there be no more disguising the perilous state of the earth, or pretending that conservation is too expensive, when we know that the cost of failure to act is far greater. Let us stop being economically defensive, and start being politically courageous".[80] Did not the Brundtland Commission also call for political will? Political will has not been in abundance or at least political will that translated into a genuine commitment to environmental integrity.

Yet, the lack of implementation of policies resulting in fundamental change should not cause us to toss *Our Common Future* into the dustbin of history as a meaningless document. Regardless of how we wish to interpret the impact of the WCED, it cannot be denied that the Brundtland Report is "one of the paradigm statements of ecological modernization".[81] The emergence of sustainable development marked a new era in the global environmental discourse – a discourse that may be rejected by some – but a discourse that has been widely adopted by others. Regardless of our "position" it is beholden upon us to seek to interpret the evolution of the discourse and to understand, or try to understand, the power of the discourse of sustainable development. If we position ourselves as critics we must understand that sustainable development has a cache that still seems to sell, and it remains a slippery, flexible and imprecise concept. If we position ourselves as incrementalists or "insiders" we need to be aware of the critiques of the concept or perhaps, more strategically, the power of the concept to legitimize certain behaviours while obfuscating others. This chapter shows that we cannot take a concept for granted. There is power in ideas even if it is a case of "greenwashing".

In terms of the dynamics surrounding the Commission itself, this chapter speaks to the importance of timing. The work of many commissions has not had the lasting impact associated with the WCED. Regardless of the diligent efforts of the Commissioners we cannot underestimate the importance of external forces. The systemic shift that led to the "New World Order" was not anticipated by many at the time of the formation of the WCED, but the systemic shift absolutely affected the promotion of items on the international agenda otherwise subsumed under Cold War hostilities. Public awareness also seems to have been a crucial variable.

One unexpected finding of this chapter is associated with the insights gleaned from Gro Harlem Brundtland's autobiography. In particular, we are made aware of the gendered nature of the internal dynamics of the Commission. We become aware of the internal obstacles to a "successful" Commission and we are made aware of the tenacity required by the Commission Chair to ensure that her voice and place were respected. In spite of all the limitations associated with the concept of sustainable development, it is important to recognize the vision of Secretary-General Pérez de Cuéllar in his appointment of Gro Harlem Brundtland. The Commission focused on the environment and development, but by its composition it challenged outmoded notions of leadership and diplomacy. Timing matters, but so do personalities.

Unfortunately, environmental degradation continues. The popularization of sustainable development has not fundamentally altered the state of the world. Perhaps, as argued by Elliott and Sachs, global environmental governance simply reinforces Western notions of progress and silences alternative voices. Nature is not part of the equation and much of international environmental governance seems nothing more than "shuffling deck chairs on the Titanic". Yet somehow, the very fact that we continue to debate sustainable development is suggestive. It is not taken for granted that we have achieved sustainable development. Businesses and governments continue to be pushed by ENGOs and academics to do more than simply identify inspirational norms. Perhaps the legacy of the Brundtland Commission lies not with the concept of sustainable development but rather in its contribution to the debate about what constitutes environmental well-being. We were asked to think about it in 1983 and we are still discussing it in 2004. The Brundtland Commission contributed to the cementing of the environment on the international agenda acting as both a site of power and a site of resistance. The World Commission on Environment and Development affected the way we see the world, the way we understand what constitutes an international issue and changed our language and ideas around the environment. Whether this is good or bad is a matter of perspective. That the Commission had an impact is not contested.

Notes

1. Wolfgang Sachs (1999) *Planet Dialectics: Explorations in Environment and Development*, London: Zed Books, p. 60.
2. World Commission on Environment and Development (1987) *Our Common Future*, Oxford: Oxford University Press, p. 8.
3. Peter M. Haas (2002) "UN Conferences and Constructivist Governance of the Environment", *Global Governance* 8: 75.
4. Sachs, *Planet Dialectics*.
5. See David Carruthers (2001) "From Opposition to Orthodoxy: The Remaking of Sustainable Development", *Journal of Third World Studies* (Fall) (accessed from Proquest Database); Maria Mies (1993) "The Need for a New Vision: the Subsistence Perspective", in *Ecofeminism*, Maria Mies and Vandana Shiva (eds.) London: Zed Books; Vandana Shiva (1993) "Homeless in the Global Village", in *Ecofeminism*, Maria Mies and Vandana Shiva (eds.) London: Zed Books.

6. Lorraine Elliott (2002) *The Global Politics of the Environment*, New York: New York University Press, p. 58.
7. Sachs, *Planet Dialectics*, p. 59.
8. Carruthers, "From Opposition to Orthodoxy", p. 3.
9. Peter S. Thacher (1992) "The Role of the United Nations", *The International Politics of the Environment*, in Andrew Hurrell and Benedict Kingsbury (eds.) Oxford: Oxford University Press, p. 188.
10. Maurice F. Strong (2000) *Where on Earth Are We Going?*, Toronto: Alfred A. Knopf Canada, p. 125.
11. Thacher, "The Role of the United Nations", p. 189.
12. Maurice F. Strong (1994) "Draft Notes for Remarks by Maurice F. Strong, Chairman, Earth Council to Royal Swedish Academy of Sciences April 9" *Earth Council: Papers and Speeches*, p. 2. See http://www.ecouncil.ac.cr/about/speech/strong/royalaca.html) (accessed 6/2/2003).
13. Jim MacNeill (1989–1990) "The Greening of International Relations", *International Journal* XLV: 19.
14. Andrew Hurrell and Benedict Kingsbury (1992) "The International Politics of the Environment: An Introduction", *The International Politics of the Environment*, Andrew Hurrell and Benedict Kingsbury (eds.) Oxford: Oxford University Press, p. 3.
15. Strong, *Where on Earth Are We Going?*, p. 2.
16. Sharachchandra M. Lele (1995) "Sustainable Development: A Critical Review", *Green Planet Blues: Environmental Politics from Stockholm to Rio*, Ken Conca, Michael Alberty and Geoffrey D. Dabelko (eds.) Boulder CO: Westview, p. 232.
17. Elliott, *The Global Politics of the Environment*, p. 14.
18. Hurrell and Kingsbury, "The International Politics of the Environment", pp. 2–3.
19. Brian Wynne, Peter Simmons *et al.* (2001) "Institutional Cultures and the Management of Global Environmental Risks in the United Kingdom", *Learning to Manage Global Environmental Risks*, Social Learning Group (eds.) Cambridge Mass: MIT Press, p. 100.
20. Brian W. Tomlin (1998) "On a fast-track to a ban: The Canadian Policy process", *Canadian Foreign Policy* 5(3): 3–23.
21. Martin W. Holgate (1995) "Pathways to Sustainability: The Evolving Role of Transnational Institutions", *Environment* (November 1995): 4. (proquest database accessed 4/22/02. See also Elliott, *The Global Politics of the Environment*, p. 15.
22. Richard Elliot Benedick (1991) *Ozone Diplomacy: New Directions in Safeguarding the Planet*, Cambridge, Mass: Harvard University Press, p. xiii.
23. Gro Harlem Brundtland (2002) *Madam Prime Minister: A Life in Power and Politics*, New York: Farrar, Straus and Giroux, p. 192.
24. *Ibid.*, p. 194.
25. *Ibid.*, p. 194.
26. MacNeill, "The Greening of International Relations", p. 12.
27. Gro Harlem Brundtland, *Madam Prime Minister: A Life in Power and Politics*, p. 198.
28. Ibid., pp. 208–209.
29. See MacNeill, "The Greening of International Relations".
30. Ibid., p. 33.
31. WCED, *Our Common Future*, p. x.
32. *Ibid.*, p. 1.
33. *Ibid.*, p. 43.
34. *Ibid.*, p. 43.
35. Elliott, *The Global Politics of the Environment*, p. 66.
36. WCED, *Our Common Future*, p. 47.
37. *Ibid.*, p. 48.

38. *Ibid.*, p. 49.
39. *Ibid.*, p. 52.
40. *Ibid.*, p. 54.
41. *Ibid.*, p. 57.
42. *Ibid.*, p. 57.
43. *Ibid.*. p. 314.
44. *Ibid.*, p. 314.
45. *Ibid.*, p. 315.
46. *Ibid.*, p. 319.
47. *Ibid.*, pp. 320–323.
48. *Ibid.*, p. 325.
49. *Ibid.*, pp. 326–330.
50. *Ibid.*, p. 330.
51. *Ibid.*, p. 337.
52. *Ibid.*, p. 343.
53. Tanvi Nagpal (1995) "Voices from the Developing World: Progress Toward Sustainable Development", *Environment* (October): 6 (accessed from Proquest Database 4/22/02).
54. WCED, *Our Common Future*, p. 9.
55. *Ibid.*, p. 9.
56. Carruthers, "From Opposition to Orthodoxy", p. 5.
57. Ibid., pp. 5–6.
58. Sachs, *Planet Dialectics*, p. 34.
59. *Ibid.*, p. 68.
60. United Nations General Assembly, "Institutional Arrangements to Follow Up United Nations Conference on Environment and Development" 29 January 1993, (A/RES/47/191).
61. Green Cross International. 2003. "History and Mission", (http://www.gci.ch/GreenCrossFamily/historymission/html) (accessed 6/5/03).
62. (World Bank, 2003).
63. (UNGA (2000): 2, 6).
64. United Nations (1997) "United Nations Earth Summit +5 Success Stories: Mozambican Refugee Camps in Zimbabwe", p. 1. (http://www.un.org/esa/earthsummit/hcrsuc.htm) (accessed 6/5/2003).
65. United Nations (1997) "United Nations Earth Summit +5 Success Stories: Santos Beaches Recovery Programme", p. 1. (http://www.un.org/esa/earthsummit/w-santos.htm) (accessed 6/5/2003).
66. International Chamber of Commerce (2003) "About the Business Charter for Sustainable Development", p. 1. (http://www.iccwbo.org/home/environment_and_energy/sdcharter/charter/about_charter/ab) (accessed 8/26/2003).
67. International Chamber of Commerce (2003) "The Business Charter for Sustainable Development – 16 Principles", pp. 1–2. (http://www.iccwbo.org/home/environment_and_energy/sdcharter/charter/principles/princi...) (accessed 8/26/2003).
68. International Chamber of Commerce (2002) "Business and Industry Intervention: 8th Conference of Parties to the UNFCCC, New Delhi, India", p. 1. (www.iccwbo.org) (accessed 8/26/2003).
69. Ibid., p. 2.
70. Marc Williams (2001) "In search of global standards: The political economy of trade and the environment", *The International Political Economy of the Environment*, Dimitris Stevis and Valerie J. Assetto (eds.) Boulder, Co: Lynne Rienner, p. 42.
71. Ibid., p. 42.
72. Haas, "UN Conferences and Constructivist Governance of the Environment", p. 73.

73. Ibid., p. 75.
74. Ibid., p. 81.
75. Ibid., pp. 81–87.
76. (UNEP 2000: 4).
77. Ibid.
78. Sachs, *Planet Dialectics*, p. 85.
79. Strong, "Draft Notes", p. 12.
80. Kofi Annan, Address to the World Summit on Sustainable Development, 2 September 2002. (http://www.un.org/events/wssd/statements/sgE.htm (accessed 6/5/2003).
81. Maarten A. Hajer (1995) *The Politics of Environmental Discourse: Ecological Modernization and the Policy Process*, Oxford: Clarendon Press, p. 26.

5

Equivocating on the future of world order: The Commission on Global Governance

*W. Andy Knight**

From its initial moment, the United Nations was consigned the lofty goals of maintaining international peace and security, developing friendly relations among nations based on principles of equal rights and self-determination, achieving international cooperation for solving transnational problems, encouraging and promoting respect for human rights and fundamental freedoms for all, and harmonizing the activities of states in the pursuit of the above common ends. Other equally high-minded goals were added later, such as protecting the global commons and facilitating the global spread of democracy.

Looking back on the twentieth century, it is now evident that this multilateral organization's record in achieving these basic "global governance" goals has been mixed, at best. In fact, some analysts have made the case that the UN's record has been one of abject failure. Even observers who are generally sympathetic to the global institution are now questioning whether the UN may have lost its relevance as a global institution of multilateral governance, and whether it can ultimately withstand the assaults on its legitimacy and credibility. Certainly, the most objective and fair-minded critics of this organization have come to the conclusion that after more than a half-century in operation, the UN has yet to deliver "the goods". The scourge of war, which the organization was created to protect humanity from, is far from eliminated. Worldwide, each and every day, we witness the trampling under foot of many of the basic principles that the UN is supposed to uphold and protect, such as fundamental freedoms, human rights, equality rights, justice, socio-economic rights, and cultural rights.

This situation has not gone unnoticed by those who wish to see the UN succeed and by those who see the institution as the best hope for countering any threat to civilization and, indeed, to the future of humankind. The Commission on Global Governance's Report, *Our Global Neighbourhood*, is representative of a number of studies and reports published at the tail end of the twentieth century that reflected on the urgent need for reform of the UN or, failing that, the development of new forms of multilateral institutions that could adequately address the transnational problems facing our globe. These more or less idealist, liberal institutional, reports all begin with the normative position that the post-Cold War global community needs an environment of peace, equity, improved socio-economic and welfare conditions, environmental and ecological preservation, and justice if humankind is to survive much longer on this planet.[1]

This chapter examines the work of the Commission on Global Governance, focusing on the intellectual and policy context within which the Commission sprung, the character and makeup of the Commission, the various positions held in its Report – *Our Global Neighbourhood* – about improving the governance of the globe, the impact which the Commission's Report has had on subsequent thinking regarding UN reform, and some of the criticisms levelled at the work of this Commission. The conclusion reached is that this particular blue ribbon panel's recommendations falls somewhere in between two competing conceptualizations of multilateralism (traditional and critical) and straddles the fence between "top-down" and "bottom-up" conceptions and practices of multilateral governance. In essence, *Our Global Neighbourhood* is an equivocal document.

Another blue ribbon panel: character and make-up of the Commission

With the dismantling of the Soviet Union and the virtual end of Cold War hostilities by the end of the 1980s, there was great optimism in the prospects that this "new" global political climate held for strengthening global cooperation and thereby renewing hope of bringing peace and security, economic development, justice and ecological sustainability to the planet. During the 1970s and 1980s there had been several blue ribbon panels, consisting of high profile global figures, which examined what was needed to address the problems confronting humanity. But the thawing of the Cold War and the warming of relations between the then superpowers in the late 1980s provided a unique opportunity to rethink governance at the global level and the place of the UN system in such governance. Indeed, this opportunity was seized upon by former West German Chancellor, Willy Brandt – who is generally credited with laying the foundation for the creation of the Commission on Global Governance.

Willy Brandt had, a decade earlier, headed up one of the blue ribbon panels referred to above.[2] He invited a number of prominent individuals from previous blue ribbon panels, including the one he chaired, to a meeting in Königswinter, Germany in January 1990 to peer into this window of opportunity presented by the end of the Cold War and the changing political climate.[3] At the Königswinter meeting, there was agreement amongst those attending that the world was indeed undergoing a fundamental structural change that was creating a propitious environment for global multilateral institutions like the UN to embark upon much needed reform and adjustment. In large part, this perceived shift offered hope for improved cooperation and collaboration among international actors. However, a significant caveat was expressed at this meeting about the fact that, as a result of the foundational alterations, there might be momentous challenges to national leaders in the future that could only be met through enhanced multilateral institutions. In other words, the challenges envisioned could not be adequately dealt with by states, acting alone.

Three prominent global leaders – Ingvar Carlsson (then Prime Minister of Sweden), Shridath Ramphal (then Secretary-General of the Commonwealth), and Jan Pronk (the Minister for Development Cooperation of the Netherlands) – were asked at the culmination of the Königswinter meeting to write a report highlighting the main global issues requiring multilateral action in the immediate post-Cold War period. Once the report was concluded, another meeting was held in Stockholm, in April 1991, to discuss it. That meeting, labelled the "Stockholm Initiative on Global Security and Governance",[4] called for the creation of an international commission to fully explore the perceived opportunities created by the Cold War's end and to construct a blueprint for a more efficient and effective system of multilateral security and governance.[5] This new blue ribbon panel, the Commission on Global Governance, was co-chaired by Ramphal and Carlsson – both of whom met in April 1992 with the then UN Secretary-General, Boutros-Ghali, to explain the goals of the Commission. The UN Secretary-General endorsed the initiative, but the Commission remained independent of the UN system. The Commission's 28 members met in the fall of 1992 to begin deliberations, each one of them acting in their own personal capacity and not under the instructions of their respective governments. Funding for the Commission's operations was secured from two trust funds administered jointly by the United Nations Development Programme (UNDP), nine national governments, and private foundations.

As Richard Falk puts it, the impulse to form blue ribbon panels like the Commission on Global Governance "is quintessentially liberal, in the American sense of the term". Supposedly, the individuals selected to these panels are wise, rational, and respected leaders who carry some clout with government leaders and have much credibility with and influence on the general public. Understanding that national leaders were being insufficiently responsive to problems of global import, these distinguished and influential liberal statesmen would use such panels as bully pulpits to urge national leaders to become more responsive to the global challenges.[6] One of the important contributions such blue ribbon panels have made through their reports is in the area of "conceptual clarification".[7]

Concepts and intellectual/policy context

With a growing number of blue ribbon panels examining ways of adjusting global governing institutions to deal with a changing global polity, one has to ask the question why did this particular Commission hit such a nerve with academics, policy practitioners and the public?

For one thing, the Commission on Global Governance's Report not only built on the analytical efforts of previous blue ribbon panels to find better ways of organizing the activities of the globe, it went beyond them in notable ways. First, it presented perhaps the clearest, most convincing conceptualization of global governance, and framed issues that required such governance in a most compelling fashion. Second, it depicted the systemic changes in global politics, since the end of the Cold War, in a manner that demonstrated the urgency of "freshness and innovation in global governance".[8] And, third, it itemized and discussed in a persuasive manner the reasons why multilateral cooperation and coordination is essential for governing the globe and building sustainable peace.

Conceptualizing global governance

What is clear from the Commission's Report is that the catalysts for interest in governance at the global level stem, in large part, from recognition of: the shrinkage of the time and space witnessed over the past 55 years or so; the emergence of a global civil society; rising interdependence among actors (state and non-state) within international society; the rise in the number and complexity of transnational issues; and, national governments' failure/inability to not only deal with these transnational issues but also provide common goods and security guarantees for their citizens.

The members of the Commission on Global Governance were all well aware that there is no overarching government at the international level. But while certainly not proposing the creation of some form of world government, the Commissioners demonstrated a desire, reflected in their analysis, for a governance regime that would control and address all levels of human activity that had transnational repercussions. The desire to control and steer such activities they labelled as "global governance". The main normative purpose of global governance, from the Commission's point of view, was to avoid "a chaotic world"[9] – that is, to steer and modify the behaviour of actors who operate on the global stage in such a manner as to avoid deadly conflicts and control intense socio-economic and political competition.[10] Thus, global governance is depicted in the Report as a purposive activity. This idea corresponds with Marie-Claude Smouts' understanding of governance when she states that "governance is order plus intentionality".[11]

Starting from the basic premise that the only way to a better world is through the collective actions of individuals and institutions across the globe, the Commission proffered the following definition of governance:

> Governance is the sum of the many ways individuals and institutions, public and private, manage their common affairs. It is a continuing process through which conflicting or diverse interests may be accommodated and co-operative action may be taken. It includes formal institutions and regimes empowered to enforce compliance, as well as informal arrangements that people and institutions either have agreed to or perceive to be in their interest.[12]

So for the Commission, governance is more than an activity, it is also a process. It is a process that can be found at many levels: local, national, regional, transnational, and global.

The issues dealt with by global governance institutions are transnational ones that transcend national frontiers. The Commission considered the tasks of global governance today to include: the maintenance of peace and security, the control of expanding economic activity, dealing with environmental problems, combating trans-border diseases such as AIDS, preserving genetic diversity, saving endangered species, curbing horizontal and vertical proliferation of weapons, deterring terrorists, warding off famine, eradicating poverty, developing fair ways to share the earth's resources, halting drug trafficking and the trafficking of women and children. No single government on its own can properly tackle these issues. Certainly, at the present time, neither the UN system nor regional organizations can hope to perform the above tasks on their own. Thus, the work of global governance, according to the Commission, requires the actions, cooperation and collaboration of a plurality of actors, and not just from a collection of nation-states.[13]

While traditional concepts of global governance were limited to intergovernmental relationships, the Commission argued that the concept now had to be broadened to include non-governmental actors as well (e.g. NGOs, citizens' movements, MNCs, and the global capital market). One is led to picture global governance, from the Commission's Report, as a complex network of activity, involving multiple actors on overlapping and shifting stages. This, of course, is a much different picture from the one that emerged out of the Second World War when the UN system was created. At that time, and for a number of decades thereafter, the activity of global governance was thought to be limited to states and the formal intergovernmental organizations (IGOs) they agree to form. State governments were considered the only entities capable of protecting in any real way the interests of their civil societies. Thus it seemed natural at the time to create a set of international, intergovernmental institutions through which to save succeeding generations from the scourge of war, to uphold human rights, and to ensure prosperity for all.

Today, however, as the Report recognizes, while national governments and the UN system are still very much central to the conduct of global governance, it has become evident that the state is no longer the only actor of significance when it comes to global decision-making. The state now has many rivals in that area. In the Commission's words, a number of "emerging voices and institutions are increasingly active in advancing various political, economic, social, cultural, and environmental objectives that have considerable global impact".[14] In some cases, their agendas may overlap. But in other cases, they may be incompatible and working at cross-purposes. In some cases, they may be working on the same stage. In other cases, they may choose to carry out their activity in different forums. Global governance is thus seen, by the Commission, as a system of rule at all levels of activity and as a vehicle for coordinating this complex governance activity; controlling and deploying the resources necessary for ensuring that the goals and objectives of these multifarious governance actors can be achieved peacefully and in a manner that would not harm the planet. *Our Global Neighbourhood* reinforces the notion, then, that the concept of global governance should be broad enough to embrace the whole patchwork of institutions, processes, and people that together make up international society.[15]

The Report of the Commission on Global Governance goes even further in delineating what ought to constitute the work of global governance. The tasks listed include: maintaining peace and order in the global neighbourhood, expanding economic activity, dealing with the problems of pollution and greenhouse warming, combating diseases, curbing horizontal and vertical arms proliferation, preserving genetic diversity, deterring terrorism, warding off famine, saving endangered species, solving economic problems, developing equitable ways of sharing the earth's resources, halting drug trafficking, tackling the HIV/AIDS epidemic. No single governing institution, acting on its own, can properly tackle this growing list of tasks, demands, and problems. Certainly, the UN system, in its present state, is unable to undertake them all. This is why the Commission makes the case that, for now and the future, global governance must therefore involve an immense, dynamic, complex process of interactive decision-making that is constantly evolving in response to changing historical circumstances and material conditions. As the Commission suggests, the task of global governance must be shared amongst global, regional, national, and even sub-national, organizations.

This model of global organization and governance is therefore not a proposal for "world government" or even "world federalism", as the Commission's Report makes quite clear. The Commissioners felt that to go down that road might ultimately result in a world that was much less democratic and much more accommodating to power and hegemonic ambition than the one we have today. It might even reinforce the roles of states and governments and diminish the rights of people. Ideally, what they wished to see was an integrated rules-based system or network of partnerships that would manage global affairs in a manner "responsive to the interests of all people in a sustainable future", guided by "basic human values" and conforming to "the reality of global diversity".[16] Such a network would draw on the skills and resources of diverse individuals, groups, and institutions operating at various levels. Due to the interconnectedness of the issues that have to be dealt with at the global level, it would be important, as the Commission asserts, for information, knowledge and capacities to be pooled so that pertinent policies and practices can be developed on matters of common concern.

Perhaps this is why the Commission still holds out hope for the UN system. After all, a close examination of the UN Charter reveals that this universal organization was created precisely to act as a rules-based network for the international community of states and "we the people". If it hasn't lived up to its Charter potential, this does not change the rational underlying its existence. The problem with the UN, as far as the Commission on Global Governance is concerned, is that it is in need of major reform. However, it is clear from the Report that the Commission wanted to distance itself from the more radical advocates of UN transformation. This gives us a clue as to the Commission's bottom line when it comes to its position on what constitutes global governance. As noted earlier, global governance for the Commission is not world government but something just short of that. It is really about developing an arrangement of partnerships and overlapping procedures that would bring a semblance of order to the globe. In many respects the overall recommendations on UN reform straddle the fence between substantial transformation of this governance entity and simple reflexive adaptation of the institution to changes occurring in international society.

For instance, the recommendation to enlarge the UN Security Council in order that it becomes more representative is one of the major reform initiatives proposed by the Commission. However, the proposal can be viewed as mere tinkering with the apex body of this organization, rather than something that would result in a true transformation of its governance structure. The reforms that the Commission would like to see in the Security Council include: establishing a new class of five "standing members" – the intent of which would be to reduce the status of permanent membership; increasing the number of "non-permanent" members from ten to thirteen; and eliminating the veto, except for very exceptional and overriding circumstances related to the national interests of the major powers. These reform proposals are not all that innovative and neither are they transformative. Similar tinkering is recommended for the UN General Assembly, the Economic and Social Council, the Office of the Secretary-General and the UN budgetary process.

On the other hand, the suggestions that the Trusteeship Council should be turned into a forum for global civil society, that there should be a deliberative body – the People's Assembly – to complement the General Assembly, and that the UN should begin to convene an annual Forum of Civil Society, are three of the more radical proposals put forward by the Commission. Not only are they recognition of the growth and influence of civil society organizations, these proposals envision the opening up of space within the UN system for non-state actors (NSAs) in the joint management of global affairs.[17] For the Commission, these NSAs include NGOs as well as the global business sector. Another far-reaching proposal, which is not really new, is the call for an expansion in the authority of the UN Security Council to intervene in the jurisdiction of states if the security of people is jeopardized by their own leadership or by a failure of their leaders to act. The Commission suggests that the time has finally come for the UN to implement Article 43 of its Charter and develop a UN-controlled volunteer force. The problem, of course, with these more transformative proposals is that they are seemingly still ahead of their time. Even the tinkering to global governance institutions envisaged by the Commission is currently unacceptable to the veto-wielding powers on the Security Council. How much more difficult will it therefore be to get the more radical reforms through?

The underlying premise on which the Commission's notion of governance rests, is found in the notion of an emerging "global civic ethic" – the appearance of a set of global "core values" to which people from varying ideological, cultural, religious, economic, and political backgrounds can adhere and support. To quote from *Our Global Neighbourhood*, "global values must be the cornerstone of global governance".[18] Without commonly accepted values the whole idea of legitimate global governance falls like a deck of cards. What are these so-called "core values"? According to the Commission, they are values "that are appropriate to the needs of an increasingly crowded and diverse planet" – respect for life, liberty, justice and equity, mutual respect, caring and integrity.[19] This list derives, as the Commission acknowledges, from the mantras of various religious teachings and is based on the so-called "golden rule" found in most world religions – that people should treat others as they themselves would like to be treated. It is one thing to aspire to such values; but it is quite another thing to claim that this set of core values already exists and forms the basis of a global neighbourhood, for there is no empirical evidence that would back this claim at this time in our human history. Yes, there may be some groups that adhere to these core values – perhaps some religious sects or humanitarian bodies – but there are also pockets of humanity that exhibit little concern for these core values. This reality makes it difficult to view *Out Global Neighbourhood* as little more than a pipe dream at this juncture in our history.

The Commission acknowledges that its complex concept of global governance would have to be anchored as well in principles that allow for inclusiveness and broad participation, that is, governance that would be "more democratic – than in the past".[20]

As a good "liberal" document, the Commission's Report promoted unabashedly the spread of democracy globally as one of the ways of addressing the problems of global governance. In doing so, the link was made between the constitutive foundation of democratic regimes and the prospects for sustained global peace. It is evident that the Report drew heavily on the literature on democratic peace, which holds that democracies seldom go to war with each other.[21]

> The spread of democracy has been one of the most heartening trends of recent years. It is democracy that can ensure that a country's affairs are conducted – and its development directed – in ways that respond to the interests and wishes of the people. Democracy provides the environment within which the protection of the fundamental rights of citizens is best safeguarded. It offers the most favourable foundation for peace and stability in international relations. Though democratic regimes may not all or always be virtuous, even recent history suggests that autocratic regimes are more likely to behave aggressively.[22]

Certainly, since the end of the Cold War, there has been a noticeable rise in democratic movements across the globe. Many autocratic regimes have been swept out of power and replaced by more or less democratic regimes. But, as the Commission admits, the "implantation of a democratic culture is, however, not an instant or easy process".[23] Basically, it takes time to develop democratic culture and traditions of democratic behaviour. Just having elections will not a democracy make, as have been demonstrated in Haiti, Angola, Cambodia, or even Afghanistan. But the Commission welcomed the spread in the desire among people all over the globe to push for legitimate and accountable governments – governments that are democratically elected. It also called for further research into ways of consolidating new democracies and for building on principles that might sustain democratic institutions in the long term.

One such principle is "subsidiarity" – the notion that any decisions reached ought to be taken as close as possible to those who will be most affected and "to the level at which they [the decisions] can be effectively implemented".[24] How this principle could be enacted in real terms is never fully explored by the Commission. A major difficulty, of course, is that regardless of where global governance decisions are taken, there will have to be some mechanism for coordinating the actions that result from those decisions. The Commission recognizes this and opts for recommending the UN system as the most logical linchpin of global governance activity. The Report states that the UN ought to remain "the principal mechanism through which governments collaboratively engage each other and other sectors of society in the multilateral management of global affairs".[25] But to play a central role in this governance, the Commission acknowledges that the UN system would have to undergo major changes that would not only make it more efficient and effective but also more relevant to the changing needs of the "new world" that has emerged since the end of the Cold War.[26]

Post-Cold War systemic changes

The call for global governance by this Commission was largely based on the premise that the world had undergone, or was undergoing, a number of systemic changes that cried out for a new governance structure and process to properly manage global issues. In other words, the members of the Commission saw a propitious moment, a window of opportunity, presented by global systemic changes, for the introduction of the global governance concept. What were these systemic changes?

It is not surprising that the Commission's Report, in describing the perceived transformational trends of the global system, exhibits elements of the observations and language of liberal internationalist scholars. After all, many such scholars contributed background papers upon which the Commission drew much of its inspiration and ideas.[27] James Rosenau, for instance, had invented the very awkward term "fragmagration" to depict the juxtaposed forces of integration and fragmentation that appeared to be at work in transforming the global system, particularly in the latter half of the twentieth century. The Commission maintained that these forces were creating a tremendous amount of flux and uncertainty in the international political environments, presenting both a challenge and opportunity for individuals and institutions involved in governance at the global level. The Commission on Global Governance highlights a number of significant trends that have brought about important changes around the globe, which call for rethinking governance arrangements.

Rapid advances in technology, particularly in the areas of information, computers, and transportation, have resulted in a noticeable shrinkage of time and space. As the Commission puts it: "The term 'global village' captured the impact of the electronic conquest of space. Technology, by telescoping distance and time, had made the world smaller".[28] Envisioning the world as a single neighbourhood would not have been possible at an earlier time in history. Certainly, this concept of the global neighbourhood adopted by the Commission captured the imagination of many who had witnessed Neil Armstrong's lunar walk and the relay of space ship and satellite imagery and photographs of the earth. The fact that one can travel easily and quickly around the globe via speedy trains, aircraft and supersonic jets only adds to the impression that the world is indeed getting smaller. When one adds the reach of radio, television and computers (e-mail and internet), it becomes evident that what occurs in some distant part of the world can resonate and reverberate almost instantaneously in one's own home location.

Linked and interacting with this trend is globalization, which has the potential of creating an integrated global market place and cultural homogenization. A truly global economy may bring citizens of the world closer together and cultural homogeneity may be what is needed to develop the intersubjective consensus around the civic values and norms that the Commission wants to inculcate globally. However, even the Commission recognizes the less than benign impact that globalization has had. With respect to economic liberalization, the Commission observes that while the North–South dichotomy is becoming less pronounced and some formerly underdeveloped countries (e.g. the Asian Tigers) may have benefited from being integrated into the global economy, yet there remains serious disparities within nations and regions, both North and South. Furthermore, the "financial liberalization that seems to have created a borderless world is also helping international criminals and creating numerous problems for poorer countries".[29] In addition, there is a backlash against globalization and homogenization coming from anti-globalization forces around the world – something the Commission acknowledged. Finally, the intensification of globalization combined with technological advances are making state borders increasingly porous and actually helping to erode the authority of governments and their ability to govern. To address these problems, the Commission suggests that a rules-based global economic structure is even more vital today than it has ever been.

A second trend identified by the Commission is the transformation in the global military strategic terrain, particularly since the end of the Cold War. While the lessening of tensions between the US and the USSR in the 1980s had led to some major reductions in nuclear stockpiles (vertical proliferation), the culmination of East–West confrontation did not stop horizontal nuclear proliferation (as we can see now with India and Pakistan declaring nuclear power status, and North Korea claiming to be also a member of the nuclear club). The Commission, in fact, predicted that the world was on the verge of another arms race involving not only nuclear but also chemical and biological weapons, and that this new arms race would involve not only states but also non-state actors (e.g. drug syndicates, political movements, terrorist groups, etc.).

The revelations since September 11, 2001 certainly indicate that on this subject the Commission was very close to the mark. However, the solutions proposed by the Commission for the global nuclear problem were at best unrealistic. The Commission set the goal of progressively eliminating nuclear arms and other WMDs in "ten to fifteen years".[30] To accomplish this, the Commission recommended: the establishment of an equitable and universal nuclear non-proliferation regime that would include both nuclear and non-nuclear states as participants and build upon the efforts of the Non Proliferation Treaty (NPT); the conclusion of a comprehensive nuclear test ban treaty with universal membership accompanied by an immediate moratorium on testing and use of existing stockpiles; and the establishment of regional nuclear-weapons-free zones. This kind of comprehensive denuclearization programme could never be accomplished without the aid of global governance arrangements and institutionalization.

The proliferation in weapons of mass destruction is accompanied by another troubling trend – the horizontal proliferation in small arms, particularly in the less developed regions of the world. The surfeit of small arms left over from the Cold War era was, in the opinion of the Commissioners, "a key enabling factor in many conflicts now scarring the world".[31] The fact that the permanent members of the UN Security Council[32] are responsible for approximately 86 per cent of the small arms exported to countries in the Third World places the problem squarely on the agenda of the apex governing body of the UN. The major powers are clearly implicated in a great number of the civil conflicts that have erupted in many parts of the developing world since the end of the Cold War. True, several of these conflicts have been precipitated by social cleavages, long-standing ethnic, clan and religious tensions, personal ambition and structural factors (such as the collapse of a regional power balance or a geopolitical shift), but there is no question that glut in small arms obtained from the major powers has helped to fuel these conflagrations. In the opinion of the Commission, this problem requires a global governance solution.

However, the solution offered by the Commission on Global Governance to the above problem is essentially utopian, flawed, and suspect. The Commission proposed that all governments reduce their national military spending and redirect money saved into economic and social projects. While this may seem all well and good on the surface, this proposal papers over the difficulties involved in unilateral disarmament and conversion. The Commission suggested a number of levers and incentives that might induce state leaders to move in this direction. One lever comes in the form of linking the distribution of international aid and development assistance to downsizing in national defence spending. Of course the problem with this strategy is that it targets poor, underdeveloped states and does nothing to slow down military spending in advanced industrialized countries. An incentive proposed by the Commission for reducing military spending comes in the form of a call for a "Demilitarization Fund". But here again, this "incentive" is intended for developing countries only, and would be managed by a multilateral institution like the World Bank. The Commission seemed oblivious to the fact that these suggestions would only serve to create major inequities and would most likely be ignored by leaders who feel that their states' military spending is necessary for the self-defence of their territory and population.

In any event, demilitarization strategies only tackle one particular aspect of the global insecurity problem. A third disturbing trend, linked to the above issue, is identified by the Commission as the spread of a culture of violence. This trend can be seen in the exponential increases in brutal civil wars since the end of the Cold War, the systematic utilization of rape as a weapon of war, genocidal and ethnic cleansing activity, the use of children as soldiers by both government and irregular forces, and the increase in terrorist attacks worldwide. What is even more insidious is that violence is oft-times "perceived as an end in itself".[33] When violence becomes so pervasive in a society it can even threaten the survival of governments and the functioning of the state. It can leave deep scars in the lives of children and seep into homes, particularly affecting women. Violence tends to beget violence and can become the breeding ground for criminal and covert activity. The Commission on Global Governance recognized it as a main hurdle for global governance institutions to overcome.

By emphasizing the need to sow the seeds of "a culture of nonviolence", the Commission demonstrated a desire to tackle root causes of violence and human insecurities. In the words of the Report:

> The task of promoting security in the global neighbourhood will be immeasurably harder if in societies around the world a culture of violence is on the rise and personal insecurity is pervasive.[34]

The task here, according to the Commission, is one for global governance.

A fourth trend identified by the Commission is the global overpopulation. The Report points out that "more people have been added to the world's population in the past five decades than in all the previous millennia of human existence".[35] This development raises the distinct possibility of a Malthusian-like crisis, occurring particularly in the poorest and most economically fragile regions of the world. It also could lead to other problems such as overcrowded cities, urban squalor, unsanitary conditions, high unemployment, environmental and ecological degradation, desertification, dwindling fisheries and other resources, disappearing species, pollution, ozone layer depletion, global warming, and violence. According to the Commission,

> Global governance has an important contribution to make in tackling causes of excessively rapid population growth and urbanization, and in strengthening regional, state, and local capacities to cope with their consequences.[36]

The problems associated with overpopulation require at minimum "a systematic, long term, global approach" that is guided by the principle of sustainable development. Addressing the problem in this way is considered by the Commission as one of the essential tasks of global governance.

The above systemic trends and changes do present a window of opportunity for global governance. But they also remind us of the fact that major obstacles will lie in the path of any attempts at establishing such governance. Therefore, unlike the implication made by the Commission, global governance is not a foregone conclusion, it is an idea that will have to be nurtured and negotiated if it is to become a reality.

The impact of the Commission on Global Governance Report

Our Global Neighbourhood is a prescriptive document aimed at finding a way forward for the world as it makes the transition from Cold War to post-Cold War era. It offers a normative vision and strategy that could help humanity in its quest to better manage its affairs. Therefore, it is really a blueprint for the governance of the globe, an aspiration rather than a fact, at least during the transitional phase between what was seen as an "old" world order to a "new" world order.

The Commission's Report is clearly a liberal-biased document. It portrays the concept of a liberal internationalist order that revolves around the reform of existing institutions, like the UN system, with the potential of embodying the vision and purpose of governance at the global level. It has synthesized, and in some ways extended, proposals presented by other blue ribbon commissions – particularly with respect to global security, the world economy, and the global environment.[37] This should not be surprising considering the overlap in the membership of these blue ribbon panels. It also builds on the ideas of liberal internationalist scholarship – ideas of complex interdependence, the advance of democracy globally, the reform of existing global institutions and the role and place of a growing and revitalized global civil society.

The Report has been cited in volumes of academic papers and books since its publication in 1995. In some respects, its analysis and content has struck a chord among supporters and critics of the Commission's work. Certainly some recommendations of the Commission have been taken seriously within national, regional and global policy making bodies and by non-state actors. Just to give the reader a sense of the impact of the Report on policy makers, I will focus on one of the specific recommendations – the Global Compact – that were taken up by Kofi Annan, the UN Secretary-General.

It is evident that Annan drew upon the following quote in the Report to make the case for what he has called "the Global Compact":

> The international community needs to enlist the support of transnational business in global governance and to encourage best practices, acknowledging the role [the] private sector can play in meeting the needs of the global neighbourhood: wide acceptance of these responsibilities is likely if the business sector is drawn in to participate in the processes of governance.[38]

The UN Secretary-General introduced at the World Economic Forum in Davos (1999) the idea of a "Global Compact"[39] as a means of improving, or recovering, the UN–private sector relationship. In doing so, he showed that he had bought into the Commission's notion that global governance was about developing a network of partnerships for managing global problems. Kofi Annan's main goal was to get business leaders to practice corporate responsibility and adhere to humanitarian values at a time when there was widespread perception that international businesses are uncaring – putting profits ahead of human rights protection and socio-economic progress, especially in the developing world. In other words, the UN Secretary-General rationalized that the UN was willing to get into bed with multinational corporations and other major international business organizations as long as they promised to uphold key UN values and principles.

Corporate business leaders also bought into the Commission's idea of global governance partnerships, but for an entirely different reason. They had begun to realize that if the momentum of globalization is to be sustained (and the backlash against liberalization stemmed), then something had to be done urgently about the cultural and social side effects of globalization that are generally perceived negatively by a growing segment of the world's population. They immediately saw Annan's idea of a Global Compact as a way to spruce up the damaged image of international business. In some respects, by going into partnership with the UN, global business leaders realized that the UN would also have to make some compromises and support, and even embrace, globalization – the engine that propels capitalist profit-making. So the Global Compact soon became acceptable to most business organizations. It would appear as well that Annan, in calling for a Global Compact of "shared values and principles" between the UN and international business, was motivated not only by the tremendous groundswell against globalization but also by the UN's need for cold hard cash. Both the Secretary-General and major corporate business leaders began to claim that the goals of the UN and international corporate bodies were more or less the same with respect to, for instance, the elimination of poverty.

This claim has been disputed by many, including Carol Bellamy (UNICEF's Executive Director) who in 1999 warned of the danger of assuming that the goals of the private sector are somehow synonymous with those of the UN, "because they most emphatically are not". Profit motive drives business and at times this has clashed with UN values. For many years, many within the UN have had a jaundiced view of the corporate world precisely because of the callous actions of certain businesses. Companies like Rio Tinto, UNOCAL, Dow Chemical, Disney and McDonalds have been clamouring to be part of the "Global Compact", but they are also examples of corporate worst practices. It should be borne in mind that the Global Compact is not a binding code of conduct for international business. "The voluntary nature of newly adopted corporate standards and codes of conduct means that multinationals are in a position to structure these rules in ways that restrict them the least, fit the best their comparative advantages and operations, and evade pervasive control and monitoring mechanisms".[40]

Thus, getting into bed with international business is a risky venture for the UN. The UN will be forced to borrow some values from the business world if the partnership is to succeed. Some of the values of transnational capital threaten the very values the Global Compact is supposed to uphold – principles of human rights, sustainable development, fair labour practices, and environmental protection. Herein lies the problem. The road ahead for UN–business collaboration is "paved with political hurdles, psychological roadblocks, and cultural chasms". There are competing visions between these two entities of the future of global order. There is lingering suspicion within the UN of the private sector's motives. In addition, the ideological differences as well as practical and legal hurdles to this partnership seem insurmountable.[41] Resistance to this idea of a Global Compact is also coming from several developing states fearful of the prospect that their economies will be dominated by a new wave of neo-colonialism – aided and abetted by the UN. Resistance also comes from within the ranks of the UN Secretariat who fear that many jobs within the UN will be lost as a result of outsourcing and secondment practices.

So while the impact of the Commission on Global Governance on Kofi Annan's thinking was critical in this case, this example also reveals that not all of the recommendations of the Commission were fully thought through, and some of them will most likely be rejected by critics of liberal internationalist ideology.

Criticisms of the Report

The fact that there have been major critiques of *Our Global Neighbourhood* coming from several quarters is an indication of the broad impact this blue ribbon panel has had. Clearly scholars and practitioners have taken the Report seriously enough to challenge its main assumptions and test its primary arguments against the harsh realities of this moment in history. Space limitations will not permit an elaboration of all of the criticisms levelled at the Report. I will only provide a sampling of some of them.

Carol Prager, for instance, notes that the most striking traits of *Our Global Neighbourhood* are "the cosmopolitan neo-Kantian features of its vision: the focus on people rather than states, and the assertion of the existence of a global civil society".[42] In a nutshell, Prager gets to the heart of the essence of this Report. However, as she correctly points out, the Commission's view of global civil society is questionable. It certainly can be contrasted with the communitarian position (e.g. Hegel, Waltzer) that civil society is only possible within the state. She is backed by other critics such as Waterman who questions whether there is such a thing as a global civil society. As he puts it, civil society presumes a state of some form that can rein in the behaviour of its "citizens". Waterman points out that just a few years ago most people would have argued that since there is no state at the international level, there can be no global civil society.[43] Of course, he was also one of the first to present civil society as a tentative ideological formulation back in 1992, but he is quick to criticize the Commission's use of the term as "an international policy slogan".[44] Waterman concludes that *Our Global Neighbourhood* is an example of "utopian reformism" that will soon be relegated to the dustbin along with similar past efforts.[45]

Claims by the Commission of the existence of a global neighbourhood are also considered as more wishful thinking then anything else. As Prager notes: "It not only presupposes membership in a single political unit, but the much more intimate relationship of neighbours" entails "stunning leaps of logic". She argues that this is "an excellent example of the attempt to bring something into existence by naming it".[46] And, she is not the only one who is critical of the Commission on this score. Upendra Baxi in agreement with Prager submits that the Commission, in its enthusiasm with positing the existence of global civil society and the civic values of a global neighbourhood, masks "the plurality and multiplicity of worlds within this 'world'".[47] Baxi is particularly critical of the Commission's concept of a global neighbourhood, suggesting that the world is really composed of the established (advanced industrial societies) and the marginalized (the recently decolonized but repauperized nations and societies of the underdeveloped world). To put it another way, there are in fact at least two neighbourhoods – a "gated one" and a "ghetto".

> As economic globalization proceeds, the local becomes the ghetto of the global marketplace; spaces for plurality and diversity shrink as the entire world becomes a series of shopping malls and arcades and human beings become market-mutated lustful consumerists (à la the Gremlins). And yet globalization of consumerism does not transform "aliens" into "neighbors". They remain "socially distant" even after they acquire the likeness of appetite to consume.[48]

Baxi calls this division "universal otherhood," which contrasts significantly with the Commission's notion of "global neighborhood".

He goes on further to argue that the "unproblematic construction of governance" by the Commission "is designed to facilitate an articulate discourse on *global* governance". Yet, this construction, in his opinion, was ultimately flawed for several reasons. First, it is regressive to conceive of "governance" in the "iconic languages of corporate power". As an example, Baxi points to the problematic management of "relations" between "predator peoples and indigenous peoples". In the case of the former, assimilation, even forced, constitutes "good" governance for the latter. He also points out that patriarchal governance "is a grid of power worked out in a mutually reinforcing way by key state and civil society agents/institution".[49] Clearly governance at any level is not unproblematic. At times it can be viewed as hegemonic domination. Even if we consider governance a process, it must be realized that that process may be "permeated by structures-in-dominance, both in states and civil societies".[50]

Clearly, Baxi is right to point out that conflict, contradiction and "victimage" characterize the structures as well as processes of governance. In other words, governance is a process of shaping (in Foucault's words) "the conduct of conduct". And the conduct (governance) as shaping the conduct (submission, subjugation, collaboration, obedience, apathy) arises precisely because "to govern ... means to govern things"[51] – including human beings, in their relations, their links, their imbrications, with those other things which are wealth, resources, means of substance, the territories; men in their relations to other kinds of things, customs, habits, ways of acting and thinking; in their relations to other kinds of things like accidents and misfortunes such as famines, epidemics, death. It is these imbrications of men and things that constitute the dynamics of governance, according to Baxi. The Report's construction of governance thus overlooks comprehensively both the "thingification" of human beings and the materiality of power itself. Baxi concludes that, "In every single sense, then, one might say that the report's enunciation is cognitively malnourished".[52]

Regardless of whether or not the work of the Commission on Global Governance is utopian or realistic, it is clear that *Our Global Neighbourhood* has had a major impact on supporters and critics alike.

Conclusion

Whether or not one agrees with the notion of global governance, it is important for us to treat blue ribbon panels like the Commission on Global Governance seriously. The ideas generated from these important and influential individuals should not be taken as givens and should not simply percolate into public debate without deconstruction and criticism.

There are at least two competing conceptual approaches to the study of multilateralism and global governance. The first is a traditional one which accepts uncritically the existing configuration of state and economic power and opts for piecemeal reforms to existing multilateral and governance structures so long as they are in accordance with the overall vision of "status quo" elements within the international system. In other words, it proposes the reform or adaptation of the existing multilateral institutional framework without questioning the constitutive principles or underlying ideas of world politics embodied within that framework. The second emphasizes the importance of analysing the nexus between evolving global order and changes to the concrete manifestations of the multilateral process (i.e. the activity of institutions and organizations of involved in governance at the global level).[53] Advocates of this second approach first ask, "What are the ways in which global order is changing?" and "Do we have the correct institutional structures and arrangements to deal with the new demands that are bound to emerge from such changes?"

Clearly traditional approaches to the study of multilateralism and global governance, while important in terms of helping to establish a successful academic research programme, have proven insufficient for making these concepts relevant in our changing world. Neo-realism, with its state-centric, static and generalized assumptions, does not allow for the progression of thought and praxis, while liberal institutionalism with its focus on interstate institutionalization at times finds itself disconnected from the changes taking place in the global system and from the realities of governance at the global level. Regime theorists and neo-liberal scholars have tried to repair the damage by re-linking institutional practices with the broader issue of regional and global governance. However, the main failings of the traditional approaches to the study and practice of multilateralism and global governance, besides their state-centrism, are their fetishism with current events, their underlying rationalist/problem-solving epistemology, and their inability to adequately reflect the new realities of the complex and turbulent world in which we live.

The Report of the Commission on Global Governance offers a slightly different perspective on global governance from the dominant neo-realist and liberal institutional paradigms. In recognizing the historicity of the concept of governance, the Report demonstrates the extent to which the multilateral stage has broadened to include multiple actors, in essence pluralizing global governance. At the same time, it remains firmly wedded to a state-centric bias that leads one to conclude that the Commissioners have a major stake in maintaining existing institutions of governance. The end result is a seemingly schizophrenic work that is at the same time "traditional" as well as "critical". To be in such a position is not necessarily a bad thing. After all, at this juncture in our history we cannot speak with certainty as though we have arrived at any coherent, or viably aggregated, form of global governance. What we have can best be described as inter-national governance, with the UN system acting as a sort of linchpin with the potential to give that governance a truly holistic and global shape sometime in the future. At the same time, as the Commission on Global Governance makes clear, there is a noticeable evolution in governance activity at the global level and within human society whose trajectory bears evidence of a progressive, albeit not consistently linear, development in the direction of what might eventually be called true "global governance". In answer to the critics, the Commissioners would probably say that their efforts, therefore, reflect this ambiguity.

In many respects, this particular blue ribbon report figuratively straddles the fence that separates traditional and critical approaches to global governance and multilateralism. While the authors demonstrate a propensity to acknowledge and appreciate the need for "new" multilateralism, they appear equally unwilling to distance themselves totally from the "old" multilateralism practised in state-centric "international" organizations like the UN system. As such, *Our Global Neighbourhood* is little different from its predecessors, that is, the Brandt, Palme, Brundtland, and Nyerere blue ribbon panels. As Richard Falk incisively points out:

> *Our Global Neighbourhood* continues the commission tradition of being sufficiently ingratiating to the established order so as not to provoke an explicit rejection at high levels of officialdom.[54]

Notes

* The author wishes to thank Tony Bhurjee for his research assistance.

1. For some examples see, Michael G. Schechter (1996) *Multilateralism and Global Change: Prospects for Reform and Innovation*, Tokyo: United Nations University Press; Eric Fawcett and Hanna Newcombe. (eds.) (1995) *United Nations Reform: Looking ahead after fifty years*, Toronto: Dundurn Press; (1995) "Organizing International Relations: Fifty Years after the United Nations Charter", *International Social Science Journal* XLVII(2); *The Report of the Independent Working Group on the Future of the United Nations, The United Nations in its Second Half-Century*, New York: Ford Foundation, 1995; Chadwick Alger, Gene Lyons, and John Trent (eds.) (1995) *The United Nations System: The Policies of Member States*, Tokyo: United Nations University Press; Keith Krause and W. Andy Knight (eds.) (1995) *State, Society and the UN System: Changing Perspectives on Multilateralism*, Tokyo: United Nations University Press; Erskine Childers (with Brian Urquhart) (1994) *Renewing the United Nations System*, Development Dialogue 1994: 1 Upsalla, Sweden: Dag Hammarskjold Foundations; Rosemary Righter (1995) *Utopia Lost: The United Nations and World Order*, New York: Twenti-

eth Century Fund Press; James Sutterlin (1995) *The United Nations and the Maintenance of International Security: A Challenge to be Met*, London: Praeger; Mihaly Simai (1994) *The Future of Global Governance: Managing Risk and Change in the International System*, Washington, DC: United States Institute of Peace Press; Oran Young (1994) *International Governance: Protecting the Environment in a Stateless Society*, Ithaca: Cornell University Press; and Robert Cox (1992) "Multilateralism and World Order", *Review of International Studies* 18(2) (April).
2. The Independent Commission on International Development Issues.
3. These individuals were members of the Independent Commission on Disarmament and Security Issues (the Palme Commission), the World Commission on Environment and Development (the Brundtland Commission), and the South Commission.
4. Here is a list of the 37 individuals who attended the Stockholm meeting: Ali Alatas, Indonesia; Patricio Aylwin Azocar, Chile; Benazir Bhutto, Pakistan; Willy Brandt, Federal Republic of Germany; Gro Harlem Brundtland, Norway; Boutros Boutros-Ghali, Egypt; Manuel Camacho Solis, Mexico; Fernando Henrique Cardoso, Brazil; Ingvar Carlsson, Sweden; Jimmy Carter, United States; Bernard Chidzero, Zimbabwe; Reinaldo Figueredo Planchart, Venezuela; Bronislaw Geremek, Poland; Abdlatif Al-Hamad, Kuwait; Mahbub ul Haq, Pakistan; Václav Havel, Czech and Slovak Federal Republic; Edward Heath, United Kingdom; Enrique Iglesias, Uruguay; Hongkoo Lee, Republic of Korea; Stephen Lewis, Canada; Michael Manley, Jamaica; Vladlen Martynov, Soviet Union; Thabo Mbeki, South Africa; Robert McNamara, United States; Bradford Morse, United States; Julius Nyerere, Tanzania; Babacar Ndiaye, Senegal; Saburo Okita, Japan; Jan Pronk, Netherlands; Shridath Ramphal, Guyana; Nafis Sadik, Pakistan; Salim Salim, Tanzania; Arjun Sengupta, India; Edward Shevardnadze, Soviet Union; Kelevi Sorsa, Finland; Maurice Strong, Canada; Brian Urquhart, United Kingdom.
5. The Commission members made it clear, however, that they were not offering "a blueprint for all time". They considered their work "no more than a transit stop" on the journey of the development of better global governance – an on-going effort to organize life on the planet. See *Our Global Neighbourhood*, p. xvi.
6. Richard Falk (1995) "Liberalism at the Global Level: The Last of the Independent Commissions?" *Millennium*: *Journal of International Studies* 24: 565.
7. *Ibid.*, p. 566.
8. See *Our Global Neighbourhood*, p. xvi.
9. *Ibid.*, p. xvii.
10. One should note that during the 1980s the term "governance" was used by international financial institutions to justify the political conditionalities imposed on developing countries. Used in that sense, the term "global governance" has particular ideological overtones. See Marie-Claude Smouts (1998) "The proper use of governance in international relations", *International Social Science Journal* 155 (March): 81.
11. Marie-Claude Smouts, p. 82.
12. *Ibid.*, p. 2.
13. See Leon Gordenker and Thomas G. Weiss, "Pluralizing Global Governance: Analytical Approaches and Dimensions", in Thomas G. Weiss and Leon Gordenker (eds.) (1996) *NGOs, the UN, and Global Governance*, Boulder, Co: Lynne Rienner publishers, pp. 17–47.
14. *Ibid.*, p. 4.
15. W. Andy Knight (1995) "Straddling the Fence: An Equivocal Proposal for Future Multilateral Governance", *Third World Quarterly* 16(3) (September): 564.
16. *Our Global Neighbourhood*, p. xvii.
17. *Ibid.*, p. 253.

18. *Ibid.*, p. 47.
19. *Ibid.*, pp. 48–49.
20. *Ibid.*, p. 5.
21. See for instance, Michael Doyle (1986) "Liberalism and World Politics", *American Political Science Review* 80; and Bruce Russett (1993) *Grasping the Democratic Peace*, Princeton: Princeton University Press.
22. *Our Global Neighbourhood*, pp. 57–58.
23. *Ibid.*, p. 58.
24. *Ibid.*, p. 5.
25. *Ibid.*, p. 6.
26. It should be noted that *Our Global Neighbourhood* was released in 1995 to coincide with the 50th anniversary of the United Nations' founding. This was no coincidence as it became clear that the members of the Commission wanted to use this anniversary to kick-start what they considered as needed reforms to this universal organization that was created to address precisely the kinds of transnational issues discussed in the Commission's Report.
27. On this point also see Michael Barnett (1997) "Bringing in the New World Order: Liberalism, Legitimacy, and the United Nations", *World Politics* 49 (July): 526–551; Richard Falk (1995) "Liberalism at the Global Level: The Last of the Independent Commissions?", *Millennium* 24(3): 563–576.
28. *Our Global Neighbourhood*, p. 41.
29. *Ibid.*, pp. 10–11.
30. *Ibid.*, p. 115.
31. *Ibid.*, p. 14.
32. The United States, the United Kingdom, France, Russia, and China.
33. *Our Global Neighbourhood*, p. 16.
34. *Ibid.*, p. 131.
35. *Ibid.*, p. 27.
36. *Ibid.*, p. 28.
37. See, in particular, the World Commission on Environment and Development (1987) *Our Common Future*, New York: Oxford University Press; and the South Commission (1990) *The Challenge to the South*, New York: Oxford University Press.
38. *Our Global Neighbourhood*, p. 256.
39. See Sandrine Tesner, with the collaboration of Georg Kell (2000) *The United Nations and Business: A Partnership Recovered*, Hampshire: Macmillan.
40. Ibid., p. 116. Also see W. Andy Knight (2002) "The United Nations and Business: A Partnership Recovered", *Pacifica Review* 14(3) (October): 256–257.
41. Sandrine Tesner, pp. 84 and 108.
42. Carol Prager (1995) "The New World Order: Global Neighbourhood or Ethnic Cleansing Zone?" *Queen's Quarterly* 102(4) (winter): 933.
43. Peter Waterman (1996) Review Article, "Beyond Globalism and Developmentalism: Other Voices in World Politics", *Development and Change* 27: 166.
44. *Ibid.*, p. 170.
45. *Ibid.*, p. 169.
46. Prager, p. 933.
47. See Upendra Baxi (1996) Review Essay, "'Global Neighbourhood' and the 'Universal Otherhood': Notes on the Report of the Commission on Global Governance", *Alternatives* 21: 531.
48. *Ibid.*, p. 540.
49. *Ibid.*, n. 17, p. 547.

50. *Ibid.*, p. 532.
51. Quote in Baxi from Graham Burchell, Colin Gordon, and Peter Miller (eds.) (1991) *The Foucault Effect: Studies in Governmentality*, Chicago: University of Chicago Press, p. 93.
52. Baxi, p. 533.
53. See Robert W. Cox (1992) "Towards a Post-Hegemonic Conceptualization of World Order: Reflections on the Relevancy of Ibn Khaldun", in James Rosenau and Ernst-Otto Czempiel (eds.) *Governance without Government: Order and Change in World Politics*, Cambridge: Cambridge University Press, p. 137.
54. Richard Falk, "Liberalism at the Global Level: The Last of the Independent Commissions?" p. 575.

6

Regulating the possession and use of nuclear weapons: Ideas, commissions, and agency in international security politics – the case of the Canberra Commission

Marianne Hanson

Various studies have been commissioned in recent years that seek to influence the role of nuclear weapons and the pace of nuclear arms control and disarmament in international security. These studies have helped to reflect and also to generate a profound rethinking of the place of nuclear weapons in international security. Significantly, as independent studies drawing on the expertise of key academics, analysts, NGOs, and others, they represent an important shift in agency and norm reinforcement in global politics, a new area of intersection between governmental and non-governmental processes, which reflects a move away from traditional great power-based negotiations on security issues. The extent to which these initiatives can determine policy decisions on arms control or the elimination of nuclear weapons remains uncertain, but they have undeniably helped to articulate and reinforce the idea of disarmament at a diplomatic and policy level in a way that is substantially new to the practice of international relations.

Notable studies issued in the 1990s by independent bodies included the Stimson Center Steering Committee Reports, especially its final report, *An American Legacy: Building a Nuclear Free World* (March 1997), and the report of the Committee on International Security and Arms Control of the US National Academy of Sciences, *The Future of Nuclear Weapons Policy*. Also notable was the *Statement on Nuclear Weapons by International Generals and Admirals* in 1996 and a similar *Statement by International Civilian Leaders*.[1] Perhaps most substantial are the reports sponsored by individual states. The Australian government-sponsored Canberra Commission on the Elimination of Nuclear Weapons[2] in 1996 and the Japanese government-sponsored Tokyo Forum Report, *Facing Nuclear Dangers*[3] released in 1999, have been adopted as useful state-backed analyses of the feasibility of nuclear elimination. These initiatives sought to avoid the sometimes belaboured progression of bilateral and multilateral talks and formal negotiations, and to produce assessments which might have a more timely and pronounced impact than did traditional security negotiations. Relevant here also is the 1998 Canadian Parliamentary Report, *Canada and the Nuclear Challenge*, the recommendations of which were aimed at reducing the political value of nuclear weapons and advancing non-proliferation and disarmament.[4] Overwhelmingly, these studies called not for unilateral disarmament, but rather for phased, balanced, and verifiable moves towards the eventual elimination of nuclear weapons, based on calculations of the utility of such weapons. Reflecting a call for the salience of nuclear weapons to be reduced in the post-Cold War era, they revealed a general agreement that while these weapons cannot be disinvented, their possession and use – and their eventual elimination – can nevertheless be managed by strong norms and institutions within international society.

This chapter will focus on the origins and significance of what is arguably the principal state-sponsored contribution to the idea of nuclear weapons elimination, the Canberra Commission on the Elimination of Nuclear Weapons. This Commission's Report continues to play an important role in the wider arms control and disarmament debate – notwithstanding the presently unfavourable climate for these issues – and stands as a key reference point in that debate.[5] Appearing in the mid-1990s, the Canberra Commission was very much the product of a favourable international climate and developments in Australian domestic politics. But its convening was also, crucially, dependent on the aspirations and activism of two key members of the Australian government at the time, Prime Minister Paul Keating and Foreign Minister Gareth Evans, who sought explicitly to locate their foreign policy initiatives within the concept of "good international citizenship". The timely convergence of these factors produced an initiative that clearly challenged prevailing orthodoxy on nuclear strategy and postures, articulated a compelling alternative to such doctrines and placed the issue of the elimination of nuclear weapons firmly on the international agenda.[6]

The Canberra Commission: the international context

The Cold War bilateral paradigm for international arms control and disarmament efforts had ensured that the security concerns and preferences of small- and middle-sized states in the international system were always subservient to those of the superpowers. The structural changes brought about by the ending of the Cold War therefore, produced expectations that debates on security could now include the views of a broader range of states and that multilateral security mechanisms might be utilized in a way that had not been possible earlier.

This new climate saw the initiation of several new developments that strengthened international support for the elimination of nuclear weapons: the unofficial moratorium on nuclear testing after 1991, the legal prohibitions of the Chemical Weapons Convention in 1993, the indefinite extension of the nuclear Non-Proliferation Treaty (NPT) in 1995, and the completion of a Comprehensive Test Ban Treaty (CTBT) in 1996. A development concurrent with these was the World Court Project, an international citizens' initiative that sought to have the International Court of Justice consider the legal status of nuclear weapons (its advisory opinion was delivered in July 1996, a month before the Canberra Commission report was released). Each of these developments, in different ways, helped to reinforce a view that the elimination of nuclear weapons, considered impossible during the Cold War, might now be within the reach of the international community. The momentum provided by these events allowed the Australian Labor government to identify a propitious climate for international disarmament efforts. They lent weight to the argument that the context of international politics had changed sufficiently by the mid-1990s to allow for a rethinking of the place of nuclear weapons.

Despite these substantial advances, however, the arsenals of the nuclear weapon states (NWS) remained on high alert and concrete steps that would assist disarmament – such as full implementation of the Strategic Arms Reduction Treaty (START) II between the United States and Russia – remained elusive. In order to shift the agenda more favourably toward complete elimination, the Australian government sought to commission a report from an internationally recognized group of experts, to ask them to make the case, if it could be made, for the complete elimination of nuclear weapons. The government's aim was to publicize the Commission's results to the widest possible audience, to present it for formal adoption to the UN General Assembly and thus give it a priority and respected standing in international politics.

Domestic political considerations

There were domestic political developments too that favoured the launch of the Canberra Commission in 1995. Chief among these was the deliberate and self-conscious adoption of a policy of "good international citizenship" by the government (discussed at length below) but specific events within Australia also came to push the momentum for convening the Canberra Commission.

Within the domestic political context, the creation of the Commission was a useful means of achieving a number of related policy goals. The Keating government had been seeking to channel pressures from within the left of the Labor Party and from anti-nuclear groups into a practical proposal for disarmament. Underpinning this was a complex but generally low-key debate about Australia's role between support for the Western alliance system and reform of international security institutions in favour of smaller and middle-sized states. These underlying concerns were overtaken by a much more challenging and immediate development, however – the resumption of nuclear testing by first China and later France.[7] Yet while the launching of the Commission might be seen as an immediate political response to the tests, it must also be noted that the idea of a creative, new approach to nuclear matters appears to have been in gestation prior to the tests. Foreign Minister Evans had noted at least a year before the French tests that the post-Cold War environment was ripe for initiatives favouring elimination and had explicitly argued the case for a nuclear weapon-free world.[8] Keating, for his part, had been aware of the substance, if not the actual details, of the recently released Stimson and Federation of American Scientists reports favouring elimination, and the growth of the disarmament debate overseas.[9] These developments had undoubtedly shaped the Keating government's view that a bold policy initiative on the nuclear question was needed. Thus while the need to respond to widespread concerns in the Australian and regional community over French nuclear testing was a key element of the Canberra Commission initiative, it was certainly not the only consideration. The changing international environment had included the appearance of a respected intellectual debate on the elimination of nuclear weapons, one that clearly resonated with Keating's and Evans's own search for diplomatic influence.

Good international citizenship: a conceptual underpinning for the Canberra Commission

While both international and domestic factors suggested the convening of the Canberra Commission, there was also an important conceptual element to Australian foreign policy at the time that precipitated it. One of the central planks of Australia's foreign policy under the Keating government (and indeed present also to some extent under the immediately preceding Bob Hawke government) was the notion that Australia, as a good international citizen, could play a positive and constructive role in the changing climate of post-Cold War politics.[10] In crafting a response to the new international relations agenda, the Labor governments of the late 1980s and early–mid-1990s were concerned with instilling an explicitly declared sense of principle and morally informed action into foreign policy, and with the increasing opportunities afforded to middle sized powers to play a more assertive role in the restructured environment of global politics. The arms control and disarmament diplomacy pursued by the government fell clearly within the context of what the Labor government claimed was its enactment of good international citizenship. Indeed the Canberra Commission, the final – and most novel – disarmament initiative of the Labor government before it lost power in 1996, can be seen as the clearest expression of what Keating and Evans understood to be good international citizenship (GIC).[11]

GIC involved primarily the notion that principled action should be considered an objective of a state's foreign policy. Although most political leaders would claim a degree of moral basis for foreign policy decisions, and earlier Australian governments had implicitly acknowledged the place of humane principles in their policies, the ethical dimension of Australia's external relations became the site of direct attention and debate following the formal and explicit adoption of this nomenclature into the Australian government's foreign policy objectives in 1988.[12] This move represented the self-conscious adoption of a moral and principled declaratory basis to policy formulation, formally broadening the discourse to include GIC as an integral part of the state's actions. By 1991, Evans had elevated the GIC concept from a recognition of a growing ethic in international politics to one of Australia's four central foreign policy objectives. In his co-authored book[13] and in subsequent official publications from the Department of Foreign Affairs and Trade, he set down the central place that the concept held in the formulation and implementation of Australia's post-Cold War foreign policy. For Evans, GIC objectives, like political, strategic, and economic objectives were fundamental to the pursuit of a constructive and intelligent foreign policy. The issues he associated with GIC (human rights, the environment, development assistance and, later, the elimination of nuclear weapons) were central to the way in which he perceived Australia's new diplomatic role in the post-Cold War period, but these did not fit neatly into any existing conceptual paradigm. The concept of good international citizenship was thus as much about providing a framework for an important element of Australian diplomacy under Labor as it was about establishing a more overtly ethical dimension to the conduct of international affairs.

In particular, Evans's conceptualization of GIC related to an increasing utilization of multilateral processes in the conduct of international relations. He pointed to a set of policy outcomes as demonstrable evidence of Australia's middle power diplomacy as good global citizenship, the most notable of which included the Cambodian peace plan of 1990, the agreement on mining in the Antarctic, and the Chemical Weapons Convention of 1993.[14] It was towards the end of his tenure that other activities such as Australia's role in the Nuclear Non-Proliferation Treaty Review and Extension Conference (NPTREC), its intensified lobbying for a Comprehensive Nuclear Test Ban Treaty and its convening of the Canberra Commission took place.

Not surprisingly, articulation of the GIC concept was not without its critics, giving rise to views that the government's desire to be a good international citizen was little more than self-aggrandized posturing with impractical notions of an idealized form of global affairs. Other concerns centred on the presence of *realpolitik* in the conduct of foreign policy,[15] the implication being that the inconsistency of the application of GIC principles discredited the entire premise of the viability of an ethic in foreign policy, the very basis on which the GIC concept was built.

Yet criticism that GIC was unevenly applied and that the Australian government failed to take a consistently principled stand in foreign policy missed an essential point. As Evans himself argued, GIC did not imply forfeiting national interests completely for the sake of moral principles, any more than it implied that foreign policy must always be dictated by calculations of self-interest. It was a means of aiming for morally acceptable outcomes while working within the constraints inherent in government. Evans[16] and David Goldsworthy[17] have noted that far from being a purely idealistic venture, it reflected an attempt to blend the pragmatic protection of a state's national interests with policies that were also inherently good and of potential benefit to the wider global community. Clearly, proposing the elimination of a class of weapons known for their inhumane and horrific effects, and which were in any case of questionable utility, fell into this category. The convening of the Commission reflected the Evans/Keating belief that foreign policy actions based on principles and norms can be for the greater good and that ethical concerns for the rights and well-being of humans across the globe could be a realistic part of policy calculations. The fundamental ethical idea that lay at the heart of the GIC concept was the notion that states should be involved in promoting policies within the international system that were inherently valuable and not simply the expression of specific national, economic, or security interests.

Good international citizenship and the element of active leadership: a further prerequisite for the Canberra Commission

A full understanding of the motives that gave rise to the Canberra Commission requires appreciation of a further element. The specific Australian version of good international citizenship needs to be located within the broader context of Gareth Evans's notion of an *activist* middle power addressing salient issues, proposing political initiatives and leading the processes of multilateralism. In essence, Evans's conceptualization of GIC objectives in Australia's foreign policy was as much about *leadership* in multilateral diplomacy as it was about providing an ethical basis for the conduct of foreign policy. Under these terms, being a good international citizen was not so much about simply doing the right thing in international politics. It was also about the opportunities for an activist middle power to provide intellectual, creative, and sometimes risk-taking leadership as a means of addressing the ever-expanding range of issues confronting states in the 1990s.

This was confirmed and made explicit towards the end of Evans's term as Foreign Minister. He made the point that the expression of GIC multilateralist objectives in Australian foreign policy was "primarily activist rather than reflective or responsive."[18] The distinction is an important one for understanding the motivations and conceptual underpinnings of the GIC initiative as it evolved in Australian foreign policy. Central to understanding it, he claimed, was an appreciation of "the extent to which GIC is about providing international leadership and constructing a better international environment."[19] Rather than merely complying with existing norms and rules, states should pursue, in addition, innovative and active diplomatic ventures to progress those norms and rules. The ideas that led to the Canberra Commission can thus be seen as, for Evans and Keating at least, the natural progression of a responsible and activist state formulating proposals to set the direction for international policies.

A renewed interest in the question of international leadership coincided with, and acted as a catalyst for, assertions of an expanded role for middle powers in contemporary international politics. The early conceptual work on middle power leadership in post-Cold War politics was led by the work of Oran Young.[20] While not specifically concerned with the role of middle powers *per se*, Young's analysis of leadership in international negotiations nevertheless argued that structural, or hegemonic, power was less important to the outcome of negotiated political settlements and influencing the international agenda than it had been during the Cold War era. Young suggested that leadership was no longer simply a function of hegemony in the international system and that states which employed a combination of imagination and brokering skills could have a significant influence on political outcomes.[21] His work on post-hegemonic leadership styles had an important impact on the development of thinking about the expanded diplomatic role of middle powers in international politics in the 1990s. In particular, Cooper, Higgott, and Nossal[22] adopted Young's notion of non-hegemonic leadership as a conceptual foundation for their study on Canadian and Australian middle power diplomacy during the transformation of the international economic and political system in the 1980s and 1990s. Their work was the most comprehensive attempt to apply Young's various categories of leadership to the raft of post-Cold War diplomatic initiatives undertaken by these two prominent middle powers. Raino Malnes[23] has also developed Young's initial work on leadership and has added to Young's categories an emphasis on what he terms "directional" leadership, which "attempts to influence the interests, values and beliefs" of parties involved in particular issues.[24] What Malnes has identified as directional leadership involves the ability to sway participants to a particular course of action by disseminating new ideas about the desirability of certain arrangements and influencing the positions states adopt in multilateral forums.

It is perhaps this last point which has most relevance for Evans's understanding of good international citizenship and middle power diplomacy. As he noted, activism alone in foreign policy circles was a necessary but not sufficient condition of middle power leadership. In the absence of what Evans called "clout" in the international system, middle powers would need to rely on their intellectual capital for leading states and pursuing outcomes for common agenda problems. In this way, Evans' notion of good international citizenship as middle power leadership in international politics was closely akin to Malnes's dimension of directional leadership. This involved, particularly in arms control initiatives such as the Canberra Commission which sought to exercise informed influence over key security players, an attempt to shape the attitudes of other states and construct particular outcomes in the international system. If we take Evans at face value and accept that being a good international citizen was as much about actively promoting a core set of ideas to the international community as it was about merely engaging in the significant debates of the time, this notion of directional leadership becomes more apparent.

Prelude to the Canberra Commission: Australia's arms control diplomacy

It was Australia's disarmament diplomacy during the 1990s that came to conform most clearly to the Evans version of GIC: propitious for Australian security interests, serving the wider purposes of global security, multilateralist in method, reformist in tone and content, and above all, endeavouring to provide a degree of political leadership and problem-solving to one of the key post-Cold War security issues. In many ways, arms control initiatives, culminating in the Canberra Commission, came to be the most appropriate and logical vehicle for demonstrating Australia's GIC credentials. Whereas human rights, development aid, and environmental efforts had been earmarked as original targets for GIC activism, the constraints surrounding easy implementation of these policies became evident over time. Inconsistent application of a thoroughly "principled" foreign policy, particularly on human rights issues, attracted criticism that claims of GIC were little more than grandstanding, designed to promote a favourable policy image, but which ultimately could not sustain the required moral commitment required of GIC. And while this criticism was not always deserved (especially given Evans's own acknowledgment that GIC would have to be a blend of what was realistically achievable within the constraints of foreign policy and the search for ideal solutions), it undoubtedly influenced the degree to which the government could claim successful outcomes in these fields. These areas were never discarded as targets for GIC, but increasingly, Labor's foreign policy initiatives – at least those which could safely be upheld as evidence of GIC – came to focus on arms control and disarmament activities, beginning largely with the success of the Chemical Weapons Convention in 1993 and continuing up to the formation of the Canberra Commission in 1995. It was almost as if there was a tacit recognition that this was one area in which GIC initiatives could be applied without risking accusations of "selling out".

Focusing on arms control and disarmament carried little risk of bringing serious disadvantage to the government's foreign policy programme. It was an issue that enjoyed bipartisan support in Australia, at least in terms of the general ends envisaged, if not the means to go about achieving these ends. (This was notwithstanding greater willingness on the part of Keating and Evans than the conservative Coalition Government to loosen Australia's tight affiliation with US objectives, a policy justified in terms of post-Cold War security calculations.) Similarly, pursuing arms control objectives did not imperil Australia's economic and trade relations in the same way that human rights policies towards states like Burma, Indonesia, and especially China might have done. Given a significant, if diffuse, public approval of arms control objectives, pursuing this area seemed a logical means of continuing and amplifying the government's GIC programme.

Additionally, Australia's record of disarmament diplomacy over the previous two decades pointed naturally to a role for Australia on the question of the elimination of nuclear weapons, a role that could now be pursued with greater vigour. From the early 1980s, Australia had sought to play a more activist role in disarmament affairs through the Conference on Disarmament (CD),[25] but the 1990s saw heightened expectations for multilateral security agreements on nuclear arms control and disarmament. Moreover, Australia's strategic and geographic position, together with its disarmament credentials made it well-placed to commission a report on nuclear elimination. It was a state that had been both a loyal supporter of its nuclear US ally and also a firm advocate of arms control and disarmament through respected multilateral forums, the latter stance gaining it an important degree of acceptance from the non-nuclear states. It was far enough away from the centres of power to distance itself from the nuclear posturings of the Cold War era, but was nevertheless a committed member of the Western alliance. Moreover, by never seriously pursuing a nuclear weapons capability for itself, Australia could implicitly claim a position of leadership and example to other states, a committed non-proliferator urging non-proliferation and disarmament at the global level.

The Canberra Commission as implementation of active good international citizenship

The Canberra Commission on the Elimination of Nuclear Weapons, the final Keating/Evans disarmament initiative, was announced in October 1995, five months before the Labor government was removed from power. It brought together a group of 17 independent specialists on the political, legal and strategic aspects of nuclear weapons. The expertise and general standing of the individual Commissioners was a key component of the Commission's status. Included were former prime ministers, ambassadors, academics, and civilian and military leaders. Two of the most prominent Commissioners were from the US: General Lee Butler, former Commander in Chief of the US Strategic Air Command, and Robert McNamara, former US Secretary for Defense. Following a series of meetings over a ten-month period, the consensus among the Commissioners was that continuing assertions of nuclear weapons' utility were not viable and that a window of opportunity existed for the nuclear weapon states to undertake a phased programme of complete nuclear disarmament. The report argued that nuclear weapons have no strategic or political utility; this being the case, then the dangers of accidental or "irrational" use could best be countered by a programme of phased elimination, together with a strict monitoring and verification regime. An elimination of nuclear weapons would bring these weapons into line with the other two types of weapons of mass destruction, chemical and biological weapons, both of which are clearly prohibited (in terms of use and possession) by established international law upheld by the United States and other key players in the international system.

The report's analysis of the utility of nuclear weapons was a compelling one.[26] It rebutted the view that nuclear weapons are useful to deter nuclear or conventional attacks, or that they are necessary to counter chemical or biological weapon attacks. The report recommended a number of steps including taking nuclear forces off alert status, removing warheads from delivery vehicles, ending the deployment of all non-strategic weapons, ending nuclear testing, phased further reductions in US-Russian arsenals and reciprocal no-first-use agreements. It outlined the case for a ban on weapons-grade fissile material and detailed strict verification procedures that must accompany any move towards elimination. One of the report's main arguments was that maintaining the status quo of nuclear "apartheid" might encourage other states, such as India, Pakistan, Syria, Iraq, or North Korea, to develop their own nuclear capabilities if they perceived that the existing nuclear weapons states would not move towards disarmament. (Some of these fears were subsequently realized, of course: Iraq, Iran, and North Korea currently stand accused of developing nuclear weapons or a nuclear weapons programme, while India's and Pakistan's decisions to test nuclear devices in May 1998 pointed, *inter alia*, to dissatisfaction with the unwillingness of the existing nuclear weapon states to disarm as justifications for their policies. Indeed a criticism that can be made of the Commission is that it did not include representatives from India or Pakistan, states of crucial importance to the disarmament debate.)

Undoubtedly, the report put forward a highly ambitious agenda and it remains the case that there was an enormous gulf between the report's recommendations and the reality of nuclear weapon states taking steps in that direction. Indeed what the Canberra Commission's report showed was that while each of the strategic, technological, or political reasons for maintaining nuclear arsenals were less than tenable in the new strategic climate of the post-Cold War period, what was required for disarmament to occur was a dramatic shift in the thinking of nuclear weapon states' political leaders. The report conceded that the elimination of nuclear weapons, if it occurs at all, will be a long and difficult process requiring years of work as well as the full commitment of the existing nuclear weapon states.

The Commission's report was not finalized until after the Australian federal election. Published in August 1996 and presented to the new conservative Coalition Government, the report was clearly now in the hands of a government that differed markedly from its original sponsors. It was presented, although with considerable reluctance, by the new government to the 51st session of the UN General Assembly. This government did not seek to have the report formally adopted by the UN and its disinclination to provide appropriate support and impetus for the report meant that the Commission lost a key opportunity to establish itself at the international political level in a forceful and effective way. Moreover, the new government failed to emphasize with sufficient force the report's warning that unless steps were taken to adopt a programme of phased and verifiable nuclear weapons elimination, the world faced a continuing danger of further proliferation, and the risks of deliberate, inadvertent or "irrational" use.

Despite the fact that the new government did not actively promote the report, the initial international reaction to the Commission's work was generally positive, eliciting favourable comment from members of the non-aligned movement and even from the United States.[27] Over the following few years, it came to influence the disarmament debate in a steady and sustained manner. The report came to be an important step in the broader push for nuclear elimination set against the background of the end of the Cold War and the attendant change in the context of nuclear weaponry, a push which is fuelled by ongoing academic and strategic research. The Commission's report is now part of a wider debate urging elimination which includes research from a number of prestigious and respected US and other research centres, many of them mainstream organizations whose advocacy of this cause even a decade earlier would have been unimaginable. The report represented a major contribution to the then evolving debate on nuclear elimination and stands as a reference point for numerous political and military disarmament analysts. It has, for instance been incorporated into recent studies on nuclear elimination (notably the Stimson Center's 1997 Steering Committee report, the report of the Committee on International Security and Arms Control of the American National Academy of Sciences, the Carnegie Commission on Preventing Deadly Conflict and the Tokyo Forum report on Reducing Nuclear Dangers) and has generated a significant amount of diplomatic attention.[28] Individual members of the Commission have also publicized the report's findings and taken the process forward to a wider audience.[29] Especially at the diplomatic level, the report generated substantial interest; it formed the basis of the platform adopted by the New Agenda Coalition, a group of eight nations now actively pursuing nuclear disarmament in the United Nations.[30] Thus while the report did not have an impact in terms of policy change, and was not actively supported by the incoming Australian government, it has been kept as a cornerstone in the on-going academic and diplomatic attempts to advance disarmament. In any case, the deterioration of the international strategic climate after 1996 closed the door on what was seen as something of a golden age in arms control initiatives, making immediate tangible outcomes unlikely. The Commission was formed at a time when expectations for advances in arms control were high; that it was not able to fulfil these expectations but nevertheless remain central to ongoing debates in this field is an important achievement.

What lessons can be learned from the experience of the Canberra Commission? I will first consider the impact of the Commission and its report, before proposing a range of conditions conducive to the success of such initiatives. The Canberra Commission represented a novel form of disarmament diplomacy, the application of state patronage to a group of independent and respected analysts in the interest of furthering arms control and disarmament, seeking to challenge status quo thinking on nuclear weapons and provide new directions for international security discussions.

The Canberra Commission report, as with those other studies that preceded or followed it, has contributed significantly to sustaining what is termed here the non-nuclear norm. They have undoubtedly added weight to the pervasive and growing feeling among many states and their publics that nuclear weapons must be de-legitimized as instruments of security, a message that the nuclear weapon states are finding difficult to ignore. This is notwithstanding the resurgence of nuclearism shown by some of these states, and especially by the United States, recently. The nuclear weapon states are now living in, and having to justify their policies and behaviour within, the world of the non-nuclear norm, even if their strategic doctrines and practices are not yet changing.

Such commissions also serve to remind the nuclear weapon states that smaller states (and indeed non-state actors also) within the international community seek to influence security dialogues. There is a sense that more inclusive and innovative ideas such as these can help to provide assessments of threats and assist in the formulation of ideas to reduce these threats, a point noted by Robert O'Neill, a Canberra Commissioner. This new type of activity also reflects a shifting pattern of agency and legitimacy in world politics, where norms specifying behaviour and seeking to constrain behaviour are emerging *not* from the dominant powers but rather from a variety of different sources.

It is, however, hard to draw absolute conclusions about the impact of ventures such as the Canberra Commission. The Commission's report may not have affected the substantive behaviour of states in the short or even medium terms – all the nuclear weapon states continue to reserve the right for themselves to possess nuclear weapons (while seeking to deny any such possibility to other states, as we see with the US campaign against Iraq). Although the number of nuclear weapons has decreased significantly since the Cold War, and the nuclear weapon states have reiterated their promises to move towards disarmament, none of them appears to be serious about this goal. At the declaratory level at least, nuclear weapons remain central to their strategic doctrines, even if this factor poses considerable obstacles to international security.[31] The ultimate success of initiatives such as the Canberra Commission will depend on the extent to which particular sponsoring states (and individuals) can sustain the political will necessary to challenge traditional assumptions and habits. It will also depend on the extent to which sponsoring and supporting states can balance these issues with alliance loyalties and the interdependence of political and economic relations.

But it is also true that old habits and old ideas are under increasing scrutiny and are now less entrenched as "acceptable" within international society as they were even ten years ago. These processes of statecraft have become important in the past decade; they are likely to grow in significance in coming years and seek to apply further pressure on the nuclear weapon states who remain, for the moment at least, the key decision-makers of security policy. It appears that the changed strategic focus of the US after September 2001 rejects, rather than embraces, the disarmament proposals put forward by the Canberra Commission. The US invasion of Iraq in March 2003 was – at least ostensibly – for the purposes of disarmament, and it might be seen as strengthening a norm of non-possession of nuclear weapons. Such an analysis would be problematic however, as doubts continue about the US's motives, and because the Iraq campaign has only served to reinforce the divisions between the nuclear haves and have-nots. In other words, there is no indication that the NWS are themselves moving to nuclear disarmament. This chapter suggests, however, that by gradually weaving a web of normative constraints around nuclear weapons and urging a reduction of their centrality in the strategic doctrines of the NWS, we reinforce the norm of non-use and even non-possession. In sum, there is a clear opinion in favour of international norms designed to reduce the nuclear threat and to marginalize nuclear weapons. The strength of this norm is due in no small part to initiatives such as the Canberra Commission.

Conclusion: identifying the elements of success

The experience of the Canberra Commission suggests that at least five factors facilitated this initiative. And while it is essential to acknowledge that no two commissions are alike (in terms of origin, purpose, or make-up) it is nevertheless possible to make a broad case for these factors applying also to the fortunes of other commissions.

First, it seems essential that commissions require a strong and determined sponsor. In the case of the Canberra Commission, an explicitly activist government willing to invest intellectual and practical leadership in this venture was clearly evident. The Canberra Commission initiative demonstrated the active leadership element of good international citizenship, rather than a merely reflective or responsive position in international relations. It was innovative and creative; above all, and in line with Malnes's concept of directional leadership, it involved seizing the initiative and devising a previously untried method for exerting diplomatic influence. The sponsors were undoubtedly aware of the obstacles that would stand in the way of elimination; they were nevertheless intent on pursuing a course of action at the international level that would challenge the nuclear status quo and provide new directions for security discussions. Unlike Australia's previous disarmament efforts in the UN, the method chosen represented a unique form of disarmament diplomacy. Certainly multilateral efforts were not meant to be sidelined by the Canberra Commission initiative. They remain and are likely to remain the mainstay of Australian disarmament diplomacy. But this initiative effectively side-stepped many of the time-consuming and bureaucratic difficulties usually encountered in multilateral negotiations. This method of advocacy accorded well with the government's push for Australia to be seen as an innovative and constructive leader in global security issues, seeking to direct the course of negotiations and influence the thinking of other actors, as well as with Keating's and Evans's own personal styles of engaging in "big picture" issues.

A second key requirement would seem to be a propitious international environment. This does not of course reduce commissions to a mere reflection of prevailing views – as noted at the beginning of this chapter, the commissions and studies associated with furthering nuclear disarmament both reflected *and* generated a view on the need for nuclear elimination in the wake of the ending of the Cold War – but it does indicate that a substantial element of "movement" needs to have taken place in the discourse and practices of international relations pertinent to the issue under question. Certainly in the case of the Canberra Commission, the opportunities afforded by the ending of the East–West confrontation were indispensable to its establishment. The early 1990s were also notable for the extent to which the sole remaining superpower was relatively amenable to the idea of change engineered via multilateral institutions. The analyses and ideas supporting nuclear elimination found a relatively open-minded audience in the form of the first Clinton administration, with Secretary of State Les Aspin and others displaying considerable interest in the issue.[32]

But it is not of course only propitious developments that have an effect; it may well be that shocks to the system are equally important in bringing forth new ideas as are "positive" international developments. The French nuclear tests are a case in point here, providing, as they did, a compelling impetus (although certainly not the underlying reason) for the Keating/Evans initiative. Indeed it was another jolt to the international system – the nuclear tests conducted by India and Pakistan in 1998 – that were the primary catalyst for the convening of the Tokyo Forum. Clearly the timing of a commission is an important factor.

A third factor concerns the willingness of individual commissioners to promote the Commission's findings. General Lee Butler, Australia's Richard Butler (chair of the Canberra Commission) and others were active in disseminating the nuclear elimination argument, through a series of written publications and personal representations. The extent to which commissioners have a sense of ownership of the findings is important here: in the Canberra Commission there was initially no clear consensus on the desirability of nuclear elimination or what the report's message should be. One can only assume that the process of deliberation sufficed not only to achieve consensus but also to galvanize individuals to sustain the momentum of the report's findings through personal efforts also.

That the original state sponsors of a commission continue to support the Commission and its findings is a fourth point of relevance to the efficacy of promotion. In the case of the Canberra Commission, unfortunate timing meant that the Labor government had lost power by the time the Commission had completed its report. The successor government, in addition to being reluctant to promote the handiwork of its political adversary, disdained the activism of its predecessor. This point suggests the demise of the concept of good international citizenship as an underpinning of Australian foreign policy. This is not only because the new government failed to promote the Canberra Commission's report, but also because it visibly renounced what it saw as the activist "meddling" of the Labor government. Moreover, it displayed little of the innovation or intellectual leadership envisioned by Keating and Evans. Differences emerge between the conceptualization of good international citizenship developed under Labor, and the more aloof, less activist, and pro-US foreign policies put forward by the Coalition government since 1996. These differences give further weight to the argument here that middle power leadership is most effective when it is actively engaged with the central issues of the time.

The Tokyo Forum Report suffered a similar fate. Its original government sponsor, mindful of the strain that a push for elimination would by this time place on its relations with its US ally, was keen to distance itself from the report's progress and findings. Despite this point about the need for continued promotion and support however, it is remarkable that the Canberra Commission was able to achieve the status and reputation that it did. This was due in no small part to the post-Commission efforts of individual commissioners, but it was also testament to the novelty of the initiative and the standing and expertise of the Commissioners.

A final point – related to the issue of a propitious international environment – revolves around the response of the prevailing great powers in the international system, or in the case of contemporary international politics, in the reactions of the United States. This factor, however, is more to do with the prospects for implementation of a commission's findings, should this stage be reached, than with the actual impact or status of a commission's findings. In the case of the Canberra Commission, while there was initially some US interest in the report, the failure of the document to be enacted was at least a reflection of the deteriorating security environment as it was a case of great power rejection. As noted above, that the findings of reports such as those prepared by the Canberra Commission are absorbed into policy decisions was in any case an unlikely development. But that is beside the point: the real value of commissions is not what they achieve in terms of immediate implementation, but rather in the extent of their contribution to the evolving normative context of global politics. Hugely dwarfed as it might currently seem against prevailing doctrines favouring nuclear retention and even nuclear use, the Canberra Commission nevertheless stands as an important challenge to that status quo.

Notes

1. The Stimson Center Report (and its two earlier reports) can be viewed at http://www.stimson.org.legacy. The National Academy of Sciences Report can be found at http://www.nas.edu/readingroom/books/fun. Both the Statement on Nuclear Weapons by International Generals and Admirals and the Statement by International Civilian Leaders are part of the Nuclear Elimination Project at the State of the World Forum. For the full text of these statements see http://www.worldforum.org/initiatives.
2. The Canberra Commission Report can be accessed at http://www.dfat.gov.au/cc/cchome.html.
3. The Tokyo Forum Report, Facing Nuclear Dangers: An Action Plan for the 21st Century, can be accessed at http://www.mofa.go.jp/policy/un/disarmament/forum/tokyo9907/index.html.
4. The full Canadian report can be accessed at http://www.dfait-maeci.gc.ca/nucchallenge/menu-e.htm.
5. Marianne Hanson and Carl Ungerer (1992) "Promoting and Agenda for Nuclear Weapons' Elimination: the Canberra Commission and Dilemmas of Disarmament," *Australian Journal of Politics and History* 44(4, X): 533–551; Marianne Hanson and Carl Ungerer (1999) "The Canberra Commission: Paths Followed, Paths Ahead," *Australian Journal of International Affairs* 53(1): 5–17; Marianne Hanson (2001) "New Initiatives to Advance Arms Control: The Tokyo Forum Report," Carl Ungerer and Marianne Hanson (eds.) *The Politics of Nuclear Non-Proliferation*, St Leonard's, Sydney: Allen and Unwin, pp. 171–186.
6. A large body of literature has emerged in recent years exploring this idea, including Michael McGwire (1994) "Is there a Future for Nuclear Weapons?" *International Affairs* 70(2): 211–228; Joseph Rotblat (1993) Bhalchandra Udgaonkar and Jack Steinberger

(eds.) *A Nuclear-Weapon-Free World: Desirable? Feasible?*, London: Macmillan; Joseph Rotblat (ed.) (1998) *Nuclear Weapons: the Road to Zero*, London: Macmillan; John Baylis and Robert O'Neill (eds.) (2000) *Alternative Nuclear Futures: the Role of Nuclear Weapons in the Post-Cold War World*, Oxford University Press; Frank Blackaby and Tom Milne (eds.) (2000) *A Nuclear-Weapon-Free World: Steps Along the Way*, London: Macmillan. For examinations of the growth of a non-nuclear norm, Richard Price and Nina Tannenwald, "Norms and Deterrence: the Nuclear and Chemical Weapons Taboos," in Peter Katzenstein (ed.) (1996) *The Culture of National Security: Norms and Identity in World Politics*, New York: Columbia University Press; Nina Tannenwald (1999) "The Nuclear Taboo: the United States and the Normative Basis of Nuclear Non-Use," *International Organization* 53(3): 433–468.

7. For details on the Australian response to the French tests, see Kim Richard Nossal and Carolyn Vivian (1997) "A Brief Madness: Australia and the Resumption of French Nuclear Testing," *Canberra Papers on Strategy and Defence*, vol. 121, Canberra: Australian National University.
8. Gareth Evans and Bruce Grant (1995) *Australia's Foreign Relations in the World of the 1990s*, second edition, Melbourne: Melbourne University Press, pp. 86–87.
9. In his statement to the inaugural meeting of the Canberra Commission, for instance, Keating noted that "many ideas for a nuclear weapons-free world are on the table, but there has never before been a government-sponsored exercise to develop a comprehensive and practical approach to the problem." Paul Keating, *Statement by Prime Minister Keating to the Inaugural Meeting of the Canberra Commission on the Elimination of Nuclear Weapons*, Canberra, 19 January 1996.
10. The concept of good international citizenship was most clearly articulated in Evans and Grant, *Australia's Foreign Relations in the World of the 1990s*, but Evans had raised the idea as early as 1988 (see Gareth Evans, "Address to the Bicentennial Conference, Strategic and Defence Studies Centre," Research School of Pacific Studies, Australian National University, 6 December 1988).
11. The specific concept of good international citizenship remains an area on which there is relatively little scholarly analysis, although its wider context can be found in the extensive literature on ethics and foreign policy. Specific examinations include Andrew Linklater (1992) "What is Good International Citizen?" Paul Keal (ed.), *Ethics and Foreign Policy*, Canberra: Allen and Unwin in association with the Australian National University; David Goldsworthy, "Australia and Good International Citizenship," Stephanie Lawson (ed.) (1995) *The New Agenda for Global Security: Cooperating for Peace and Beyond*, St Leonards, NSW: Allen and Unwin in association with the Australian National University; Peter Lawler (1992) "The Good Citizen Australia?" *Asian Studies Review* 16(2): 241–250; Peter Lawler (1994a) "Constituting the Good State," Paul James (ed.), *Critical politics: from the Personal to the Global*, Melbourne: Arena Publications. The GIC concept has also been applied, in a revised way, to Britain's "Third Way" in foreign policy under the (early) Blair government (see Nicholas J. Wheeler and Tim Dunne (1998) "Good International Citizenship: a Third Way for British Foreign Policy," *International Affairs* 74(4): 847–870.
12. The crucial differences between Evans's foreign policy programme and that of previous Foreign Ministers were that Evans made explicit mention and adoption of GIC as informing the decisions of the Australian government, and that the changed international structures following the end of the Cold War allowed middle powers to exercise more initiative and innovation than was possible during the more constrained period of bipolarity. These factors suggest that the adoption of GIC represented a sufficiently different approach to foreign policy than had been taken earlier, although it is not to suggest that previous policies were devoid of any degree of moral consideration. On this point see Goldsworthy, "Australia and Good International Citizenship," pp. 176–178.

13. Gareth Evans and Bruce Grant (1995) *Australia's Foreign Relations in the World of the 1990s*, second edition, Melbourne: Melbourne University Press, pp. 40–41.
14. Gareth Evans (1993) *Cooperating for Peace: the Global Agenda for the 1990s and Beyond*, Sydney: Allen and Unwin.
15. In particular, the Australian government's position on East Timor was heavily criticized as tolerating the widespread abuse of human rights.
16. Gareth Evans, "Cooperating with my Critics: a Rejoinder," in Stephanie Lawson (ed.) (1995) *The New Agenda for Global Security: Cooperating for Peace and Beyond*, St Leonards, NSW: Allen and Unwin in association with the Australian National University.
17. Goldsworthy, "Australia and Good International Citizenship".
18. Evans, "Cooperating with my Critics: a Rejoinder," p. 193.
19. Ibid., p. 193.
20. Oran Young (1991) "Political Leadership and Regime Formation: on the Development of Institutions in International Society," *International Organization* 45(3): 281–308.
21. This is not to claim that the actual implementation of such negotiated agreements can always proceed without the blessing of hegemonic powers or the presence of structural leadership in the international system. Nevertheless, there have been some important recent developments, including the 1997 Ottawa Convention on Landmines and the establishment in 2002 of the International Criminal Court, which testify to the tenacity of lesser powers.
22. Andrew Cooper, Richard Higgott and Kim Nossal (1993) *Relocating Middle Powers: Australia and Canada in a Changing World Order*, Vancouver: University of British Columbia Press.
23. Raino Malnes (1995) "'Leader' and 'Entrepreneur' in International Negotiations: a Conceptual Analysis," *European Journal of International Relations* 1(1): 87–112.
24. Ibid., p. 105.
25. Although it had played a valuable role in disarmament negotiations from the time it became a member of the CD in 1979, Australia's more active involvement in disarmament issues can be dated from the appointment of a full-time Geneva-based Ambassador for Disarmament in 1983. See Evans and Grant, *Australia's Foreign Relations in the World of the 1990s*, pp. 82–90.
26. The report was released together with a selection of Background Papers commissioned from leading international academics and analysts. For a fuller analysis of the report's content, see Marianne Hanson and Carl Ungerer, "Promoting and Agenda for Nuclear Weapons' Elimination: the Canberra Commission and Dilemmas of Disarmament," and Marianne Hanson and Carl Ungerer, "The Canberra Commission: Paths Followed, Paths Ahead".
27. United Nations, UN Press Release GA/DIS/3054, 15 October 1996.
28. For a detailed examination of the report's progress and impact after its release, see Hanson and Ungerer (1999) *The Politics of Nuclear Non-proliferation*.
29. See especially Lee Butler, "At the End of a Journey: the Risks of Cold War Thinking in a New Era," in John Baylis and Robert O'Neill (eds.) *Alternative Nuclear Futures: the Role of Nuclear Weapons in the Post-Cold War World*, (Oxford: Oxford University Press, 2000), pp. 184–190.
30. Carl Ungerer (2001) "The Force of Ideas: Middle Power Diplomacy and the New Agenda for Nuclear Disarmament".
31. Marianne Hanson (2002) "Nuclear Weapons as Obstacles to International Security," *International Relations* 16(3): 361–379.
32. Michael MccGwire (2001) "Shifting the Paradigm," *International Affairs* 78(1): 1–28, p. 16.

7

Beyond temples and tombs: Towards effective governance for sustainable development through the World Commission on Dams

Sanjeev Khagram

Genesis of the World Commission on Dams[1]

Big dams are characterized diametrically as modernization and destruction, as temples and as tombs, as progress and as injustice. On the one hand, perhaps more than any other development initiative, these projects over the years symbolized the progress of humanity from a life controlled by nature and tradition to one where nature is ruled by science, and tradition by rationality. On the other hand, big dams have more recently been identified with the injustice of humanity as a result of their untold destruction of nature as well as the sacrifice of diverse peoples, cultures, and ways of life in the name of ostensible progress through science and rationality.

Big dams bring together virtually the entire set of issues and actors that are central to conflicts over sustainable development at multiple levels and scales around the world. Nowhere have the conflicts between competing approaches to sustainable development been displayed more vividly than in the contestation over the options to planning, design, appraisal, construction, operation, monitoring, and even decommissioning of these grand technological, ecological, socio-economic, and political interventions. At the heart of the debates and struggles over dams, however, lies the governance challenge of generating the institutional arrangements and decision-making processes needed for achieving sustainable development.

The world has built 45,000 big dams, mostly since 1950. The number of big dam projects built annually grew from virtually zero in 1900 to nearly 250 by mid-century. The rate exploded thereafter and peaked at around 1,000 big dams being constructed annually from the mid-1950s to the mid-1970s. But even more dramatically, the number of these projects completed per year fell precipitously to under 250 by the 1990s. This represents a 75 per cent drop in the construction rate of big dams in a little over a decade. The number of the subset of major dams completed each year declined similarly: during the 1970s, 93 of these mega-projects were constructed, while only 20 were built during the first half on the 1990s.[2]

Given the seemingly tremendous needs for water (nearly 1 billion people do not have adequate supplies of drinking water), irrigation (for increasing agricultural production as global population expands beyond 6 billion), electricity (over 2 billion people do not have access to stable sources of electricity), and flood control (witness the massive and destructive floods that have engulfed numerous river basins over the past several years), in addition to the powerful set of interests and institutions promoting and supporting big dams (governments, international agencies, multinational corporations, domestic industrialists, agricultural lobbies, and urban consumers), the rapid and dramatic decline in the construction of these projects globally over the last three decades is puzzling.

Four types of arguments can be offered to explain this trend: technical, financial, economic, and political. The technical argument highlights the decreasing availability of sites for big dam building to account for the falling completion rate of these projects. However, as of 1986, 95 per cent of big dam projects were concentrated in 25 countries which had already built more than 100, while less than 2 per cent were spread over more than 150 other countries of the world where sites are still available, if not plentiful.[3] During the 1990s, the number of big dams under construction increased slightly from about 1,500 to 1,700 per year, as the number of big dam-starts continued to average 300 per year.[4] Thus, there has been a diverging trend over time between the number of sites still available – as well as the number of dams being started and under construction – compared to the number of big dams actually being completed every year.

Financial and economic factors, such as shortages in available funding and the increasing relative viability of "conventional" alternatives to big dams are two other possible explanations for the decline in big dam building.[5] The worldwide recession during the 1980s, the growth in indebtedness of many third world states, donor fatigue among foreign lenders, and a strategy shift towards privatization all contributed to the decreasing availability of public and international financing for these projects. The decreasing costs of other conventional alternatives, particularly natural gas power plants in place of hydroelectric dams, also reduced their comparative financial and economic feasibility. The increasing time and cost overruns associated with big dam projects further detracted from expected financial and economic returns of these projects and improved the relative viability of alternatives.

These technical, financial, and economic factors have clearly made big dam building less attractive, but they do not tell the whole story. Political factors have contributed increasingly to the decreasing financial viability of, and changing economic calculations regarding big dams. Mounting public protests against these projects have caused time overruns, which in turn have produced cost overruns. Costs have also escalated because big dam builders and authorities have been compelled to investigate and mitigate negative environmental and social effects, such as improving the life chances of displaced peoples. As these environmental and social costs have been internalized more fully, economic benefit-cost or financial rate of return criteria justifying the building of these projects have become more difficult to meet. These requirements for the formulation, sanctioning, and implementation of big dams either did not exist or were not followed in the past.[6]

Site depletion, moreover, actually has been as much a cause for the generation of political opposition to big dams, as it has been a direct factor in the decline of big dam building. Particularly in North America and Western Europe, the continual loss of free flowing rivers associated with the damming of more and more sites sparked much of the initial mobilization and organization of domestic conservation groups. The success of these early campaigns around big dams played a critical role in the growth of national environmental movements in numerous countries in the West from the 1950s to the 1970s.[7] The declining opportunities for big dam building in the first world and increasing demand in the third world for the services these projects offer subsequently drove big dam builders to shift even more of their activities to developing countries. As a result, approximately two-thirds of the big dams built in the 1980s and three-quarters under construction during the 1990s were located in the third world.

But over the last two decades, coalescing from a multitude of struggles and campaigns waged at the local, national, and international levels, transnational civil society groups and organizations advocating participatory, equitable, and sustainable development have altered dramatically the dynamics of big dam building. Directly affected people, social movements, and domestic non-governmental organizations in many parts of the world have empowered themselves to reform or block the completion of big dams in their own countries, often by forming partnerships with like-minded foreign supporters. At the same time, non-governmental organizations from the first world and international non-governmental organizations working on human rights, the protection of indigenous peoples, environmental conservation and other issues, have focused their energies increasingly on slowing or halting the global spread and growth of big dam building. As a result, in contrast to the first world where historically, domestic technical, financial, economic, and political factors contributed relatively equally and interacted to cause the decline in big dam building, the primary explanation for these changing dynamics in the other countries is increasingly political-economic, having to do with the shifting transnational relations of power and meaning surrounding the construction of these projects.

Government agencies, private sector firms, and international organizations had slowly begun to reform their policies and practices with respect to big dam building globally, particularly in the 1980s and 1990s. Parts of these reforms were motivated by the scientific and practical knowledge base that had been built up from the tremendous amount of research experience with dam building over the last fifty years. But, these actors were pushed persistently, and progressively, to initiate, expedite, modify, and broaden reform efforts or often just halt building dams by growing numbers of transnationally allied critics – primarily local peoples' groups, social movements, and non-governmental organizations at the regional, national and international levels.[8]

It was clearly transnational civil society groups of various kinds that successfully pushed for an independent and comprehensive review of big dams, a demand for which they had been lobbying for several years and which was articulated most explicitly in the Curitiba Declaration. The declaration itself was drafted and approved at the historic First International Conference of People Affected by Dams held in Curitiba, Brazil, 11–14 March 1997. Nearly 100 dam-affected people and dam critics speaking more than 12 languages from 17 countries including Argentina, Bolivia, Brazil, Chile, France, Germany, India, Lesotho, Mexico, Norway, Paraguay, Russia, Spain, Sweden, Switzerland, Taiwan, Thailand, and the United States attended the meeting and endorsed the declaration.[9] The declaration demanded the establishment of an independent commission to conduct a comprehensive review of all large dams supported by international agencies, subject to the approval and monitoring of representatives of transnational civil society and especially those groups directly accountable to dam-affected peoples. Similar reviews for each national and regional agency that had supported the building of big dams would also be required.

By the 1990s, an increasingly dramatic state of affairs had clearly begun to emerge. On the one hand, while opponents had been successful in halting specific projects and generating gradual policy change more broadly, many were interested in institutionalizing mechanisms for halting unacceptable big dams early on so that more resources could be deployed for an "options" agenda rather than be drained by the continuous battles to reform or stop the next "destructive" project. On the other hand, proponents bemoaned the decline in prospects for big dam building but continued to extol the virtues and benefits of these projects. Many proponents were interested in having clear rules on when, how, and by whom big dams could be built to increase predictability and lower risks and transactions costs of their activities.[10]

Partly in response to this state of affairs, and partly to soften the harsh criticism that had been levelled against it, the World Bank invited the World Conservation Union (IUCN) to convene a workshop to bring "together leading experts and representatives of major stakeholder groups ... to initiate an open and transparent dialogue", on the future of large dams and alternatives globally.[11] In April of 1997, 39 participants from governments, international development agencies, the private sector, professional associations, non-governmental organizations, universities, and peoples' groups met at a workshop entitled, "Large Dams: Learning from the Past, Looking to the Future", held in Gland, Switzerland. After criticizing the workshop for being biased and flawed, the first ever post-evaluation of World Bank-financed big dam projects was conducted by the World Bank's own Operation Evaluation Department. Consensus emerged among participants at Gland that no existing group or organization had the legitimacy to evaluate authoritatively the historical experience with dams and alternatives, and suggested recommendations for the future. Consequently, the constitution of a World Commission on Dams was proposed to fill this vacuum of legitimate authority globally and facilitate a path forward.

The purpose and nature of the World Commission on Dams

The World Commission on Dams (WCD) was arguably one of the most innovative and even unprecedented international governance experiments in the area of sustainable development of the late 1990s. Its mandate, which it received from the "Gland Reference Group" of key stakeholder representatives, was to: a) conduct a global review of the development effectiveness of dams and assess alternatives for water resources and energy management, and b) develop internationally accepted standards, guidelines, and criteria for decision-making in the planning, design, appraisal, construction, monitoring, operation, and decommissioning of dams".[12]

The guiding principles of the WCD, also embedded in the mandate endowed to it by the Gland Reference Group, were independence, inclusiveness, openness and transparency. It was further agreed that the WCD would have a limited lifespan of two years at which time it would present its report to the global community at large and thereafter cease to exist. The WCD thus was not supposed to contribute to further long-term international bureaucratization.

It is from the process by which it emerged, its objectives, its guiding principles, and its time-bound lifespan that the WCD drew its legitimacy – and legitimacy is the primary challenge of any such endeavour. Emerging from a process that itself was quite participatory and inclusive, in which no major type of stakeholder was entirely absent, gave the idea of a commission a great deal of momentum early on.

But the way forward from Gland was hardly easy. The Gland Reference Group established a smaller Interim Working Group of selected representatives from across the spectrum of stakeholders to take the WCD from idea to reality. This negotiation process took nearly a year with virtually every decision being hotly contested, from the selection of a Chair to the number and composition of the Commission members to the appropriate role of the World Bank, IUCN, and broader reference groups once the WCD was firmly established. The fact that these decisions were negotiated by relatively representative parties, again with no major interest completely absent, was critical to the ultimate establishment and success of the WCD.[13] Certainly, the institutional, financial, and political support provided by the World Bank and IUCN also contributed to the prospects for a commission.

The twin objectives as specified in the mandate provided further legitimacy to the WCD. By combining an evaluation of experiences of the past (a global review of dams and assessment of alternatives), which was the main focus of critics with the formulation of recommendations for the future (standards, criteria, and guidelines for decision-making around big dams) which was the main concern of proponents, all stakeholders had something to gain and lose from the WCD's activities – strong incentives to stay involved. And stipulating that both the evaluation and recommendations would be completed within a specified and imminent period of two years meant that the results would be important and useful to various stakeholders because of their timeliness.

The guiding principles of independence, transparency, openness, and inclusiveness were perhaps the most important legitimating mechanisms for the WCD. Because all existing groups and organizations (including international bodies) were seen as being vested or biased in one way or another, establishing an independent body was certainly necessary. Moreover any organization, after it is established, can be co-opted or even hijacked. To minimize the likelihood of these possibilities required the WCD to be transparent. A commitment to being open to and inclusive of all, moreover, ensured that the WCD would not become an unaccountable body – a criticism levelled against many more established international institutions. One could have imagined an independent commission of eminent individuals who did not have any specific stake in the actual outcome of the process. However, this alternative model would not have satisfied the concomitant focus on inclusiveness, the acknowledgement that the WCD was as much a negotiation process as a policy formulating body, and the belief that the results of a commission which was composed of active stakeholders would be more likely to command acceptance from the broader range of interested groups.

Of course, the principles of independence, transparency, openness, and inclusiveness also had a deep ethical basis besides their functional importance, and this moral foundation further increased the legitimacy that the WCD invoked when reflecting and upholding these principles in all of its structures and activities. What was attempted through the structures and activities of the WCD was to provide independent, transparent, and inclusive arenas and processes in and through which the multiple groups and organizations that have stakes in big dams could negotiate through their differences, find areas of common ground, identify areas of continuing divergences, and formulate global public policy where possible and feasible.

The constituent structures of the WCD

The key structural elements of the World Commission on Dams were the Commissioners, the Secretariat, the WCD Forum, and the broader stakeholder constituencies (including funders). Each of these structural elements will be discussed in greater detail but it should be noted that each level was a reflection of the diversity of the broader set of stakeholders active in decision-making around big dams. Moreover, one might argue that the degree of influence over the final output of the Commission decreased as one moved away from the core, which consisted of the Commission members themselves, but that longer-term outcomes were most dependent on the leading stakeholder groups and not the Commission itself.

Undoubtedly, the set of Commission members were the most important structural element of the WCD. The twelve Commissioners were selected to represent the range of stakeholders involved in conflicts and decision-making around big dams. The Commissioners as a group represented a diversity of institutional, disciplinary, geographic, and political backgrounds. They were selected on the basis of their recognized leadership in government, the private sector, civil society, academia, professional association, etc., as well as for their significant experience and expertise with big dam projects. Roughly one-third of the members were considered historically to have been proponents of dam building, one-third were considered to be opponents of dam building, and one-third to be moderate reformers or supporters. The backgrounds of Commission members ranged from Goran Lindahl, CEO and President of the multinational company ABB, to the Chair Kader Asmal, the former Minister of Water Affairs, and now the Minister of Education of South Africa, to Medha Patkar, the transnationally acclaimed activist leader of the Save the Narmada Movement and National Association of People's Movements in India. The Commission members were also relatively evenly divided in their origins, from countries such as China, India, Brazil, South Africa, the United States, Switzerland, the Philippines, and Australia, with approximately one-half of the members coming from developing countries.[14] Importantly, five of the twelve Commissioners were women.

Debate over the balance amongst the Commission members bedevilled the WCD from its inaugural meeting held in Washington, DC in May of 1998. In particular, to convince domestically based stakeholders that the Commissioners did not represent the views of any particular country was difficult. This created problems from all sides of the dams debate. In the case of India, dam proponents (including many government officials) saw the two Commissioners from India as being anti-dam and thus questioned the overall independence of the WCD process. On the other hand, dam opponents and affected peoples from Brazil found the presence of a generally pro-dam Commissioner from that country as preempting a fair hearing for their views. The message that the Commission continually communicated was that the Commissioners were reflective of the diversity of stakeholders by sectors and issue areas *globally*, and not nationally. But this was not always sufficient nor could it ever allay fully critics of the WCD process.

The other challenge was to accommodate the full range of stakeholders given the relatively small number of Commission members that were selected. Previous World Commissions had often been too unwieldy because far too many members were selected to serve. On the other hand, the smaller number of members selected to the WCD meant that not all groups would be represented. Of course, any set of Commissioners chosen would not be beyond controversy, no matter what ultimate number was decided upon.

However, a better mapping of the political environment would have revealed early on that, partly because of the composition of the stakeholder representation in the Interim Working Group, potential commissioners with more expertise and experience with dams and alternatives for irrigation and agricultural production were ultimately left out of the set chosen. On the other hand, the WCD Forum and WCD Work Programme were safety valves for those key interests who did not find explicit and direct representation in the form of a Commission member, including such groups as those promoting irrigation dams and others promoting agricultural strategies where irrigation was less of a priority.

Moving outwards from the set of twelve Commissioners was the secretariat of the WCD, members of which were selected primarily on their experience and expertise. However, as a group they were also selected to complement one another in terms of their disciplinary, institutional, and geographical backgrounds. The Secretary-General, also an ex-officio (non-voting) member of the Commission, who was selected by the Chair but approved of by the Interim Working Group, held the pivotal function at the nexus of the Commission members, the Secretariat and broader set of stakeholders and funders of the WCD. The one concern for any Secretary-General appointee is that the person will be a dynamic leader without directly or indirectly usurping the authority of the commission members, individually or as a set.

The other, approximately ten members of the WCD Secretariat, brought disciplinary expertise as engineers, environmental specialists, social scientists, policy analysts, and communications specialists. They also ranged in their institutional backgrounds, working previously in organizations as diverse as private sector consulting firms to international development agencies to universities to nongovernmental organizations. This combination of expertise and diversity increased the comprehensiveness of the activities undertaken, contributed to the outreach capabilities of the WCD, and raised confidence in the capacity of the Commission to fulfil its mandate.

Again, creating and maintaining the balance within the secretariat was a difficult challenge for the WCD. It was quite a task to find and attract the best experts with cross-regional work experience on dams, water, and energy resources to move to another country (the Secretariat was based in Cape Town, South Africa, which gave it further legitimacy as not a Northern-driven initiative)[15] to be part of a process that was only two years long with a fate that was extremely uncertain. It was particularly difficult to find and attract such experts from developing countries as there was an extremely short supply of such qualified individuals. As a result, although there were members from developing countries, the composition of the Secretariat was still slightly weighted towards those from the first world.

In addition, some important gaps existed in the backgrounds and professional expertise of the Secretariat. For example, no member came from East or Southeast Asia, and no member could have been considered an expert on legal issues. Moreover, the gender balance within the Secretariat was far from equal, partly because of the fewer number of women working on issues of dams, water, and energy. Those women that do work on these issues were in extremely high demand. Also, women tend to have more difficulty moving their families than men do due to well-known and entrenched patriarchal norms.

These challenges of a small, time-bound, and highly specialized Secretariat were partly overcome by the WCD Work Programme through which hundreds of consultants and reviewers from around the world contributed to generating the knowledge base of the Commission. One difficulty with the appointment of consultants was the lack of individuals from developing countries with cross-regional and global expertise. This certainly led to once again a somewhat imbalanced representation of Northern consultants, but to a much less degree than in other commissions. In addition, the regional backgrounds and disciplinary expertise of both the set of Commissioners and the WCD Forum also compensated for those gaps and weaknesses within the Secretariat and consultants.

The WCD Forum was a critical structural component that also assisted in operationalizing the guiding principles of transparency, participation, openness, and inclusiveness. The Forum was an expanded version of the Gland Reference Group that initially proposed the establishment of the Commission. Approximately 60 representatives from the most important types of stakeholder groups and organizations involved in conflicts and decision-making around dam building around the world were members of the WCD Forum. Again these groups and organizations were selected from across the spectrum of civil society, private sector, academic, professional association, governmental, and intergovernmental organizations. There was also a relatively equal balance of Forum members coming from the North and South, although the gender balance was quite unequal.

The Forum acted as a sounding board and networking mechanism in the WCD process. Forum members were specifically invited to participate and comment in the various activities of the Commission. They were also a critical vehicle in the Commission's outreach to the various regional, sectoral, and issue-area networks involved in the dams debate. The Forum, furthermore, was an important mechanism for the implementation of the WCD's recommendations and other follow-up activities after the Commission ceased to exist in 2000.

While the Forum was a key structural innovation of the WCD process, as noted earlier, it was not used as effectively as it might ideally have been during the early part of the Commission's life. Part of the reason was the difficulty of coordinating a group of approximately 60 extremely busy individuals working in organizations spanning the entire globe. For example, given the resource and time constraints of the WCD, to convene a meeting of all the Forum members, required extraordinary skill and tremendous amounts of logistical planning. Just to keep Forum members informed about the ongoing work and status of the Commission was a challenge in itself. Certainly, the wide-spread availability of information technology have been indispensable in this regard. But to reach those Forum members who were from or work at the grassroots level, especially those from developing countries, e-mail and web-sites did not suffice. Indeed, an adequate mechanism for overcoming this constraint was not fully developed.

Another critical structural component of the WCD was, of course, the donors. Funding for the Commission was also sought out and received from the widest possible range of groups and organizations from the private sector (approximately one-quarter of the total budget), from governmental and intergovernmental agencies (approximately one-half of the total budget), and from non-governmental organizations and foundations (approximately one-quarter of the total budget). Moreover, to ensure that the guiding principles of the Commission were not contradicted, funders had to provide untied financial support such that the WCD's independence and thus legitimacy was not questioned. An informal rule was established that no single donor should contribute more than 10 per cent of the total budget, and donors were not automatically given membership in the WCD Forum.

Funding the WCD was perhaps the greatest challenge of all, especially given the range of funding sources and untied nature of the funding that was sought out. It would likely have been much easier if the World Bank or some small set of large organizations had donated the entire US$10 million budget of the Commission from the outset. But, as discussed earlier, the independence and legitimacy of the WCD would have been weakened if such a strategy had been pursued.

On the other hand, to convince donors to give money to an endeavour without a track record, with an uncertain future, and which might possibly generate findings and conclusions against the interests of those very donors was truly difficult. This difficulty was gradually overcome by the legitimacy created in the WCD by the various factors noted previously and by critical infusions of support and funding from key organizations at key moments. Certainly the World Bank's donation of US$1 million early on was crucial to getting the Commission underway. But the donation of an even larger amount by the UN Foundation midway through the Commission's life was just as crucial in strengthening the WCD's financial base. In addition, the WCD could not have been financially sustained without the support of a few bilateral donors (in particular from Norway, Germany, and Sweden).

The fact that fundraising continued to be a priority of the Commissioners and Secretariat throughout the life of the WCD did, however, detract from time and focus on other activities (the Work Programme, Commissioner deliberations and negotiations, and communications/outreach). The effect on the WCD fulfilling its potential by the challenges of funding cannot be underestimated. The uncertainty of an insecure financial base clearly weakened the quality of work that the WCD was able to do, especially early in its lifespan. For example, given the instability of funding, it was unclear whether several parts of the WCD Work Programme could even be undertaken let alone completed at a high level of quality for many months. Commissioner meetings spent more time on issues of fundraising than on deliberations and negotiations around key substantive issues. And the full complement of Secretariat members was not brought on board as early as needed. If all the funding had been secured prior to the establishment of the Commission, many of the other difficulties mentioned above could have been handled more easily.

In summary, the four critical structural components of the WCD were the set of twelve Commissioners, the Secretariat, the WCD Forum, and the donors. The composition of each was reflective of the broader set of active stakeholders in the dams debate and each was structured to give life to the Commission's guiding principles of independence, transparency, openness, and inclusiveness. Each component contributed to the broader WCD process, and each was critical in shaping, activating, and legitimating the outcomes of the WCD process. The intensity and importance of the functions served by each of these constitutive components of the WCD, however, varied over time in relation to the various activities that were being conducted during the WCD process.

The activities of the WCD

The activities of the Commission could be divided into three general types that were strongly interconnected: 1) the formal Work Programme, 2) Commissioner deliberations and negotiations, and 3) broader stakeholder engagement efforts. The Work Programme was the bridge between these three. Its basic objective was to develop the most comprehensive knowledge base possible to assist the Commission in achieving its objectives while fulfilling its guiding principle, thereby further increasing the legitimacy and thus potential effectiveness of the WCD. The Work Programme was composed of four components which include 10 in-depth basin and national case studies, a larger survey of 125+ dams around the world, 17+ thematic reviews of cross-cutting issues such as dams and social impacts or international trends in project financing, and the active solicitation of stakeholder views and perspectives through regional consultations, reviews, and submissions.

Each sub-component of the Work Programme contributed different types and levels of knowledge for the Commission.[16] While the survey of 125+ dams yielded information on the broader trends and patterns with respect to the performance and decision-making concerning dams on a relatively small number of issues, the case studies provided more holistic histories of the development effectiveness of a smaller number of dam-building experiences within river basins or countries. The contribution of the thematic reviews was to deepen further the knowledge base by focusing on specific cross-cutting issues. Finally, acknowledging that a significant amount of the conflicts over big dams lies not just in controversies over specific pieces of information but on broader and deeper debates about values that constitute good governance and sustainable development, the Work Programme consciously included an open and active set of invitations to all stakeholders to offer their views and perspectives through written submissions, comments on case studies, the cross-check survey and thematic reviews, and through oral presentations at the various regional and other consultations of the WCD.

The sub-component of the stakeholder inputs overlapped a great deal with the WCD's broader communications activities which included the WCD Forum gatherings, regional consultations, a web site, a regular newsletter, as well as the active participation of Secretariat members and Commissioners in various meetings, conferences, and other events around the world. The primary purpose of the communications activities was to ensure that the all stakeholders who wanted to be informed about, participate in, and contribute to the WCD were able to do so. In addition, a comprehensive communications programme increased the likelihood that the WCD reached "beyond the usual suspects". But another, perhaps equally important, purpose of the communications activities was to generate greater awareness of the Commission's mandate, structure, and activities in order to increase the WCD's profile and legitimacy among various stakeholder groups and networks.

The third core, and perhaps the central activity of the WCD process, was the ongoing deliberations and negotiations of the Commissioners. While the Secretariat members worked full time at managing the Work Programme and implementing the broader stakeholder engagement activities, Commissioners met every three or four months to discuss the progress of the Commission, evaluate the emerging knowledge base, and negotiate through divergent views and perspectives. In between these meetings, individual or small sub-sets of Commissioners often attended meetings, reviewed specific areas of the Work Programme in which they had deep interest or expertise, and communicated through e-mail, regular mail, telephone, and fax. But the most important work of the Commissioners was their active and serious involvement in the discussions and negotiations at their regular meetings.

Given the diversity that existed among Commissioners and the extremely active professional lives all of them led, their continuing and active involvement in the Commission was a persistent challenge. And as the focus of their meetings moved from the stage of identifying priorities and formulating the WCD Work Programme and stakeholder engagement activities towards more substantive discussion and negotiation, the possibilities for greater levels of conflict increased significantly.

A tactic that was helpful early on was to have Commissioners focus on process issues rather than substantive debate, especially on formulating a common set of strategies to raise the profile and budget of the WCD. A second tactic was to have the Commissioners present themselves as a corporate unit through various joint activities (such as at Forum meetings, regional consultations or with selected field trips) rather than as individuals representing different constituencies. A third tactic was to have Commissioners focus on the findings and conclusions to be derived from the common knowledge base that was being assembled through the Work Programme, rather than negotiate on the basis of their own personal experience. A fourth tactic was to identify areas of convergence (of which several existed but which had been previously excluded from the public discourse because of the sub-optimal stalemate that had emerged) to build a basis from which the remaining divergences could be addressed. But as the Commissioners moved forward towards negotiating the more difficult and conflictual sets of substantive issues, the need for other tactics to be utilized increased. Clearly greater use could have been made of best practice negotiation and mediation techniques as the process unfolded.

In summary then, the WCD involved three core sets of activities that served different functions but were interlinked and often overlapped. The Work Programme was geared towards developing the formal knowledge base that would provide the raw materials for both the Commissioners' deliberations/negotiations as well as the final outputs of the WCD. The communications activities contributed to the implementation and enrichment of the Work Programme and Commissioners' deliberations/negotiations by encouraging submissions and participation, which raised the profile through disseminating information about the progress of the WCD. The Commissioners' deliberations/negotiations shaped the direction of the Work Programme and communications activities and ultimately determined the content of the WCD's recommendations, final products, and follow-up agenda.

WCD challenges and results

The range of challenges faced by the WCD was vast and many have already been highlighted. Additional challenges included: 1) the need to acquire at least the cooperation if not the broader engagement of governments; 2) the difficulty of getting the private sector to take a more proactive role; 3) the constraints on outreach to affected people at the grassroots in the developing world; 4) the potential inability to capture best knowledge and best practice globally; and 5) the question of how the WCD's recommendations could be activated and implemented after the Commission ceased to exist.

As an independent global commission with an advisory and not adjudicatory role, the WCD was often rebuffed by governments as being "self-appointed" or as being without "locus standi". Moreover, the WCD was on occasion just ignored by governments who did not see why they should be interested in this "maverick" international experiment. Because implementation of the WCD Work Programme required at least the approval if not the cooperation of governments, cold shoulders from governments slowed down the assembly of the knowledge base a great deal. Moreover, implementation of the WCD recommendations ultimately involved governments to a certain degree and thus the long-term prospects of WCD impact could have been curtailed significantly by the early stages of insufficient or antagonistic government involvement with the Commission.

Several tactics were utilized to engage governments. Commission members, and in particular the Chair, as well as Secretariat members communicated directly and in a sustained way with various government officials to persuade them of the WCD's importance. Various Forum members, such as the World Bank, urged governments to allow the Commission entry into their countries to implement Work Programme activities. And certainly, the strength of the Commission as evidenced by its survival, its increasing success with fund raising, and its progressively wider coverage in the media convinced more governments of its importance.

Other tactics to engage governments were also critical during the implementation phase after the final report of the Commission was completed. For example, perhaps the most successful Commission – the World Commission on Environment and Development, or Bruntland Commission – conducted meetings with more than 100 governments (heads of states and relevant ministries) to promote its recommendations. The WCD had to do the same. However, the challenge of getting key governments to "buy in" to the WCD process and results remains a continuing challenge for post-WCD advocacy and implementation efforts.

The private sector was also a difficult nut to crack for the Commission. Despite their "formal" participation throughout the WCD process (from the Gland meeting onwards) and in all of the WCD structures (Commission, Secretariat, Forum, and Donors), their involvement in the ongoing Work Programme was patchy. For example, submissions from non-governmental organizations poured into the WCD, while those from the private sector were few and far between. Representatives from the private sector were also the least forthcoming and most reluctant to present their views and perspectives at the WCD's regional consultations and case study stakeholder meetings. Several more examples such as these can be offered.

The WCD utilized similar tactics with the private sector as it had with governments and other stakeholders. These included, for example, direct, face-to-face Commissioner, Secretariat and Forum member meetings with private sector firms although not to the extent that they were perhaps necessary. The private sector was sent specific outreach materials (at considerable cost in terms of money and time) encouraging greater involvement. A significant percentage of the consultants commissioned to conduct Work Programme activities were selected from the private sector. And, as with governments, the WCD conducted a massive outreach to the private sector with is final report and recommendations.

But much of the problem lay within the private sector itself. Most firms have not yet caught up with the new ways of doing business with the rise and growth of civil society organizations domestically, internationally, and transnationally. Ironically, they just do not have the capacity. Moreover, because of the market environments that many private sector firms are in, many refuse to coordinate their activities with their competitors. Finally, while companies in the North are far from perfect and generally have very little capacity, businesses in most developing countries in general have grasped the changes that have occurred in their external environment even less.

A major problem of all ostensibly global organizations and processes is the general inability to fully integrate developing countries at an equal level, especially those living and working at the grassroots. The WCD, while being considerably more effective, was no exception in this regard. The significant numbers of individuals who were selected as Commissioners (as well as the Chair), Secretariat staff, and Forum members was one indicator of success. On the other hand, the search for individuals from the South to conduct various Work Programme activities (research, writing and review) was somewhat less effective.

A second piece of evidence indicating relative success in geographical balance was the numbers of stakeholders who participated in the WCD's regional public consultations. Four multi-stakeholder consultations, at which broad representation from different sectoral groups was achieved, were held as part of the WCD Work Programme (in South Asia, Latin America, Africa/Middle East, and East/Southeast Asia). In addition, the several WCD case studies located in developing countries encouraged further participation from developing country stakeholders.

But the involvement of stakeholders at the grassroots in the developing world was relatively low. The case studies involved, by far, the most interaction with these individuals, groups, and organizations, primarily because of the conscious solicitation of their participation. Even in the case studies, however, the speed with which the Commission had to complete its work (one of the costs of the stipulated two-year time limit), and the limited resources available for such critical activities as translation into local languages, meant that few people at the grass roots were active and equal participants in the WCD process. Part of the responsibility for increasing the involvement of grass-roots people and groups, however, lay with the national and international civil society organizations that often claimed to represent these stakeholders. If the internal mechanisms of participation and accountability within these non-governmental organizations were weak, and they were working with grass-roots people for a much longer time period than a new and time-bound international arrangement like the WCD, then the WCD cannot be faulted completely for a gap it did not have the resources or mandate to fill. On the other hand, the WCD certainly did have the moral obligation, and the self-interest, to marshal a larger amount of resources than it had to improve the chances for those at the grass roots in the developing world to participate effectively in a process that would undoubtedly affect them.

The short time period and limited resources of the WCD also lessened the likelihood that the Commission would be able to conduct as high a quality and as comprehensive a knowledge-gathering process as was hoped for. Although the Commission implemented its Work Programme with vigour, and actively sought out the best research and expertise worldwide, there was only so much that could be done in a two-year time period. More importantly, the difficulty with acquiring the full budget of the WCD not only reduced the resources available for implementing the Work Programme and facilitating outreach worldwide, it also reduced the effective time of the Commission to complete its activities perhaps by at least one-third. In other words, resource constraints reduced the originally estimated 18-month time period for conducting knowledge-gathering work to less than one year.

The actual time available to conduct investigations and outreach was further curtailed by the highly charged political environment in which the WCD was located. Virtually any decision to focus on a particular topic, or select a particular consultant, or invite a particular individual or group to present their views was seen by one side or another in the dams debate as potentially detrimental to their extant interests. Thus, decision-making and implementation of knowledge-gathering activities proceeded haltingly at times. The ultimate effect of these various constraints to the quality and depth of the knowledge base that was eventually assembled, and to the legitimacy and, thus, impact of the WCD's final report and recommendations is, predictably, hard to determine.

The final uncertainty that became a primary question for the WCD was what should be done and what will happen after the WCD completed its work? Besides mandating that the Commission presents its report to the international community at large and thereafter cease to exist, neither the Gland Reference group nor the Interim Working group predetermined the answer to this query. The record of previous global commissions in directly motivating broader changes as a result of their work, final report, and recommendations has not been extremely strong. And while the indirect effects of these previous Commissions should not be underestimated – in contributing to the development of global norms, in supporting the growth of domestic, international and transnational civil society, in assembling knowledge from around the world – most stakeholders agreed that much more was expected from the WCD.

To the WCD's credit, the topic of post-Commission follow-up was focused on seriously and intensively from its formal establishment in February 1998 and the first meeting of Commissioners three months later in May. The final report of the WCD was completed in September 2000 and, issued in November – three months behind schedule, was presented to the WCD Forum and the broader "international community" as required by its mandate. It was signed by 11 Commissioners and the Secretary-General (the Commissioner from China resigned without replacement). One of the remaining 11 Commissioners – the leading Indian social activist – signed, but only with the inclusion of a note of dissent that the WCD report did not go far enough or deep enough in its analysis and recommendations. The WCD implemented relatively extensive, immediate follow-up activities to promote the final report's findings and recommendations, including a third meeting of the WCD Forum; a Dams and Development Unit was established within the United Nations Environment Programme to push the agenda forward for an additional two years.

The report met the first part of the WCD mandate with an extensive review of the effectiveness of large dams, of their financial, economic, environmental and social impacts, an assessment of water and energy options, and an analysis of the state of governance arrangements in this area. It claimed neutrality on the subject of whether or not large dams should be built in the future, but strongly urged that these projects be considered as only one of many options for water and energy development – including the option of improving the utility of already built large dams. The final report very consciously embedded its review of large dams in a wider discussion about options for water and energy development.

The WCD process achieved enough legitimacy that all relevant groups have reacted to its report and recommendations.[17] Judging by the responses to date, the report seems to have been welcomed by many large dam critics from civil society, who are concerned about democratizing governance and having a voice in decision-making processes for sustainable development. A letter from a transnational coalition of 109 nongovernmental organizations, community-based groups, and social movements from 39 countries notes that the report vindicates many of the concerns they have previously raised and calls upon decision-makers to incorporate all the recommendations of the report before funding more large dams. Many aid agencies such as bilateral funders as well as regional development banks have generally been publicly supportive, and the World Bank has accepted the WCD normative framework but not formally adopted its recommended guidelines. Numerous private sector multinational companies now formally, or at least informally, link their practices to the WCD's recommendations.

Criticism of the final report, of its accuracy, and the recommendations' emphasis focusing on decision-making process have been levelled by some of the most powerful proponents of large dams, primarily from particular associations of industry professionals and private sector firms as well as some developing country governments. The International Hydropower Association objected that the overall tone of the report cast a negative light on large dams and claims that its conclusions were based on inadequately researched data in that only a fraction of the world's 45,000 dams were studied. But a newer association of other hydropower companies was formed to support the activation of the report's recommendations.

For some actors from a range of perspectives on large dams, the report skirted the second part of the WCD mandate by developing guidelines for decision-making processes in which large dams may be involved, rather than providing clear economic, social, environmental, and technical criteria for their sanctioning. A posting from the International Commission on Large Dams (ICOLD) protested that, in only offering guidelines for "consultations" with stakeholders, the report failed in its mandate to offer technical criteria and standards for the planning, construction, and operation of dams. Moreover, it argues the kind of negotiation and decision-making process suggested would be so cumbersome that it would stall any new large dams.

But the WCD process and final report are certainly now a central focal point in the dynamics around big dams and sustainable water resources development. The actual role the Commission will have played with respect to broader, underlying dynamics in this issue area remains to be seen. Moreover, the WCD is clearly looked upon as offering a model and set of lessons for current and future global governance processes and institutional arrangements.

Conclusion: WCD lessons for making global commissions successful

Based on this review of the WCD, it is clear that several strategic issues must be effectively addressed for global commissions to be successful, including: 1) legitimacy; 2) external stakeholder engagement and knowledge generation; 3) internal structures and processes; and 4) final report/recommendations formulation and advocacy. Critical is that these challenges be discussed and strategies agreed upon at the commissioners' first meeting for early resolution, both to guide commission priorities as well as to generate widespread internal and external support for the commission's work. It is critical for early resolution that these challenges are discussed and strategies agreed upon at the commissioners' first meeting in order both to guide the commission's priorities as well as to generate widespread internal and external support for its work.

Legitimacy is the primary challenge of any global commission. This involves effectively and consistently answering the following questions:

1. *Where did this commission come from?* Some are born out of requests by the heads of international agencies, particularly the UN Secretary-General, others from pressure by and/or negotiation with civil society organizations like the WCD, and still others from the actions of visionary leaders. Whatever the genesis, a common and compelling narrative requires formulation.
2. *Why is this commission needed at this time?* Perhaps more important than the genesis of the commission is the rationale and justification for its need at this particular time? It may be needed to find innovative solutions to a seemingly intractable policy problem, or to solve a conflict that has become deadlocked, or to provide a broad new moral and philosophical vision. In some sense the WCD was needed for all these reasons. Whatever the needs, they must capture the public imagination.
3. *Why a commission and why these commissioners?* To put the first of these two queries another way: why not just use an existing institutional arrangement? And once a case for the global commission

"form" is made: why and through what process were specific commissioners selected? It could be because of their eminence, because of their prior engagement with an issue, because they have deeply relevant knowledge, because they represent specific constituencies. The WCD commissioners were selected for a combination of all of these criteria and through a stakeholder consultation process. Whatever the selection criteria and the process, the world wants to know.

4. *What are the commission's goals?* Some global commissions have mandates given to them by "authorizing" constituencies, others receive them from their chairpersons, and still others formulate them through commissioner deliberation. The way in which the goals and objectives are determined, and ensuring that they are sufficiently clear and agreed upon by commissioners early on and repeatedly, are critical factors to success. The WCD's mandate was given to it by the Gland meeting participants, but certainly was modified and adapted by the Chair, Commissioners, and Secretariat.
5. *What will be the commissions guiding principles?* Most recent global commissions state that their work will be based on the principles of independence, openness, inclusiveness, and transparency. From the WCD case, being independent suggests not being captured by vested interests, including funding agencies; being open implies that all ideas and information will be seriously considered; being inclusive entails the participation of all stakeholders; and being transparent requires constant communication through a variety of mechanisms and media.

The importance of external stakeholder engagement and knowledge generation/synthesis overlap with the challenge of legitimacy, as both widespread stakeholder engagement and a sound knowledge-base contribute to legitimacy. Those commissions that have relied upon only one or the other have been less successful than those commissions that have included both – which the WCD attempted to do. However, balancing both is difficult in terms of organizational capacity and financial resources, as well as the formulation and advocacy of the final report and recommendations (discussed further below).

- To the extent that inclusiveness, transparency, and openness become guiding values of a global commission, widespread and sustained stakeholder engagement becomes a fundamental task it must fulfil. This can take different forms such as regional hearings/consultations (usually involving some if not all commissioners), open submissions, the commissioning of position papers, mandatory web-site communication but also lower-tech forms of engagement (newsletters), etc.

A combination of mechanisms for stakeholder engagement must be established that makes the commission publicly visible by reaching out broadly (not just the usual suspects) but also strategically to those individuals and organizations the commission is directly trying to influence. In other words, the advocacy strategy of the commission must be embedded within its broader stakeholder engagement strategy. This requires a careful political mapping of stakeholders to determine who might be supportive and who might be against the commission's work, as well as who might be easier to engage and who more difficult (for example, engaging those at the grass roots in developing countries as well as private sector companies requires much creative thought).

- Linked to stakeholder engagement is the strategic issue of knowledge generation and synthesis. Will the commission rely solely on existing materials and try to synthesize these in a new way, or will it solicit new research and analysis? One can certainly think of these as sequential activities: an overview and synthesis of existing stock of knowledge, followed by a gap analysis linked with commission priorities will provide key areas for specifically commissioned research and analysis.

  But three key questions in terms of knowledge generation remain regardless of how the commission answers this broader issue of stocktaking versus new research. The first is how will the knowledge generation process be connected to the stakeholder engagement process? Correspondingly, who will manage these linked processes? And finally, how will the results of these two processes feed into the deliberations of the commissioners leading to the final report and recommendations?

Internal commission structures and processes are a large subset of the broader strategic challenge of organizational capacity. The other major aspect of organizational capacity is of course funding for the commission's work, an issue that is always challenging. The one lesson from the WCD experience that should be noted, however, is that not having the full or majority of the funding in hand at the outset severely hinders success. But returning to the topic of commission structures and processes, there are several issues that should be addressed:

1. The first is to what extent there will be a permanent research/administrative secretariat and secretary general that manages a commission's "work programme". The experience of the WCD in light of other global commissions suggests that those that rely almost exclusively on the commissioners to manage the process are less robust than those that have a high-level but lean secretariat staff. The more a commission wants to engage stakeholders in conducting a comprehensive knowledge base, the more a solid secretariat is needed – especially communications professionals. Commissioners do not have the time to do this work, although they must advise/oversee the formulation of the work programme and monitor it regularly (through meetings and regular contact with the secretariat, for example).

   Moreover, to the extent that the commissioners are not directly involved in implementing the work programme on a daily basis, it shields them from any criticism that the commission's final recommendations have been formulated *ex ante* – in essence, that the "books have been cooked". With the secretariat administering the work programme, the main responsibilities of commissioners are to oversee the secretariat, to represent the commission to the world, and to review and deliberate upon the knowledge base – a good division of labour in the case of the WCD. But this also requires active and committed communication between the secretariat and commission members – a major leadership task for an effective Secretary-General.

2. The second issue involves how the commissioners will arrange their interactions and deliberations. How actively engaged will commissioners be? How many meetings will there be? Will there be virtual interactions between meetings via electronic means? Will there be subcommittees of commissioners who oversee parts of the work programme? How will decisions be taken and recommendations formulated? In the case of the WCD, there was a high level of opportunity of interaction among commissioners as a set and as sub-sets but the degree of involvement of individual commissioners varied. Virtually all attended most if not all of the quarterly general meetings, and decisions were usually taken on the basis of consensus.

   The most successful global commissions have been those where commissioners were actively engaged from beginning to end. Those commissions that were dominated by a few individuals, often the chairperson, were rarely successful. Active engagement results in commissioners offering more of their time to advocating for the commission as well as to thinking creatively about the commission's work. This suggests that decision-making through full consensus or sufficient consensus might be an entry point for commissioner deliberations, perhaps followed by voting procedures and majority/minority opinions. Differences and conflicts should be seen as opportunities for creativity rather than as constraints on effectiveness.

It may seem early to raise the issue of final report/recommendations formulation and advocacy at the commission's first meeting, but experience shows that it is not. Commissioners lead incredibly busy lives, so that early discussion of the type of report and other final products needed is essential. This discussion is tightly coupled with consideration of the goals and objectives as well as the decision-making procedures of the commission.

Indeed, in a world of information overload, the need to strategize the advocacy and follow-up phase for whatever outputs and outcomes the commission decides to work towards from the beginning cannot be overemphasized. The number of good reports and recommendations that lie in the dustbins of history are far too many to count. If substantial resources, including commissioner time, as well as funds are utilized for the commission's work, no one wants the processes and products to be lost in the noise of our cluttered policy world. There are issues of human capacity (who will plan and implement the advocacy and follow-up), funding, time horizons (short- to longer-term tactics), targets and arenas, and so on, that must all be worked through long before the final report and products/recommendations are formulated. The principle in this area is certainly one of "don't delay or it will be too late"! The WCD did address these issues early on, and the UNEP post-report process has accomplished many of its dissemination and advocacy goals, but the jury is still out.

Notes

1. This section is derived from Sanjeev Khagram (2004) *Dams and Development: Transnational Struggles for Water and Powers and Development: Transnational Struggles for Water and Power*, Ithaca: Cornell University Press.
2. The number of big dams being completed decreased partially as a result of the larger size of the projects that were initiated during this time. For example, 10 major dams were built before 1950, 35 during the 1950s, 64 during the 1960s, and 93 during the 1970s. Figures calculated from T.W. Mermel (1993–1996) "The Worlds Major Dams and Hydro Plants", *International Water Power and Dam Construction Handbook*.
3. ICOLD, *World Register of Dams*, Paris: ICOLD, p. 1. Only slightly more than 10 per cent of the world's technically available hydropower potential has been developed. See Jose Roberto Moreira and Alan Douglas Poole (1993) "Hydropower and Its Constraints", in Thomas B. Johansson, *et al.*, *Renewable Energy: Sources for Fuels and Electricity*, Washington, DC: Earth Island Press.
4. ICOLD, Circular Letter 1427, December 1995, Circular Letter Number 1388, 16 January 1995, and Circular Letter 1342, 4 October 1993, Paris: ICOLD. "Under construction" and "starts" can mean anything from receiving formal approval from authorities to actually being in the process of development with a reasonable certainty of completion.
5. This does not include non-conventional and renewable sources of energy production such as wind or solar power.
6. The World Bank estimates that a one-year delay in completion will reduce the benefit–cost ratio of projects by one-third and a two-year delay by over one-half, and that costs associated with resettlement can increase project costs by up to 30 per cent (World Bank, *The Bankwide Review of Projects Involving Involuntary Resettlement*, 8 April 1996).
7. For the United States, see Tim Palmer (1986) *Endangered Rivers and the Conservation Movement*, Berkeley: University of California Press; and R. Gottlieb (1993) *Forcing the Spring: The Transformation of the American Environmental Movement*, Washington, DC: Earth Island Press.
8. See, for example, the various policy reforms of the World Bank during the 1980s and 1990s.
9. See the various documents presented and generated at the conference, found in *Pro-*

ceedings: First International Meeting of People Affected by Dams (June 1997) Berkeley: International Rivers Network.

10. "With a multi-million dollar dam the costs of long political delays are enormous", said Mr. Jan Strombland of ABB, the dam-building multinational that had received a beating from pressure groups for its involvement in the Bakun Dam and other similar projects throughout the world. See Stephanie Flanders, "Truce called in battle of the dams", *Financial Times*, 14 April 1997.
11. Actually, the World Bank's Operational Evaluation Department approached IUCN to co-sponsor the workshop with the objective of reviewing its draft review of the development effectiveness of World Bank-funded dams. IUCN representative agreed to co-sponsor on the condition that the full range of stakeholders be invited and that the agenda be broadened beyond a focus solely on the review.
12. See IUCN (August 1997 and February 1998) "Large Dams: Learning From the Past, Looking at the Future", Workshop Proceedings, and "WCD Mandate", Cambridge: IUCN.
13. Perhaps the most important victory for the WCD process at this early stage was the invitation and acceptance by Professor Kader Asmal to be Chair of the WCD. Asmal had impeccable credentials as a Professor of International Law, leader in the international Anti-Apartheid movement, as the then Minister of Water Affairs and Forestry in South Africa, and as a member of the ongoing World Commission on Oceans. While he was not immune to criticisms from various stakeholders, his expertise, experience and stature not only prevented any side from blocking his selection but also greatly contributed to the respectability and legitimacy of the WCD.
14. For more information on Commission members see The World Commission on Dams (August 1999) "Interim Report", Cape Town: WCD.
15. The Secretariat was based in Cape Town, South Africa, for organizational and political reasons. Organizationally, it was seen to be much more efficient way for the Chair, Kader Asmal of South Africa, to oversee the work of the Secretariat. Politically, the choice of South Africa was important because most previous World Commissions have been located in the North, as are most international organizations; in addition, it was seen as another mechanism for welcoming the new South Africa back into the international community.
16. See World Commission on Dams (December 1999) "Work Programme", Cape Town: WCD.
17. See the website of the commission for an overview of ongoing reactions, endorsements, criticisms, etc., based on the commission's report and efforts of the UNEP Dams and Development follow-up initiative. See also Navroz K. Dubash, Mairi Gupar, Smitu Kothari, and Tundu Lissi (2001) *A Watershed in Global Governance? An Independent Assessment of the World Commission on Dams*, Washington DC: World Resources Institute; and Jeremy Bird (2000) "Nine Months after the Launch of the World Commission on Dams Report," *Water Resources Development* 18(1): 111–126.

8

Fair assessment: The Independent International Commission on Kosovo

Richard J. Goldstone and Nicole Fritz

The armed interventions that have occurred in Afghanistan and Iraq in the past years have been subject to heated public debate. For good or bad, they are said to be representative of a new type of international intervention. In light of these developments, the events in the Kosovo in 1999, specifically NATO's armed intervention, seem almost of a different age. Yet they too precipitated widespread public comment, were the subject of polarizing debate, were also said, for good or bad, to have ushered in a new type of international intervention.[1]

There is much that divides the intervention in Kosovo from those undertaken in respect of Afghanistan and Iraq – most obviously the specific circumstances surrounding these interventions, the actors involved, and the targets of the attack. However, even at an abstract level it seems easy to distinguish what happened in Kosovo from that which took place in Afghanistan and Iraq. Broadly speaking, the motivation prompting NATO's actions was altruistic or humanitarian, even if the means employed were not always consistent with that purpose.[2] Afghanistan and Iraq were much more self-interested endeavours on the part of the intervening powers, even if certain humanitarian objectives were invoked as justification. Nonetheless one can speak of commonality in the sense that each of these initiatives was styled as a watershed – they represented unusual international action on such a grand scale that they were said to frame new or emerging international norms, but without much consideration given for how these purported "norms" would fit within the accepted or orthodox template of international law.

In the immediate aftermath of contested actions of this sort, with opponents and supporters having so much at stake in the way in which these events are transmitted and received by the general public, it is particularly difficult to find clear-sighted, non-partisan and independent perspectives. The absence of non-partisan perspectives has the following repercussions: it not only negatively impacts any assessment of the needs of those inhabiting the intervened territory, but the lawfulness or legality of the intervention may come to be determined not so much by settled or evolving norms and principles in international law, but by those most powerfully positioned to influence public opinion. Without more, these impressions may settle into historical consensus.

This chapter looks at the establishment of the Kosovo Commission, which was an initiative designed in the context of the Kosovo intervention to offer independent, non-partisan analysis and appraisal not only of the needs of Kosovo itself, but of the way in which future, similar interventions should be addressed. It examines the principles and objectives prompting the establishment of the Commission and argues that it may be understood as a contribution to the increasingly prevalent discourse of fairness within international law.[3] The Commission's Report issued a number of recommendations: two among them – that the intervention was technically illegal, but nonetheless should be considered legitimate, and that Kosovo should be given the status of "conditional independence" – generated most comment and debate. This chapter examines whether initiatives such as the Kosovo Commission are appropriately positioned to make recommendations of this sort. The second of the Commission's primary conclusions was substantially readdressed in the Commission's "Follow-Up of the Kosovo Report"[4] – the Commission concluding that, despite changed circumstances, the recommendation of "conditional autonomy" for Kosovo remained the most compelling. The chapter also takes the opportunity to re-examine, in light of recent interventions in Afghanistan and Iraq, the Commission's other conclusion, that "humanitarian intervention", subject to certain strict qualification, should be recognized as lawful.[5]

The establishment of the Commission

Swedish Prime Minister Goran Persson had, in the wake of the NATO's intervention in Kosovo, become increasingly alarmed at the intensity of the debate surrounding the intervention and at the absence of clear-sighted, non-partisan analysis or a forum in which such analysis might be formulated. He raised his concern with a number of heads of state and, with their encouragement and the support of his own government, he initiated the establishment of the Independent International Commission on Kosovo. However, in the interests of the Commission's independence, the Swedish government's direct involvement was minimal. It extended only to the appointment of the chairperson, Justice Richard Goldstone, and the co-chairperson, Mr. Carl Tham,[6] and to the provision of financial resources utilized by the Commission.[7]

It was the task of the co-chairmen to appoint the other members of the Commission. This selection was made with due regard for the sensitive nature of the inquiry – the diverse substantive and procedural issues involved and the great number of international actors who stood to be scrutinized by the Commission. In the end eleven individuals, all with expertise relevant to the Commission's work, were selected. They were: Dr. Hanan Ashwari from Palestine, Grace d'Almeida from Benin, Senator Akiko Domoto from Japan, Professor Richard Falk from the US, Ambassador Oleg Grinevsky from the Russian Federation, Professor Michael Ignatieff from Canada, Professor Mary Kaldor from the UK, Professor Martha Minow from the US, Professor Jacques Rupnik from France, Mr. Theo Sommer from Germany and Mr. Jan Urban from the Czech Republic.[8] It should be emphasized that none of these individuals were asked to serve on the Commission in their capacity as representatives of their respective nation-states; however, given the importance of securing globally representative viewpoints, geographic composition of the Commission did play a role in the selection of Commission members.

The Swedish government had approached the co-chairmen with a broadly phrased scope of inquiry, but it was left to the Commission, once constituted, to define its mandate and terms of reference.[9] In the year preceding publication of the Commission's Report, the Commission held five plenary meetings (although more informal meetings between Commission members took place more frequently) – in Stockholm, New York, Budapest, Florence and Johannesburg. In intervals between meetings, different Commission members took the lead in investigating and researching the various aspects of the Commission's mandate, but findings and results were always brought back for full plenary discussion. The chair and co-chair also travelled extensively throughout the year, meeting with key players in the conflict. The Commission was assisted in its deliberations by obtaining a large number of expert views. At three of its meetings – in New York, Budapest and Johannesburg[10] – the Commission invited a number of prominent experts to attend public seminars and deliver their own views on questions relevant to the work of the Commission. Subsequent to publication of the Report, a large number of meetings were also held to discuss the Commission's finding and recommendations.

Contributing to a discourse on fairness

The Commission's own report followed close on the heels of the publication of two groundbreaking reports commissioned by the United Nations. The first, *The Report of the Secretary-General Pursuant to General Assembly Resolution 53/35 (1998)*, subjected the UN's failure to deter the Bosnian-Serb attack on Srebrenica in July 1995 and the subsequent massacre of 8,000 Muslim men and boys to sustained scrutiny. The second, *The Report of the Independent Inquiry into the Actions of the United Nations during the 1994 Genocide in Rwanda*,[11] undertook a similar inquiry in regard to the genocide in Rwanda. Both of these reports focused on situations in which the UN was accused of doing less than it could have done to prevent those tragedies. Neither report, however, shied away from apportioning blame to the UN and demonstrated the UN Secretariat's commitment to take seriously its own shortcomings.

These reports also evidenced a new civic-mindedness within the international community – a sense that, even absent, definable legislative, executive and judicial powers within the international sphere, there was nonetheless a definable constituency to whom international institutions like the UN were accountable. In a sense, one could speak of a new international ethos of transparency, justification, and accountability. This new ethos becomes that much more important in the international context where prevailing rules and standards are rarely backed by force of a coercive authority, but must instead depend for their observance on the cogency of the reasoning underpinning these norms. Much of that cogency will depend on the perceived fairness of the reasoning.[12] Thomas Franck argues that this notion of fairness encompasses "two different and potentially adversary components: legitimacy and distributive justice. These components are indicators of law's, and especially fair law's, primary objective: to achieve a negotiated balance between the need for order and the need for change".[13] Fairness may be one of any number of responses to these two often conflicting demands: "what matters is how that tension is managed discursively through what Martti Koskenniemi calls 'the social conception' of the legal system".[14] This "social conception" – an understanding of the international realm as a community[15] to whom accountability is owed – manifests itself in the discursive pursuit of fairness: "an interlocutory process of exhortation, expiation, explanation and exposition".[16] Viewed in this light, the two UN reports, and the subsequent *Report of the Panel on United Nations Peace Operations*, can be seen as credible contributions to the international interlocutory enterprise.

It should, nonetheless, be recognized that these reports were authored sometime after the events had occurred, in large part prompted by growing criticisms of the UN's egregious omissions in both situations. Certainly, the UN's willingness to commission these reports and release them to public scrutiny is admirable, and neither report shrank from directing hard-hitting criticism at the respective, responsible UN authorities. Ideally, however, if impartiality is to be guaranteed, those charged with undertaking extensive review of an international institution's activities, should be independent of that same institution.

In Kosovo it was less a case of any single international player. NATO deployed its armed forces for the express purpose of implementing UN Security Council resolutions, but without Security Council authorization. It was an action that appropriately framed the decentred, multipolar nature of authority structures at the international level and which, in the subsequent analysis, required examination of several transnational actors. It would thus have seemed particularly insufficient had examination thereof been left to the initiation of and confined to only one of the actors involved. An independent Commission, composed of non-affiliated individuals was better placed to examine the situation and the interlinking actors holistically.

Also, given their independence from any institutional affiliation or association, the individual members of the Commission were more freely able to perceive and respond to the calls for change that became manifest in the treatment of the Kosovo conflict. Institutional affiliation may too often work to favour precedent and stability, at the expense of desperately needed reform.[17] Paradoxically, however, the Commission's position outside any established institution also made it particularly conscious of the desire for order, stability, and precedent. If its conclusions and recommendations were to be taken seriously by international organizations, if they were to stand a chance of being implemented and realized, it had to be sensitive to demands for consistency and clarity. The Commission therefore made every effort to ensure that its recommendations and conclusions found support in settled, observed norms and standards of international law. As a discursive enterprise, the Commission was suitably constituted to ensure that full consideration was given to both order and substantive justice (change) claims.

The nature of the Commission's establishment also protected it, in its investigations and subsequent publication of the Report, from accusations of bias, making it much less easy for those implicated by the Commission's recommendations and conclusions to attempt to discredit the Commission and so avoid the apportionment of responsibilities.[18] The nature and composition of the Commission was also particularly suited to the type of broad mandate with which the Commission was charged. It imposed a searching examination of the context in which the Kosovo conflict and intervention took place and the subsequent repercussions, so demanding multiple spheres of expertise. The ad hoc, independent nature of the Commission's establishment meant that the demand for diverse spheres of expertise could be fully accommodated.

Significantly, the Commission's own composition both reflected and reinforced the multilateral character that international initiatives must assume if a genuine international community is to be instantiated. Franck writes that "for rules to be subject to a meaningful scrutiny from the perspective of fairness, they must be seen to operate in the context of a community: a social system of continuing interaction and transaction. It is only in a community that the bedrock of shared values and developed principles necessary to any assessment of fairness is found".[19] The Commission was at once both evidence of this community and an attempt to elucidate the shared values and developed principles that constitute the belief system within which the community could develop.

The Commission's establishment, and that of other similar initiatives, nonetheless raises certain issues of concern. They ultimately depend for their establishment and existence on an initiating body, which will need to guarantee at least the initial organizational costs. In order to make this undertaking, the initiator will have to be prompted by political will or benevolent foresight, neither of which can be guaranteed in every instance; thus one faces the prospect (a general dilemma in international law) that these types of initiatives appear random and arbitrary. This new era of international community may come to be undermined by only selective establishment of fair assessment initiatives. In fact, the ad hoc, selective character of these types of assessment or review may push the international lawyer back to questions of whether international law is really law at all, and not, given that selectivity reveals it so clearly not to be the case, whether international law is fair.[20]

Additionally, while the absence of any institutional affiliation guaranteed the Kosovo Commission the independence it required, it came at the risk that the Commission's conclusions and recommendations would not be treated with the seriousness they would have been given had its report been commissioned by a single or a number of institutions. For instance, organizations like the UN and NATO – complex, cumbersome, with a host of competing priorities and demands that their own authorities have determined – may too readily assign low priority to reports of this kind.

The nature of the Commission's findings

The Commission's Report provided a comprehensive documentation of the origins of the crisis, efforts undertaken to resolve the crisis, the ultimate intervention of NATO and the role played by ancillary domestic and international actors. There can be little doubt that this itself was a valuable endeavour. All too often in conflicts of this nature, little effort is made to obtain nuanced, detailed understandings of specific local contexts. This failure bedevils subsequent humanitarian efforts within the afflicted area, not only hampering the delivery of effective provisions, but in some cases employed as justification for offering no protection at all.

The Commission's report, however, went further than documentation – it also issued a discrete set of far-reaching recommendations, including most notably the recommendation of "conditional autonomy" for Kosovo and advocating the lawfulness of humanitarian intervention in certain exceptional circumstances. As has already been noted, both these recommendations generated substantial public comment.

In light of this debate, it might be asked whether it is appropriate that ad hoc initiatives, like the Commission, issue recommendations of this type – recommendations that may alter the delicate stability achieved in Kosovo, for instance, or the accepted terms and conditions of attempts at negotiated settlement. We could go further and ask whether this high-profile endorsement of humanitarian intervention might not serve to make it more difficult to police an already substantially weakened international order? Might it not be better for actors with substantial investments in the international order, nation-states, and international or transnational institutions – that is, those that must address international crises – to issue recommendations that they will ultimately be required to meet? After all, the Commission is not expected to take responsibility for managing or addressing the altered dynamics.

We argue that notwithstanding these circumstances, forums like the Commission are exactly those most suited to the formulation of recommendations that privilege change over stability. The Commission's recommendations should be understood as part of a discursive enterprise, consisting "primarily of advancing claims and testing them against rival claims based on alternative values: national security, self-interest, economic efficiency, and others".[21] Once these recommendations are placed in the public domain, a global conversation can take place in which the suitability or, more accurately, the fairness of the particular recommendations is debated.

Admittedly, many claims can be advanced on behalf of fairness, but determination of the agreed formulation will depend on the types of claim that present themselves for selection. If claims are only to be advanced by institutions or nation-states, they will generally incline towards interests of stability and order. Few proposals that take account of the need for reform, for an enhanced conception of substantive justice, would be offered up for discussion in this global conversation. We would then be left only with proposals that privilege stability.

The lawfulness of humanitarian intervention

The final section of this chapter re-examines the Commission's advocacy of humanitarian intervention in light of recent developments, and addresses the question of whether in its formulation of this recommendation, the Commission embraced the call for change but paid insufficient heed to the demand for stability.

Speaking to the UN General Assembly in September 1999, Secretary-General Kofi Annan cautioned that the crisis in Kosovo "revealed the core challenge to the Security Council and to the United Nations as a whole in the next century: to forge unity behind the principle that massive and systematic violations of human rights – wherever they may take place – should not be allowed to stand".[22] The Commission shared the Secretary-General's conclusion, and having weighed the evidence in Kosovo, came to the conclusion that in certain circumstances vindication of human rights would require the use of force – that a "humanitarian intervention" should take place. The Commission conceded that "a 'right' of humanitarian intervention is not consistent with the UN Charter if conceived as a legal text",[23] but went on to argue that "it may, depending on the context, nevertheless, reflect the spirit of the Charter as it relates to the overall protection of people against gross abuse".[24] Its argument supported a conclusion that the NATO campaign was illegal but legitimate.

It reasoned further that if this gap between legality and legitimacy was to be closed, a first step would require the elaboration of a framework of principles that could then be used to assess whether proposed military action fell within the justifiable limits of humanitarian intervention. The Commission's suggested framework consisted of a set of threshold and contextual principles.

The first of the threshold principles posits two valid triggers for humanitarian intervention: the occurrence of severe violations of international human rights or humanitarian law on a sustained basis or substantial suffering on the part of a civilian society due to state "failure".[25] The second insists that the overriding objective of the intervention at all stages must be cessation of the human suffering,[26] and the third principle requires that the means employed be reasonably calculated to bring an end to the crisis as soon as possible, that the instigators be vigilant in their protection of civilians and abstain from collateral damage or any measures which might be characterized as punitive or retaliatory against the target government.[27]

These threshold principles are accompanied by eight contextual principles which further specify when intervention may justifiably be understood as humanitarian in character, and the Commission suggests revisions to the UN Charter which would bring the doctrine within the Charter's parameters but without making it appear as anything but an exceptional, final-resort occurrence.[28]

Yet despite the Commission's efforts to tailor the limits of humanitarian intervention very narrowly and carefully, this recommendation has met with a fair degree of criticism. Iris Marion Young, addressing specifically the Commission's conclusion, argues that war can never be legitimated, although it may perhaps be justified by appeal to consequences but not to any authorizing covenants or principles. She argues further that it is dangerous to assume that "stronger institutions of international law themselves can and should authorize the use of violence. Just as in the domestic case, violence must be justified by arguing that it is the only means available to do good, that it does more good than harm, and that it is effective without having undesirable long-term consequences. By such reasoning, I submit that the NATO war was not justified".[29] David Rieff, speaking at a Commission seminar after the publication of the Commission's report, characterized the recommendation as a "call to war", suggesting it would facilitate pretextual resort to hostilities.[30]

In light of the actions taken in Afghanistan and Iraq, these criticisms perhaps prompt more serious evaluation. Has the Commission's recommendation contributed to a more permissive global attitude towards armed interventions? Is the international community now more prepared to sanction assaults on states' sovereignty? Did the Commission accommodate the need for change and reform without paying sufficient heed to demands for consistency and clarity?

Our argument is that these charges are unsupported. Had there been no after-the-fact analysis by the Commission and others, had there been no attempt to limit this type of action within defined parameters – as the Commission did in formulating its principles – it would have been relatively easy to claim that the interventions in Afghanistan and Iraq represented but one logical step from the action in Kosovo. As it is, these later interventions might claim validity under the doctrine of self-defence, but they cannot do so under the rubric of "humanitarian intervention". The overriding aim of all phases of the intervention must be the direct protection of the victimized population. This cannot be claimed by the intervening forces in either Afghanistan or Iraq.

Obviously, this does not stop the intervening forces from claiming that aspects of the intervention were consistent with humanitarian objectives, even if the overriding objective was not humanitarian, but here too the Commission's formulation of principles serves to make the appeal more onerous for the intervening forces, rather than facilitating such appeal. These claims can now be tested against expressly articulated principles and the integrity of the claimants will be judged by the extent to which they keep faith with these principles – for instance, the extent to which the intervening powers commit sufficient resources, once the intervention is complete, to sustain the population in the target society and to ensure speedy and humane reconstruction of that society in order for the whole population to return to normality.[31] Consequently, the Commission's recommendation sufficiently caters to the demand for stability and order by framing its proposed reform within expressly defined and narrowly drawn parameters.

However, if the Commission's endorsement of humanitarian intervention does not run the risk of opening the door to and legitimating all manner of interventions, the viability of its endorsement might risk being undermined by the selectivity of the enforcement of this norm.[32] Political will on the part of national governments for enforcing humanitarian norms remains highly selective, and in most cases half-hearted. Thus, while much comment and outrage attended to the violence perpetrated against Kosovar Albanians, the arguably worse atrocities carried out during the same time-frame in Sierra Leone were receiving very little attention, and certainly not prompting international intervention of a nature seen in Kosovo. Edward Luck writes, in this context of humanitarian intervention, "Kosovo and East Timor may well prove to be the exception, with Rwanda and Sierra Leone closer to the rule".[33]

This disparity (and occasional duplicity) in the treatment of conflicts by the international community was a fact of which the Commission was particularly conscious, and was the incentive for its public seminar in Johannesburg in September 2000. Participants invited to address this conference were asked to examine possible lessons from Kosovo in treating conflicts in Africa. The seminar also led to the publication of the collected papers in a book: *A Continent Apart: Kosovo, Africa and Humanitarian Intervention*. It is hoped that the Commission, in framing the discrepancy in international response and urging more equal treatment of conflicts throughout the globe, will go some way to making Kosovo the norm and not merely the exception.

Conclusion

As international law increasingly shrugs off misguided claims that it is not, in fact, real law and as the international community becomes less a hortatory term than a real phenomenon, issues of fairness will come to dominate the global debate. But a "discourse solely and exclusively reflecting the views of those who govern nations cannot be expected to produce rules that are fair or can only be expected to do so haphazardly".[34] The Independent International Commission on Kosovo represents an attempt to ensure that the views of non-state actors are also taken into account in that global discourse – non-state actors, that is, of a kind different from those constrained by institutional affiliation and by limited and shrinking budgets, from those as likely to act in self-interest as nation-states.

Importantly, however, the Commission was not free to abandon the dictates of consistency and clarity in framing its recommendations. In fact, its inquiry went to the heart of fairness discourse – an attempt to negotiate a balance between the demands for change and those of stability within the specific context of Kosovo.

None of this means that the Commission's recommendations will necessarily settle into accepted and observed international rules – but it does mean that within the discursive enterprise that constitutes the international community, parties will have a much wider choice of their sanctioned rule/norm and that the chosen norm, even if not consistent with the Commission's proposals, is much more likely to reflect or be conditioned by its recommendations.

Notes

1. See Edward C. Luck (2001) "The Enforcement of Humanitarian Norms and the Politics of Ambivalence", in Simon Chesterman (ed.) *Civilians in War*, Boulder, Colo.: Lynne Reinner, p. 197: "The international military responses to repression in Kosovo and East Timor in 1999 encouraged some observers to announce the arrival not only of a new doctrine but also a new era of humanitarian intervention", and cited references.
2. See the Independent International Commission on Kosovo (2000) *Kosovo Report: Conflict, International Response, Lessons Learned*, Oxford: Oxford University Press, p. 94, citing the Human Rights Watch Report, *Civilian Deaths in the NATO Air Campaign*: "as few as 488 and as many as 527 Yugoslav civilians were killed as a result of NATO bombing".
3. See Thomas M. Franck (1995) *Fairness in International Law and Institutions*, New York: Oxford University Press, p. 6: "The questions to which the international lawyer must now be prepared to respond, in this post-ontological era, are different from the traditional inquiry: whether international law is law. Instead, we are now asked: is international law effective? Is it enforceable? Is it understood? And, the most important question: Is it fair?"
4. *The Follow-Up of the Kosovo Report: Why Conditional Independence?*, Oxford: Oxford University Press, 2001.
5. Obviously this reassessment is limited to only one member of the Commission writing in his personal capacity and is not necessarily reflective of the Commission's views.
6. Mr. Carl Tham is currently Sweden's ambassador to Germany. At the time of his appointment to the Kosovo Commission, he was Secretary-General of the Olof Palme International Center in Stockholm.
7. Other financial contributions were also made to the Commission by the Government of Canada, the Ford Foundation, the Carnegie Foundation and the Sasakawa Foundation. Contributions by way of hosting Commission meetings and holding seminars for

the Commission were made by the Swedish Cooperative Union, New York University School of Law, the Carnegie Endowment for Peace, the Soros Foundation, the Central European University, ABA/CEELI, the United States Institute for Peace, the University of the Witwatersrand, and the South African Institute for International Affairs.

8. Dr. Ashwari was ultimately prevented from participating in the work of the Commission due to her commitment to peace initiatives in the Middle East and ill health prevented Ambassador Grinevsky from participating in the deliberations of the Commission.
9. The Kosovo Commission's Mission Statement, formulated in September 1999, reads as follows:

   The Independent International Commission on Kosovo will examine key developments prior to, during and after the Kosovo war, including systematic violations of human rights in the region. The Commission will present a detailed, objective analysis of the options that were available to the international community to cope with the crisis. It will focus on the origins of the Kosovo crisis, the diplomatic efforts to end the conflict, the role of the United Nations and NATO's decision to intervene militarily. It will examine the resulting refugee crisis including the responses of the international community to resolve the crisis. The effect of the conflict on regional and other states will also be examined. Furthermore, the Commission will assess the role of humanitarian workers, NGOs and the media during the Kosovo war. Finally, the Commission will identify the norms of international law and diplomacy brought to the fore by the Kosovo war and the adequacy of present norms and institutions in preventing or responding to comparable crisis in the future. In addition the Commission will take up: The future status of Kosovo, lessons learned for Kosovo, and lessons learned for the future.

10. In Johannesburg, the seminar focused on lessons to be learnt from Kosovo for treating conflicts in Africa and papers presented at this seminar resulted in the publication of a separate book: Elizabeth Sidiropoulos (ed.) (2001) *A Continent Apart: Kosovo, Africa and Humanitarian Intervention*, Johannesburg, South Africa: South African Institute of International Affairs.
11. This report was commissioned by UN Secretary-General Kofi Annan under authority of a Security Council resolution.
12. See Thomas M. Franck (2002) *Recourse to Force: State Action Against Threats and Armed Attacks*, Cambridge: Cambridge University Press, p. 175: "The capacity of the law to pull towards compliance those to whom it is addressed depends first and foremost on the public perceptions of justice".
13. Franck, *supra* at n. 5 at p. 23.
14. *Ibid.*
15. *Ibid* at p. 478. Franck posits that "our world of states has consolidated to form a community with systemic, systematic interactions and utilitarian regimes. What was an anarchic rabble of states has transformed itself into a society in which a variety of participants – not merely states, but also individuals, corporations, churches, regional and global organizations, bureaucrats, and courts – now have a voice and are determined to interact".
16. *Ibid.*
17. Franck, *supra* at n. 5 at p. 24: "[F]airness discourse does not invariably favour stability".
18. However, accusations of bias are not entirely avoided by commissions of this nature. High-profile participants will often attract negative comment. The government of the Federal Republic of Yugoslavia, then led by Slobodan Milsoevic, refused to meet with the Kosovo Commission, in part because of Judge Goldstone's alleged anti-Serb bias, purportedly demonstrated during his tenure as Chief Prosecutor of the International Criminal Tribunal for the former Yugoslavia.

19. Franck, *supra* at n. 5 at p. 10.
20. *See* Luck, *supra* at n. 3 at p. 214, noting in a different context: "'Ad hockery' does little to reinforce, and may actually undermine the authority of international law and organization".
21. Franck, *supra* at n. 5 at p. 478.
22. Cited in Luck, *supra* at n. 3 at p. 197.
23. Kosovo Report, *supra* n. 4 at p. 186.
24. *Ibid.*
25. *Ibid* at p. 193.
26. *Ibid* at p. 194.
27. *Ibid.*
28. *Ibid*, elaborated on pages 194–198 of the Report.
29. "Despite its conclusion that the war was legitimate, the Independent Commission also offers much evidence that the war did not achieve its objectives of saving the lives and society of the Albanian Kosovars, and that, in general, it wreaked more destruction than it prevented": Iris Marion Young (2002) "Power, Violence, and Legitimacy", in Nancy L. Rosenblum (ed.) *Breaking the Cycles of Hatred: Memory, Law and Repair*, New Jersey: Princeton University Press.
30. Kosovo Commission Seminar at the State University of New York, New Paltz, 7–8 December 2000. See Franck, *supra* n. 14, in response to this type of argument, citing Judge Rosalyn Higgins: "there have been countless abusive claims of the right to self-defence. That does not lead us to say that there should be no right of self-defence today.... We delude ourselves if we think that the role of norms is to remove the possibility of abusive claims ever being made".
31. See principle 11 of the Contextual principles elaborated by the Commission, Kosovo Report, *supra* at p. 4, at p. 195.
32. Franck, *supra* n. 14, argues that the accusation of selectivity, even if valid, is irrelevant. However, selectivity raises the presumption that states undertaking "humanitarian" interventions are prompted by self-interest. Although a certain amount of self-interest – i.e. the desire to stop refugees from flooding neighbouring states – will not render the humanitarian motivation void, the more stark and repeated the pattern – intervention in Kosovo, not Sierra Leone; in East Timor, not Rwanda – the more cynically will we view claims to humanitarianism on the part of the interveners. Ultimately, respect for law and norms in the international sphere, their ability to pull towards compliance, depends on the public's perception of their fairness.
33. Luck, *supra* at n. 3 at p. 198.
34. Franck, *supra* at n. 5 at p. 484.

9

Intervention, sovereignty, and the responsibility to protect

Ramesh Thakur

The debate on intervention was ignited in the closing years of the last century by the critical gap between the needs and distress felt in the real world in Somalia, Rwanda, Srebrenica, and East Timor, and the codified instruments and modalities for managing world order. There has been a parallel gap, no less critical, between the codified best practice of international behaviour as articulated in the UN Charter and actual state practice as it has evolved in the 57 years since the Charter was signed. The responsibility for protecting the lives and promoting the welfare of citizens lies first and foremost with the sovereign state. There is a gap – a responsibility deficit – if the state proves unable or unwilling to protect citizens, or itself becomes the perpetrator of violence against its own citizens. Can the slack in responsibility be picked up by agents outside the country concerned? If so, by whom, under what authority, in what circumstances, and subject to what procedural and operational safeguards?

The community-sanctioning authority to settle issues of international peace and security was transferred from the great powers in concert in the nineteenth century to the United Nations in the twentieth century. While Rwanda in 1994 stands as the symbol of international inaction in the face of genocide, Kosovo in 1999 raised many questions about the consequences of action when the international community is divided in the face of a humanitarian tragedy. The United Nations is the only organization with universally accepted authority to validate such operations. The Security Council lies at the heart of the international law-enforcement system. But the only military coalition with the capacity to engage in robust and sustained enforcement action, in and outside its area of operations, is the North Atlantic Treaty Organization (NATO). In 1999, on the one hand, there were claims of a compelling humanitarian tragedy in Kosovo that was an affront to an internationalized human conscience. On the other hand, there was every prospect of Security Council action being blocked by one or two vetoes. But this was never put to the test, and NATO launched a "humanitarian war" without UN authorization. The justification for a collective defence organization bypassing the international organization in order to wage an offensive war remains problematic, and the precedent that was set remains deeply troubling to many observers and countries for having posed a fundamental challenge to the normative architecture of world order.[1]

The dilemma can be summarized thus:

1. To respect sovereignty all the time is to risk being complicit in humanitarian tragedies sometimes;
2. To argue that the UN Security Council must give its consent to international intervention for humanitarian purposes is to risk policy paralysis by handing over the agenda either to the passivity and apathy of the Council as a whole, or to the most obstructionist member of the Council, including any one of the five permanent members determined to use the veto clause;
3. To use force without UN authorization is to violate international law and undermine world order based on the centrality of the UN as the custodian of world conscience and the Security Council as the guardian of world peace.

Under the impact of contrasting experiences in Rwanda[2] and Kosovo, Secretary-General Kofi Annan challenged member states to come up with a new consensus on the competing visions of national and popular sovereignty. Responding to the challenge, Canadian Foreign Minister Lloyd Axworthy set up the International Commission on Intervention and State Sovereignty (ICISS) to wrestle with the whole gamut of difficult and complex issues involved in the debate.

The Report of the Commission,[3] published with formal presentation to Annan on 18 December 2001, seeks to achieve three things. First, it seeks to reposition the existing normative consensus on the subject by replacing the language of humanitarian intervention with the concept of the responsibility to protect. Second, it seeks to locate that responsibility with state authorities at the national and the Security Council at the global levels respectively. Third, it seeks to ensure that when intervention for human protection purposes does take place, it is carried out with efficiency, effectiveness, and due authority, process, and diligence.

This chapter is devoted principally to an exposition of the first of the three goals.[4] The key to the attempt to move the existing consensus forward is a change in the conceptual vocabulary, from the right and duty of "humanitarian intervention" to the responsibility to protect. The mandate of ICISS was to eschew polemics and find a formula for reconciling the urge to humanitarian intervention with the persisting reality of state sovereignty. The concept of the responsibility to protect does just that. The rest of the chapter is divided into five parts. The next section describes the added value of the Commission's work. In the two sections after that, relatively greater attention is paid to elaborating the concepts of the responsibility to protect and sovereignty as responsibility. The fourth section alludes briefly to other parts of the Commission's report, while the fifth and final section considers the tension between UN and great power responsibility to protect deriving from lawful authority and military capacity.

Added value of ICISS

There is already a vast literature on the subject that ICISS was set up to address.[5] Why bother with another study? What could we do that would be a substantial advance? We believe that ICISS has six distinguishing features: balance, outreach, independence, comprehensiveness, innovativeness, and political realism.

The Commission was balanced in composition, starting with the co-chairs, with regard to professional backgrounds (former heads of state and cabinet ministers, UN officials, generals, scholars, journalists), continents-cum-civilizations, industrialized-developing country perspectives, and initial starting positions on the intervention–sovereignty debate.[6] Mohamed Sahnoun wears the inherited wisdom of an entire continent very lightly on his shoulders, and has long and great experience as a national and UN diplomat. He has a wonderful and seemingly inexhaustible repertoire of African animal stories with a moral for every occasion. Gareth Evans is as passionate about justice and human security as Sahnoun, and driven by a restless energy that is astonishingly creative when harnessed to a pet cause. The excellent personal chemistry between the Commissioners, combined with their willingness to listen to one another and adapt and evolve their thinking, without necessarily giving up bottom lines,[7] enabled us to come up with a unanimous report that is more than a collection of clichés and platitudes. If just twelve reasonable, experienced, and intelligent people had failed to come to an agreed report, the prospects of the international community forging a new consensus on the contentious subject of military interventions would have been bleak indeed.

The willingness to listen and adapt was put to the test in an extensive outreach exercise that was one of the most valuable parts of the ICISS process. Commission meetings and round tables were held in almost all continents and major capitals, involving continent-wide representatives, over 200 in total, from all sectors and cross-section of views.[8] The Report reflects a genuine effort to incorporate many of the views that were expressed in Cairo, New Delhi and Santiago as well as Beijing, London, Paris, and Washington. The views presented during the outreach exercise were sometimes used as tie-breakers during deadlocked discussions in the Commission.

There would not have been much point to the regional consultations if the Commission was working to a secret agenda. If the Canadian government had a hidden agenda and a predetermined outcome for ICISS, as mooted by some, they neglected to tell the Commissioners. ICISS was notable for the lack of "shrinking violets", and this reinforced the independent nature of the Commission. The Report reflects our combined and collective thinking as it evolved over the year's deliberations.

The Report is comprehensive in three senses. First, it includes separate chapters on prevention, intervention, reconstruction, lawful authority, and the operational dimension of military interventions. The "responsibility to protect" provides conceptual, normative and operational linkages between assistance, intervention, and reconstruction. The inputs from the round table discussions contributed greatly to the comprehensiveness of the Commission's final product, which consists of a supplementary research volume in addition to the main report.[9] The Commission was assisted by a Secretariat provided by Canada's foreign ministry, plus a research team under the co-direction of Stanlake Samkange and Thomas W. Weiss. While the primary responsibility for the second volume lay with Weiss and Don Hubert, they were helped by several especially commissioned essays, plus submissions and contributions from over 50 specialists. The research volume is supported by an extensive and annotated bibliography that contains more than 2,200 entries, and the entire report and volume is available on CD-ROM that is key-worded and indexed to facilitate ease of research.

Fifth, the "Responsibility to Protect" formulation is, we believe, genuinely innovative, as was "sustainable development" of the Bruntdland Commission whose success in reconciling the previously opposed concepts of development (which is exploitative) and conservation had formed an inspiring model for us from the start of our deliberations. (Co-chair Sahnoun was a member of the Brundtland Commission.)

Sixth, the ICISS discussions and report were always grounded in political realism. For example, we were not interested in solving all the world's problems, but stuck narrowly to our mandate. Thus we resisted the temptation to recast our report in the light of the terrorist attacks of 11 September 2001, concluding that horrific and urgent as the latter was, self-defence is conceptually and operationally distinct from the protection of at-risk foreign populations. Similarly, we resisted the temptation to urge amendments to the UN Charter, for example, with respect to the composition and functioning of the Security Council.

In retrospect, as a final contextual comment, the one-year time-frame was probably a very useful discipline. This meant the momentum never flagged, we worked to a tight deadline, and we remembered where we had got to at the last meeting and the progress that had already been made.

Shifting the terms of the debate

"Humanitarian Intervention" is what humanitarian agencies like the International Committee of the Red Cross (ICRC) and the UN High Commissioner for Refugees (UNHCR) do; they object to the phrase being appropriated by states engaged in military intervention. "Humanitarian Intervention" conveys to most Western minds the idea that the principle underlying the intervention is not self-interested power politics but the disinterested one of protecting human life. It conjures up in many non-Western minds historical memories of the strong imposing their will on the weak in the name of the prevailing universal principles of the day, from the civilizing mission of spreading Christianity to the cultivation and promotion of human rights.

The traditional terms of the debate focus attention on the claims, rights, and prerogatives of the potentially intervening states much more so than on the urgent needs of the intended, putative beneficiaries of the action. By focusing on the "right to intervene" they do not adequately take into account the prevention and follow-up assistance components of external action. The phrase "humanitarian intervention" is used to trump sovereignty with intervention at the outset of the debate: it loads the dice in favour of intervention before the argument has even begun, by labelling and delegitimizing dissent as anti-humanitarian.

Where humanitarian intervention raises fears of domination based on the international power hierarchy, the responsibility to protect encapsulates the element of international solidarity. Moreover, it implies an evaluation of the issues from the point of view of those seeking or needing support, rather than those who may be considering intervention. Our preferred terminology refocuses the international searchlight back on the duty to protect the villager from murder, the woman from rape, and the child from starvation and being orphaned.

Sovereignty

Crucially, the responsibility to protect acknowledges that responsibility rests primarily with the state concerned; only if the state is unable or unwilling to fulfil this responsibility, or is itself the perpetrator, does it become the responsibility of others to act in its place. In many cases, the state seeks to acquit its responsibility in full and active partnership with representatives of the international community. Thus the responsibility to protect is more of a linking concept that bridges the divide between the international community and the sovereign state, whereas the language of the right or duty to intervene is inherently more confrontational.

Internally, sovereignty refers to the exclusive competence of the state to make authoritative decisions of government with regard to all people and resources within its territory. Externally, it means the legal identity of the state in international law, an equality of status with all other states, and the claim to be the sole official agent acting in international relations on behalf of a society. *National sovereignty* locates the state as the ultimate seat of power and authority, unconstrained by internal or external checks; *constitutional sovereignty* holds that the power and authority of the state are not absolute but contingent and constrained.[10] Domestically, power sharing between the executive, legislature, and judiciary, at federal and provincial levels, is regulated by constitutional arrangements and practices. Internationally, states are constrained by globally legitimated institutions and practices.

Sovereignty has its philosophical and political roots in European thought and practice. Ironically, while aspects of sovereignty are being progressively superseded in the construction of the increasingly borderless European Union, some of its most passionate defenders are to be found among developing countries (although the US is second to none in the jealous defence of national sovereignty against international encroachments).

At one level, the developing countries' attachment to sovereignty is deeply emotional. The colonial experience traumatized many of them, and the long shadows cast by this are yet to disappear. In the age of colonialism, most Afro-Asians and Latin Americans became the victims of Western superiority in the organization and weaponry of warfare. Most developing countries are former colonies who achieved independence on the back of extensive and protracted nationalist struggles against the major European powers. The anti-colonial impulse in their worldview survives as a powerful sentiment in the collective consciousness of the nation. The continuing scars in the collective memory are difficult for many Westerners to comprehend and come to terms with.

At another level, the commitment to sovereignty is functional. The state is the cornerstone of the international system. State sovereignty provides order, stability, and predictability in international relations. It mediates relations between the strong and weak, rich and poor, and former colonizers and colonized. With independence, and following the globalization of the norm of self-determination, the principle of state sovereignty was the constitutional device used by newly decolonized countries to try to reconstitute disrupted societies and polities, and to restart arrested economic development. As Mohammed Ayoob notes, the developing countries typically sought order within and justice between states. By contrast, the industrialized Western countries have given primacy to order between states and justice (that is, civil–political human rights) within.[11]

A condition of any one state's sovereignty is a corresponding obligation to respect every other state's sovereignty. In the era of decolonization, the sovereign equality of states and the correlative norm of non-intervention received their most emphatic affirmation from the newly independent states. Even during the Cold War state practice reflected the unwillingness of many countries – not just the two power blocs, but also some former colonies like India and Tanzania – to give up complete intervention as an instrument of policy. But the many examples of intervention in actual state practice throughout the twentieth century did not lead to an abandonment of the norm of non-intervention. Indeed, often the breaches provoked such fierce controversy and so much nationalistic passion that their net effect was to reinforce, not negate, the norm of non-intervention.

UN membership was the final symbol of independent sovereign statehood and thus the seal of acceptance into the community of nations. The organization was also the principal international forum for collaborative action in the shared pursuit of the three goals of state building, nation building, and economic development. The UN was therefore the main arena for the jealous protection of state sovereignty, not its casual abrogation.

The Commission's core principle is that state sovereignty implies responsibility,[12] and the primary responsibility for the protection of its people lies with the state itself. But if it should default, a residual, fallback responsibility also lies with the broader community of states. Where a population is suffering serious harm, as a result of internal war, insurgency, repression, or state failure, and the government in question is unwilling or unable to halt or avert it, the principle of non-intervention yields to the international responsibility to protect. The foundations of that responsibility lie in obligations inherent in the concept of sovereignty; the responsibility of the Security Council for the maintenance of international peace and security; specific legal obligations under human rights and human protection declarations, covenants and treaties, international humanitarian law and national law; and the developing practice of states, regional organizations, and the Security Council itself.[13]

The international order is based on a system of sovereign states because this is seen as the most efficient means of organizing the world in order to discharge the responsibility to the people of protecting their lives and livelihoods, and promoting their well-being and freedoms. If sovereignty becomes an obstacle to the realization of freedom, then it can, should, and must be discarded. But sovereignty need not be such an obstacle. While some elements of sovereignty have devolved downwards and inwards to civil society within the state, others have been subsumed in transnational flows, activities, and institutions across borders. In today's seamless world, political frontiers have become less salient both for international organizations, whose rights and duties can extend beyond borders, and for member states, whose responsibilities within borders can be held to international scrutiny.

The steady erosion of the once sacrosanct principle of national sovereignty is rooted in the reality of global interdependence: no *country* is an island unto itself anymore. The increasing internationalization of the world has widened the gap between the legal status and actual reality of states acting and interacting in the international arena. As a result of agreements that they have signed voluntarily, states now accept many external obligations and international scrutiny. The norms of human rights and international humanitarian law in particular are widely acknowledged and honoured in and among states. As memories of colonialism dim and become increasingly distant, the salience of sovereignty correspondingly diminishes. Citizens and domestic groups instead begin to use the international human rights norm and cross-national global coalitions to subject the actions of their own governments to increasingly critical scrutiny.

For these reasons, and based on changes in the real world and evolving best practice international behaviour, the Commission concluded that it is necessary and useful to reconceptualize sovereignty as responsibility. This has a threefold significance. First, it implies that the state authorities are responsible *for* the functions of protecting the safety and lives of citizens and promotion of their welfare. Second, it suggests that the national political authorities are responsible *to* the citizens internally and to the international community through the UN. And third, it means that the agents of the state are responsible for their actions – that is to say, they are *accountable* for their acts of commission and omission. Would-be perpetrators of mass atrocities should fear the growth of universal justice as a result of which they will ultimately have nowhere else to run, no place left to hide.

The goal of intervention for human protection purposes is never to wage war on a state in order to destroy it and eliminate its statehood, but always to protect victims of atrocities inside the state, to embed the protection in reconstituted institutions after the intervention, and then to withdraw all foreign troops. Thus military intervention for human protection purposes takes away the rights flowing from the status of sovereignty, but does not in itself challenge the status as such. It does supplant the rights of the state to *exercise* protective functions if the state has proven incapable or unwilling to do so with respect to genocidal killings, humanitarian atrocities, and ethnic cleansing; or to suspend the right of the state to conduct itself free of external interference if such conduct is the cause of the above atrocities. The prevention of the exercise of sovereign rights under intervention for human protection purposes is always limited in time to a temporary period, until the capacity of the state itself to resume its protective functions can be restored and institutionalized.

Intervention for human protection purposes may also be limited in two further respects. It may be confined to a particular portion of the target state's territory rather than all of it, for example Kosovo and not all of Yugoslavia, where the abuses are actually occurring; or it may be limited with respect to a particular group that is the target of abuse, rather than to all citizens.

The UN Charter is itself an example of an international obligation voluntarily accepted by member states. On the one hand, in granting membership to the UN, the international community welcomes the signatory state as a responsible member of the community of nations. On the other hand, the state itself, in signing the Charter, accepts the responsibilities of membership flowing from that signature. There is no transfer or dilution of state sovereignty. But there is a redefinition from sovereignty as right of exclusivity to sovereignty as responsibility in both internal functions and external duties. The United Nations is the symbol and the arena for the shared management of pooled sovereignty.

Doing it right, doing it well

Conflict prevention and peacebuilding

Action in support of the responsibility to protect necessarily involves and calls for a broad range and wide variety of measures and responses in fulfilment of the accompanying duty to assist. These may include development assistance to help prevent conflict from occurring, intensifying, spreading, or persisting; rebuilding support to help prevent conflict from recurring; and, in extraordinary cases, military intervention to protect at-risk civilians from harm.

Prevention is the single most important dimension of the responsibility to protect, so prevention options should always be exhausted before intervention is contemplated. Moreover, the exercise of the responsibility to prevent and react should always involve less intrusive and coercive measures being considered (although not necessarily attempted) before more coercive and intrusive ones are applied. The responsibility to prevent requires addressing both the root causes and direct causes of internal conflict and other man-made crises putting populations at risk. The responsibility to react requires us to respond to situations of compelling human need with appropriate measures, which may include coercive measures like sanctions and international prosecution, and in extreme cases military intervention. The responsibility to rebuild requires us to provide, particularly after a military intervention, full assistance with recovery, reconstruction, and reconciliation, addressing the causes of the harm the intervention was designed to halt or avert.

Threshold criteria and cautionary principles

Military intervention for human protection purposes is an exceptional and extraordinary measure. To be warranted, there must be serious and irreparable harm occurring to human beings, or imminently likely to occur, of the following kind:

- Large-scale loss of life due to deliberate state action, neglect, or inability to act, or a failed state situation; or
- Large-scale ethnic cleansing, actual or apprehended, whether carried out by killing, forced expulsion, acts of terror, or rape.

We concluded that it would be futile to try to anticipate every contingency and provide a uniform checklist for intervention. Rather, the decision on intervention would have to be a matter of careful judgment on a case-by-case basis. Even when the just cause threshold is crossed of conscience-shocking loss of life or ethnic cleansing, intervention must be guided by the cautionary principles of right intention, last resort, proportional means, and reasonable prospects.[14] The primary purpose of the intervention, whatever other motives intervening states may have, must be to halt or avert human suffering. Right intention is better assured with multilateral operations, clearly supported by regional opinion and the victims concerned. Military intervention can only be justified when every non-military option for the prevention or peaceful resolution of the crisis has been explored, with reasonable grounds for believing that lesser measures would not have succeeded. The scale, duration, and intensity of the planned military intervention should be the minimum necessary to secure the defined human protection objective. And there must be a reasonable chance of success in halting or averting the suffering which has justified the intervention, with the consequences of action not likely to be worse than the consequences of inaction. Military intervention against major powers is ruled out, therefore, not as a matter of double standards at the level of principles, but due to a prudential consequentialism: under no conceivable circumstances would humanitarian goals be advanced by launching an external military intervention against Russia in order to protect, say, the people of Chechnya.

Finally, the Report also seeks to identify the operational principles to guide interventions. The chapter outlining these should be of particular interest to military staff colleges.

Right authority and due process

War is itself a major humanitarian tragedy that can be justified only under the most compelling circumstances regarding the provocation, the likelihood of success – bearing in mind that goals are metamorphosed in the crucible of war once started – and the consequences that may reasonably be predicted. And the burden of proof rests on the proponents of force, not on dissenters. In particular, we cannot accept the alternative doctrine that any one state or coalition can decide when to intervene with force in the internal affairs of other countries, for down that path lies total chaos. The sense of moral outrage provoked by humanitarian atrocities must always be tempered by an appreciation of the limits of power, a concern for international institution-building, and a sensitivity to the law of unintended and perverse consequences. The NATO intervention in Kosovo in 1999 remains hotly disputed over the question of whether it triggered more carnage than it averted.

Intervention for human protection purposes occurs so that those condemned to die in fear may be rescued to live in hope instead. Even so, military intervention, even for humanitarian purposes, is just a nicer way of referring to the use of deadly force on a massive scale. Given the enormous normative presumption against the use of deadly force to settle international quarrels, who has the right to authorize such force? On what basis, for what purpose, and subject to what safeguards and limitations? In other words, even if we agree that military intervention may sometimes be necessary and unavoidable in order to protect innocent people from life-threatening danger by interposing an outside force between actual and apprehended victims and perpetrators, key questions remain about agency, lawfulness, and legitimacy: that is, about international authority that can override national authority.

Attempts to enforce authority can only be made by the legitimate agents of that authority. What distinguishes rule enforcement by criminal thugs from that by police officers is precisely the principle of legitimacy. The chief contemporary institution for building, consolidating, and using the authority of the international community is the United Nations. Set up as the principal element of order and stability in the revolutionary post-World War world, it was meant to be the framework within which members of the international system negotiated agreements on the rules of behaviour and the legal norms of proper conduct in order to preserve the society of states.

The Commission concluded that there is no better or more appropriate body than the Security Council to authorize military intervention for human protection purposes. The task therefore is not to find alternatives to the Security Council as a source of authority, but to make it work better than it has. Its authorization should in all cases be sought prior to any military intervention. Those calling for an intervention should formally request such authorization, or have the Council raise the matter on its own initiative, or have the Secretary-General raise it under Article 99 of the UN Charter.

UN authority and great power capacity

The formal authority for maintaining international peace and security is thus vested in the Security Council. But the burden of responsibility, from having the power to make the most difference, often falls on the US and other leading powers. The conceptual connecting rod that links power to authority is legitimacy. The legitimacy of the Security Council as the authoritative validator of international security action has been subject to a steady erosion as it has been perceived as being unrepresentative in composition, undemocratic in operation, unaccountable to anyone "below" (e.g. the General Assembly) or "above" (e.g. the World Court), and ineffective in results. Western countries often chafe at the ineffectual performance legitimacy of the Council, and their desire to resist the Council's role as the sole validator of the international use of force is the product of this dissatisfaction at its perceived sorry record. On the other hand, if it were to become increasingly activist, interventionist, and effective, then the erosion of representational and procedural legitimacy would lead many developing countries to question the authority of the Council even more forcefully.

The UN is just as powerful a symbol of what member states must not do. In the field of state–citizen relations *within* territorial borders, the totality of Charter clauses and instruments like the Universal Declaration of Human Rights restrict the authority of states to cause harm to their own people. In the sphere of military action *across* borders, UN membership imposes the obligation on the major powers to abjure unilateral intervention in favour of collectively authorized international intervention.

The legal debate on a clear, consistent, and workable set of codified criteria for intervention is largely sterile. The political debate quickly degenerates from rational discussion to highly charged polemics. Morally, many fear that any codification of the rules of intervention would relegitimize the use of force in international relations. This would be a major step backward, in that over the course of the twentieth century the international community placed increasing legislative and normative fetters on the recourse to military force as a means of settling international disputes. The United Nations is both the symbol and the major instrument for moderating the use of force in international relations, not blessing it and sanctifying a major expansion in its permissive scope.

The response from those with little patience for claims of UN primacy (let alone monopoly) on the legitimate use of international force is that the UN system of collective security was fatally flawed from the start. Peace was preserved and justice advanced by the operation of institutions and the pursuit of values by coalitions of the right-minded, able and willing to defend the international order against all challenges.

The real debate is between those who support the development of guidelines for use by the Security Council in authorizing international intervention but remain firmly opposed to criteria for circumventing the UN, and those who wish to retain the right to unilateral intervention. The first group, comprising mainly (but neither exclusively nor all) developing countries, is fearful that the norm of non-intervention could become roadkill on the highway of international power politics, taking us back to the nineteenth-century system of a concert of great powers.

Among those who wish to retain the flexibility to launch military intervention without UN authorization if necessary, there is a further division of opinion between those who would like a "doctrine" approach and others who want merely an "exception" approach[15] – a signposted emergency exit from the existing norms as embedded in the UN Charter.

Yet another variation would be to distinguish a "red light" from the entrenched "green light" approach. Under the latter, intervention may not proceed until and unless it has been duly authorized by the Security Council. Under the former, interventions can take place unless and until specifically prohibited by the Council. In Kosovo in 1999, a draft resolution condemning NATO bombing was defeated by 12 to 3, despite two permanent members voting in the affirmative. Many interpreted the failure to flash the red light as tacit or de facto authorization. The difficulty with this is not just that it subverts the Charter and turns the principle of authorization on its head. As well, the veto clause would still come into play. Even if the vote in support of a "red light" resolution was 14 to 1, the resolution would fail, and the red light therefore could not be flashed, if that one solitary negative vote was that of a permanent member. Equally, when the vital interests of global or regional major powers are engaged, interventionary forces may go crashing through an entire forest of flashing red lights without paying any heed to them.

Alternatively, it may be argued that the intersection of international law and ethics creates a space where the precautionary principle can be borrowed from environmental ethics and law. Developed especially in Germany and France with regard to environmental law and the legal protection of health, it seeks to provide policy guidance in situations of inherent uncertainty. The equivalent of the prudential driving adage "If in doubt, don't," the precautionary principle states that the absence of certainty must not delay the adoption of measures aimed at preventing the risk of serious and irreversible damage.[16] For if we wait until certainty (for example with respect to the scope, magnitude, and gravity of impact, or causal links between anthropogenic activities and environmental degradation), then irreversible damage may already have been caused. Therefore, as per the precautionary principle, the legal responsibility to protect applies not only to those domestic public authorities who failed to take preventive measures against *known* risks and hazards, but also to those who did not take *precautionary* measures because of existing margins of doubt and uncertainty. Humanitarian atrocities, genocidal killings, and ethnic cleansing occur against the backdrop of chaos, confusion, and lack of real-time reliable information. If we wait until clarity and certainty obtains, our task may become restitution and retribution, not protection. It should be protection and therefore, in the face of uncertainty, the default bias should be to avoid risk.

This is why it is important for the Security Council to deal promptly with any request for authority to intervene where there are allegations of large-scale loss of human life or ethnic cleansing. The ICISS Report recommends that the Permanent Five members of the Security Council should agree not to apply their veto power in matters where their vital state interests are not involved, so as not to obstruct the passage of resolutions authorizing military intervention for human protection purposes for which there is otherwise majority support. Action in selected cases outside a veto-paralysed Security Council framework is less defensible by those who refuse to accept any dilution of the veto power as a matter of general principle.[17]

If the Security Council rejects a proposal or fails to deal with it in a reasonable time, alternative options are: consideration of the matter by the General Assembly in Emergency Special Session under the "Uniting for Peace" procedure; and action within area of jurisdiction by regional or subregional organizations, subject to their seeking subsequent authorization from the Security Council.

The Security Council should take into account in all its deliberations that, if it fails to discharge its responsibility to protect in conscience-shocking situations crying out for action, concerned states may not rule out other means to meet the gravity and urgency of that situation. This carries a double risk. Their actions may not be guided by the just cause and cautionary principles identified in the ICISS Report, and so their interventions may not be done well, with due authority, diligence, and process. Alternatively, they may do it very well and the people of the world may conclude that their actions were necessary, just, and proper, in which case the stature and credibility of the United Nations may suffer still further erosion. (So where do we go from here?)

Conclusion

The Commission's Report deals succinctly with the full range of issues involved in the debate. The fact that a dozen people of diverse background and varied starting positions were able to agree on a challenging, substantial, and wide-ranging report encourages us to believe that an international consensus can indeed be forged around these ideas and principles. If and when the world is once again confronted by challenges on the scale of Rwanda, Kosovo, and East Timor, we hope it will be better prepared to act with principled force. Too often in the past UN peace operations have fallen victim to coalitions of the unwilling, unable, and unlike-minded. It is time to put collective might to the service of individual and international right.

How might this be done? What are the next steps? At a seminar in New York on 15 February 2002 organized by the International Peace Academy, most Security Council members seemed supportive of the main thrust of the Report. In May, Kofi Annan convened a Security Council retreat for discussing the policy and operational implications of the ICISS Report. The Report itself also calls for a declaratory resolution by the General Assembly affirming the just cause threshold criteria that would trigger intervention, and the four cautionary principles of right intention, last resort, proportionality, and reasonable prospects.

If imitation be the sincerest form of flattery, it is interesting that Ambassador Jayantha Dhanapala, the UN Under-Secretary-General for Disarmament and a member of the Canberra Commission on the Elimination of Nuclear Weapons, recently proposed the creation of a new commission on the elimination of all weapons of mass destruction, drawing explicitly on the model of ICISS.[18]

To the extent that our primary goal is to reposition the normative consensus, the Secretary-General is uniquely important to our task. The office is the custodian of the world conscience and the embodiment of the international interest like no other. In the 15 February seminar, in his opening address for the public record, Kofi Annan put the authority of his office behind the ICISS Report. He described it as an "extraordinary and eloquent Report", "a remarkable accomplishment", and the "most comprehensive and carefully thought out response to date" to his challenge of humanitarian intervention. He said it takes away the last remaining excuses for the international community to sit back and do nothing when confronted with atrocities again. While there were doubts and hesitations about some of the nuances of the Commission's Report, and agreement that many serious hurdles were yet to be overcome, the consensus at the seminar was that if we are going to get any progress on this vexed and deeply divisive issue, then the Commission's Report is the way to go.

Three caveats should be noted about this article. First, it reflects the personal opinion of the author, and does not necessarily reflect the views of the United Nations University. Second, it does not even purport to speak in the name of ICISS: only the consensus Report of the Commission does that. Third, it has nevertheless benefited enormously from the debates and discussions with the other members of the Commission, and from the extensive reading material collected by the research team as background material to assist the Commission's deliberations.

Notes

1. For a full treatment of the Kosovo debate from a variety of perspectives, see Albrecht Schnabel and Ramesh Thakur (eds.) (2000) *Kosovo and the Challenge of Humanitarian Intervention: Selective Indignation, Collective Action, and International Citizenship*, Tokyo: United Nations University Press. See also *The Kosovo Report: Conflict, International Response, Lessons Learned. Report of the Independent International Commission on Kosovo*, Oxford: Oxford University Press (2000).
2. On Rwanda, see in particular Alan J. Kuperman (2001) *The Limits of Humanitarian Intervention: Genocide in Rwanda*, Washington: Brookings; Linda Melvern (2000) *A People Betrayed: The Role of the West in Rwanda's Genocide*, London: Zed Books; and Gérard Prunier (1997) *The Rwanda Crisis: History of a Genocide*, New York: Columbia University Press.
3. *The Responsibility to Protect: Report of the International Commission on Intervention and State Sovereignty*, Ottawa: International Development Research Centre for ICISS (2001). The Report is available also on the website at ⟨www.iciss.gc.ca⟩.

4. Clearly, as a Commissioner, I am writing as a partisan advocate, not an independent critic.
5. The Commission's own supplementary volume (see n9 below) provides 16 pages of bibliographic entries under "Humanitarian Intervention" and "Sovereignty and Intervention", plus many more entries under specific case studies including Kosovo and East Timor.
6. The co-chairs were Gareth Evans and Mohamed Sahnoun, the remaining ten Commissioners being Gisele Côté-Harper, Lee Hamilton, Michael Ignatieff, Vladimir Lukin, Klaus Naumann, Cyril Ramaphosa, Fidel Ramos, Cornelio Sommaruga, Eduardo Stein, and Ramesh Thakur. Their biodata can be found in the Report or on the Commission's website (n3 above).
7. As is noted in the foreword from the co-chairs, "[t]he Commissioners brought many different personal views to the table, and the report on which we have agreed does not reflect in all respects the preferred views of any one of them. In particular, some of our members preferred a wider range of threshold criteria for military intervention than those proposed in our report, and others a narrower range. Again, some Commissioners preferred more, and others less, flexibility for military intervention outside the scope of Security Council approval" (p. viii).
8. Commission meetings were held in Ottawa (November 2000), Maputo (March 2001), New Delhi (June 2001), Wakefield, Canada (August 2000), and Brussels (September 2001). Round tables and consultative meetings were held, in chronological order, in Ottawa, Geneva, London, Maputo, Washington DC, Santiago, Cairo, Paris, New Delhi, Beijing, and St. Petersburg.
9. The Responsibility to Protect: Research, Bibliography, Background. Supplementary Volume to the Report of the International Commission on Intervention and State Sovereignty, Ottawa: International Development Research Centre for ICISS (2001).
10. See Hideaki Shinoda (2000) *Re-examining Sovereignty: From Classical Theory to the Global Age*, New York: St. Martin's Press.
11. Mohammed Ayoob (2002) "Humanitarian intervention and state sovereignty", *International Journal of Human Rights* 6(1): 81–102.
12. On this we owe an intellectual debt to Francis M. Deng, et al. (1996) *Sovereignty as Responsibility: Conflict Management in Africa*, Washington DC: Brookings. See also Francis M. Deng (1995) "Reconciling Sovereignty with Responsibility: A Basis for International Humanitarian Action," in John Harbeson and Donald Rothchild (eds.) *Africa in World Politics: Post-Cold War Challenges*, Boulder, Colo.: Westview, pp. 295–310.
13. As the Report puts it, "While there is not yet a sufficiently strong basis to claim the emergence of a new principle of customary international law, growing state and regional organization practice as well as Security Council precedent suggest an emerging guiding principle – which in the Commission's view could properly be termed 'the responsibility to protect'" (p. 15, para. 2.24).
14. These are clearly derived from the just war doctrine. But because the doctrine is rooted in the Christian tradition, acknowledging its religious roots would not necessarily have been the wisest political decision. This is just one example, albeit an interesting one, of the clash of academic and policy cultures.
15. For a review of this debate, see in particular Simon Chesterman (2001) *Just War or Just Peace? Humanitarian Intervention and International Law*, Oxford: Oxford University Press, pp. 226–232, and Nicholas Wheeler (2000) *Saving Strangers: Humanitarian Intervention in International Society*, Oxford: Oxford University Press, pp. 33–51.
16. See David Freestone and Ellen Hey (eds.) (1996) *The Precautionary Principle and International Law: The Challenge of Implementation*, London: Kluwer Law International; James Cameron (2002) "The Precautionary Principle," in Gary P. Sampson and W.

Bradnee Chambers (eds.) *Trade, Environment, and the Millennium*, 2nd ed., Tokyo: United Nations University Press, pp. 287–319.

17. This normative inconsistency is fatal to the moral majority proponents of coalitions of the willing. Yet it is an obvious flaw – so much so that one may question whether failure to address it reflects intellectual laziness or moral duplicity. Can an intellectually coherent or morally consistent argument be advanced for any one or several of the P5 to lead such coalitions when faced with an actual or apprehended Security Council veto, if they are not prepared to give up the veto right?
18. Jayantha Dhanapala, "The Canberra Commission: Lessons Learned for a Future Commission", keynote address at the UN University and University of Waterloo Conference on the Ideas–Institutional Nexus, Waterloo, Ontario, 18 May 2002; and Jayantha Dhanapala and Ramesh Thakur, "Let's get together against terrorism," *International Herald Tribune*, 4 June 2002. See also Appendix.

10

The responsibility to protect: Assessing the report of the International Commission on Intervention and State Sovereignty

Jennifer Welsh, Carolin J. Thielking, and S. Neil MacFarlane

[I]f humanitarian intervention is, indeed, an unacceptable assault on sovereignty, how should we respond to a Rwanda, to a Srebrenica – to gross and systematic violations of human rights that affect every precept of our common humanity? (Kofi Annan)[1]

The controversial principle of non-intervention is much older than the United Nations system that enshrines it. Indeed, debates about the extent and limits of state sovereignty have been an integral part of the evolution of modern international society since the Treaty of Westphalia in 1648.[2] Since 1945, the debate has focused on the alleged incompatibility of two principles of the United Nations system: sovereign equality and human rights. The former, enshrined in articles 2(1), 2(4), and 2(7), suggests that states should enjoy sovereign equality – defined *internally* as exclusive jurisdiction within a territory and *externally* as freedom from outside interference. The latter, identified in the preamble and article 1(3) and elaborated in subsequent declarations and conventions, suggests that individual rights are inalienable and transcend sovereign frontiers.

Several features of contemporary international relations have sharpened this conflict and provided added impetus to those calling for more interventionism: the weakness (or complete failure) of state structures in many conflict-ridden societies, which provides opportunity for criminal activity, arms proliferation, and terrorism; the increased vulnerability of civilians in the context of civil conflict; the "CNN effect", in which global and instantaneous access to information heightens popular awareness of human suffering; the strengthening of human rights norms and proliferation of human rights organizations; the fear of refugee flows; and the search by Western governments for new forms of political legitimacy and "moral authority" to replace the ideologically driven agenda of the Cold War. In short, today's debate about the legitimacy of intervention is conducted in a climate of heightened expectations for action.

This permissive context for intervention provided the backdrop for Kofi Annan, the Secretary-General of the United Nations, to issue a challenge to the international community to prevent "another Rwanda". At the General Assembly in 1999, Annan called for a new consensus on the age-old problem of intervention and a plan of action for responding to humanitarian tragedies.[3] Canada's response to this call, led by former minister of foreign affairs, Lloyd Axworthy, was the International Commission on Intervention and State Sovereignty (ICISS).

ICISS was announced at the United Nations Millennium Summit in September 2000 by Canada's prime minister, Jean Chrétien, and received funding, thought leadership, and organizational support from the Canadian government.[4] In fact, a great deal of the Commission's language and concepts reflect the human security agenda that was so prominent a part of Canadian foreign policy in the 1990s.[5] ICISS was modelled on the 1987 Brundtland World Commission on Environment and Development and had three goals: to promote a comprehensive debate about humanitarian intervention; to foster a new political consensus on how to reconcile the principles of intervention and state sovereignty; and to translate that consensus into action. The Commission was co-chaired by Gareth Evans, a former foreign minister of Australia, and Mohamed Sahnoun, a senior Algerian diplomat and former special adviser to the United Nations secretary general.[6] An advisory board of serving and former foreign ministers provided a political reference point and follow-up mechanism for the ICISS recommendations. Eleven regional roundtables and national consultations, engaging members of the academic community and civil society, took place around the globe. The consultations were intended to take the issue beyond the confines of Western liberal internationalism and to ensure a broader consensus on the Commission's findings. Finally, the work of the Commission received substantial assistance from a comprehensive programme of research, led by Thomas Weiss, a professor at the CUNY Graduate Centre, and Don Hubert, a senior policy adviser in the Peacebuilding and Human Security Division of Canada's Department of Foreign Affairs and International Trade.[7] According to the ICISS final report, the consensus reached by this process reflects "the shared views of all Commissioners as to what is politically achievable in the world as we know it today".[8]

We begin this chapter with a summary of ICISS principles and priorities and identify its two main contributions to the debate on humanitarian intervention: the conceptual move from a "right of intervention" to a "responsibility to protect"; and the creation of a spectrum of action for the international community – prevention, non-military coercion, military action, and post-conflict rebuilding. In the second section, we highlight some of the challenges in implementing the ICISS recommendations and suggest how the "responsibility to protect" poses problems for policy-makers. Third, we analyse the operational dimension of the Commission's findings, particularly those related to mandates and force command. We conclude with a discussion of the Report's impact in the wake of the events of September 11, 2001 and the Iraq war of 2003. Our overall assessment is that although the ICISS goes a long way to meeting its first objective, it underestimates the countervailing political forces that will impede both the achievement of a broad consensus and the realization of its prescriptive agenda.

Intervention and state sovereignty

The work of ICISS centred around a central question: "when, if ever, it is appropriate for states to take coercive – and in particular military – action, against another state for the purpose of protecting people at risk in that other state".[9] Before the terrorist attacks of 9/11, this was one of the most prominent issues facing international policy-makers. The action of the North Atlantic Treaty Organization (NATO) in Kosovo in 1999 was for many the apex of the problem, illustrating the tension between Western leaders such as Britain's prime minister, Tony Blair, who insisted that the world had to "do something" in the face of evil acts in Kosovo,[10] and representatives of powerful countries such as China, who condemned the intervention as an illegitimate attempt to force Serbians and Kosovars to change their government and their political system.[11]

The ICISS report offers an apparently compelling solution to this dilemma: the international community should view the relationship between sovereignty and intervention as complementary rather than contradictory. Reconciliation is achieved by reshaping the very notion of sovereignty and linking it more closely to the responsibility of states to their citizens.[12] Hence, sovereignty is no longer conceived as undisputed control over territory, but rather as a conditional right dependent upon respect for a minimum standard of human rights. In the words of the ICISS: "It is acknowledged that sovereignty implies a dual responsibility: externally – to respect the sovereignty of other states, and internally, to respect the dignity and basic rights of all the people within the state. In international human rights covenants, in UN practice, and in state practice itself, sovereignty is now understood as embracing this dual responsibility. Sovereignty as responsibility has become the minimum content of good international citizenship".[13] For the Commission, it logically follows that intervention is permissible – and indeed necessary – if it is aimed at protecting civilians and restoring the effective sovereignty of states.

Right vs. responsibility

Seen in this way, coercive external engagement inside a state no longer appears illegitimate. The central conclusion of the ICISS is that sovereign states have a responsibility to protect their own citizens from avoidable catastrophe. But, when they are unwilling or unable to do so, that responsibility must be borne by the broader community of states: "Where a population is suffering serious harm, as a result of internal war, insurgency, repression or state failure, and the state in question is unwilling or unable to halt or avert it, the principle of non-intervention yields to the international responsibility to protect".[14]

The Commission offers several reasons why its formulation, centred on "responsibility" and "protection", is much more than a clever twist of words. First, it argues that "sovereignty as responsibility" implies that state leaders and representatives are accountable for their actions – both internally to their citizens and externally to the international community.[15] Second, it insists that the notion of protection shifts the focus to where it belongs – on the victims of suffering who seek assistance, rather than on the claims or rights of intervening states.[16] Third, the Commissioners believe that the narrow legal concept of intervention fails to consider the importance of prior preventive actions or post-intervention rebuilding,[17] a theme we will address further below. And, lastly, the rejection of the term "humanitarian intervention" responds to the concerns expressed to the Commission by humanitarian organizations, which oppose any attempt to militarize the word "humanitarian".[18]

A spectrum of responsibilities

For some, the evolution in language from "right" to "responsibility" is the central achievement of the Commission. It should be noted, however, that the notion of sovereign responsibility is not new – arguments about conditional sovereignty have been made previously by international relations scholars.[19] Nor is it without its detractors. Commentators such as Henry Kissinger, Hedley Bull, and Robert Jackson have counselled against linking domestic conditions to the maintenance of international order.[20] Instead, they argue that states should "agree to disagree" about the right way to organize their own political systems and respect the norm of non-intervention as the best way of maintaining stability in the international system. Many states share this view of international order, particularly China and Russia, who are both permanent members of the United Nations Security Council. As Ramesh Thakur argues elsewhere in this volume, developing countries also emphasize the link between "sovereignty as responsibility" and the "standard of civilization" that fuelled policies of neo-colonialism. For much of the post-1945 period, the developing world has championed the protection offered by the norm of non-intervention as a means of preventing interference by Western powers.[21]

In our view, the more significant contribution of the Commission's report is its focus on a spectrum of action. According to ICISS, if there is a responsibility to protect, there is also a responsibility to *prevent* and to *rebuild*. Furthermore, when faced with evidence of human suffering inside the domestic jurisdiction of another state, policy makers have a wider array of choices between inaction and military invasion.

Given the considerable difficulties surrounding the use of force in international society, the Commissioners give priority to the task of prevention. In a direct challenge to states and international organizations, they claim that "it is more than high time for the international community to be doing more to close the gap between rhetorical support for prevention and tangible commitment".[22] The Commission recognizes that the resources devoted to preventive measures are dwarfed by the money allocated to war preparation, war fighting, humanitarian assistance to victims of violence, and peacekeeping.

The ICISS report does not profess novelty in its recommendations on prevention. Following the Carnegie Commission on Preventing Deadly Conflict,[23] it distinguishes between two sets of preventive strategies: those directed at so-called root causes of conflict (development assistance and support for good governance and human rights); and those targeted at immediate triggers for violence (good offices and mediation, inducements such as conditional assistance, and punishments such as economic sanctions or suspension of membership in international organizations).[24] It also identifies three conditions for successful prevention: effective early warning mechanisms; a well-stocked "preventive toolbox" that combines political, economic, legal, and military measures; and sufficient political will to act.

Nevertheless, the Commission acknowledges that conflict prevention is not foolproof. It also concedes that some states have been reluctant to accept any kind of externally sponsored prevention efforts for fear that internationalizing the problem will lead inevitably to intervention.[25] When the situation on the ground develops into full-scale conflict, and civilians are placed at serious risk, the option of military action must be considered and evaluated. The ICISS employs a just war framework of six principles to guide decision-makers contemplating such action:

- Just cause: military intervention is an exceptional measure, to be undertaken only in extreme humanitarian emergencies.
- Right intention: the primary motive of the military action must be humanitarian.
- Last resort: all non-military options must be explored before force is used.
- Proportional means: the nature of the force used must be proportionate to the humanitarian objective and limited in scale and intensity.
- Reasonable prospects: the operation must have a reasonable chance of success, and negative consequences of force must not outweigh the consequences of inaction.
- Right authority: military action should be authorized by the United Nations Security Council (but authorization can be found elsewhere if the Council fails to act).

Finally, ICISS calls upon intervening states to commit to a long-term process of rebuilding. The recommended priorities are economic reconstruction, the establishment of legitimate and effective institutions of governance, the restoration of public safety, and sustainable development.

Assumptions and controversies

The findings of ICISS rest on a series of assumptions about international politics and about the behaviour of individuals, states, and international organizations. It is these assumptions that, upon closer analysis, raise the greatest challenges for the implementation of the report's recommendations.

State responsibility

The first, relatively uncontroversial, assumption is that sovereign states are still the first port of call in providing for their citizens. Although countless books and articles published in the late 1980s and 1990s predicted the end of the nation-state in the face of globalization, the pendulum is swinging back towards recognition of the sovereign state as the cornerstone of international order. In the words of Canada's minister of foreign affairs, Bill Graham, "it is an effective, functioning State that can best protect its own citizens. Indeed, it is in the State that the international community has vested primary responsibility for the protection of humanitarian standards".[26] The Commission goes even further when it suggests that "effective and legitimate states remain the best way to ensure that the benefits of the internationalization of trade, investment, technology and communication will be equitably shared"[27]. Rather than decrying the strength of national institutions and practices as impediments to transnational forces, today we worry about weak and failed states as the greatest source of international instability.[28]

But sovereignty is not a static concept. The conditions under which it is exercised have evolved substantially, especially since the Second World War. Nor is sovereignty absolute. As the report states: "The defence of state sovereignty, by even its strongest supporters, does not include any claim of the unlimited power of a state to do what it wants to its own people".[29] Put simply, states should no longer be allowed to get away with murder.

The threshold for intervention

A second and more problematic assumption is that states and international organizations can come to agreement on when a sovereign state has lost the capacity to protect its citizens. Here, there are two sets of issues.

The first involves determining a clear threshold of atrocities that would justify the use of military force. In other words, what constitutes an extreme humanitarian emergency? The Commission's report consciously excludes situations that some have argued are just cause for intervention: for example, systematic racial discrimination, repression of political opponents, or overthrow of a democratic regime.[30] In the ICISS formulation, a moral defence of intervention can be mounted in two cases only: where there is a large-scale loss of life – with or without genocidal intent – that results from deliberate state action or the massive failure of state structures; and where there is large-scale ethnic cleansing carried out by killing, rape, torture, or mass expulsion. In both cases, the danger to civilians can be "actual or apprehended".[31]

The report does not attempt to quantify "large-scale" and suggests that in most cases there is unlikely to be major disagreement in interpretation.[32] It quickly becomes clear, however, that this threshold is riddled with controversy. In 1999, Kosovo certainly was "extreme" for some in the international community, though not for others (notably China, India, and Russia). Chechnya has not crossed the threshold for anyone, despite the fact that the level of abuse of civilians was and is substantially higher there than it was in Kosovo prior to intervention. Indeed, it is intriguing that there is no reference to Chechnya anywhere in the ICISS report.[33] Finally, while humanitarian rationale have risen to prominence in the aftermath of the war to unseat Saddam Hussein (in light of the failure to find weapons of mass destruction), the Commissioners are divided amongst themselves as to whether Iraq met the ICISS criteria for justifying intervention.

The threshold becomes more problematic when ICISS adds the words "actual or apprehended" to its definition. On the one hand, its list of conditions that would trigger a judgement appears sound: actions identified by the 1948 Genocide convention and Geneva conventions; different manifestations of ethnic cleansing (including killing, forced removal, and rape); exposure to mass starvation or civil war; and overwhelming natural or environmental catastrophes. Yet, on the other hand, it is difficult to imagine a reliable apprehension of these conditions. In the latter two cases, accurate intelligence information might foreshadow the humanitarian emergency, but what about genocide, crimes against humanity, or ethnic cleansing? And who would we trust to provide an objective assessment of their likelihood? As Kosovo demonstrates, actors on the ground who are desperate for external assistance have a massive stake in how atrocities are categorized and may be tempted to inflate their representations so as to secure intervention. They might also be tempted to provoke the very conditions that are required for intervention.

In most cases the problem is not lack of evidence but rather how it is assessed. Thus, the Commissioners might have distinguished between the internal assessment (made within government circles) and the public assessment (announced at public forums or at press briefings). It is the latter that carries the most significant consequences for decision-makers. For example, large-scale loss of life in Rwanda in April 1994 was widely acknowledged within the ranks of government. However, members of the Security Council (particularly the United States) were not prepared to use the word genocide publicly because of the obligations that would have followed from using the term.[34] Similarly, there has been little dispute over whether the threshold for lives lost has been crossed in Chechnya; rather, the public statements of major states cannot be separated from the pursuit of their own national interests or their concern for international stability.

These kinds of trade-offs – which states frequently make in international politics – do not sit easily with the criteria for intervention set out by ICISS. In place of a linear checklist, policy makers require a more complex web of considerations that takes account of the interdependent relationships among various criteria. In the end, assuming the criteria can be operationalized, the ICISS checklist can only represent necessary, and not sufficient, conditions for a decision to intervene.[35] States will take into account order, stability, and self-interest even when the facts regarding lack of protection are reasonably clear.

Another issue with the threshold is the tension between the state's role as protector and its role as provider of group and individual rights. In other words, it may not always be possible to treat the responsibility to protect in a homogeneous way. What would the international community do in a situation in which a state attempts to fulfil its responsibility to protect a majority by targeting a minority that is perceived to be a threat to society? The campaign by the Russian government against Chechen rebels is one such case. Another might be the recent practice in the United States regarding "People of Middle Eastern Aspect" (PMEAs), including preventive detention, denial of rights to travel, and deportation without due process. As September 11 revealed, even Western states see protection of the community as a whole as requiring some restrictions of the rights of a visible minority. It is also noteworthy that a large proportion of the population supports these measures. We elaborate further on this theme in the conclusion.

Law and morality

As suggested earlier, the Commission assumes it can avoid the conundrum surrounding the so-called right of humanitarian intervention[36] by substituting the notions of "responsibility" and "protection". In other words, it rests its case on a moral rather than a legal foundation.[37]

There are two challenges to this approach. First, the idea of protection rests on the broader and fuzzier concept of human security, defined by the ICISS as "the securing of people – their physical safety, their economic and social well-being, respect for their dignity and worth as human beings, and the protection of their human rights and fundamental freedoms".[38] By broadening security to include such diverse facets, the Commission risks losing focus on what may be the most pressing threats to security – and therefore the most urgent tasks of protection.

Second, ICISS cannot escape the same normative connotations that it claims plague the idea of humanitarian intervention. "Responsibility" and "protection", like "humanitarian", have positive evaluative content. Furthermore, the notion of a responsibility to act – which is related to the stronger concept of duty – implies that the Commissioners believe interventions for humanitarian purposes *should* be undertaken (in extreme cases). Although this is not the same as saying that states *can* act (that is, that they have a legal right to intervene), it does raise the question of whether morality and law should be more closely aligned. In other words, the question of right cannot be avoided entirely.

The "responsibility to protect" therefore moves us beyond the state of play that existed at the time of the Kosovo bombing. Indeed, even Hugo

Grotius, the first modern Just War theorist, sought to avoid the language of duty and responsibility in writing about the use of force for humanitarian purposes. Unlike his medieval predecessors, Grotius believed that war waged on behalf of the oppressed was a right rather than a duty: "if danger is evident, it is certain that a man is not so bound, for he may prefer his own life and interests to those of others".[39] As it is with individuals, so it is with states: statesmen are entrusted with the fate of those who form part of their political community and must do nothing that will jeopardize their well-being and interests. The international morality that Grotius defends "*permits* ... intervention but *does not demand it*".[40]

The ethical perspective that supports the ICISS position is not explicitly outlined in the report. However, the logic resembles the Kantian notion of "common morality", which is discernible by reason rather than by custom or consent. As Terry Nardin explains, the principles of this Kantian position "constitute a common moral world in which human beings have rights not as members of this or that community but as members of the human community". Applied to the particular issue of humanitarian intervention, the Kantian logic runs like this: human beings, as rational agents, are owed respect; and respecting other human beings means not only refraining from interfering with their freedom, but also assisting them in achieving their ends. As Nardin shows, this "implies that we must not allow anyone to be harmed by violence if we can reasonably prevent it".[41] But the devil is in the details – particularly in the meaning of "reasonably". On what basis does the responsibility to protect others trump the responsibility to one's own citizens or to one's soldiers who would be put in harm's way?

Effectiveness and legitimacy

Another controversial assumption in the report is that the international community can agree on an effective and legitimate course of action. This critique applies to preventive strategies as well as to military action.

1) Prevention

If the Commission's emphasis on root causes is taken to its logical conclusion, it implies massive economic engagement by states and international organizations. Securing this level of involvement is hampered by a continuing controversy over the most effective development strategy. It also presupposes that states and societies have adequate absorptive capacity for this kind of assistance and can uphold their end of the bargain. When states are weak or corrupt, dealing with root causes through development assistance – to be effective – might well require the suspension of the sovereignty of the state in question.[42] Thus, we are left with a paradox: efforts to build state capacity and prevent conflict lead to a short-term erosion of state sovereignty.

A further issue with prevention is that it is difficult to determine whether and which preventive strategies have been effective because, as two recent commentators have noted, prevention successes are "often a non-event".[43] A successful effort is often limited in scope (containing a conflict) or of very limited duration.

Third, advocates of preventive strategies have minimized the political nature of both information-gathering and analysis. For example, the assessment of a brewing conflict by a body such as the United Nations may differ from that of national intelligence services or critical domestic constituencies.[44] Or, as in the case of Rwanda, opinions may vary on how to interpret the information gathered. As that instance showed, categorizing a situation as a "threat to international peace and security" or "genocide" is in the end a *political* decision.

This leads to the final problem with preventive action: its violation of basic political principles. Prevention requires a level of attention and a commitment of resources that are difficult to generate in the absence of a clear crisis or overwhelming domestic pressure. Given competing demands on limited resources, states will not commit resources unless clearly perceived interests are at stake. It may well be that comprehensive, root-cause prevention strategies are inconsistent with politics as we know it in the developed world.

2) Military action

In terms of the ICISS principles for military action, three are particularly problematic. The first is the requirement of "right intention". As some commentators on humanitarian intervention (including the Commission) have noted, it may be counter-productive to insist that interventions have a purely humanitarian motive. Given the inevitable mix of interests and values in international relations, we would search forever for such a pure case. Furthermore, as the Commissioners themselves acknowledge, "the budgetary cost and risk to personnel involved in any military action may in fact make it politically imperative for the intervening states to be able to claim some degree of self-interest".[45] Their solution is for intervening states to convince their citizenry that "these days, international citizenship is a matter of national self-interest".[46] In our view, however, this does not take sufficient account of the serious political barriers that decision-makers face. As suggested above, in democratic political systems the general population, as well as organized interest groups, pressure their leaders to sacrifice long-term interests for short-term ones. Constituents also play the "us vs. them" card, and question the legitimacy of placing the welfare of foreigners ahead of domestic priorities.[47] Finally, as Nicholas Wheeler explains, the problem with relying on motive "is that it takes the intervening state as the referent object for analysis rather than the victims who are rescued as a consequence of the use of force".[48] As we saw earlier, this reference point is something ICISS had explicitly hoped to move away from. A better approach to evaluating the pros and cons of military action is to concentrate on the prospects for a humanitarian *outcome*. As long as the motives and means do not undermine that result, then a military intervention may be consistent with the responsibility to protect (even if it is accompanied by more strategic rationale).

The second challenge in the ICISS principles for military action is the notion of "reasonable prospects of success". The action in Kosovo has raised complications for this criterion because so much of the criticism levelled at NATO claimed that the situation for individual Kosovars was made *worse* by the bombing. One obvious counter to this charge is that decision-makers cannot know what would have happened in the absence of action. The Kosovo-inspired debate over consequences reveals a number of difficulties with measuring success. Take, for example, the time-frame for measurement. One could argue that in the short run the negative humanitarian consequences of the Kosovo action (both in Kosovo itself but also in the rest of Serbia) exceeded the positive ones. In the longer term, however, the benefits associated with return and autonomy for the Albanians and political changes in Serbia have to be weighed against the ethnic cleansing of the Serbs. How do you balance short against long term? And how do you balance one group against the other? And if you can't answer these questions, what does "reasonable prospect of success" mean?

The third problem is with the approach to the question of "right authority". Despite misgivings from some members of the Commission, the report insists that the UN Security Council is the appropriate body to authorize intervention for human protection purposes. Perhaps the impetus for the Commission, and the strong influence of Secretary-General Annan, influenced this conclusion. The Commissioners are well aware of the objections to such a recommendation: the slowness of Security Council decision-making; the under-representation of key regions; and the political nature of vetoes of the five permanent members. In the wake of the breakdown in diplomacy within the Council in the lead-up to war in Iraq in the spring of 2003, these hesitations about the legitimacy and effectiveness of the Council have become even more pronounced.

On the issue of politicization, the ICISS solution is that the five permanent members of the Security Council should agree not to veto interventions in cases in which their vital interests are not engaged. There are two clear objections to this recommendation. First, if a permanent member is engaged in an act that might occasion intervention, this rule would not preclude that member's use of the veto. Cases that come to mind include Chechnya, Xinjiang, and Tibet. Does the Commission really want to dilute the larger norm of the responsibility to protect by sanctioning this rule of behaviour? Secondly, permanent members have very different views on what constitutes a vital interest. Examples include China's use of the veto on extending peacekeeping operations in Guatemala and Macedonia because it objected to the decisions of both countries to establish diplomatic relations with Taiwan, and the threatened use of the veto by the United States over the continuation of the Bosnian mission due to concerns about subjecting American peacekeepers to the jurisdiction of the International Criminal Court. The latter example is an important reminder that vital interests are not only generated by systemic pressure on states (as realists would argue) but also by domestic politics.

In the end, the report warns that if the Security Council "fails to discharge its responsibility to protect in conscience-shocking situations crying out for action, concerned states may not rule out other means to meet the gravity and urgency of that situation – and that the stature and credibility of the United Nations may suffer thereby".[49] Aside from the question of UN legitimacy, there is a deeper dilemma: claims about the lack of authorization do not absolve those who have the capability to act from their moral responsibilities, which is why others who have employed just war criteria do not include the principle of "right authority".[50]

In defence of the ICISS, it should be noted that alternative sources of authority that are more representative could be even slower to act in situations of supreme humanitarian emergency. Consensus in a body larger than the Security Council will likely be more difficult and even more prone to political considerations.

The responsibility to rebuild

Underlying the ICISS recommendations is a final assumption: that states and international organizations have the capacity to assume the responsibilities outlined in the report. This assumption becomes particularly problematic when one looks at the last section, the responsibility to rebuild. Inevitably, the question arises: if the international community assumes this responsibility inside a country, how and when should it leave? The creation of international administrations in former zones of conflict has become one of the hottest issues in contemporary international relations.[51] In the wake of rebuilding efforts in Bosnia, Kosovo, East Timor, Afghanistan, and now Iraq, doubts are being raised about the ability and willingness of states to sustain long-term reconstruction. Moreover, thorny questions about accountability and democracy have arisen, as the "subjects" of international administrations raise alarm bells about the erosion of their right of self-determination and a new generation of imperialism.

Before concluding this section, it is worth pointing out the risks of reading the ICISS framework of "preventing, responding, and rebuilding" as a continuum. It may be that the most effective strategy is one that simultaneously seeks to prevent, react, and rebuild within a single conflict zone. Thinking in terms of a clear sequence might stall the development of an appropriate mix of policies for dealing with a specific case. Here, the Commissioners might have paid closer attention to the lessons learned by those in the development community, who previously conceived of a "relief-to-development" continuum – that is, humanitarian relief while the conflict was raging and development once there was a peace settlement. Several conflicts (most notably in Angola) were protracted and settlement processes were frozen – leaving a generation of civilians to face severe poverty and underdevelopment. Others (such as in Georgia) occurred in small sections of a country that was otherwise at peace. Analysis of these and other cases led the United Nations Development Programme to abandon the notion of sequentiality implicit in its continuum.

Operational challenges

ICISS takes pains to distinguish military interventions for humanitarian purposes from traditional warfighting. According to the Commissioners, the main difference is that the former seeks to protect populations and the latter aims to defeat or destroy the enemy militarily.[52] In practice, however, the distinction is not so clear-cut. Take the Kosovo bombing again: it may be that coercing a regime that threatens human security means attacking the things most valued by the offending regime – military and industrial infrastructure, for example. Although human protection operations should achieve quick success, and not damage the state's capability to recover economically, the means used and the targets chosen may evolve as a military campaign progresses. Similarly, while civilian lives should be spared – especially since the objective of the campaign is humanitarian – the intervening states must accept that any use of force carries the potential for collateral damage.

There are two other operational issues in the report. The first is the statement that a "clear and unambiguous mandate is one of the first and most important requirements of an operation to protect".[53] This recommendation draws heavily on the findings of the UN-sponsored Brahimi Report on peacekeeping, which stressed the danger to military forces in the field in the absence of clear instructions and commitment from the Security Council.[54] Although quite sensible, the ICISS statement about clarity of mandate is difficult to square with its earlier discussion of the political obstacles to getting any resolution at all within the Council in some situations.[55] There is also tension between the call here for focus and clarity and the recognition elsewhere of the inevitable "vagueness and incrementalism" of multilateral efforts.[56] Ambiguity is often the price of consensus.

The second issue, unified command, is one that ICISS is not alone in grappling with. We have no argument with the claim that "unity of command is essential for the successful conduct of operations".[57] The challenge, however, is that the major powers have shown little willingness to put their national forces under the exclusive command of others. The problem of national contingents taking orders from home rather than from UN force commanders was chronic in United Nations military operations in the 1990s, and there is little evidence of improvement in recent years. Where there is unified command, it tends to be in well-established alliance military structures (such as NATO) where relationships of trust and habits of cooperation are strong. Alternatively, tighter command structures can exist in "coalitions of the willing" led by one state that contributes the bulk of the resources (such as the Australia-led force in East Timor). Given these realities, the ICISS call for unified command implies that interventions for human protection are likely to occur outside formal UN frameworks.

The same criticism could be made about the ICISS's indeterminate comments on civil–military co-ordination. The commissioners are correct to highlight its importance[58] and to recognise its difficulty.[59] Nevertheless, they provide no guidance on how to improve coordination or on what specific obstacles need to be overcome.

There is one area where the ICISS deserves particular praise: its recommendation that intervening nations establish codes of conduct for the behaviour of their troops. Accountability mechanisms for external forces and associated personnel have become increasingly important in the wake of a variety of scandals (including abuse of civilians and the involvement of foreign troops in narcotics and human trafficking). As the Commission acknowledges, maintaining the legitimacy of an intervention for protective purposes is critical. Nothing would delegitimize the enterprise more quickly than situations in which civilians are perceived to need protection from the protectors.

A new consensus?

In Kofi Annan's view, the Commission has delivered on its promise of reconciling the principles of intervention and state sovereignty: "How to protect individual lives while maintaining and even strengthening the sovereignty of States has become clearer with the publication of this report. You are taking away the last excuses of the international community for doing nothing when doing something can save lives. I can offer no higher praise".[60] The real test, of course, is whether the ICISS can meet the Secretary-General's objective of providing practical guidelines for policy makers charged with responding to conscience-shocking situations around the globe.

The aftermath of 9/11

As the Commission was completing its analysis and drafting its recommendations, the world's attention was captured by the horrific attacks on New York and Washington on September 11, 2001. Undoubtedly, those events and their aftermath have affected the pace of the response to the ICISS findings – especially the energy and focus of the Secretary-General. In the foreword to the report, the Commission was also forced to distinguish the kind of military action it was analysing (military action in another state for human protection purposes) from the war in Afghanistan (an act of self-defence designed to respond to terrorist attacks in one's own state).

On one reading, September 11 appears to reverse some of the gains of the Commission. In the course of waging war on terrorism, the powers of sovereign states within their jurisdictions have been increased. Furthermore, states that were previously subject to international criticism for internal repression have skilfully deflected attention by labelling their actions as "counter-terrorist". As John Lewis Gaddis recently put it, in the world after September 11, justice has taken a back seat to concerns about order and security.[61] Before September 11, Western states by and large rejected Russia's branding of its war in Chechnya as a counter-terrorist operation. Russia's rapid closing of ranks with the United States in the struggle against Al-Qaeda, however, quickly resulted in a marked diminution in official criticism from Western states. China likewise has sought to deploy the discourse of anti-terrorism to deflect criticism of its campaign of repression in Xinjiang. And Israel has effectively associated its campaign against Palestinian groups in the Occupied Territories with the global campaign against terror. There is, however, an alternative reading that suggests a greater relevance for the ICISS and its view of sovereignty in a post-September 11 world. We see three main areas where the "responsibility to protect" is linked to the larger war on terrorism.

The first is the Commission's observation that instability within or collapse of a state anywhere in the world can have implications that reach far wider than that particular region. This is true not only for collapsed states such as Somalia or Afghanistan, but also for a country like Pakistan, which has had to accept the "assistance" of outside powers that have a stake in its ability to control rebel and terrorist forces. Second, the ICISS focus on the "responsibility to rebuild" and "responsibility to prevent" has contributed to discussions about the importance of long-term reconstruction efforts for Afghanistan – the first state target in the US war on terror. This position has been pushed strongly by the Secretary-General: "We are confronting these questions right now in Afghanistan, where we are desperately trying to ensure that the international community stays engaged. Prevention, in the case of Afghanistan today, means ensuring that security is provided throughout the country, and not just in Kabul. Otherwise we risk a return to violence and conflict".[62] It is almost two years since Annan made these remarks, and security remains elusive for large sections of the Afghan population. While NATO has been applauded for its decision in the summer of 2003 to take charge of the stabilization forces in Afghanistan (its first mission of this kind outside of Europe), concerns continue to be expressed about the lack of a robust security presence outside the country's capitol.

The final link between "the responsibility to protect" and the events of September 11 relates to the treatment of foreign residents and refugees. As one scholar aptly put it: "A shiver ran down the spine of many people in the West on September 11. The world they looked out upon now seemed a much less secure and much more uncertain place. This changed world provided the rationale for new measures of exclusion and control on refugees, asylum seekers and, in some cases, foreign residents generally".[63] In the United States, the new USA PATRIOT Act allows the government to detain aliens without charge for seven days. Members of identified terrorist organizations (that is, organizations on the Justice Department list) can be deported or barred from entering the country without judicial review. In Britain, the Anti-Terrorism Crime and Security Act allows the Secretary of State to reject asylum claims of people deemed to be a threat to national security, broadens the state's authority to detain suspected terrorists, and curtails appeals by asylum seekers. In Canada, the government's recent Anti-Terrorism Act creates new detention places for foreigners suspected of terrorist activities, provides tighter screening systems to ensure that those involved with terrorist groups do not enter asylum systems, and allocates more resources to deportation. We would argue that asylum is a quintessential recognition of the responsibility to protect. Yet, the state's responsibility to protect its own citizens has caused many of them to limit this fundamental right for others. The defenders of Western governments frequently argue that such "targeted" measures do not threaten "legitimate" asylum seekers. But is that targeting always accurate? If not, then the effort to protect implies the violation of the right of others to protection.

Progress within the United Nations

As part of their strategy for implementing the ICISS report, the Commissioners envisaged a series of initiatives within the United Nations: a General Assembly resolution embodying the basic framework of the "responsibility to protect"; Security Council guidelines for responding to military interventions with a humanitarian purpose and Security Council agreement to suspend use of the veto in such situations; and leadership by the Secretary-General to advance the report's findings.[64] To date, only the final area has seen significant activity.

Within the UN General Assembly, hopes had been raised that there might be a declaration affirming the ICISS approach and principles – akin to the 1970 Declaration on Friendly Relations among States – which could serve as a normative framework for changed behaviour on the part of states and international organizations. But, despite positive responses to the report, there has yet to be any significant work on a substantive resolution. As one official within Canada's Department of Foreign Affairs told us, the general consensus in the General Assembly is that the Commission recommendations constitute a multi-year agenda.

For its part, the Security Council devoted two days at its retreat in May 2002 to discussing the ICISS findings. While the Secretary General claimed that the report was received favourably, the concrete results of the meeting were more mixed. According to the British and French ambassadors, there was widespread opinion in the meeting that if new situations emerged – for example, in Burundi or the Congo – the five permanent members and broader Council would lack the political will to deliver troops and would restrict themselves to condemnatory resolutions. In the case of the Congo, this prediction proved too pessimistic: western states have mobilized to supply military forces to this troubled region through the organizational umbrella of the European Union. Nonetheless, there remains very little appetite in the Security Council to commit to principles *in advance* that would force its hand. Similarly, while some suggest that the ICISS report has made use of the veto more difficult, the Russians have continually resisted any idea of restraint in their veto power.[65] Most troubling of all is the Security Council member that has not engaged substantially in discussions about the ICISS recommendations: the United States. Clearly, its energies have been focused elsewhere, most notably on Iraq.

By the autumn of 2002, as the pressure for war against Saddam Hussein mounted, the proponents of ICISS had conceded that any formal kind of codification – whether a legally binding convention or amendment to the UN Charter – were both unlikely and unwise in the current international climate. Instead of pushing for the issue to be placed on the UN agenda, the Canadian government changed its tactics and attempted to gain support for the ICISS recommendations on a regional basis, particularly in Africa and Asia. In the former case, the inclusion by the African Union and the Southern African Development Community (SADC) in their organizational charters of explicit provisions for intervention to curb genocide, war crimes, and crimes against humanity is potentially very significant.

The war in Iraq

In the summer of 2003, following the end of the military phase of the US-led war in Iraq, Canadian Prime Minister Jean Chrétien once again took up the cause of the "Responsibility to Protect" – this time at the Progressive Governance Summit hosted by Tony Blair in London. But even at this gathering of left-of-centre government leaders – an audience usually amenable to discussions about humanitarian intervention – very little progress was made in moving the debate forward. Developing countries continued to express reservations about the international community bypassing the UN system in authorizing the use of force – a fear that has particular resonance in the aftermath of the Iraq war. Similarly, the Germans expressed concern that the ICISS concept of the responsibility to protect would be twisted to provide an ex *post facto* justification for the campaign to unseat Saddam Hussein (a campaign that the German government consistently opposed). In reality, both of these fears are exaggerated: the Commission report clearly reiterates the importance of UN authorization and restricts the scope for intervention to situations of large-scale loss of life or ethnic cleansing.[66] Nonetheless, the reluctance to embrace the ICISS framework for intervention is symptomatic of the deep divisions that have been created within international society by the Iraq crisis. Even within liberal and left-leaning circles, where a consensus had developed during the 1990s about the principles that should underpin a progressive foreign policy, there is now "open warfare" about whether the ICISS criteria of just cause, right intention, and last resort were fulfilled in the case of Iraq. For some, such as former British Foreign Officer adviser David Clark, the Faustian bargain between liberal proponents of war in Iraq and US neo-conservatives threatens to discredit the concept of humanitarian intervention altogether.[67]

Conclusion

While the Commission made a concerted effort to take account of diverse geographical perspectives, the debate over its recommendations is still largely an *internal* one – within the liberal internationalist community. Despite the claim of its two co-chairs that sovereignty as responsibility is "sufficiently accepted in practice to be regarded as a *de facto* emerging norm",[68] this concept has yet to find its way into the diplomatic vocabulary of the actor identified by ICISS as the appropriate body to authorize intervention for human protection purposes – namely, the United Nations. Ultimately, the significance of the ICISS report lies more in the realm of advocacy than analysis. Its treatment of a broad range of issues related to the responsibility to protect (prevention, criteria for intervention, mandates, command, rebuilding) reflects international politics as the Commissioners think it should be rather than as it is. ICISS does not fully recognize that international politics remains a web of contending normative principles and contingent political interests. Taking the desirability of protection as given, what we need now is a better sense of how to get from where we are to where we want to be.

Notes

1. Kofi Annan (2000) "We the peoples", *Millennium Report*, New York: United Nations, p. 48.
2. For a detailed history of the principle of non-intervention, see R.J. Vincent (1974) *Non-Intervention and International Order*, Princeton NJ: Princeton University Press.
3. Secretary-General's Annual Report to the General Assembly, Press Release SG/SM7136, 20 September 1999.
4. Other funders included the Carnegie Corporation of New York, the William and Flora Hewlett Foundation, the John D. and Catherine T. MacArthur Foundation, the Rockefeller Foundation, and the Simons Foundation.
5. This agenda is summarized by Lloyd Axworthy (2001) "Introduction", in Rob McRae and Don Hubert (eds.) *Canada's New Diplomacy: Protecting People, Promoting Peace*, Montreal and Kingston: McGill-Queen's University Press, pp. 3–13.
6. The other commissioners came from diverse regional backgrounds and perspectives: Gisèle Côté-Harper (Canada), Lee Hamilton (United States), Michael Ignatieff (Canada), Vladimir Lukin (Russia), Klaus Naumann (Germany), Cyril Ramaphosa (South Africa), Fidel V. Ramos (Philippines), Cornelio Sommaruga (Switzerland), Eduardo Stein Barillas (Guatemala), and Ramesh Thakur (India).
7. See *The Responsibility to Protect: Research, Bibliography, Background, Supplementary Volume to the Report of the International Commission on Intervention and State Sover-*

eignty, Ottawa: International Development Research Council (2001). This article considers only the primary report and not the supplementary volume.

8. *The Responsibility to Protect: Report of the International Commission on Intervention and State Sovereignty*, Ottawa: International Development Research Council (2001), p. viii.
9. *Ibid.*, p. vii.
10. Rachel Sylvester (1999) "The Blair Doctrine: this is an ethical fight", *Independent on Sunday* (London), 18 March.
11. For a review of the Chinese position, see Zhang Yunling (2000) "China: whither the world order after Kosovo?" in Albrecht Schnabel and Ramesh Thakur (eds.) *Kosovo and the Challenge of Humanitarian Intervention*. Tokyo: United Nations University Press, pp. 117–127. Russia and India also opposed the NATO action.
12. Three notable examples of the extensive literature on changing norms of sovereignty are Stephen D. Krasner (1999) *Sovereignty: Organized Hypocrisy?*, Princeton NJ: Princeton University Press; Gene M. Lyons and Michael Mastanduno (eds.) (1995) *Beyond Westphalia? State Sovereignty and International Intervention*, Baltimore: Johns Hopkins University Press, pp. 21–42; and Robert Jackson (1990) *Quasi-states: Sovereignty, International Relations and the Third World*, Cambridge: Cambridge University Press.
13. *The Responsibility to Protect: Report*, p. 8
14. *Ibid.*, p. xi.
15. *Ibid.*, p. 13.
16. *Ibid.*, p. 15.
17. *Ibid.*, p. 16.
18. *Ibid.*, p. 9.
19. Forerunners of the current notion include Metternich's Holy Alliance against revolutionary change and Theodore Roosevelt's doctrine of qualified sovereignty at the beginning of the twentieth century. Earlier articulations of "sovereignty as responsibility" can be found in Francis M. Deng, *et al.* (1996) *Sovereignty as Responsibility: Conflict Management in Africa*, Washington: Brookings Institution Press; Fernando Teson (1997) *Humanitarian Intervention: An Inquiry into Law and Morality*, 2nd ed, Dobbs Ferry, NY: Transnational; and Samuel Barkin (1998) "The evolution of the constitution of sovereignty and the emergence of human rights norms", *Millennium* 27(2): 229–52.
20. Henry Kissinger (1957) *A World Restored*, London: Weidenfeld and Nicholson; Hedley Bull (1977) *The Anarchical Society*, London: Macmillan; and Robert Jackson (2000) *The Global Covenant*, Oxford: Oxford University Press.
21. See, for example, Mohammed Ayoob (2002) "Humanitarian intervention and state sovereignty", *International Journal of Human Rights* 6(1): 81–102.
22. *The Responsibility to Protect: Report*, p. 19.
23. *Preventing Deadly Conflict: Final Report* (1997) New York: Carnegie Corporation of New York.
24. *The Responsibility to Protect: Report*, p. 19.
25. *Ibid.*, p. 25.
26. Cited in Simon Chesterman (2002) "Discussions at the Release of *The Responsibility to Protect*", International Peace Academy, February (www.ipacademy.org).
27. *The Responsibility to Protect: Report*, p. 7.
28. See, for example, Robert I. Rotberg (2002) "Failed states in a world of terror", *Foreign Affairs* 81 (July–August): 127–140.
29. *The Responsibility to Protect: Report*, p. 8.
30. *Ibid.*, p. 34.
31. *Ibid.*, pp. 32–33.

32. *Ibid.*, p. 33.
33. It is, however, mentioned in the supplementary volume, where the research team excludes the possibility of an intervention on utilitarian grounds (*The Responsibility to Protect: Research*, p. 143). In view of the Commission's desire to create and sustain a broad consensus, the omission is understandable. On the other hand, one could be forgiven for wondering whether such compromises irretrievably compromise the very norm they are attempting to embed.
34. See Michael Barnett (2002) *Eyewitness To A Genocide: The United Nations and Rwanda*, Ithaca: Cornell University Press, ch. 4. The legal implications of how the United Nations categorized the killing are analysed by William Schabas (2000) in *Genocide in International Law: The Crimes of Crimes*, Cambridge: Cambridge University Press, pp. 459–464.
35. Adam Roberts, "Intervention: suggestions for moving the debate forward", submission to the International Commission on Intervention and State Sovereignty, Roundtable, London, 3 February 2001.
36. The legal debates are summarized in Independent International Commission on Kosovo (2000) *The Kosovo Report*, Oxford: Oxford University Press; and Simon Chesterman (2001) *Just War or Just Peace? Humanitarian Intervention and International Law* (Oxford: Oxford University Press.
37. The moral arguments date back to the medieval Just War tradition and are given modern expressions by Michael Walzer (2000) *Just and Unjust Wars*, 3rd ed., New York: Basic Books; Nicholas Wheeler (2000) *Saving Strangers: Humanitarian Intervention in International Society*, Oxford: Oxford University Press; Terry Nardin (2002) "The moral basis of humanitarian intervention", *Ethics and International Affairs* 16(1): 57–70; and Jennifer M. Welsh (2003) "Taking consequences seriously: objections to humanitarian intervention", in Jennifer M. Welsh, *Humanitarian Intervention and International Relations*, Oxford: Oxford University Press.
38. *The Responsibility to Protect: Report*, p. 15.
39. Cited in Chesterman, *Just War or Just Peace*, p. 14.
40. Nardin, "The moral basis of humanitarian intervention". This moral position is also outlined in Charles Beitz (1979) *Political Theory and International Relations*, Princeton NJ: Princeton University Press.
41. Nardin, "The moral basis of humanitarian intervention", pp. 64–65.
42. David Williams (2000) "Aid and sovereignty: quasi-states and the international financial institutions", *Review of International Studies* 26 (October): 557–573.
43. Fen Osler Hampson and David M. Malone (2002) "Improving the UN's capacity for conflict prevention", *International Peacekeeping* 9(1): 78.
44. *Ibid.*, p. 81.
45. *The Responsibility to Protect: Report*, p. 36.
46. *Ibid.*, p. 36.
47. For further analysis of the democratic constraints on humanitarian intervention, see Allen Buchanan (1999) "The internal legitimacy of humanitarian intervention", *Journal of Political Philosophy* 7 (March): 71–87.
48. Wheeler, *Saving Strangers*, p. 38.
49. *The Responsibility to Protect: Report*, p. xiii.
50. See, for example, Walzer, *Just and Unjust Wars*, and Wheeler, *Saving Strangers*.
51. Two recent contributions to the debate are Richard Caplan (2002) *A New Trusteeship? The International Administration of War-torn Territories*, IISS Adelphi Paper 341; and Simon Chesterman (2002) "East Timor in transition: self-determination, state-building and the United Nations", *International Peacekeeping* 9(1): 45–76.
52. *The Responsibility to Protect*, p. 57.

53. *Ibid*., p. 60.
54. *Report of the Panel on United Nations Peace Operations* (New York: United Nations, 2000), Section F, paras 56–64.
55. *The Responsibility to Protect*, pp. 53, 59.
56. *Ibid*., p. 59.
57. *Ibid*., p. 61.
58. *Ibid*., p. 61.
59. *Ibid*., p. 62.
60. Kofi Annan, Address to the International Peace Academy Seminar on "The Responsibility to Protect", Press Release SG/SM/8125, 15 February 2002.
61. John Lewis Gaddis, "And now this: lessons from the old era for the new one", in Strobe Talbott (ed.) (2001) *The Age of Terror: America and the World After September 11*, New York: Basic Books, p. 14.
62. Kofi Annan, Address to the International Peace Academy.
63. Matthew Gibney (2002) "Security and the ethics of asylum after September 11", *Forced Migration Review* 13 (June): 42.
64. *The Responsibility to Protect*, pp. 74–75.
65. "La Russia s'oppose à un 'usage raisonné' du droit de veto", *Le Monde* (Paris), 3 juin 2002.
66. For one Commissioner's attempt to win over the sceptics, see Ramesh Thakur (2003) "Chrétien was right: It's time to redefine a 'just war'", *Globe and Mail* (Toronto), 22 July.
67. David Clark, "Iraq has wrecked our case for humanitarian wars", *Guardian* (London), 21 August 2003. Michael Ignatieff, an ICISS Commissioner, is a prominent example of a liberal supporter of the US-led war in Iraq.
68. Gareth Evans and Mohamed Sahnoun (2002) "The Responsibility to Protect", *Foreign Affairs* 81(6): xx.

11

The responsibility to protect: Humanitarian intervention and the principle of non-intervention in the Americas

Jorge Heine

Since the end of the Cold War, internal conflicts – in many cases plain and simple civil wars – have erupted, increased, or multiplied all over the planet. From Colombia to Kosovo, from Rwanda to East Timor, some seventy such conflicts have shaken the world. In the absence of the bipolar structure that provided a semblance of order for the international system post-World War Two, and that forced countries to choose sides between East and West, the newly emerging – largely unipolar – system has "liberated" many ethnic and religious tensions that had been submerged under the ideological mantle of the conflict between capitalism and socialism. The result has been a veritable frenzy of tribal wars, "ethnic cleansing", and genocidal massacres that can be compared to some of the worst war crimes of the twentieth century. Scientific and technological progress has made it possible for humankind to make a quantum leap into what has been called the Third Industrial Revolution (largely because of breakthroughs in the areas of IT and telecommunications), which has the potential to improve radically the standard of living of most people on Earth. At the same time, though, we seem to have regressed to forms of human cruelty that would seem to belong to the Middle Ages or earlier – such as the systematic amputation of limbs of innocent civilians in Sierra Leone.[1]

While widespread, these human rights violations have also become much more visible to the rest of the world – through CNN, among other media – thus making people much more aware of the suffering that is being inflicted on their fellow human beings. The plight of the 25 to 30 million Internally Displaced Persons (IDPs) because of various types of conflicts worldwide is thus watched, not just on the evening news, but around the clock by people all around the globe. Not surprisingly, human rights law and humanitarian law have become perhaps the fastest growing area in international law. The European and the Inter-American Human Rights systems, though not without their limitations, are perhaps the most elaborate expressions of these advances in international justice, with formal courts and commissions that routinely look into matters that only a few decades ago would have been considered strictly domestic affairs. The Special Tribunal for War Crimes in the former Yugoslavia and the one for Rwanda are good examples of the unwillingness of the international community to tolerate massive human rights violations and/or let the main perpetrators of such violations get away with it.

The arrest of General Pinochet in London in October 1998 was another landmark event in customary human rights law: for the first time a former head of state was arrested abroad for human rights violations committed in his own country. And although he was eventually allowed to return to Chile after having been detained in England for 16 months, it was his arrest abroad that opened the doors for a full-scale trial for murder and kidnapping in Chile, leading to the lifting of his parliamentary immunity, indictment, and eventual sentencing.[2] A key (albeit unsuccessful) element in the defence of General Pinochet, both by his own lawyers and by the Chilean government, was that of sovereignty and of sovereign immunity. Yet, the degree of scepticism with which this was treated, both by the British courts and international public opinion, was revealing of the remarkable shift we have seen over the past few decades on matters related to sovereignty. No longer can the latter be invoked as a shield behind which the perpetrators of human rights violations can hide with impunity. And there is, of course, a cascading effect. The arrest of General Augusto Pinochet, a former head of state, in London in October 1998, was followed in May 1999 by the indictment of President Slobodan Milosevic, the then head of state of former Yugoslavia, by the Special Tribunal for War Crimes in the former Yugoslavia in The Hague, and his subsequent arrest and imprisonment in Belgrade in April 2001.

There is, then, a problem. On the one hand, a veritable flood of internal conflicts in many countries around the world (including, of course, Europe, which many thought would have been immune from these types of troubles) in which human rights violations are not just a by-product of the fighting, but a key tool for terrorizing target populations and for publicizing the various parties' capacity to inflict damage on each other. And the extent to which it is civilians that are increasingly the victims becomes evident when we realize that whereas civilians constituted only 10 per cent of all casualties in World War I and half of all casualties in World War II, this figure reached 75 per cent in the largely internal conflicts of the 1990s. There are, then, many more "innocent bystander" victims in today's conflicts, and their plight is much more apparent and obvious to the rest of the world. The international community will simply no longer stand idly by while such atrocities take place. The 1999 NATO bombing of Kosovo, which marked a real turning point in this matter, can largely be explained because of the enormous pressure being exercised by Western public opinion, which would not stand for "another Bosnia".[3]

Yet, such actions fly in the face of national sovereignty, the very bedrock of the international state system ever since the Treaty of Westphalia in 1648. The Westphalian meaning of sovereignty entails essentially non-interference by states in the internal affairs of other states. Despite the United Nations Charter of Human Rights and international conventions on crimes such as genocide and torture, it was not until the last quarter of the twentieth century that the notion of human rights violations as "crimes beyond borders" became more or less established – among other things, because of the activities of NGOs such as Amnesty International and Human Rights Watch.[4]

The tension between the need to intervene to protect human lives and the sovereign right of a nation state to handle its internal affairs as it sees fit is thus evident. The very United Nations system is based on sovereignty – it is predicated on the existence of sovereign member states. New members can only join the United Nations once they have become independent – that is, when they too have become sovereign states. Once universal international organizations (like the UN), or regional ones (like the Organization of American States), or even individual states, start deciding on their own when the sovereignty of another state should be respected and when not, the very foundation of the international system is endangered, and the elaborate international legal framework – the *ius gentium* – that guides state behaviour may collapse, or so it is argued.

As should be apparent from the preceding discussion, there is possibly no single more vital and urgent international legal issue facing us than the one that, for want of a better term, has come to be known as humanitarian intervention. In fact, at the Millennium Assembly of the United Nations in September 2000, the Secretary-General, Kofi Annan, put it before the heads of state and government that met in New York, as a key challenge for the United Nations and the international community in years to come.[5] As he put it, "if humanitarian intervention is, indeed, an unacceptable assault on sovereignty, how should we respond to a Rwanda, to a Srebrenica – to gross and systematic violations of human rights that offend every precept of our common humanity?" After which he went on to argue,

> But surely no legal principle – not even sovereignty – can ever shield crimes against humanity. Where such crimes occur and peaceful attempts to halt them have been exhausted, the Security Council has a moral duty to act on behalf of the international community. The fact that we cannot protect people everywhere is no reason for doing nothing when we can. Armed intervention must always remain the option of last resort, but in the face of mass murder, it is an option that cannot be relinquished.

To draw out the appropriate lessons from Kosovo (which, as already mentioned, has been a key turning point in the debate on humanitarian intervention) and as a result of a Swedish initiative, the International Commission on Kosovo met through 1999 and 2000, delivering its report to the United Nations Secretary-General in November 2000.[6]

On the other hand, the International Commission on Intervention and State Sovereignty, a Canadian-led initiative designed to respond to the challenge issued by Secretary-General Annan has also submitted its report. Its purpose was "to build a broader understanding of the problem of reconciling intervention and sovereignty and to foster global political consensus on how to move from polemics, and often paralysis, towards action within the international system, particularly through the United Nations",[7] and it did its work through round tables held around the world, and independently commissioned research. Aimed at reconceptualizing the debate on the issue, somewhat along the lines the Brundtland Commission followed in the 1980s with the notions of development and environmental sustainability, it set out to recast the terms of debate from an alleged (and highly controversial) "right to intervene", to a "responsibility to protect".

The purpose of this paper is to provide a conceptual discussion of the issue, as well as an assessment of extant perspectives on the subject in Latin America, where it has had a much lower profile than in Europe, Africa, or Asia, and where the debate is therefore still very much in its infancy.

The nature of the problem

The polarization and passion that the issue has triggered can be ascertained from the fact that no agreement exists even on the very term to be used for it. While Humanitarian Intervention (HI) is the most widespread expression, it evokes strong reservations, if not outright resistance, and it is symptomatic that the ICISS decided not to use it.

By joining two seemingly disjointed terms – one associated with benevolent assistance and the other with the use of (often illegal) military force across international borders – HI runs the risk of sounding like an outright oxymoron. Needless to say, resistance to the use of the term is especially strong among those who oppose what it entails – among which the Non-Aligned Movement (NAM) has taken a very vocal lead, with three resolutions of the G-77 condemning the very notion of HI. Many human rights activists have historically been strongly opposed to military intervention, no matter what its objectives. "Intervention for humanitarian purposes", "intervention for humanitarian action", "intervention for humanitarian assistance" are some of the alternatives that have been suggested.

There is, no doubt, something jarring about the term HI, and one can fully understand the reservations many people have about it. In a way, it seems almost designed to cleanse the notion of "intervention" of its rather unsavoury connotation and history and give it a new lease on life, as it were. Yet, new realities demand new concepts and new analytical tools to examine and act on them. In a sense, precisely because the term HI evokes such strong reactions, it is especially apposite to describe this new phenomenon of the post-Cold War world. There is an edge to it, a provocation that gets people thinking. The seeming contradiction in terms embodied by the notion of humanitarian intervention captures nicely the policy and political dilemmas the issue puts squarely on the table. None of the more elaborate and less concise formulations does so, at least not to the same degree.

What exactly is the nature of the dilemma we are confronting? On the one hand, the ethical imperative makes it very difficult, if not outright impossible, for the international community to stand idly by while thousands or even hundreds of thousands of innocent lives are brought to an end; we are, after all, part of a common humanity. On the other hand, elaborate international institutions have been created, anchored on principles such as national sovereignty, the peaceful resolution of controversies, and the non-intervention in the internal affairs of states. In fact, many of the developments in international human rights law and international humanitarian law over the past few decades have emerged as a result of efforts to somehow make the defence of these rights compatible with the latter principles.

In strictly abstract terms, then, the essence of the problem boils down to one of "humanity versus institutionality". If so put, the choice is obvious; yet, in descending from the lofty heights of ethics and morality in general terms to the concrete policy choices to be made by statesmen and diplomats in often highly ambiguous specific situations, answers become less clear cut. To put it succinctly, there would seem to be a gap between the needs that exist wherever and whenever massive and systematic human rights violations take place and the modalities available to the international community to deal with the situation.

On the one hand, there is Article 2 of the United Nations Charter, which establishes the sovereign equality of all member states and that they all shall refrain from the threat or use of force against the territorial integrity or political independence of any state, as well as that "nothing contained in the present Charter shall authorize the United Nations to intervene in matters which are essentially within the domestic jurisdiction of any state", while also stating that "this principle shall not prejudice the application of enforcement measures under Chapter VII". On the other, the latter measures need to be approved by the Security Council.

To ask for the authorization of the government of the affected state – as was done for example (successfully) of the Indonesian government in the case of East Timor in 1999, about which more is mentioned below – is often beside the point. In many situations, it is the very government that is behind these human rights violations, as was the case in Kosovo. In such circumstances, any intervention, by definition, would have to be against the will of the government. A somewhat different situation obtains in the case of failed or disintegrated states – such as Somalia or Sierra Leone – in which there is no authority with effective control over the national territory, and roving bands do as they please, a case in which the rationale for HI is even stronger.

If a state fails to fulfil one of its primordial duties, that is, to protect the human rights of its citizens, and in fact, may be the main agent behind those very violations, it would lose the right to hide behind national sovereignty to continue to commit those very atrocities. At the same time, as will be seen below, these violations must be massive and systematic. Isolated, trivial, or occasional human rights violations would not qualify for HI.

On the other hand, under whose authority would HI take place? And this leads us directly to the heart of the matter. For the international community to act – that is, send troops that would put an end to the genocide or other atrocities being committed – it needs authorization from the United Nations Security Council. There are a number of cases in the recent past where this authorization to prevent further bloodshed in highly conflictual situations came forth relatively quickly: the cases of Haiti in 1994 and East Timor in 1999 come to mind, with both having what could be considered a successful outcome. In the case of Rwanda – where the genocide of half a million Tutsis in 1994 in the face of constant procrastination by the United Nations, the Security Council, and the main powers, has come to embody the very worst type of abuse HI is designed to prevent – simple inaction proved fatal (as United Nations Secretary-

General Kofi Annan put it, "the genocide in Rwanda will define for our generation the consequences of inaction in the face of mass murder"). But the real problem emerges when, in the face of a quickly deteriorating situation of human rights violations in a given country, authorization to intervene is not forthcoming because of opposition within the Security Council. That, of course, is exactly what happened in Kosovo, where both Russia and China opposed the use of force to end the human rights violations in that province by the government of Yugoslavia. In the end, NATO acted on its own, thus giving an added impetus to HI as a policy tool, albeit making it even more controversial.

The key question thus revolves around the commitment of the Security Council to put an end to massive human rights violations wherever they occur. And that commitment is not obvious. As a Presidential Statement issued by the Council put it,

> The Council emphasizes the need fully to respect and implement the principles and provisions of the Charter ... and norms of international law ... It affirms its commitment to the principles of political independence, sovereign equality and territorial integrity of the States. The Council *also* [my emphasis] affirms the need for respect for human rights and the rule of law. It will give special attention to the humanitarian consequences of armed conflicts. The Council recognizes the importance of building a culture of prevention.[8]

This text reflects in many ways the ambiguities and tensions inherent in HI, and the many questions it raises. In fact, a standard critique of treatments of the issue is that they are much better at raising questions than at providing the tough answers many observers feel the matter deserves at this point.

In this context, and before moving on to a more detailed discussion of the very thorny legal and political issues raised by HI, one critical objection to it needs to be confronted. This is the one of selectivity, or, as it has been summarized so aptly, "If Kosovo, why not Chechnya?" Behind this question lies the obvious perception in some quarters, mainly in the South, to which we will return, that HI is largely an instrument of the big powers, to be used for their own ends – in other words just another expression of neo-colonialism. As President Abdelaziz Bouteflika of Algeria has put it, "Sovereignty is the last defense in an unequal world".

As appealing as this view may be in many quarters, and as useful as it may be to dismiss the whole notion of HI as just another plot of the big powers, conniving once again to gain advantage of developing nations, it does not hold up under close analysis. In the first place, two of the P-5 (i.e. the five permanent members of the United Nations Security Council) – that is Russia and China, which are certainly among the big powers in today's world – have been adamantly opposed to any version of HI that does not go through all the formalities of Security Council approval. And, despite Kosovo, the United States itself has by no means been on the forefront of the HI debate, with many observers having the distinct impression that the last thing the United States government wants or needs is another set of rules for multilateral action that would stand in the way of US unilateral initiatives. In fact, it has been the Northern European countries, with a long tradition of international humanitarian involvement, and countries such as Canada, Australia, and New Zealand that have been especially active in the development of the theory and practice of HI (especially valuable doctrinal and conceptual work has been done in countries such as Denmark and the Netherlands, which few would categorize among today's big powers).

In fact, it could be argued that HI, rather than being a tool of the big powers (at least one of which in today's world can act unilaterally without any recourse to the protective umbrella of international law), should be categorized as an instrument of "soft power", allowing smaller countries, which have traditionally relied on multilateral organizations and the rule of the law of nations to achieve their objectives, to stand up for certain humanitarian values.

Moreover, the fact that you cannot intervene everywhere does not mean you cannot intervene anywhere. An obvious requirement for HI is that, as a result of it, more good than harm is created – which would hardly be the case if, say, NATO bombers were to be dispatched to bomb Moscow to stop the fighting in Chechnya.

The evolving debate on humanitarian intervention

The very different perspectives extant on the issue are well reflected in the following summary of the United Nations General Assembly 1999 debate:

> On the notion of humanitarian intervention, there were those speakers who observed that respect for human rights has become more important than the sovereignty of States. Against this background, it was argued that the international community should intervene in the face of gross and systematic violations of human rights, with or without prior approval of the United Nations, particularly the Security Council. Other Member States expressed the view that the new notion of humanitarian intervention has the potential for destroying the Charter, undermining the sovereignty of States and overthrowing legitimate governments. They stressed that the protection of human rights is an obligation incumbent upon all governments within the context of the exercise of their sovereignty and constitutional order. Still, other delegations, recalling the spirit of the Charter of the

world body, emphasized that nations could not intervene in the internal affairs of others without a specific Security Council mandate. They observed that any massive violations of human rights leading to humanitarian emergencies required the coordinated action of the international community through the United Nations, and not by a fiat of unilateral action and creation of faits accomplis that would set bad precedents.[9]

It is against this background of polarized opinion that we must set the evolving debate in international law on HI. As Nicholas Wheeler has observed, through its action in Kosovo, NATO set a very important doctrinal challenge to the non-intervention rule in international law.[10] It did not argue that it ought to be jettisoned – just that it ought to be modified. The notion emerged that Kosovo would open the floodgates to all sorts of interventions, yet that has not been the case. Nonetheless, the point is not so much to discuss the merits or demerits of the action taken in Kosovo (or, later that year, in East Timor), but to develop a framework for thinking how a particular case fulfils the HI requirements.

A first premise of the discussion is that the problem only arises if there is opposition to take concerted action by the international community within the Security Council – in other words if there are not nine votes (including the concurring votes of the five permanent members) out of the fifteen member states that form the Council. Under such circumstances, what is to be done?

A standard response has been to develop a set of guidelines that would allow the international community to establish whether HI is warranted or not. Some have argued that it would be impossible to come up with legally binding guidelines (for which an obvious question would be "binding to whom?") and the most one can do is to develop some morally binding ones. The difficulties of reconciling international opinion and that of the people directly affected by interventions were highlighted by the invasion of Cambodia by Vietnam in 1978, arguably not necessarily of a humanitarian nature. Although condemned by the United Nations Security Council and the General Assembly, it was welcomed by the Cambodians, who were thus able to free themselves of the dictatorial and bloody rule of Pol Pot.

In this context, some of the guidelines that have emerged for deciding whether HI should take place or not are the following:

- That there should be a clear pattern of massive and systematic human rights violations. The murder of several thousand Tutsis in Rwanda in April 1994 would certainly qualify under this heading. The potential danger to US citizens of a tense political situation (an argument used by the United States in the 1965 invasion of the Dominican Republic, and then again in Grenada in 1983) would not.

- A second condition would seem to be there be some regional support for HI. If it is only extraregional powers that see a dangerous situation, there may be something wrong with their perceptions, or so the reasoning goes.
- A third condition is what we might call the proportionality rule: that the force to be used be proportionate to the problem at hand. According to some views, the massive bombing of Yugoslavia was somewhat out of sync with the human rights violations of the Albanian Kosovars.
- Finally, as already mentioned, it is important that HI causes more good than harm. The overall effects of intervention have to be assessed before deploying any troops. In the opinion of some observers, Somalia before HI was split into three or four parts; after US troops left, it was split into 100 pieces.

In this context, the question of thresholds becomes significant. For some, the more specific one can get, the better. The scope and intensity of the humanitarian crisis at hand is thus a vital reference point; prospects for early domestic resolution would lead to withholding any HI decisions. Another key element would be what we might call "the spillover factor", in other words, the degree to which the situation can spread to neighbouring countries, which would point towards accelerating intervention.

For others, getting too specific in these matters can end up being counterproductive. According to this view, the establishment of certain criteria can be of help, but should never be the sole determining factor, in a situation in which ambiguity is of the essence. By creating, say, a situation in which one of four or five criteria is not met, a party to a conflict may want to inoculate itself against the possibility of HI, but otherwise feel free to act in a highly inhumane fashion. International politics, like domestic politics, is ultimately a dynamic process based on strategic interaction, and no static listing of circumstances can fully account for it, and even less so manage to avoid undesirable outcomes on the basis of criteria such as these.

Having identified these criteria for HI, the next question is who would actually be the agent to take action. Several possibilities come to mind:

- The United Nations itself. This, of course, can only happen if the Security Council has given the go-ahead for any such operation.
- Regional organizations like the Organization of American States (OAS), the Organization of African States (OAU), or other such bodies.
- An alliance of several countries, as was done by Australia, Thailand, and other countries in East Timor.
- A single state.

For a time the prevailing notion was that regional organizations and regional powers were somehow better suited to such operations than universal organizations (like the United Nations) or extraregional powers. Yet, that may or may not be the case. For one, such action may open the doors to "regional bullies"; in addition, regional organization may simply not have the resources (and here we are referring to political as much as to material resources) to deal with such complex situations as those calling for HI. Key criteria in this regard are effectiveness, military suitability, and speed with which action can be undertaken. On the other hand, the United Nations may well be overburdened with demands for its presence in crisis situations, and some delegation of authority to regional bodies or coalitions to deal with them may be the only way to cope.

Latin American perspectives on HI

Yet, while the debate on HI gets more and more polarized both in international fora and in the pages of international law journals, Latin America, despite a distinguished tradition of significant contributions to many areas of international law, is perhaps the one region in the world which has shown the least interest in the matter.[11] While it is difficult to pinpoint a single reason for this, I would like to put forward at least four.

One of them is the historical pattern of US interventionism in Latin America since the days of "dollar diplomacy". This, of course, led to the development of a highly elaborate doctrine of non-intervention. The respect for national sovereignty and that of the juridical equality of states became key principles in the region, later established as such in the charter of Organization of American States, albeit often honoured more in the breach than in its observance. Upon hearing the word intervention, Latin Americans automatically think of "gunboat diplomacy", and the repeated invasions of Cuba, Puerto Rico, Haiti, and the Dominican Republic, as well as of US intelligence actions to destabilize the governments of Joao Goulart in Brazil and of Salvador Allende in Chile, rather than of humanitarian actions on behalf of the Albanian Kosovars or the East Timorese. This necessarily clouds their view of the issue.

The fact is that, more than most regions in the world, Latin America has formalized a rather elaborate set of doctrines, treaties, and protocols designed precisely to avoid interventions of one sort or another, which does not mean it has always succeeded in doing so. The Drago doctrine rejected the coercive collection of debts by foreign powers, and the Estrada doctrine opposed the practice of "recognizing" new governments as a manifest violation of national sovereignty.[12]

Hemispheric security, built on the OAS Charter, the Inter-American Treaty of Reciprocal Assistance and the Inter-American Treaty for

Peaceful Conflict Resolution, was based on the notion of collective security, that is, "all against the aggressor".

Secondly, over the past two decades or so, a rather complex and sophisticated set of legal instruments to deal with human rights violations in the region has emerged, leading to what has been called the Inter-American Human Rights System. This included the Inter-American Human Rights Court and the Inter-American Human Rights Institute (both based in San José, Costa Rica) and the OAS Human Rights Commission (headquartered in Washington, DC), a body which has raised its profile quite highly since the mid-seventies. Anchored in the Pact of San José (signed in 1969, but which only came into effect in 1979, after being ratified by the requisite number of states) this system of human rights protection, though not without loopholes and difficulties, has made some progress in eroding old-fashioned notions of national sovereignty in the region.

If the idea of HI (or "the responsibility to protect", as the ICISS put it) is to find some favour within the Latin American community of nations, something that still remains to be seen. One likely place for it to be "nested", or embedded, at least in its monitoring if not the decision-making dimension, would be within the Inter-American Human Rights System, where early warning and other such capabilities to prevent massive loss of life could be installed.

On the other hand, after the almost universal return of democracy to the Hemisphere by 1990, considerable progress in formalizing the region's commitment to democratic rule has also been made. This was ratified at the OAS Assembly held in Santiago in July of 1991, as well as in the various "democratic clauses" enshrined in regional and sub-regional integration schemes such as MERCOSUR, not to mention the three Summits of the Americas (held in Miami in 1994, in Santiago in 1998, and in Quebec City in 2001, respectively). With massive human rights violations often the product of authoritarian regimes and/or generalized institutional breakdowns, the regional return to democracy and the fact that the process has been sustained for more than a decade now is seen by many observers as important guarantors that no massive human rights violations are in the offing. In fact, as one Brazilian official put it, "There is no situation in Latin America right now that would justify a humanitarian intervention. The only one that came close to it was Haiti a few years ago, which was dealt with accordingly".[13] Latin Americans, then, see no immediate threat of genocide-like situations in the region. On the other hand, massacres such as the ones obtaining in Rwanda and Sierra Leone, or such bloody conflicts as the one occurring presently in the Democratic Republic of the Congo, which have raised such concern in Western Europe, are seen as far removed and quite marginal to regional priorities.

Finally, and quite apart from the principle of non-intervention itself, there is an additional legal element that stands in the way of Latin American appreciation of HI. Like much of contemporary international law, the very notion of HI is ultimately based on precedent and custom; the present discussion of it is strongly grounded in the Kosovo and East Timor cases, rather than in abstract considerations of what is desirable in humanitarian law. Yet, such discussions raise enormous difficulties in a region in which treaties and formal protocols provide the basis for international obligations, and the Napoleonic code constitutes the anchor for domestic law. Thus it is ironic that for a region with no permanent members in the Security Council, it boasts a number of small and weak states that are the biggest champions of the unalloyed prerogative of the veto exercised by the P-5 when it comes to the possibility of HI, a subject to which we shall return.

At the same time, there is an emerging awareness that "context matters" – that is, that it is different to talk about intervention in general and HI in particular in the age of globalization than to do so in the era of gunboat diplomacy or that of the Cold War. And quite apart from the reservations many Latin American governments and academics may have about HI, the fact is that over the past decade (i.e. since the end of the Cold War) three interventions of sorts have taken place, albeit with mixed results: Haiti (from 1994 until now); Peru (with the special OAS mission tasked with supervising the 2000 presidential elections) and Colombia (through the so-called "Plan Colombia" initiated by the Clinton administration in close coordination with the government of President Andrés Pastrana). Although the one in Haiti comes closest to it (and it was also the only one that had United Nations Security Council support), none of them really qualifies as HI. Both in Haiti and in Peru, the key concern of the international community has been to establish and/or restore proper democratic procedures and institutions; in Colombia, it has been to help the government restore law and order in the vast swaths of national territory presently under control of the Fuerzas Armadas Revolucionarias de Colombia (FARC) and other guerrilla movements and of the various drug cartels.

Most observers would agree to the proposition that significant steps toward democratization have taken place as a result of those interventions, both in Haiti and in Peru; the situation in Colombia remains unresolved, although polls indicate a remarkable swing in favour of international intervention over the past few years, which many Colombians see as the only way to overcome the deep crisis the country is facing.

Given the highly unequal relationship with the Hemisphere's big power (the United States), for most of the twentieth century Latin America tried, as best it could, to rely on the doctrine and principle of non-intervention as one way to hold unilateral interventions by the United States at bay. This principle was often honoured more in the breach than in its observance. Yet, it constituted an important element in the emerging architecture of the Inter-American system, although one that continued to pit the United States vis-à-vis its Southern neighbours, that often split up in various coalitions marked by the degree of subservience to or independence from Washington.

Yet, one of the hallmarks of Inter-American diplomacy over the past twenty years or so has been the emergence of much more forceful and assertive mechanisms of regional political cooperation, starting with the Contadora Group in 1983 and culminating in the Rio Group in 1990 (to which one could add the Iberoamerican Summits that started in 1991, and the American Summits that did so in 1994). One of the leitmotivs of this regional political cooperation has been the promotion of democracy in the Americas, often with quite overtly interventionist tools.

In short, although the sort of large-scale humanitarian disasters that have occurred in Africa, Southeastern Europe or Asia – thus triggering calls for HI – have not taken place in Latin America in the recent past, other, less dramatic situations, mostly related to the need to restore democratic rule have led to the use of a variety of mechanisms just short of overt military force (the Haitian exception notwithstanding). This "creeping interventionism" may be laying the foundations for a somewhat different perspective on the changing nature of intervention and state sovereignty in the Americas in the post-Cold War era, an argument buttressed by the interesting evolution of the debate on the subject over the past two years.

This debate has to be set against the background of the increasing significance of the concept of Human Security, which has been gaining widespread support in Latin America, leaving behind the doctrine of National Security, so dear to the military regimes of the seventies and eighties. As defined in United Nations Development Programme (UNDP) in its Human Development Report 1993, it puts people (as opposed to the state) at the very centre of national priorities: "The concept of human security must change in such a way that from relying exclusively on national security it does so on the security of people, from security through weapons to security on human development, from territorial security on food, employment and environmental security".[14]

In subsequent documents and reports, the UNDP further developed this notion of security as an integrative concept that blends seven key components: economic, food, health, personal, community, environmental and political security. Since then, the concept has had a widespread impact on relevant actors in the international system, reframing the debate on economic development as well as on security issues. Canada has played an important role in its promotion, at a time when it has also considerably increased its diplomatic presence and activity in Latin America.

In addition to the key elements mentioned above, the notion of human security also includes the use of military force when needed. It was on that basis that Canada fully supported NATO's actions in Kosovo. Arguably, humanitarian intervention could be described as a policy tool within the human security doctrine.

In that context, the latter has been making some headway in Latin America. In the Central American Democratic Security Treaty signed in San Pedro Sula in 1995, Central American countries subscribed to the notion of human security.[15] Within the OAS, there have also been some acknowledgment of its significance by Secretary General César Gaviria (who has described it as "an important contribution to the discussion and definition of ... the Hemisphere's political agenda").

Within the Rio Group's 2001 agenda, both the notions of human security and that of humanitarian intervention were among the key themes to be discussed by member countries in their various meetings leading to the Presidential Summit held in Santiago, Chile, in August 2001. Some background information on the way HI has so far been considered by various Latin American governments may shed some light on how the debate is likely to be framed in the future.

The first reference to HI in any address by a Latin American head of state or foreign minister to the United Nations General Assembly was made by Chilean Foreign Minister Soledad Alvear in her September 2000 address to the United Nations. While Chile reiterated its adherence to the principles of non-intervention and self-determination, it also recognized that they must be made compatible with post-Cold War realities. As Minister Alvear put it: "We cannot stand idly by in the face of humanitarian catastrophes provoked by great conflicts, which is why we propose that in such circumstances, and according to the UN Charter, help for those that are suffering can quickly be undertaken through concerted multilateral action".[16]

Two days later, after a meeting in New York between the Rio Group and the European Union (EU), the then Mexican Foreign Minister Rosario Green asked their fellow Latin American colleagues to stay on to discuss a matter of great concern to her. This was whether, in the light of some references to HI in the speech of one colleague, the Rio Group was still fully committed to the principle of non-intervention, so dear to the countries of the region, and so vital to Latin American diplomacy. In this, she was fully supported by the Foreign Minister of Uruguay, Didier Opertti, himself a distinguished international lawyer, who at that meeting also came out very strongly against HI, pronouncing himself against NATO's actions in Kosovo, which in his view were totally against the most basic norms of international law and the United Nations Charter.

Mexico pressed the Group for a clear-cut statement reaffirming its support for non-intervention, but did not succeed. Brazil, represented at the meeting by Deputy Minister Pericaz, demurred, since this was a complex issue that required further consideration, and although countries like the Dominican Republic, referring to the 1965 US invasion, also supported the Mexican position, no consensus was achieved on the matter. It was concluded, however, that the matter deserved further study, and it was tabled for the Iberoamerican Heads of State Summit that would take place in Panama in November 2000.

Ironically, the Mexican effort to have Latin American countries reject HI had backfired, and ended putting the issue squarely on the regional agenda. As a compromise, it was Minister Opertti who was asked to present a formal document on the subject in Panama, which he did. In any event, during the remainder of the 55th Session of the United Nations General Assembly, several Latin American countries expressed their views on HI. Venezuela took a very strong stand against any use of force not authorized by the United Nations.[17] Much the same could be said about Mexico, a country that had previously insisted on its view that the use of force in international affairs, even if apparently motivated by the most noble causes, can only be a source of greater instability, uncertainty, and violence.[18] Cuba was also adamant in its position: it stated that the so-called "right of humanitarian intervention" was today the greatest threat to peace and international security; according to Cuba, this was something being promoted by a small group of Northern countries led by the United States, which were trying to promote this notion in various international organizations.

Argentina, on the other hand, while reiterating its support for the principle of non-intervention, expressed its concern about outbursts of violence against vulnerable groups like women and children during armed conflicts and underscored that the international community cannot remain indifferent to humanitarian crises.[19] Costa Rica also shared this concern, saying that humanitarian crises constituted themselves a threat to international peace and security, and that in such cases the United Nations could not ignore their responsibility.[20]

As has been pointed out, then, at the beginning of this discussion on HI, Latin American perspectives on it could be distributed along the following spectrum. Cuba and Venezuela were at one end of it, strongly opposing the very notion and denouncing it as a tool of Northern countries bent on violating the sovereignty of developing nations. Close to that, but in a more legalistic rather than political argumentation, were Uruguay and Mexico, with Colombia in a more ambiguous position, as was Brazil. Much closer to an open-minded consideration of the issue was Argentina, a country that has played a very active role in peace-keeping operations. Costa Rica and Chile, in turn (especially the latter), have taken the lead in putting HI on the regional agenda.

The Uruguayan position on HI represents one extreme in the spectrum of views taken by Latin American countries with, revealingly, the other extreme being represented by Chile, which has not taken a position, but, rather, would simply like to open the discussion on a matter very much on the agenda of many universal and regional fora. It is the Uruguayan position though which endorses the initiation of a collective discussion on the issue that can be summarized as follows:[21]

- With the exception of legitimate defence, the use of force or the threat of its use has been banned in international law. The only way to overcome this is through a proper authorization of the United Nations Security Council. HIs would need such an authorization. Military operations undertaken by a State or group of States without such authorization place themselves outside international law.
- Any delegation by the Security Council of its powers to States or groups of Member States to undertake coercive actions is not exempt from this authorization. Such would be the case of NATO's actions in Kosovo.
- To keep peace and international security are, by definition, essential and unavoidable objectives of the international system based on the United Nations Charter and international law more generally. For that reason, those objectives cannot be delegated in violation of the international legal order.
- To respond quickly and effectively to a situation of flagrant violation of human rights is a duty of the international community, which must be fulfilled according to existing norms. Notwithstanding this, one must realize that because of the veto in the Security Council, authorization of the use of force may not be viable, undermining the standing of the organization before public opinion because of inaction.
- The debate on the very definition of humanitarian interference and its legal basis, as well as the possible inclusion of the latter as a new enabling hypothesis for the use of force, is unavoidable if one wants to protect the prestige and credibility of the international system in general and that of the United Nations in particular. A key issue in any such debate would be the delicate question of the delegation of the powers related to the use of force to regional organizations, and particularly the right of the latter to dispose freely of them.
- What cannot be allowed is a highly visible and often dramatic, but in

the end *de facto*, situation that ends up with the adoption of selective criteria for intervention that can put into question the very universality of the humanitarian cause that is being invoked.
- The question of regional defence mechanisms deserves a special and detailed treatment.

Given the novelty of the issue and the reluctance of most Latin American countries to depart from established norms and principles of international law, including the one of non-intervention and the peaceful resolution of disputes, it is not surprising that most other countries in the region do not have fully elaborated positions on HI.

The way forward: a research agenda on HI

As should be apparent from the preceding section, not many definitive answers on HI have been forthcoming from Latin America, and those that have, have been rather conventional restatements of traditional notions of international law. However, a useful exercise was undertaken by the Permanent Representatives to the United Nations of the Rio Group member countries in two meetings held on 11 and 25 October 2000 in New York. Although very preliminary and tentative, they came up with a document on HI to be submitted to the foreign ministers of the Rio Group. It provides as much a list of questions of the matters that worry diplomats of the region about HI as it does a research agenda of sorts from a Latin American perspective.[22] The document refers to the following key subjects:

1. Conceptual aspects

a) Definition and its key elements
No universally accepted definition of HI is available, nor have its key constituent elements been identified. The need to discuss and analyse the concept at some length with the participation of all Member States should be apparent.

2. Predominant perceptions

b) HI as military intervention
The assimilation of HI to the use of force through military intervention is present in some quarters and ought to be clarified.

c) HI and humanitarian assistance
Humanitarian assistance is a universally accepted mechanism that must have the express assent of the recipient state and is regulated by various resolution of the United Nations General Assembly. The need to draw a

sharp distinction between humanitarian intervention and humanitarian assistance should be apparent.

3. The non-intervention principle in Latin America

d) The Latin American and Caribbean tradition

The region's contribution to the non-intervention principle in the Inter-American System and more generally is a significant asset, very much worth referring to in the context of HI.

4. Universality of HI

e) Scope of acceptance

Is it possible to come up with a definition and a set of key elements of HI that will enjoy universal acceptance? If its acceptance is only at a regional level, what should be the reaction of extraregional states?

f) Scope of application

What would be the scope of application of HI? In other words, can a Northern, developed country be the subject of HI, or is the concept to be applied only in the South?

5. Causes and justification of HI

g) Causes

What can cause an HI? Would it be because of genocide, crimes against humanity and war crimes – that until now fall under the jurisdiction of the International Criminal Court – or would there also be other motives, and which ones would those be?

h) Justification and the ethical imperative

Once you have established the objective causes leading to HI, would the latter be justified in all cases? How would you find a balance between the urgency of responding adequately to humanitarian crises and the need to respect the sovereign integrity of States?

i) Decision-making

Who decides whether the objective causes for HI exist or not? Who determines whether HI is justified or not? What are the risks that threaten the universal application of the concept?

6. HI and the United Nations

j) Respect for the United Nations Charter

Respect for the UN Charter is a sine qua non requirement for whatever is accepted as HI.

k) Treatment in the General Assembly
Although Secretary-General Kofi Annan has unofficially introduced the concept, HI is not a subject that has been dealt with in the General Assembly. For that purpose, are the working mechanisms of the Assembly such as open working groups, informal consultations at the plenary session, or other formats agreed on by consensus valid?

l) Treatment in the Security Council
In practice, the Security Council has made decisions on matters that have been referred to as HI. Can it continue to make these decisions without previous consultation to the Member States who are not part of the Council?

m) Relations with other bodies of the system
What would be the relationship between HI and the work of the international courts created by the Security Council and eventually bodies such as the International Criminal Court? What would be the relation with the work of the Human Rights Commission, the Special Rapporteurs of the High Commissioners for Human Rights and for Refugees, among others?

n) United Nations reform
How will this debate on HI affect United Nations reform?

7. Competent body to authorize HI

o) United Nations Security Council
Is the Security Council the only competent body to authorize a HI? How can we make compatible the wish to be able to rely on a concept of HI of universal validity with the existence of a veto by five members of the international community?

p) Regional organizations
Do regional organizations play some role in HI in the light of the United Nations Charter?

At the Foreign Ministers meeting of the Rio Group held in Panama in November of 2000, it was thus decided to establish a working group that would look into the matter and come up with some specific proposals for the Santiago Summit of August 2001. This group met in Santiago on 5 May 2001 in a session that had a slight overlap with a round-table discussion of the International Commission on Intervention and State Sovereignty (ICISS) held in Santiago on 4 May at the invitation of the Chilean government.

The Rio Group Working Group

The first thing that became apparent in the discussions of the working group was how uncomfortable most Latin American governments are with the very use of the term humanitarian intervention. Several of them were of the opinion that the term ought to be restricted to cases where the use of force had been fully authorized by the United Nations, but even then, some preferred not to use the term at all. As a result, it was decided to "freeze" the matter, as it were, by postponing any decision on the use of the term for later on.

A distinction was also made between interventions designed to avoid (or stop in their tracks) humanitarian crises that conform to the definition of genocide and those that arise from massive human rights violations or from the need to avoid the breakdown of democratic institutions. There was generalized agreement that, while some form of intervention was warranted in all three cases, the only one that justified the use of military force was the first one. While mediation efforts, diplomatic pressure, and other forms of international actions were quite acceptable for the other two, the use of force was not.

The use of force is, of course, at the very heart of the current debate on HI. And on this, the position of the Rio Group is that it can only be undertaken within the rules and boundaries of the United Nations system (countries like the United States, of course, take a different position, reserving for themselves the right of unilateral intervention). Having said that, there was also agreement that this system has not worked in a very satisfactory manner, and the question thus becomes how this might be changed.

In the United Nations Charter the use of force is only authorized in self-defence (which can be individual or collective) or when there is a threat to international peace and security. Traditionally, the latter had been interpreted as referring to an international conflict, but more recently the view that it can also apply to a situation extant in only one country has been gaining ground (although this is not a perspective that is fully accepted within the Rio Group).

However that may be, a key challenge becomes how to come up with a more objective (and measurable) definition of what constitutes an HI that would embody a threat to international peace and security – which, was acknowledged, can happen in Latin America. Even after having done so, though, the decision would have to be made by the Security Council. Aware of the inaction of the Council on critical occasions in the past (such as in Rwanda), the issue thus turns on how to ensure a more proactive role for it. Tinkering with the UN Charter was seen by most countries as an unlikely possibility, and a somewhat different approach was thus put forward:

- If there is a humanitarian crisis and the Security Council is unwilling to act, one possibility would be to strengthen the hand of the Secretary-General by enabling him to enlist endorsements for it by the High Commissioner for Human Rights and the High Commissioner for Refugees, as well as by the International Red Cross (although whether the latter would be willing to take part in what some might construe as a political action remains an open question). Such prestigious, high-level support might sway the Council, or so the reasoning goes.
- On the other hand, if the Council is unable to act, because of the actual or potential exercise of the veto by one of the five permanent members (which is precisely what happened in Kosovo in 1999) and an impasse is created within the Council, the proposal would be to take the decision on HI directly to the General Assembly, the most democratic of all the UN organs – which would be taking the matter to the very limit of UN legality. Given the reliance on precedent and customary law within the UN system, this suggestion, if taken up and implemented, might lead not only to a more effective United Nations on matters related to HI, but also to a somewhat different distribution of power within the Council and the organization more generally.

In the end, although much progress took place in Latin America in the discussion of HI during the period 2000–2001, the Rio Group was unable to reach agreement on the issue at the Santiago Summit of August 2001, largely because of opposition by Colombia. And after September 11 of that year, other international issues have come to the forefront of the Inter-American system, leaving little room for HI.

Conclusion

The debate on HI in Latin America is still in its very early stages. Most governments are rather reluctant to get involved in it, as it questions many of the key assumptions of the existing international system. Within civil society, though there are exceptions, most NGOs, academics, and other organizations do not see within the foreseeable future the occurrence of massive human rights violations like the ones we have seen in some African countries in the nineties, and therefore do not envision the need for any sort of HI, however it is framed or justified. At the same time, as the cases of Haiti, Colombia and Peru illustrate, the intervention of the international community in the internal affairs of various Latin American countries is taking place in the post-Cold War era in any event, despite the reservations about the legacies of dollar diplomacy. Perhaps the most dramatic shift in this regard can be found in Colombia, where, from an outright rejection of any form of foreign meddling in internal affairs, public opinion polls now show an overwhelming majority of Colombians support any form of international intervention that would bring to an end the violence that is crippling their country.

As in so many other international issues, while grappling with HI Latin America would seem to be torn between its Southern realities and its Northern aspirations. To the degree that HI has become somewhat of a North–South issue (with the NAM taking a very strong stand against it), some countries, including such unlikely partners as Uruguay and Cuba (two countries so far apart on other issues that they recently broke off diplomatic relations), see it in stark black and white terms as a quite unacceptable breaking of the established rules of international society. Others (like Chile and Argentina), aware that it is an issue that will not go away, would rather deal with it in ways that are not simply a restatement of the relevant articles of the United Nations Charter, but that actually confront the very real human rights violations problems faced in so many places by the international community today. However that may be, it should be evident that HI will remain with us as one of the most critical and controversial issues on the international agenda at the beginning of the twenty-first century.

Notes

1. This chapter draws on research and analysis undertaken for a study on the subject commissioned by the Ford Foundation. It is based on interviews on the subject done in Brasilia, Mexico City, Lima, Bogotá, Washington DC, and Santiago between September 2000 and May 2001, as well as on the deliberations of the conference "Humanitarian Intervention: How Can We Do It Better?", Wilton Park, England, 19–22 February 2001; at the Regional Roundtable Discussion of the International Commission on Intervention and State Sovereignty (ICISS) held in Santiago, Chile, on 4 May 2001; and on briefings of the Chilean Ministry of Foreign Affairs on the Rio Group Working Group on Humanitarian Intervention on 23 May 2001.
2. See Ruth Wedgewood (2000) "Augusto Pinochet and International Law", *McGill Law Journal* 46: 241; Curtis A. Bradley and Jack L. Goldsmith (1999) "Pinochet and International Human Rights Litigation", *Michigan Law Review* 97: 7; and J. Craig Barker (1999) "The Future of Former Head of State Immunity after Ex Parte Pinochet", *International and Comparative Law Quarterly* 48: 937–949.
3. See Tim Judah (2000) *Kosovo: War and Revenge*, New Haven: Yale University Press; Independent International Commission on Kosovo (2000) *Kosovo Report: Conflict, International Response, Lessons Learned*, Oxford: Oxford University Press; and Elisabeth Sidiropoulos (ed.) (2001) *A Continent Apart: Kosovo, Africa and Humanitarian Intervention*, Johannesburg: South African Institute of International Affairs. For a broader discussion of the use of US military force in the nineties, see Richard N. Haass (2000)

The Use of American Military Force in the Post Cold War World, Washington DC: Brookings Institution.

4. See Jack Donnelly (1998) *International Human Rights*, 2nd edition, Boulder, Colorado: Westview Press.
5. For a full statement of Secretary-General Kofi Annan's position on HI, see his "Human Rights and Humanitarian Intervention in the Twenty First Century" (2000) in Samantha Powers and Graham Allison (eds.) *Realizing Human Rights: Moving from Inspiration to Impact*, New York: St Martin's Press, pp. 309–320.
6. Albrecht Schnabel and Ramesh Thakur (eds.) (2000) Kosovo and the Challenge of Humanitarian Intervention: Selective Indignation, Collective Intervention and International Citizenship, Tokyo: United Nations University. See also Michael O'Hanlon (2000) *Saving Lives with Force: Military Criteria for Humanitarian Intervention*, Washington DC: Brookings Institution.
7. Pamphlet of International Commission on Intervention and State Sovereignty (ICISS), n.d.
8. UN Document S/PRST/1999/34. Quoted in Henry J. Steiner and Philip Alston (2000) *International Human Rights in Context: Law, Politics and Morals*, Oxford: Oxford University Press, pp. 651–652.
9. UN Press Release, GA/SM/105, 2 October 1999. Quoted in Steiner and Alston, *ibid.*, p. 653.
10. Nicholas Wheeler (2000) *Saving Strangers: Humanitarian Intervention in International Society*, Oxford University Press.
11. It may be worth noting that this writer was the only Latin American participant at a major international conference entitled "Humanitarian Intervention: How can we do it better?", held at Wilton Park, England, a UK Foreign Office conference centre, 19–22 February 2001, which was attended by some 90 government officials, academics, and NGO representatives from all over the world.
12. This and the following paragraphs draw on the informative paper "Reflexiones para la formulación de una posición nacional sobre la llamada 'intervención humanitaria'" by Colombian analyst Adolfo García (Bogotá: mimeo, n.d., but approximately April 2001; author's files). Highly sceptical of the whole endeavour, the outlook of Mr. García is in itself emblematic of what we might call the "predominant perspective" in much of Latin America on this issue.
13. Interview with Dr. José Humberto de Brito Cruz, Assistant to the President, Brasilia, 19 September 2000.
14. See Programa de Naciones Unidas para el Desarrollo, Desarrollo Humano 1993, Santiago: United Nations (1993).
15. See title II of the Treaty. For an excellent discussion of the notion of human security more generally and its relevance to Latin America, see Miriam Villanueva (2000) "La seguridad humana: ¿una ampliación del concepto de seguridad global?", *Revista Mexicana de Política Exterior*, 59 (February): 106–113.
16. Speech by Chilean Foreign Minister María Soledad Alvear to the 55th General Assembly of the United Nations, New York, September 2000.
17. Speech by Venezuelan Foreign Minister Ignacio Arcaya to the 55th General Assembly of the United Nations, New York, September 2000.
18. Speech by Mexican Foreign Secretary Rosario Green to the 55th General Assembly of the United Nations, New York, September 2000.
19. Speech by Ambassador Enrique Candiotti, Secretary of State for Foreign Affairs of Argentina to the 55th General Assembly of the United Nations, New York, September 2000.

20. Speech by Costa Rican Foreign Minister Roberto Rojas to the 55th General Assembly of the United Nations, New York, September 2000.
21. This draws on the document circulated by Foreign Minister Opertti at the Iberoamerican Summit Meeting in Panama City, November 2000, "Documento del Ministerio de Relaciones Exteriores del Uruguay, Didier Opertti, Intervenciones Humanitarias", Montevideo, 8 November 2000 (author's files).
22. "Issue paper", sobre Interención Humanitaria presentado a consideración de los Ministros de Relaciones Exteriores del Grupo de Rio por parte de los Representantes Permanentes ante Naciones Unidas, New York, October 2000 (author's files).

12

Ideas, institutions, and the evolution of women's human rights

Elizabeth Riddell-Dixon

The symbiotic relationship between ideas and institutions is clearly evident in the United Nation's efforts to promote women's rights. Ideas serve as the impetus for the creation of UN bodies promoting gender equity and as the bases for their conceptual approaches, policies, and programmes. Institutions, in turn, develop ideas, market them and translate them into practice. This chapter examines the evolution of ideas, concepts, and institutions pertaining to women's rights. It begins with a brief historic overview of UN efforts to develop women's rights. This discussion provides a backdrop for the focus of the chapter, which is to examine the evolution of ideas and concepts and the role of institutions and institutionalization in the UN's efforts to promote gender equity. It concludes by identifying and discussing some of the factors that have promoted the development of ideas and institutions in this area.

Historical overview

The UN Charter specifies the promotion of human rights as one of the organization's key objectives and it prohibits discrimination against women.[1] Nonetheless, it took the UN 30 years to convene the first World Conference on Women. The UN Commission on the Status of Women and NGOs had been pushing for years to have a conference held; but their pressure was not enough. Instead, it took the growing realization that the failure to consider women had seriously undermined the effectiveness of several important UN programmes, including the Green Revolution, to prompt the General Assembly in 1972 to proclaim 1975 to be International Women's Year and to convene the first intergovernmental conference ever held on the status of women. In 1975 the First World Conference on Women was held in Mexico City. On its recommendation, the General Assembly declared 1976 to 1985 to be a Decade for Women. In 1979 – half way through the Decade – a second conference on women was held in Copenhagen to assess the progress made in implementing the goals established in Mexico City. A third conference was convened in Nairobi in 1985 – at the end of the Decade – to assess the progress that had been made in promoting and protecting women's rights in the preceding ten years and to recommend strategies for overcoming obstacles to women's advancement in the political, economic, and social spheres. Ten years later, in 1995, a fourth conference was convened in Beijing, to examine the major obstacles to the advancement of women in 12 interconnected, critical areas of concern: poverty, decision-making, education, human rights, health, media, violence, environment, armed conflict, girl-child, economic equality, and national machinery for the advancement of women.[2] The conference prescribed objectives and strategies for removing the barriers that prevent women from enjoying the full range of their human rights and from participating fully and equally in all spheres of life. "Equality, development and peace" served as the themes for the Decade as well as for each of the four UN conferences on women.

In between the Third World Conference on Women and the Fourth World Conference on Women, a series of world conferences and summits were convened, each of which addressed women's issues.[3] Although the documents they produced were not legally binding, they did reflect a growing consensus on women's issues and women's rights, and precedents set in one set of negotiations were often used as bases for moving the agenda ahead at subsequent conferences and summits.

Since the First Conference on Women was convened, significant progress has been achieved in the development of ideas and concepts pertaining to women's rights and in the establishment of institutions to promote gender equity. For the sake of clarity, ideas and institutions are discussed separately below; however, the linkages between them are important and extensive.

Ideas

A major conceptual shift has taken place from the "add women and stir" mentality, that was all too prevalent at the time of the First World Conference on Women, to the concept of gender and gender analysis. A key motivation for holding the 1975 conference on women was the recognition that women had to be considered if other objectives, particularly economic development, were to be addressed effectively. By the end of the Decade, women's rights were seen as being important in their own right. Furthermore, the focus was shifting from women as a category of people to gender as a concept that examines the socially constructed roles of men and women.

Gender is not about women per se. Instead, it is about the socially constructed roles of men and women and the impact that these roles have on the respective abilities of men and women to enjoy the full range of their political, economic, and social rights. We know, for example, that conflict affects both men and women but that it affects them differently because of the roles that they are assigned in society. Most societies ascribe the role of warrior to men. Thus in war, male combatants face the threat of death and wounding. A man who has been badly wounded may no longer be able to provide for his family; hence he may not be able to fulfil the culturally defined responsibility of a man to be a breadwinner. As a result, not only may his family face hardship but the man, himself, may suffer a major loss of prestige in his family and in the community, more broadly, and his own sense of self-worth may be badly eroded. Rape is all too commonly used as "tool of war" and its usage is closely related to gender-defined roles. The belief that men are by nature aggressive and sexually demanding and women are naturally passive and sexually submissive encourages other beliefs ("men can't help it", "women actually want it") that legitimate systemic sexual abuse.[4]

Women are frequently seen as the mothers of their race; hence to defile them violates a whole people. In cultures where women are seen as the property of men, to degrade a woman is a direct affront to the men to whom she is seen to belong. A woman who has been raped may face a host of serious problems: emotional trauma, HIV infection and other sexually transmitted diseases, unwanted pregnancy, and ostracism within her own community. It is because of gender roles that women are more likely to be refugees than are men. As refugees, men and women often face very different problems. Men are often separated from their wives and children, which deprives them of their ability to assume their socially prescribed roles of protectors and providers for their families. Women must seek to care for their children as well as for themselves. They may face demands from male officials for sexual favours in exchange for safe passage, food, clothing, and documentation for themselves and their children. If the UN is to promote the well-being of people worldwide, then it must understand and address their respective needs which are profoundly affected by gender roles.

In addition to the major conceptual breakthrough that came with gender analysis, the past 25 years has also seen a tremendous expansion in the breadth of entitlements classified as women's rights and in the depth of analysis that is devoted to them. For example, at the Third World Conference on Women in 1985, governments were just beginning to recognize rape and domestic violence as social problems.[5] In contrast, one of the 12 critical issue areas addressed in the 1995 Beijing *Platform for Action* was the violence against women that occurs in all societies (e.g. domestic violence, predatory assaults). The *Platform for Action* not only holds states responsible for protecting women from violence but it also prohibits "invoking any custom, tradition or religious considerations"[6] as excuses for neglecting this responsibility.

Although considerable advancements have been made over the past 25 years, it would be naive to assume that there has been a steady progress towards enhancing the status of women in society. The language adopted at one conference or summit has not always been accepted automatically at subsequent sets of negotiations.

Although the term "gender" had been used in the Rio (Conference on the Environment and Development), Vienna (Conference on Human Rights) and Cairo (Conference on Population and Development) documents, a group of Catholic, Islamic, and other countries insisted it be bracketed in the Beijing draft on the basis that its meaning was unclear and that it would be interpreted to endorse lesbianism and bestiality. The issue was resolved just prior to the Beijing conference by the formation of a special Gender Contact Group attended by 60 nations, chaired by Selma Ashipala of Namibia, which affirmed that "gender" was to be interpreted and understood as it is in ordinary, generally accepted usage![7]

The report of the Informal Contact Group on Gender was accepted by the Fourth World Conference on Women and hence the concept is once again understood in terms of the socially constructed roles ascribed to men and women. Nonetheless, the term "gender" does not exist in every language; thus, the concept is by no means universally understood, let alone applied.

The issue of cultural relativism provides a further illustration of halting progress, where gains made in one forum were later reversed in subsequent sets of negotiations.[8] The controversy revolves around the question of whether the universality of women's human rights should take precedence over respect for religious, cultural, and social rights. If priority is given to the universality of women's rights, a state cannot refer to cultural, religious, or social traditions as justification either for passing legislation that contravenes its obligations to uphold international human rights or for failing to exercise due diligence in preventing and punishing violations of women's rights by non-state actors. On the other hand, if religious, cultural, or social traditions are accorded priority, then a state can use them as justification for ignoring and for violating women's human rights. The 1993 Vienna Conference on Human Rights, while recognizing the need to consider historical, cultural, and religious backgrounds, agreed that states were required to promote and protect all human rights regardless of their own political, economic, and cultural systems. One year later, at the 1994 Cairo Conference on Population and Development, however, the balance shifted in favour of cultural relativism. The Cairo conference stressed the sovereign rights of states rather than their duties to uphold international human rights and specified that religious, cultural, and ethical values were to be given full respect. The Cairo language, which implied precedence for cultural, religious, and social backgrounds, was picked up at the 1995 Copenhagen Summit for Social Development and was included in the draft Beijing *Platform for Action* as a "chapeau" to all the critical areas of concern, including health, education, and violence against women. On the very last day of the Fourth World Conference on Women, this highly controversial issue was resolved and those championing women's human rights prevailed over those advocating deference to cultural and religious values. The battle was won in Beijing but the war continues as debates over cultural relativism continue to plague UN discussions of women's rights.

Significant advances were made on reproductive rights at the Fourth World Conference on Women. Seven years later, at the 2002 World Summit for Sustainable Development, the US, Argentina, and fundamentalist Islamic states sought to roll back progress that had been made on reproductive rights at previous negotiations. After an arduous struggle, a coalition comprising Canada, Norway, Australia, Switzerland, and the European Union succeeded in preventing such rollbacks; however, the issue is far from being resolved and is likely to keep surfacing in the foreseeable future.

The evolving debates over cultural relativism, gender, and reproductive rights exemplify the often tortuous path of progress that is frequently marked by the one step forward and then one (if not two) steps back. The economic, social, and political well-being of women around the world remains inferior to that of men, and in many cases the well-being of women has actually deteriorated.

Of the 1.3 billion people living in poverty, 70 per cent are women; the majority of the world's refugees are women; female illiteracy is invariably higher than male illiteracy. Women and girl-children are treated as commodities in cross-border prostitution rackets and the pornography industry. Millions of girls are still subject to genital mutilation, while women in every country are regular victims of domestic violence. In many countries, women lack access to reproductive health care and every day women are targeted in armed conflicts. Women's economic, social, and cultural rights continue to be neglected.[9]

Cuts to social programmes in both the North and the South are negatively affecting women in several important ways. Women are deprived of programmes, such as day care and health care, that are vital to their well-being. When social services are cut, gender roles defining women as care givers dictate that it is women who will be expected to take care of children in the absence of daycare programmes and to take care of sick relatives for whom there are no longer hospital beds. Cuts to social services mean fewer jobs in sectors where women are frequently employed. Sadly, the strides made in the evolution of thinking about women's rights and gender issues often have not been matched by tangible improvements in the daily lives of women around the world.

Institutionalization

As we saw with the evolution of ideas, the path to greater institutionalization has neither been smooth nor straight. Ideas become institutionalized when they are translated into international norms – both those that are legally binding and those that are not legally binding – and when they provide the basis for creating and expanding offices and bodies devoted to gender equity.

Ideas about women's rights were translated into concrete legal norms in the 1979 Convention on the Elimination of all Forms of Discrimination Against Women, which is one of the six principal human rights treaties. The Convention, which had been ratified by 165 states, addresses systematic discrimination against women and specifies state responsibilities to promote women's equality in all spheres of life, including political, economic, social, and cultural realms, both in the public domain and within the family. Former UN Secretary-General Boutros Boutros-Ghali described the Convention on the Elimination of All Forms of Discrimination Against Women as "a landmark treaty in the struggle for women's rights" and "an international bill of human rights for women".[10] State Parties to the Convention are required to submit a national report at least every four years to the Committee on the Elimination of Discrimination Against Women. The Committee meets annually to review the reports and works with State Parties to assist them in overcoming barriers to full compliance. The committee's findings are submitted to the General Assembly in an annual report.

The hope of getting a second treaty – this time dedicated specifically to eradicating violence against women – has not yet been achieved.[11]

There is, however, a Declaration on the Elimination of Violence against Women,[12] which the United Nations General Assembly adopted by consensus in 1993. Although not legally binding, the Declaration recognizes a state's obligation to prevent violence against women, to investigate cases involving violence against women, and to punish the perpetrators.

Since the First Conference on Women, there has been a marked improvement in the quality of the documents that each successive conference has produced. The *Plan of Action*, which was adopted at the 1975 conference, was described as a "shopping list of issues related to women".[13] In contrast, the 1995 *Platform for Action* outlined specific objectives for each of the 12 critical issues of concern and provided detailed strategies for their attainment. As such, the latter provides a comprehensive programme to enhance the social, economic, and political status of women and to secure gender equality. Over time the conference documents covered increasingly broad ranges of issues and they addressed these issues more concretely, subjected them to more in-depth analysis and proposed strategies for overcoming roadblocks to progress. Although the existing norms could always be stronger and more all encompassing, the quality and quantity of the norms is not the principal problem. If one had compliance with the existing norms, gender equity would be close to being a reality.

Within the United Nations, several significant programmes and bodies have been established to promote women's rights and gender equity. Created in 1946, the Commission on the Status of Women is an intergovernmental body, whose 45 Member States meet annually to develop policies and recommendations for the advancement of women's political, civil, economic, and social rights. In addition to presenting its recommendations to the Economic and Social Council, the Commission makes the Council aware of serious situations requiring immediate attention and recommends action to address such problems. Within the UN system, the Commission is responsible for monitoring the implementation of the Beijing *Platform for Action* and acts as a catalyst in mainstreaming of a gender perspective throughout United Nations activities.

1946 also saw the establishment of the Division for the Advancement of Women, which seeks to ensure that women are able to participate and benefit, as equal partners with men, in all aspects of life, including governance, peace and security, sustainable development, and human rights. It promotes the inclusion of women's issues on the global agenda and the mainstreaming of a gender perspective within the UN system and in regional and national bodies. The Division provides support services, such as supplying advice, conducting research, and developing policies and programmes, for other UN bodies (e.g. the Commission on the

Status of Women, the Committee on the Elimination of Discrimination against Women and the Economic and Social Council) as well as for member states.

The Development Fund for Women and International Research and Training Institute for the Advancement of Women were established on the recommendation of the First World Conference on Women. The former works to ensure that women are full and equal participants in all phases of development activities, from the planning through the implementation and subsequent evaluation to, if necessary, the redesigning of programmes. It has funded many projects and initiatives to help empower women throughout the South, politically, economically, and socially. Within the UN system, the Development Fund for Women serves as a catalyst to ensure that the needs and concerns of women are on the agenda when international, regional, and national development issues are being discussed.

The International Research and Training Institute for the Advancement of Women conducts research and training programs to promote the participation of women in all levels of the development process. It functions as an autonomous body within the UN system, whose budget is funded by voluntary contributions from member states, intergovernmental organizations, NGOs, and private donors. To promote networking, information sharing, and collaborative research and training, it has developed the Gender Awareness Information and Networking System to assist UN bodies, other intergovernmental organizations, NGOs, foundations, and various private organizations in using the new information and communications technologies to promote gender equity.

The position of Special Rapporteur on Violence Against Women was created in 1994 to investigate violence against women, its causes and its consequences, and to recommend strategies for eradicating this violence.[14] The Special Rapporteur works closely with other special rapporteurs, special representatives, working groups, and independent experts of the Commission on Human Rights and the Sub-Commission on Prevention of Discrimination and Protection of Minorities, and committees set up to administrate the main human rights treaties.

At the national level, 146 states now have government agencies devoted to the advancement of women. Yet in spite of these national and international bodies, much remains to be done: "in all cases women's programmes and policies remain marginal in the system and rarely have the resources or authority to match the mandates given".[15] As of 2 July 2002, 46 countries still lacked national machineries for the advancement of women. Furthermore, one cannot assume that once created an institution will be maintained, and support for its work will continue to flow. At the 1995 Conference on Women, the Holy See and its allied states, as well as the fundamentalist Islamic states, sought to narrow and weaken the mandates of the Commission on the Status of Women and the Division for the Advancement of Women, and to reduce the resources allocated to them. Canada responded by proposing language both to review and strengthen the mandate of the Commission on the Status of Women and to request that the UN Secretary-General provide adequate resources from the regular UN budget to enable the Division for the Advancement of Women to function effectively. With the support of the European Union, the United States and the Group of 77, Canada secured the adoption of its proposal. The end result was positive but the fight was tough and there was no prior assurance of a favourable outcome. While women's issues have never been central on international, regional, or national agendas, the awareness of women's issues has grown over the past 25 years, as evidenced by the creation of programmes and offices to facilitate the advancement of women.

The concept of gender is being increasingly mainstreamed within the UN system, although the process is far from complete. Mainstreaming involves making a concept central to the work of an organization by incorporating it into the pre-existing frameworks and structures. The concept of mainstreaming is usually understood to exist in juxtaposition to the concepts of marginalization and being relegated to the sidelines – concepts which all too aptly describe the position of women's rights within the United Nations.[16] In March 1993, the Commission on Human Rights passed the first resolution to integrate women's human rights with the UN human rights mechanisms.[17] The commitment for such integration was reiterated in the 1993 Vienna Declaration and Programme of Action[18] and again in 1995 in stronger and more specific language in the Beijing Declaration and Platform for Action.[19] In 1997 UN Secretary-General Kofi Annan mandated mainstreaming gender analysis throughout the UN system.[20] Since 1997, the Secretary-General has presented annual reports to the Economic and Social Council on the steps being taken to mainstream a gender perspective within the UN system and on the progress being made.[21] Calls to integrate a gender perspective in UN plans, policies, programmes, and activities are increasingly common not only in documents emanating from the bodies that first took up the cause (e.g. Commission on the Status of Women, Division for the Advancement of Women, Human Rights Commission, and Economic and Social Council) but also in such organs as the Security Council.[22] The mandates of the International Criminal Court and the International War Crimes Tribunals for Rwanda and the former Yugoslavia all explicitly require that sexual crimes against women be considered when deciding on the jurisdiction and when judging cases.

Factors facilitating the promotion of women's rights

Our conference on the theme of "Ideas-Institutional Nexus" identified a variety of factors that promote the establishment of commissions and help determine the longer-term significance of their work. The factors include individual leadership; state leadership; the type of issue being addressed; the level of support from civil society, generally, and NGOs, in particular; and the impact of developments in the external environment. All these factors are also important determinants of progress in the development of women's rights.

Individual leadership

The role of individual leadership has received relatively little attention from scholars,[23] although its importance is frequently highlighted by practitioners in private discussions. Long-time scholars of, and practitioners in, the UN system, Brian Urquhart and Erskine Childers describe individual leadership as "an essential ingredient in the successful conduct of most great enterprises".[24] The attributes of an effective leader include sound judgement, the ability to inspire confidence in others, the use of conciliatory language, a keen sense of timing, the capacity to reformulate provisions so as to make them generally acceptable, and tireless efforts to persuade. Clearly, not all people are equally skilled at deciding how and when to present what to whom.

Individuals have played pivotal roles in the struggle for gender equality, both as intellectual leaders and as activists.[25] There is now a rich body of feminist scholarship, whose ideas have exerted influence in UN circles as well as among academics.[26] There have also been many courageous activists who have struggled to promote women's rights. Bella Abzug is remembered as a civil rights and labour lawyer, a congresswoman, a prominent NGO leader, and a feminist pioneer. She was a leading figure in campaigns, both within the United States and internationally, for greater gender parity in government, equity in education, women's reproductive rights, gay and lesbian rights, universal health care, and equal pay for women. In 1990 she co-founded the Women's Environment and Development Organization, which encourages and assists women to develop their leadership and advocacy skills and strongly advocates for the rights of women worldwide to enjoy equitable, safe, and healthy living conditions. Under the leadership of its president, Bella Abzug, the Women's Environment and Development Organization helped to galvanize women's groups around the world into a more coherent, effective lobbying force at UN negotiations.

Particularly in recent years, the United Nations has benefited from women, such as Mary Robinson, Louise Arbour, Sadako Ogata, and Gro Harlem Brundtland, who have headed increasing numbers of its operating agencies. As Ireland's first female president, Mary Robinson worked hard to improve the status and welfare of women in her country. In particular, she is remembered for her crusades to liberalize the laws prohibiting divorce and abortion. In 1997 Robinson became the first female High Commissioner for Human Rights, a position in which she again demonstrated dedication, courage, and integrity. In addition to publicizing the hardships faced by women around the world, she was an outspoken proponent, in many political forums, of measures to empower women so that they could define their own needs and design appropriate programmes to meet them. In the post-September 11 discussions about Afghanistan, Mary Robinson strongly advocated that women be given better access to education, employment, and full participation in the political process. In short, she had a good sense of timing and she effectively linked the promotion of women's human rights to the dominant concerns on the international agenda.

The recently appointed High Commissioner for Human Rights, Louise Arbour, came to office having had a distinguished career as a scholar and member of the Supreme Court of Canada. From 1996 to 1999, she served as the chief prosecutor for the International Criminal Tribunals for the former Yugoslavia and Rwanda. Her effectiveness in bringing perpetrators of war crimes, genocide, and crimes against humanity to justice contributed greatly to the success of the tribunals, and their successes, in turn, facilitated the creation of the International Criminal Court. Although it is still early in her tenure, Louise Arbour is expected to make major contributions to the promotion of human rights, generally, and women's rights, in particular. Being High Commissioner for Human Rights gives one a highly visible platform from which to promote women's rights; however, as was all too evident with Mary Robinson's predecessor, not all individuals holding that position campaign vigorously for the cause.

Like Mary Robinson, Gro Harlem Brundtland was a political leader at home before becoming a significant actor within UN circles. As three-times prime minister of Norway, she actively encouraged the participation of women in political life and her administration had a higher percentage of women in senior government positions than that of any other country in the world. Brundtland chaired the World Commission on the Environment and Development, whose 1987 report, *Our Common Future*, promoted a major conceptual shift from thinking about economic development and environmental protection as separate entities to the recognition of their symbiotic relationship, as expressed in the term "sustainable development". In 1998 Brundtland became the first female Director-General of the UN World Health Organization, where she continues to battle against barriers to women's full participation in the decision-making process.

Sadako Ogata, professor, diplomat and UN High Commissioner for Refugees from 1991–2000, is another example of an individual who used her position effectively to promote women's rights. Ogata brought to the position a longstanding commitment to human rights, an ability to empathize with those she was seeking to assist – the majority of whom are women – and the courage and determination to advocate on their behalf.

Bella Abzug, Mary Robinson, Louise Arbour, Gro Harlem Brundtland and Sadako Ogata are only five of many sung, and many more yet unsung, heroes in the crusade to advance women's human rights. Behind the scenes, the agenda has been advanced on many fronts by individuals working diligently. Their stories demonstrate that individuals who are capable and dedicated can, and do, make significant differences.

The reticence on the part of most scholars to undertake in-depth analysis of the individual leadership may be due to the difficulty in conducting the necessary research. In compiling information on individuals, the researcher must rely heavily on interviews with participants who may be reluctant to discuss their own performance or that of other individuals, who may be inclined to exaggerate, and whose perceptions of events and developments may be faulty. In light of the importance of individual leadership, it is essential that ways be found of addressing these methodological difficulties and that more analyses of this salient factor be conducted.

State leadership

While the role of individual leadership has received relatively little attention from scholars, a great deal has been written about the role of state leadership.[27] Internationally, Canada is seen as a leader in the promotion of human rights, generally, and women's rights, in particular. At the Fourth World Conference on Women, Canadian delegates chaired the majority of the working groups that were established to negotiate particularly contentious issues, such as parental rights, unpaid work and sexual rights. In other words, over half of those chosen to chair working groups were drawn from one – out of 189 – participating states. Canadian initiatives, moreover, resulted in several major precedent-setting advances being incorporated into the Beijing Platform for Action, including the definition of rape as a war crime and crime against humanity, the requirement to develop international, gender-sensitive classifications for measuring unpaid work, and the recognition that violence and gender-related persecution are legitimate grounds for claiming refugee status. At the Fourth World Conference on Women, Canada – along with its profeminist allies, including the European Union, Australia, the Caribbean countries, and most of the international NGOs – was active in cultivating support for other key provisions in the Platform for Action. These provisions included the recognition of the universality of women's human rights, the agreement to mainstream women's human rights and a gender perspective throughout the UN system, and the broadening and strengthening of women's sexual and reproductive rights. As Canada and its allies were seeking to move the agenda ahead, they faced vocal opposition from religious/conservative forces: the Holy See[28] and its allies (most notably Guatemala, Ecuador, Honduras, Argentina, and Malta) as well as fundamentalist[29] Islamic states (in particular, Iran, Sudan, Algeria, and the Gulf states). Their anti-feminist stances were supported by conservative NGOs, such as Catholic Campaign for America, Focus on the Family, and Canada's REAL Women. There is a tendency to think of state leadership in terms of advancing an agenda – in this case expanding the breadth and depth of existing norms – however, states can also take active roles in impeding progress or even in rolling back progress.

The issue

The degree to which positions are polarized varies from issue to issue. In short, it is much easier to reach consensus on some issues than on others. There is widespread support for granting women and girls the right to at least some level of education. In contrast, reproductive rights and sexual rights continue to engender bitter differences of opinion. Yet even on issues where there is a considerable degree of consensus, women's rights cannot be assumed. Most countries formally recognize a girl's rights to attend primary school. Nonetheless, in Asia, the Middle East, and North Africa, the majority of girls of primary school age do not attend school.[30] While paying lip service to the right to education, governments are often negligent in addressing the impediment to education, which include culturally defined expectations that encourage girls to marry early and that discourage girls from pursuing education, generally, or education in certain – usually highly valued – fields, such as mathematics, science, engineering, and technology. Culturally defined roles, such as care of children and the sick, homemaking, subsistence farming, and the collection of fuel and water, make it very difficult for girls and women to pursue education. Even on issues where there is a large degree of consensus among states, women may still be far from full enjoyment of their human rights.

Civil society

NGOs comprise a principal vehicle through which citizens can aggregate and articulate shared concerns to political leaders, both nationally and internationally. Today NGOs play significant roles within the UN system: establishing parameters within which decisions must be taken; influencing the agendas; affecting policy outcomes; monitoring compliance; and implementing policies and programmes. There is probably no other area of UN activity that has attracted more NGO attention and where NGOs have been more influential than the human rights field. The initiative for including human rights in the Charter of the United Nations came from NGOs, which successfully lobbied for their inclusion.[31] Likewise, the idea and the initial impetus for an International Women's Year came from an NGO.[32] The year began a process that included the Decade for Women, four UN conferences on women, and the adoption of a legally binding convention on women's rights as well as numerous substantial documents outlining norms and strategies for promoting gender equity.

Although women's NGOs were active long before the UN was established, their numbers have proliferated greatly in the past 25 years. The 1995 NGO Forum on Women that was held parallel to the Fourth World Conference on Women attracted 30,000 participants, making it "the largest NGO Forum as well as the largest international gathering of women ever".[33] Vast networks of experienced NGOs dedicated to the advancement of women's rights now exist worldwide. Largely as a result their participation at UN venues, women's groups have become much more sophisticated in their lobbying strategies. Experienced NGOs seek input early in the process when UN documents and states positions are being formulated. Their ability to orchestrate massive campaigns at short notice was illustrated when the Chinese government decided to move the NGO Forum from Beijing to a resort town 42 kilometres from the site of the intergovernmental conference.

UN Secretary-General Boutros Boutros-Ghali's office was flooded with calls, faxes, petitions, and letters from around the world. Women engaged in a global conversation about strategies to ensure an adequate site while simultaneously debating whether to boycott the Forum. The alacrity with which women responded to calls for action and the numbers who entered the debate reflected how seriously women took this event.[34]

The campaigns waged by the international women's movement were instrumental in having the General Assembly adopt the Declaration on the Elimination of Violence against Women by consensus; the World Conference on Human Rights recognize that the "human rights of women and of the girl-child are an inalienable, integral and indivisible part of universal human rights"; and the World Conference on Population and Development affirm women's reproductive rights.[35] NGOs have made major contributions to getting issues on to the international agenda and to ensuring that these issues receive in-depth treatment and that specific strategies are developed to overcome barriers to gender equity. Their importance is noted in the Beijing Platform for Action:

> Non-governmental organizations, women's organizations and feminist groups have played a catalytic role in the promotion of the human rights of women through grass-roots activities, networking and advocacy and need encouragement, support and access to information from Governments in order to carry out these activities.[36]

Programmes to assist women are frequently contracted out to NGOs, which generally implement them more efficiently and cost-effectively than could state governments or intergovernmental organizations. NGOs also play a vital role in monitoring compliance after agreements are reached. International Women's Rights Action Watch, for example, is an important source of information for the Committee on the Elimination of Discrimination Against Women as it prepares its annual reports.

NGO participation not only affects agendas, policies, and programmes but, over the longer term, it also results in changes to the process itself. In the 20-year period between the First World Conference on Women and the Fourth World Conference on Women, the numbers attending the NGO Forum increased sixfold. Attendance facilitated gaining a deeper understanding of the issues and the realities of international negotiations, enhancing lobbying strategies, and expanding international NGO networks. It also brought demands for greater efficacy. Today NGOs with expertise, credibility, and sophistication can be either valuable allies or formidable foes, and their ability to be both is widely recognized. Increasingly, numerous and sophisticated women's groups demand to be included in UN negotiations pertaining to the well-being of women around the world and the system has become more inclusive in response.

Developments in external environment

Timing plays a major role in determining which ideas are seen as valuable, which ideas get institutionalized, and the extent to which policies, programmes, and norms are effectively implemented. For instance, at the Second World Conference on Women, geopolitical issues, such as the Arab–Israeli conflict and apartheid in South Africa, frequently took precedence and women's issues were relegated to the sidelines. Furthermore, when geopolitical issues came to the fore, female delegates yielded the microphones to male spokespersons from their respective countries. The preoccupation with such geopolitical considerations detracted significantly from the success of the conference. When the idea of holding a Fourth World Conference on Women was first considered, its mandate was to assess the progress made since the Third World Conference on Women and to eliminate barriers to achieving the objectives prescribed by the latter. Yet the progression from Nairobi to Beijing was less linear than had been the case between the previous three conferences. The world conferences and summits held in the 1990s exerted major influences over the text of the Platform for Action and hence over the agenda in Beijing. Many negative aspects of globalization and of structural assistance programmes have undermined many women's opportunities to enjoy their full economic rights. Thus developments in the external environment, such as economic recession, Cold War preoccupations, and other threats to security, dramatically affect the political will to negotiate and implement agreements.

Conclusion

The progress made over the past 25 years in the development of international norms on women's human rights has been remarkable and the advances in development of institutions to promote gender equity have been significant. The focus of this chapter, as for the book as a whole, has been on norm development and institution-building. Were the focus to be on compliance, the picture would be much less encouraging. No governments – not even the strongest proponents of women's rights – have fully lived up to the commitments they made in Beijing, nor is there the political will to provide the UN bodies with the technical and financial resources necessary to adequately promote and protect women's human rights. As a result, many questions require more in-depth consideration and more substantial answers. Most importantly, what can be done to ensure that the now considerable body of norms promoting women's human rights are in fact translated into practice so that gender equity becomes a reality around the world? What is needed is not additional conferences and ad hoc committees of experts convened to develop further norms. Instead, what is needed is action to ensure compliance with the extensive and substantive body of existing norms. There is also the question: why, in spite of the many mandates to mainstream a gender perspective, do issues of gender continue so often to be relegated to the sidelines, if they are considered at all? In the context of the theme of this conference on the Ideas/Institutions Nexus, the discussions, just like the work of the international commissions themselves, were remarkably silent on gender. Why?

Through the development of ideas and institutions, much has been done to promote women's human rights. These very considerable gains need to be recognized and celebrated. At the same time, it is essential to recognize that the record of protecting women's human rights is, in most cases, abysmally weak. Strategies for enhancing compliance already exist as do institutions to facilitate the task. What continues to be lacking is the political will to ensure compliance. Yet there are some causes for cautious optimism: each time ideas are institutionalized and offices are created and strengthened, the pressure for compliance intensifies and the cost of violations increases.

Notes

1. The Preamble to the Charter of the United Nations reaffirms "faith in fundamental human rights, in the dignity and worth of the human person, in the equal rights of men and women and of nations large and small", while Article 1.3 gives as one of the basic principles of the UN "promoting and encouraging respect for human rights and for fundamental freedoms without distinction as to race, sex, language, or religion".
2. For a discussion of the conference, see Elizabeth Riddell-Dixon (2001) *Canada and the Beijing Conference on Women: Governmental Politics and NGO Participation*, Vancouver: University of British Columbia Press, especially chapters 2, 5, 6, and 7.
3. The 1990 World Summit for Children established objectives for promoting the health, nutrition, and education of women and their children. The 1992 Rio de Janeiro Conference on the Environment and Development recognized the vital roles played by women in safeguarding the environment and in promoting sustainable development. Hence it pressed for their full participation in political and economic decision-making. The 1993 Vienna Conference on Human Rights declared women's rights to be human rights and called for the mainstreaming of women's rights and gender concerns within the UN human rights system. It stressed the importance of eliminating violence against women both in the private as well as in the public domain and called for the establishment of the new position of Special Rapporteur on Violence Against Women – a position that was created in March 1994. The same year, the Cairo Conference on Population and Development addressed issues of gender and recognized women's empowerment as being a prerequisite for health, population control, and economic development. The 1995 Copenhagen Summit for Social Development recognized that macro-economic policies have highly detrimental effects on women, that women have a crucial part to play in the eradication of poverty and in fostering social integration, and that gender equality is an important component of sustainable development.
4. V. Spike Peterson and Anne Sisson Runyan (1993) *Global Gender Issues*, Boulder: Westview Press, p. 26.
5. Charlotte Bunch, Mallika Dutt, and Susana Fried (1996) "Beijing '95: A Global Referendum on the Human Rights of Women", *Canadian Woman Studies* 16(3): 8.
6. United Nations, Fourth World Conference on Women, *Report of the Fourth World Conference on Women (Beijing, 4–15 September 1995)*, A/Conf. 177/20, 17 October 1995, Annex II, paragraph 124(a), p. 54.
7. Hilary Charlesworth (1996) "Women as Sherpas: Are Global Summits Useful for Women?", *Feminist Studies* 22(3): 543.
8. My thanks to Kerry Buck, Deputy Director, Human Rights, Humanitarian Affairs and International Women's Equality Division, for her valuable insights into this issue, the debate it sparked and its final resolution at the Fourth World Conference on Women.

9. United Nations Office of the High Commissioner for Human Rights (2000) *Women's Rights are Human Rights: Special Issue on Women's Rights – Spring 2000*, Geneva, p. 2. ⟨www.unhchr.ch/html/menu2/womenpub2000hts⟩.
10. Boutros-Ghali (1996) "Overview" in Commission on the Status of Women, *The United Nations and the Advancement of Women, 1945–1996*, United Nations Blue Books Series, vol. 6, revised edition, New York, p. 3.
11. At the Beijing Conference on Women, Canada sought unsuccessfully to get agreement on establishing a convention on the elimination of violence against women.
12. United Nations, General Assembly, Session 85, *Declaration on the Elimination of Violence against Women*, A/Res/48/104, New York, 20 December 1993.
13. Rounaq Jahan (1975) "The International Women's Year Conference and Tribune" *International Development Review* 3: 38.
14. United Nations Commission on Human Rights, 50th Session, Resolution 1994/45, 4 March 1994.
15. Stienstra (1994) *Women's Movements and International Organizations*, New York: St. Martin's, p. 152.
16. See Anne Gallagher (1997) "Ending the Marginalization: Strategies for Incorporating Women into the United Nations Human Rights System", *Human Rights Quarterly* 19(2): 283–333.
17. "Integrating the Rights of Women Into the Human Rights Mechanisms of the United Nations", E/CN.4/Res/1993/46, 8 March 1993.
18. United Nations World Conference on Human Rights, *Vienna Declaration and Program of Action* (A/Conf. 153/23), 25 June 1993, Section II, B3, par. 37.
19. United Nations Fourth World Conference on Women, *Report of the Fourth World Conference on Women*, Chapter IV (I), par. 213–231, pp. 93–99.
20. In essence, the Secretary-General told the heads of all units within the UN system (e.g. heads of departments, programmes, funds, specialized agencies, international financial and trade institutions, and regional commissions) to implement the Agreed Conclusions of the 1997 meeting of the Economic and Social Council [1997/2], which called for the consideration of gender issues in all mainstream activities, the systematic gathering of gender disaggregated data and the conducting of gender analysis. All plans and programmes are now expected to reflect a gender perspective.
21. For example, see United Nations Commission on Human Rights, 54th Session, *The Question of Integrating the Human Rights of Women throughout the UN System: Report of the Secretary-General*, E/CN.4/1998/49, 25 March 1998.
22. On 31 October 2000, the UN Security Council unanimously passed a resolution on Women, Peace and Security that recognized "the urgent need to mainstream a gender perspective into peacekeeping operations". United Nations, Security Council, S/2000/1044, 31 October 2000, p. 2. www.frauen.spoe.at/download/uno_resolution.pdf.
23. The most notable exception is Oran Young. See, "Political Leadership and Regime Formation". The nature and role of individual leadership is also discussed by Roger Coate in "Leadership Dynamics in International Institutions", paper presented to the Annual Meeting of the International Studies Association, Washington, DC, April 1990; and by Elizabeth Riddell-Dixon (1997) in "Individual Leadership and Structural Power", *Canadian Journal of Political Science* 30(2): 257–283.
24. Brian Urquhart and Erskine Childers (1990) *A World in Need of Leadership: Tomorrow's United Nations*, Uppsala: Dag Hammarskjold Foundation, pp. 7–8.
25. For a seminal discussion of the importance of individual leadership, see Oran Young (1991) "Political Leadership and Regime Formation: On the Development of Institutions in International Society", *International Organization* 45(3): 281.

26. The list of scholars making significant contributions in this field is extensive and includes Charlotte Bunch, Hilary Charlesworth, Rebecca Cook, Mallika Dutt, Cynthia Enloe, Susana Fried, Elisabeth Friedman, Arvonne Fraser, Jane Jaquette, Spike Peterson, Jan Pettman, Hilkka Pietilä, Anne Sisson Runyan, Vandana Shiva, Gayatri Chakravorty Spivak, Deborah Stienstra, Irene Tinker, Jill Vickers, Sandra Whitworth, and Anne Winslow.
27. Andrew F. Cooper (1997) *Canadian Foreign Policy: Old Habits and New Directions*, Scarborough, Ontario: Prentice-Hall, especially pp. 1–34; Andrew Cooper, Richard A. Higgott, and Kim Richard Nossal (1993) *Relocating Middle Powers: Australia and Canada in a Changing World Order*, Vancouver: University of British Columbia; Robert Gilpin (1987) *The Political Economy of International Relations*, Princeton: Princeton University Press; Robert Gilpin (1981) *War and Change in World Politics*, Cambridge: Cambridge University Press; Charles P. Kindleberger (1981) "Dominance and Leadership in the International Economy: Exploitation, Public Goods and Free Riders," *International Studies Quarterly* 25: 242–254; Charles P. Kindleberger (1973) *The World in Depression, 1929–1939*, Berkeley: University of California Press; Stephen D. Krasner (ed.) (1983) *International Regimes*, Ithaca: Cornell University Press; Marci McDonald (1995) *Yankee Doodle Dandy: Brian Mulroney and the American Agenda*, Toronto: Stoddart; Joseph S. Nye (1990) *Bound to Lead: The Changing Nature of American Power*, New York: Basic Books.
28. The Holy See is the Roman Catholic Church's supreme organ of government whose membership comprises the Pope, the College of Cardinals, and the Church's central government bodies. It is considered by the United Nations to be a non-member state with permanent observer status. Nevertheless, at most recent UN conferences, including the Beijing Conference on Women, it has been a full participant with a vote. In Beijing, the contrast between the Holy See's status as a full participant and the observer status of the UN Committee on the Elimination of Discrimination Against Women did not go unnoticed. The Holy See did not oppose all provisions in the *Platform for Action*. For example, it supported education for the girl-child. On the other hand, it opposed many of the provisions related to sexual and reproductive rights.
29. Marie-Andrée Roy, Professor of Religious Studies at the University of Quebec in Montreal, defines fundamentalism as "a religious movement which tries not only to resist modernity, secularity, separation of Church and the state, but also wants to impose its values and belief system on the whole population. Religious Fundamentalism rejects all other interpretations of tradition – in fact it positions itself as the only thinking authorized interpreter". See, "Fundamentalism at the NGO Forum" *Onward to Beijing: For Equality, Development and Peace*, Ottawa: Canadian Beijing Facilitating Committee, December 1995, p. 16.
30. The percentage of girls not attending primary school is 62 in Asia and 72 in the Middle East and North Africa. World Bank, *2000 World Development Indicators*, Washington, DC (2000), p. 88.
31. Felice D. Gaer (1996) "Reality Check: Human Rights NGOs Confront Governments at the UN", in Thomas G. Weiss and Leon Gordenker (eds.) *NGOS, the UN, and Global Governance*, Boulder: Lynne Rienner, pp. 51–66.
32. Marta Alter Chen (1996) "Engendering World Conference: The International Women's Movement and the UN", in Thomas G. Weiss and Leon Gordenker (eds.) *NGOS, the UN, and Global Governance*, Boulder: Lynne Rienner, p. 140.
33. United Nations, NGO Forum on Women Secretariat, *NGO Forum on Women*, p. 4.
34. Charlotte Bunch, Mallika Dutt, and Susana Fried (1996) "Beijing '95: A Global Referendum on the Human Rights of Women", *Canadian Woman Studies* 16(3): 8.

35. Christine Chinkin (2001) "Human Rights and the Politics of Representation: Is There a Role for International Law?" in Michael Byers (ed.) *The Role of Law and International Politics: Essays in International Relations and International Law*, Oxford: Oxford University Press, p. 133.
36. United Nations Fourth World Conference on Women, *Report of the Fourth World Conference on Women*, paragraph 228, p. 95.

13

Ideas, think-tanks, commissions, and global politics

Jon Pedersen

Where do correct ideas come from? Do they drop from the skies? No. Are they innate in the mind? No. They come from social practice, and from it alone. (Mao Tse Tung 1966 [1963])[1]

In late 1999, Joseph Stiglitz – then Chief Economist at the World Bank – told researchers participating in the Global Development Network conference in Bonn that they were participating in the experiment of "a closely integrated global economy which is striving for global governance without global government". He went on to say: "If this experiment is to be successful, it will be based on a process of global consensus building". Researchers would be key actors.[2]

This is a vision that rests on three premises. First, that ideas are among the forces that shape global politics. Second, that researchers may generate ideas that may be useful in policy debate and formulation. Third, that it is possible to design networks and institutions so that the ideas that researchers generate can have impact on policy decisions and outcomes. It is in the third premise that Stiglitz joins Mao, namely, that there are some social situations that do a better job of stimulating "correct thoughts", and Stiglitz sees networking among think-tanks and other research institutions as the key. Mao, of course, goes on to name the "the class struggle, the struggle for production and the scientific experiment". The topic of this chapter is to consider some specific actors and their social situations, namely think-tanks and international commissions.

The relation between the structure of society and its ideas is beyond the scope of this chapter. Suffice it to say that global politics and local comments on global politics form a particular type of knowledge economy, which is a social organization of actors and ideas. A characteristic of a knowledge economy such as the global policy arena is the organization of ideas through what Ortner calls "key symbols".[3] According to Ortner, symbols deserve the designation "key" when some or all of the following features are present: The locals tell the anthropologist that the symbols are important; they generate strong positive or negative feelings rather than indifference; they recur in the culture in many different settings; there are many ways to describe them; and there are rules surrounding their use. These symbols summarize or elaborate complex bodies of thought. As Ortner uses the term, key symbols are comparatively stable. In the international discourse of global politics I will argue that key symbols exist, but many are transient.

Typical recent examples of such symbols are "poverty", "sustainable development", "human development", "peace process", "root causes", and "rights-based approach". They are mainly of the elaborating type, as they refer to what is often complex schema for interpretation of events and guidelines for actions.

Key symbols, and the successful establishment of such symbols, are one of the most important products of intellectuals, researchers, think-tanks, and commissions. Thus, the Brundtland commission made "sustainable development" a household word in development policy circles and beyond. The Carnegie Commission on Preventing Deadly Conflict probably has had an important hand in making the concept of the "root cause of conflict" popular, although the idea certainly existed before then, as did the idea of sustainable development in the case of the Brundtland commission.

Nevertheless, key symbols are not the only product of research in global politics. Most of us do not manage to dominate the thoughts of many, but aspire only to more modest contributions. Social science generally provides four types of products. One product of social science is concepts. A second product is that of empirical descriptions using the concepts. A third is that of explanations or theories. Sometimes these explanations and theories become so all-embracing that I would call them key-symbols. Social science is often merged with policy formulation, so that the fourth product is reflections on policy.

The triumph of particular concepts or key symbols is not an everyday occurrence. Think-tanks are rather engaged in more low-key insertions into the policy process. One example is aspects of the work of Fafo, a Norwegian think-tank that has been closely involved in the Middle East peace process, partly in conjunction with the Refugee Working Group.

The Refugee Working Group is one of the working groups that were established as an outcome of the Madrid Peace Conference in 1991. Their purpose is to establish areas of discussion between the parties and interested countries that can be used to find solutions to issues of contention in a piecemeal fashion. The groups were envisaged as a vital part of the multilateral track of the Middle East Peace Process. The Refugee Working Group's purpose is to enhance the living conditions of the refugees without prejudicing final agreements regarding the rights of Palestinian refugees. The participants in the Refugee Working Group are the core parties (PLO and Israel), the co-sponsors of the peace process (the United States and the Russian Federation), as well as interested regional and extraregional countries. It is presided over by Canada, the coordinator or "gavel". The Refugee Working Group has several sub-groups known as "shepherds" that are each responsible for a particular area of interest to the group. Norway has the role of "shepherd for databases", and Fafo (the Institute for Applied Social Science in Norway) is the executive agent of that role. The role entails a specific responsibility for producing and systematizing policy relevant data on Palestinian refugees. It has also entailed participation in Refugee Working Group meetings of various types and presentation of data and analyses in such contexts.

At the Cairo Plenary in 1994 of the Refugee Working Group, Norway agreed to act on the group's recommendation for an anthropological study of living conditions of refugees. This was partly in response to criticisms of Fafo's previous quantitative studies of the refugees that held that the statistical analysis could not depict the real-life situation of the refugees. The Fafo staff present at the meeting initially formulated the proposal for the study, agreeing to study refugee camps in the West Bank, Jordan, and Lebanon. Palestinians in urban Amman were also covered. The resulting study, *Finding Ways*,[4] looked at the different forms of adaptation to host countries that Palestinian refugees have made.

The study was partly an attempt to deconstruct the somewhat essentialist notion of the economic and social integration of the Palestinian refugees that is current in much of the existing research on the subject. In this notion the Palestinian refugee is construed as a "generalized other" with a fixed set of characteristics. Said has been particularly fond of the essentialism found in Arab studies.[5] The construction of the Palestinian refugee as a particular type of refugee with certain characteristics is very much one of a kind with classical essentialist description of the Arab, and one that Said himself may be accused of harbouring.

In contrast, the central idea that structured *Finding Ways* was that of a multiplicity of ways in which Palestinians adapted to their life as refugees. The idea was influenced by Clifford,[6] whose concept of different paths through modernity was a useful idiom for how refugees had found their ways both literally and metaphorically from flight to adaptation in the host countries. Integration was considered as several quite dissimilar processes: assimilation, segregation, and incorporation. Assimilation denotes the complete merging of the refugees and the host society. Segregation the encapsulation of the refugees from the host society, such as was the situation in Lebanon during the civil war with very limited contact between the two. Incorporation refers to continuation of a separate identity, and interaction with the host society in specific limited ways. The key point in this was that it had to be possible to discuss various forms of adaptation and the differences between them, both in order to explain how refugees adapted and to be able to provide services for them.

At the Refugee Working Group plenary session in Antalya in December 1994 where the study was presented, the Jordanian delegation took some exception to that perspective, citing the need to treat refugees as one group in order not to prejudice their rights. However, the Jordanian position has changed since then. Moreover, the notion of different adaptations and opportunity situations for Palestinian refugees has become more accepted. It is, for example, a basis for the Palestinian notion of choice for Palestinian refugees that appears to have been an aspect of the Taba negotiations between the Israelis and Palestinians in January 2000.[7] Thus, the example of the concept of refugee adaptation is one of establishment of a concept in the policy formulation process.

The most well-known piece of Fafo's work is the living condition survey of the West Bank and Gaza carried out in 1992 and presented at the Refugee Working Group meeting in Oslo in May 1993. It is a typical example of the second type of scientific work, namely, that of empirical description. The study presents a comprehensive view of Palestinian living conditions, but does not go much beyond that in analytical terms.

Fafo's current studies of Palestinian refugee camps is an example of the third type of social science research for policy – that of explanations and theory. These studies aim at discovering whether the observed poorer conditions in camps than among Palestinians living outside camps are a function of one or more of three main mechanisms. These are: reproduction of poverty within the camps, selection effects because successful households move out of the camps and poor households into the camp, and discrimination by the surrounding society. The policy options following from this are relatively clear. If internal reproduction is the main process, then strategies that aim at improving, for example, the infrastructure of the camps, the educational level of the inhabitants, and other camp internal measures should be tried. If selection processes are at work, then it may be helpful to improve the camp infrastructure if this is bad, although the end effects of this may prove to be contrary to intentions if this encourages an increase in the numbers in the camp, thereby reducing the overall benefits. If discrimination is the main problem, then policies should aim at reducing discrimination, while ameliorating in the short term the effects of discrimination.

In the last example, the work of Fafo borders into the explicit formulation of social policy, that is, the fourth product of social science mentioned previously. This is an area that some see as one of the important arenas of think-tanks internationally, in particular in the form of policy transfer, which is the transfer of ideas and reasoning about policy.[8]

Fafo has done several other studies in conjunction with Norway's role in the Refugee Working Group and the Middle East peace process more generally. The role of Fafo and other Norwegian think-tanks and NGOs in the Middle East must be seen in the light of the general foreign policy consensus that was formulated by Foreign Minister Stoltenberg, who was in office from 1987–1989 and from 1990–1993, and his Political Advisor, and later State Secretary, Jan Egeland.[9]

The policy, which was formulated in part in 1985 by Egeland in his Master's thesis and developed by the Stoltenberg administration of the Foreign Ministry through a government white paper in 1989,[10] can to some extent, and somewhat irreverently, be termed a "saturation-of-kindness-policy". Briefly, the idea is that, first, Norway as a small country has limited assets to bring to bear in the international community. For that reason, it has to find a niche, and one such niche is that of peace-broker, facilitator, and general do-gooder. It can take that role because there is little reason for countries to fear Norway. It has few pressures to bear, yet is politically close enough to the United States – meaning any Norwegian-brokered solutions are likely to be acceptable to the superpower. It also has sufficient wealth to finance such operations on its own. Second, this policy can only be successful if a situation of cross-cutting links is achieved. The Norwegian presence must be a community consisting of multiplex relations in which actors incur costs if they break the links to the process sponsored by the Norwegians. In this respect, whether the vehicle was a think-tank or a humanitarian NGO did not matter much. The insights that the think-tank might produce would be an added value, but it is the process itself that was important.

This originally was conceived as a way of exploiting comparative advantages that Norway already possessed in various conflict and crisis areas because of the wide net of Norwegian NGOs all over the world. The Norwegian support to the peace process in Guatemala and to that of Mali are examples of this, since the already well-established Norwegian Church Aid was an important vehicle in both cases. In Mali for example, the Norwegian Church Aid had employed a number of Tuaregs who were close to the leaders of the rebellion, as well as a government minister.

The Foreign Ministry also developed a more activist stance, where organizations that were not already present in a country would be asked or allowed to become established in a country or region in the hope of stimulating the overall process. In many cases, where a process had been started, the foreign ministry has supported a number of organizations, increasing the Norwegian civil society presence dramatically.

Nevertheless, in order to fulfil the role the think-tank or NGO has to have legitimacy and authority. Some have automatic or semi-automatic legitimacy and authority. This is especially the case for religious organizations. But with think-tanks this is not the case; their legitimacy has to be established. In the case of Fafo in the Middle East, legitimacy was originally established through Fafo's link with the labour party and trade union movement, as well as by Norway, thus allowing Fafo to play a role in the Refugee Working Group. The legitimacy was significantly enhanced by Fafo's hosting of the secret back-channel leading to the Declaration of Principles between Israel and PLO in 1993.

Legitimacy as discussed above is mainly political legitimacy in the sense of having a voice and access to policy fields. However, the extent to which access and voice is matched with ears depends also on how the think-tank performs, its products, and its establishment of reputation. Different think-tanks have taken various approaches to this and the different ways follow largely the typology that Weaver and McGann have developed for think-tanks: academic, contract research, advocacy and party-affiliated.[11] In the typology, the two first types focus on academic and scientific credibility as a source of legitimacy and differ mostly on who sets the agenda for the research: the institution itself, in the academic case, and the contractor in the second. The advocacy and party think-tanks, on the other hand, are more concerned with marketing specific ideas. Therefore, they derive their credibility from their effectiveness in communicating their ideas and influencing the policy agenda rather than from the scientific validity of their reports.

Fafo has typically evolved in its strategy of legitimation and establishment of authority. Initially, as described above, it was close to the party-affiliated end of the scale, and that was a legitimacy that was first and foremost used to establish its presence. Since then it has steadily distanced itself from the party strategy of legitimacy, especially in its international work, and is now firmly in the contract research/academic end of the scale. This is probably a quite common strategy, although the specific means to establish a presence often varies. For example, many think-tanks in the successor states to the Soviet Union have depended on gaining access and voice through alliances with international funders, and then built on that for their continued existence in a more independent manner. In general, networks are extremely important to the establishment of think-tanks, regardless of who are the nodes of the network. Other think-tanks, such as the successful Institute for International Economic Studies, have focused nearly exclusively on the academic track, linking the success of think-tanks to international peer-reviewed publications. Moreover, its network of individual researchers is linked to an established university, granting it visibility with the popularization of its research.[12] Here, of course, the success is measured in terms of the survival of the institution, rather than with respect to its impact on the policy arena.

As indicated above, the ideas that think-tanks try to get across are often quite limited in scope. Fafo, for example, has mainly been in the business of providing data, and, as indicated above, some specific ideas about the interpretation of those data. In this regard, most, but not all, think-tanks differ from the international commissions, which I will now consider.

The international commissions, such as the World Commission on Environment and Development (the Brundtland Commission, created in 1983), the Carnegie Commission on Preventing Deadly Violence (created in 1994), the Commission on Global Governance (established 1992), WHO's Commission of Macroeconomics and Health (created in 2000), the ILO's Commission on the Social Dimension of Globalization (created in 2001) and the Government of Canada's International Commission on Intervention and State Sovereignty (created in 2000) carry out work that is similar to that of think-tanks along some dimensions. Most importantly they enter into policy arenas and present analysis and synthesis within a particular area of policy. Nevertheless, they approach the legitimacy question differently than do the think-tanks. In part that is because they may be conceived of as instant, and ad hoc, advocacy think-tanks.

The most obvious difference between the establishment of legitimacy between a think-tank and a commission is the fact that the commission is dependent on instant recognition while a think-tank can establish itself gradually. Since the commission is supposed to present one product – its report – it cannot depend exclusively on that report to secure interest for its activities. In order to be able to carry out its activities, it must be interesting in itself. The way to achieve this has invariably been to constitute the commission from personas of undoubted fame and competence. Thus, the Carnegie Commission, established in May 1994, had among its sixteen members the Executive Director of UNICEF, the United Nations High Commissioner for Refugees, two former members of the Cabinet of the United States of America and a former Secretary-General of the

United Nations. The very high level membership of the Commission was probably a reflection of its need to assert legitimacy, having been established by the Carnegie Corporation rather than by an international body such as the United Nations. In contrast, the membership of the Macroeconomics and Health Commission established by the WHO had a more scientific background, although far from exclusively so.

A major difference between the commissions and the think-tanks lies in the details of the products. Most commissions do not present new insights. Rather, they present a linkage between insight and policy. "Sustainable development" is one of the more successful examples, perhaps the most successful example. With this concept the commission managed to turn debate away from the issue of zero-growth versus economic growth into one of sustainable growth, a concept that both growth adherents and environmentalists could subscribe to and that, at the same time, was not completely devoid of meaning.

Thus, a first success criterion for an international commission is the extent to which it manages to develop a key symbol in Ortner's terms. The arena of global politics is not homogenous; a key symbol cannot be a key symbol for all. But it must be sufficiently broad. To reiterate the definition: people must believe that the concept is important; they must have strong feelings about it, use it in many contexts, describe it in many ways, and try to regulate its use. As noted, the product of commissions is a linkage between insight and policy. A second success criterion is that the key symbol which epitomizes this linkage represents or establishes a policy consensus among key actors, preferably actors that before the commission could not agree on policy or had not been able to formulate their agreement.

The Carnegie Commission on Preventing Deadly Conflict has not developed such concepts. This may have been a matter of timing: the commission's work took place during a period where several conflicts developed, raged, and spread, and where the response of the international community was less than perfect. This, however, was partly because the international community simply did not know what to do.

It is illuminating to compare the Brundtland Commission, which entered a stage that had been set for a synthesis. At least two factors were crucial. First, the debate on environment had matured considerably before the commission was launched. The major lines of conflict and policy agendas were already well known. Second, there was an interested public in the West: a large number of NGOs involved in environmental issues and therefore governments that needed to relate to environmental issues. The Brundtland Commission provided both an arena for public dialogue and a language that governments could use in policy formulation.

When read with a critical and somewhat cynical eye, the Carnegie

Commission presents a list of comparatively obvious observations: that preventive action should focus on preventing emergence, spread, and recurrence of violent conflict. Furthermore, one should have the ability for early reaction to signs of trouble, one should have a comprehensive balanced approach to alleviate the pressures that lead to conflict, and one should try to remove the root causes of conflict.[13] The commission then went on to discuss a large number of important concerns in the prevention of deadly conflict.

Nevertheless, the Carnegie Commission could not command the interest of the public as the concern for deadly conflict in distant lands has created a less intense debate than was that on the environment in the 1980s – and which the Brundtland Commission was able to take advantage of. Moreover, the commission could not present a policy argument and consensus together with an expression of this in a symbolic form that would make its message recognizable.

The International Commission on Intervention and State Sovereignty (ICISS) represents an interesting twist on the purpose of international commissions.[14] First, it is comparatively narrow in scope and addresses a very specific topic, namely, whether or not there exists a right and duty to "humanitarian intervention" in other countries when the country in question cannot or will not protect its citizens. In form, it is a mixture between a typical commission report and the report of an advocacy-type think-tank.

Second, the process of work was somewhat different from many of the other commissions: the ICISS did try to engage a broad range of scholars and NGOs from a wide range of countries. Somewhat cynically, one might say that this was necessary to establish legitimacy and authority since the commission was, after all, established by the Canadian government and therefore liable to the suspicion that it would represent solely a Canadian or Western view on the issue. Less cynically, one might say that it was an attempt to secure the broad base and public debate that had proved important in the case of the Brundtland Commission. Regardless of motives, it was an attempt to establish legitimacy by means other than simply depending on the reputation of the core members of the commission.

The Brundtland and Carnegie Commissions and the ICISS all tried to establish their legitimacy and authority in related ways that were all founded on the actors involved. As noted, the think-tanks have depended more on networks in the initial phase, and then shifted gear into securing legitimacy on the grounds of academic reputation.

Some think-tanks are explicitly engaged in setting policy agendas on a level that is close to that of the commissions. For example, the Council on Foreign Relations' report on the Ferghana Valley[15] is a plea for a shift in American (and other countries') foreign policy towards flash-points in the Central Asian region. Even closer to the commissions are the task force reports of the Council on Foreign Relations, such as that titled *Strengthening Palestinian Public Institutions.*[16] Part of an extraordinary series of other task forces likewise give detailed policy advice to (American) policy makers on a wide range of topics that in generality are on the level of the ICISS report. It is significant that in setting up their task forces, the Council on Foreign Relations follows strategies that resemble that of commissions, namely, securing high-profile participation and embedding the project with the relevant actors. For example, in the Palestinian project extensive consultation with Palestinian civil society, academics, and the Palestinian Authority were part of the project.

Considering large-scale think-tanks such as the Council on Foreign Relations, it becomes clear that in some ways there exists a continuum from the small-scale think-tank that markets ideas within limited fields to the commission. Along this continuum from think-tank to commission, the freshness of ideas decreases, while the embeddedness in policy increases.

One should also bear in mind that think-tanks and international commissions are but two of the actors that peddle ideas in the global politics arena. The NGOs, the World Bank, UN organizations, governments, and groups of governments are also key players. For example, the World Bank, in particular through its World Development Reports, functions in much the same ways as the successful international commissions. It also functions in a similar manner to think-tanks, as it is constantly pouring out ideas and analysis of varying orders of generality into the debate on economic and social development.

Where do the correct thoughts come from? Like Mao, I have argued that the correct thoughts come from social practice, but that the social practice required depends on the kind of thoughts. The flexible ability to insert small ideas into the policy area is the domain of the manifold think-tanks. To formulate key symbols with extensive policy implications and make them heard are more the domains of the commissions. Thus, it is perhaps wrong to focus on the origin of the thoughts themselves. But the specific positioning of think-tanks and commissions in relation to other actors, a positioning into which the successful ones invest considerable work, is what determines the success or failure of think-tanks and commissions. This, of course, is a conclusion that pertains to any organization, not just think-tanks and commissions.

Notes

1. Mao Tse Tung (1966) *Quotations from Mao Tse Tung*, Beijing: Foreign Languages Press.

2. Stiglitz (2000) Stortingsmelding nr. 11 (1989–90): Om utviklingstrekk i det internasjonale samfunn og virkninger for norsk utenrikspolitikk. Oslo: Utenriksdepartementet. Legg til diskusjon av ulike basisgrupper og nettverk.
3. S.B. Ortner (1973) "On Key Symbols", *American Anthropologist* 75(5): 1338–1346.
4. S. Gilen, A. Hovdenak, R. Maktabi, J. Pedersen, and D. Tuastad (1994) *Finding ways*, Oslo: Fafo.
5. E. Said (1978) *Orientalism*, New York: Pantheon Books.
6. J. Clifford (1988) *The Predicament of Culture*, Cambridge: Harvard University Press.
7. A. Eldar (2002) "Moratinos Document: The peace that nearly was at Taba", *Ha aretz*, 14 February.
8. D. Stone (2001) "Think-tanks, Global Lesson-Drawing and Networking Social Policy Ideas", *Global Social Policy* 1(3): 338–360.
9. H. Henriksen Waage (2000) "Norwegians? Who needs Norwegians?", *Explaining the Oslo Back Channel: Norway's Political Past in the Middle East*, Series: *Evaluation Report* 9/2000, Oslo: Ministry of Foreign Affairs.
10. Government of Norway (1989).
11. R. Kent Weaver and J.G. McGann (2000) "Think-tanks and Civil Societies in a Time of Change", in R. Kent Weaver and J.G. McGann *Think-tanks and Civil Societies*. New Brunswick: Transaction Publishers, pp. 1–35.
12. A. Lindbeck (1995) "Principles for successful research institutes: Assar's ten commandments", in *Annual Report 1993/94*, Stockholm: Institute for International Economic Studies.
13. *Carnegie Commission on Preventing Deadly Conflict* (1997) New York: Carnegie Corporation, pp. xvii–xviii.
14. ICISS, The Responsibility to Protect – Report of the International Commission on Intervention and State Sovereignty, Ottawa: IDRC (2001).
15. N. Lubin, K. Marting, and B.R. Rubin (1999) *Calming the Ferghana Valley*, Washington: Brookings.
16. Council on Foreign Relations, *Independent Task Force Report: Strengthening Palestinian Public Institutions*, 1999. See www.cfr.org.

14

UN Reform Commissions: Is anyone listening?

Edward C. Luck

It is instructive, if not always reassuring, for those of us in the business of producing ideas and policy proposals to check from time to time whether anyone is listening. Are we making a difference in terms of influencing policymaking at the United Nations and/or in member state capitals? If we learn more from our failures than from our successes, then I am unusually well qualified to speak on this topic. In twenty years with the United Nations Association of the USA (UNA-USA), I was involved in well more than my share of blue ribbon panels and binational reports on how the United Nations could do its job better or the United States could be a more constructive player in multilateral fora. Most of these were quite respectable pieces of work, and at times even innovative. Though widely regarded as influential, our reports hit the mark in terms of policy implementation only occasionally and then not always with the ideas we valued the most highly.

From 1995 to 1997, I backstopped much of the reform effort at the UN, including with the Strengthening Working Group in the General Assembly, with Razali Ismail when he was President of the Assembly and pushed Security Council reform, and with the Secretary-General's team in helping to assemble the 1997 reform package. My group of researchers at the UN produced an enormous compendium of reform proposals from inside and outside the UN, literally thousands of recommendations, for use by the member states and secretariat officials. Yet, again, only a handful of these ideas found their way into the inter-governmental deliberations and even fewer were adopted. So, were most of these authors and commissions simply wasting their breath espousing lost causes to a disinterested and deaf audience of jaded and narrow-minded policy makers?

Standards of success

Before jumping to conclusions, or jumping off the policy-wonk bandwagon altogether, some perspective would help on what would constitute a reasonable set of standards for success. Would a mid-level bureaucrat in Washington, Moscow, London, or Beijing have much higher expectations for getting his or her pet policy innovations adopted as national policy? Probably not. Quite simply, there are relatively few opportunities for policy change, particularly when this would have to entail institutional reform, and large numbers of individuals and groups attempting to push this or that idea for change. Many of these suggestions, of course, contradict what others are espousing. This is true in national capitals, and even truer in multilateral organizations with hundreds of member states, dozens of institutional actors, and endless agendas. Even if one-tenth of the thoughtful and relevant reform ideas were adopted, the result would be institutional chaos at the UN. It can only absorb so much at one time. The politics of change can be very sensitive, especially in the UN, and it wouldn't take long for too many cooks to spoil the reform broth.

I would suggest three standards for success:

- Did the report affect how policy makers, opinion leaders, and publics think about an issue, weigh policy options, or prioritize interests and values?
- Did the report set forth fresh concepts and proposals for change and/or reform, even if they were not achieved in the short run?
- Did the report spur the process of change, speed the ripening process, help build constituencies for change, or expand the boundaries of what is widely considered to be feasible or reasonable? If, as Secretary-General Kofi Annan has declared, reform is a process, not an event, then perhaps one should not assess a report's impact until a decade after its release.

Of course, it is gratifying to see one's proposals expeditiously translated into national or UN policy. But that doesn't assure that they will prove to be sustainable or ultimately successful in producing the kinds of results one had anticipated. Given the number of times the UN has been "reformed", for example, it would seem that many of the reforms did not prove out over time. And should our goal be to get our proposals adopted or to achieve real results in terms of ultimate effectiveness? It may be better, in that sense, to have spurred a process of reflection and negotiation that in the end produced somewhat different but more sustainable policy innovations.

Lessons

Looking back at past commissions and reports, what lessons might be derived about what works and why? The lessons enumerated here are drawn from three exercises in which I participated in recent years: 1) a review conducted for the MacArthur Foundation and the Commission on Global Governance on the impact of its report, *Our Global Neighbourhood*; 2) a study of a number of projects, undertaken for the Better World Fund and the UN Foundation and published as "Blue Ribbon Power: Independent Commissions and UN Reform" in the inaugural issue of *International Studies Perspectives* (2000); and 3) a 2001 review for the Ford Foundation of eight reform projects it supported between 1985 and 1996. Based on these research efforts, a dozen lessons come to mind:

- In every successful case, the project had committed leadership and a quality staff. Views differ as to which is more crucial, but it clearly helps to have both.
- In terms of getting high-level and/or sustained attention, nothing counts like follow-up, follow-up, and follow-up. The release of a "final" report should be around the mid-point of the project, not its culmination.
- It is very helpful – though not a prerequisite – to have the project based at an institution that is prepared and equipped to carry the report's key proposals forward as part of its ongoing agenda. If a particular government is ready to carry the ball over an extended period, then that almost always helps as well.
- Careful planning and preparatory work is needed before a commission is formed or a project is launched. This is when the biggest mistakes are made. This would seem obvious, but it is remarkable how many policy projects are launched on the equivalent of a wish and a prayer. Enthusiasts, in particular, should be encouraged to stop and ask themselves candidly a) whether a market exists for the product they intend to produce and b) whether their commission or study will truly bring added value to the subject.
- The best reports have both vision and practical proposals. Too many groups try to get away with having one or the other.
- It is critical to have a sober understanding of the political and institu-

tional realities that will define the context within which the project and report will be seen.

- It helps, sometimes greatly, to line up potentially supportive constituencies early on. This gives them a sense of ownership and an incentive to help with the marketing and salesmanship.
- Likewise, it pays to reach out to those who will be key to actually implementing your proposals, even if they are not initially enthusiastic. Again, such a dialogue should be opened at an early stage and maintained throughout the project. Whatever else you do, take care to avoid surprises – don't drop the report on the desk of policy makers and expect them to be taken with the brilliance of your ideas and the persuasiveness of your prose.
- In most cases, the process of getting one's ideas absorbed by policy makers does not seem to follow either a top-down or bottom-up model. Rather, much of this osmosis seems to flow horizontally, from one side of the process to the other, as commissioners or key staff move laterally into positions of policy responsibility. While much of the focus in organizing panels tends to be directed to distinguished former officials – which may be wise for credibility reasons – it is often the future policy makers who actually carry the ideas forward into policy circles. So remember to think about "futures" as well as "formers".
- Big ideas are exciting, of course, but it helps to have some smaller or less innovative ones as well. Having some readily achievable proposals may boost the credibility of a report, as well as the morale of its authors.
- It almost always pays to be flexible, to look for openings and niches, twists and turns, both in what commissioners may be thinking over time and in the potential environment in which their ideas will be thrust. What will the market bear at any point? Which ideas might be held in reserve for more propitious times ahead? It is striking, in this regard, how often reports are remembered for ideas or proposals that may have seemed rather secondary to the authors at the time.
- It may well be true that money can't buy you love, and it is certainly true that money cannot guarantee a good report. We have seen more than one example where the expensive promotion of a second-rate report has been doubly embarrassing. However, it is also a fact of life that commissions do not get very far without sufficient funding and staff. Poorly funded projects cannot take advantage of unexpected opportunities, adjust to unforeseen contingencies, or – and this can be fatal – do proper follow-up.

Most of these lessons, it would seem, are little more than common sense. Yet it is remarkable how often they are overlooked in planning or carrying out high-profile panel projects.

Missing links

In assessing the independent UN-reform studies over the past 15 or so years, four shortcomings recur so often as to qualify as missing links. As these four points suggest, the shortcomings of these efforts generally lay more with what they did not attempt than with what they did.

One, there was a repeated failure to identify, understand, or plan for overcoming the obstacles that could be expected to interfere with achieving the desired policy outcomes. Perhaps it is just too difficult or out-of-character for advocates to accept that others may not share either their sense of urgency or their enthusiasm for a particular course of action. The very process of selling their project proposals to funding sources (and to potential panellists) may lead both to over-heated expectations and to believing one's own rhetoric. In any case, while I have seen many thoughtful expositions of ways to make the UN a better place, I have yet to come across a single cogent analysis of how to move the political and bureaucratic processes to get all of these glorious ideas implemented.

Two, though a few projects did far better than the rest, in general these efforts were plagued by weak or insufficient follow-up. This was especially true when it came to lobbying legislators and policy makers in major capitals. Effective follow-up tends to be expensive, time-consuming, and staff intensive. Someone needs to be in residence over an extended period of time, whether it is an individual associated with the project, a professional hired for that purpose, or a volunteer who is simply sympathetic to it. Funders, moreover, are more likely to call for effective follow-up than to fund it.

Three, in almost every case, the project leaders failed to establish effective and sustainable communication links with Washington policy makers. True, reaching key figures in the US capital for UN-related issues can be a frustrating exercise, but usually little effort was made in this direction and, tellingly, strategies were not even formulated for involving US policy makers. At times, there seemed to be a distinct preference for bypassing or ignoring what were assumed to be political obstacles in Washington. Not surprisingly, the latter tended to become a self-fulfilling prophecy.

Four, given these predilections, it should come as no surprise to learn that very few conservative voices were included in the various commissions or staff. By and large, these projects have facilitated the exchange of ideas among confirmed internationalists. Therefore, with a few exceptions, most of these reports spent relatively little time addressing larger questions of strategy, history, priorities, or the relationship between national sovereignty and global governance, since it was assumed that there was – or should be – a consensus on core goals and principles. Too often, however, it has been differences over these fundamental questions that have interfered with the implementation of designs for stronger international institutions.

Examples

Before commenting on a few specific projects, two caveats are in order. One, it is awkward to provide a candid public assessment of any of these efforts, since they all involved individuals for whom I have great respect and, in many cases, with whom I have worked in the past. Two, evaluations may well change over time. Sometimes reports that make a big initial splash due to good public relations work, the prominence of the personalities associated with them, or apt timing, do not ultimately enjoy a long shelf-life. The opposite can also be true. Some proposals may not appear ripe when first released, but then gain relevance and credibility over time, as political and contextual conditions evolve. The gestation period for a significant reform proposal, for example, may be a decade or longer.

These caveats aside, it is worth pondering why certain initiatives that had a great deal going for them appear to have fallen below expectations or at least achieved rather uneven results. Four over the past decade come to mind, in part because they were undertaken with the encouragement, even in several cases the endorsement, of the UN Secretary-General and had not only the funding, but also the active involvement, of one or more major foundations.

First, in 1993, at the behest of Secretary-General Boutros Boutros-Ghali (or at least of his staff on his behalf), the Ford Foundation convened a blue ribbon panel to study the perennial problem of UN funding. The group, ably led by Shiguro Ogata and Paul Volcker, was composed of top-flight former finance ministers from around the world, who reportedly worked together very smoothly and amiably. They produced their report, *Financing an Effective UN*, in less than six months. It was a model of brevity, accessibility, and common sense. While the report was generally well received, however, certain recommendations apparently were not to the liking of top UN officials and others to key member states. The follow-up efforts were relatively modest, especially in capitals, where the report stirred relatively little interest. Relatively few of the recommendations, however sensible, were ever implemented.

In this case, there appears to have been two basic flaws in planning the study. First, it had been assumed that the common voice of respected financial officials would be sufficiently authoritative to overcome whatever political obstacles had been in the way of a reliable system for financing the UN. Political figures were excluded from the panel to permit a relatively quick and broad consensus. Financing the UN, however, has always been an acutely political issue and national decision-makers wanted to keep it that way. Two, it seems that no market testing was done beforehand. Other than a smattering of officials in the UN and in sympathetic missions, there was relatively little interest in solving this "problem", so even a distinguished and cogent report got little play.

Second, two years later, the United Nations would mark its fiftieth anniversary. Secretary-General Boutros-Ghali, among others, urged the preparation of a high-level and independent study of the future of the world body and of ways it might be strengthened. Again the UN turned to the Ford Foundation, which in turn provided Yale University with a major grant to organize and oversee the project. The two well-respected institutions, working in close collaboration, chose Moeen Qureshi and Richard von Weizsäcker to head a geographically balanced commission with strong intellectual and policy credentials. It was decided, however, that to get fresh ideas the group should not include figures with too much UN experience.

In retrospect, this was either a misjudgement or one that was carried out too rigorously and uniformly. The panel's final report, *The UN in Its Second Half Century*, presented a well crafted, concise, and compelling account of the challenges before the world body. But its recommendations, while often original and innovative, did not show a good feel for how the organization operates or what would fly politically. With the emphasis on brevity, moreover, several of the more innovative proposals were not explained adequately and no supporting papers or materials were provided. The timing might have been ideal – since the member states and the secretariat were just launching the broadest reform debate in the history of the UN – but the report gained little attention from the membership and was virtually ignored by the Secretary-General who had been so instrumental in its launch.

Three, by far the most costly of all of the projects reviewed was that of the Carnegie Corporation of New York on conflict prevention. In part, this was due to the scope of the work undertaken, which included the commissioning and publication of a series of individually authored papers in addition to the report of the Carnegie Commission on Preventing Deadly Conflict. Unlike the two reports noted above that may have erred on the side of brevity, the Commission, itself an unusually large group, produced a final report of over 200 pages in 1997. Led by two widely respected internationalists, David Hamburg and Cy Vance, the Commission sought both to underline the importance of prevention as a way of thinking about policy choices and to put forward specific recommendations for the UN and member states. The group appears to have done much better on the former than the latter tack.

Aided by an ample outreach budget and enthusiastic co-chairmen, the prevention mantra became a regular component of the UN's vocabulary under Secretary-General Kofi Annan, one of the report's biggest boosters. Yet Boutros-Ghali had emphasized prevention in his *Agenda for Peace* report five years before and it was already widely accepted in both scholarship and policy making that prevention was highly preferable to reaction after conflict had already broken out. Whether the Carnegie report and its supporters have provided sufficient guidance in terms of specific policy steps that would translate the concept of prevention into workable, effective policy making remains to be seen. Like the other reports being reviewed, *Preventing Deadly Conflict* failed to reach out convincingly to more conservative figures or to Washington policy makers. Many in the academic and policy research communities, however, benefited from the related funding undertaken by the Carnegie Corporation, giving this project a much wider research legacy than the others.

Four, prior to the Carnegie project, an award for the most expensive, as well as ambitious, study would have gone to the Commission on Global Governance. Headed by Ingvar Carlsson and Sonny Ramphal, the membership of the large Commission read like a liberal internationalist all-star team. It, too, produced a book-length final report. *Our Global Neighbourhood*, in fact, was produced by Oxford University Press as a surprisingly readable 400-page book in 1995. Carlsson was elected to his second round as Prime Minister of Sweden over the course of the project, which benefited from the political and material support of that government as well as of several major foundations.

Addressing the whole scope of global governance was an enormous undertaking, and it could be said that the scale of this substantive ambition determined both the success and the failure of the enterprise. Some parts of the report necessarily were far better received and far more influential than others. Though the commissioners and organizers expected their recommendations for UN reform to be the centrepiece of the study, it turned out that most of their proposals in that area were well outside the mainstream of international debate at that point and had little influence at the UN. For more conservative audiences, these proposals, plus what they saw as a denigrating of sovereignty concerns, reduced the credibility of the whole exercise. On the other hand, the report was prescient about the future course of arms control and about the growing role of civil society within and between countries. Perhaps because it flagged rising issues of how the world should organize to handle transnational challenges, the report has shown considerable durability, even if many of its findings remain controversial with some groups.

As these four cases illustrate, clearly it is not enough to throw either money or blue ribbon commissions at a problem. Some high quality products, like the Ogata/Volcker report, the series produced by Brian Urquhart and Erskine Childers at the Ford Foundation, and the *Successor Vision* study headed by Elliot Richardson for UNA-USA, cost only a fraction of the last three projects discussed above. Urquhart and Childers demonstrated, as well, that it does not necessarily require a large blue-ribbon panel to get attention and results. In this field, bigger is surely not always better.

Caveats, worries, and provocations

While I remain a booster of independent international studies of how the United Nations and other international institutions can be strengthened, it does seem to me that we need to rethink how to go about this. In each of the four cases addressed above, decisions made in the planning stages – who, what, when, and why – proved critical in terms of determining the project's eventual impact. The political context in which these efforts are made is changing, which makes such strategic choices even more critical. In this regard, I have five concerns.

First, while most of the organizers have paid attention to geographical diversity, they have either ignored or rejected the need for political diversity. Surely it is more fun to work with the like-minded and it certainly both eases and broadens the process of consensus-building within the group. But the larger question is how a report will fare outside of the group, and that is where all of these projects ran into trouble. Sooner or later our ideas will be challenged and it might well be better to have a few devil's advocates within the process of deliberation than to face them only after the ideas and phrases are fixed and potential critics are doubly upset at being excluded from the process. One option would be to include dissents and reservations in the reports, a practice that has largely been lost in recent years with the stress on consensus. More thought needs to be given to how to incorporate a broader range of views without destroying either the chemistry within a group or the possibility for a meaningful and specific result.

Second, the trend to mega-studies – those costing over a million US dollars – in the latter half of the 1990s is worrisome for several reasons. Not only is there a question of cost effectiveness, but it suggests that there will be fewer studies and hence less of an intellectually competitive and stimulating environment. If mega-projects with sweeping mandates, authoritative leadership, and consensus rules come to dominate the production of well-publicized ideas on UN reform, security, or global governance, for example, where are the dissident voices going to come from and how are they going to be financed? It is not coincidental, in this regard, that all of the major projects reviewed were sponsored and organized by bodies based in the North. Some of these groups, of course, were much better than others at including voices from the South, but then only those known to and selected by the northern organizers.

Third, at times, it can be difficult to tell whether some of the projects were established for the purpose of advocacy or inquiry. In several cases, it appeared as if the organizers assembled a study or commission basically to add a degree of authority to a position or orientation they already held. These groups seemed to be independent only within the confines of a set of stated or unstated assumptions, and their conclusions were largely predictable from the outset. To some extent, of course, panels will be self-selecting and organizers need to have a sense of where they are going before launching a panel study. But if the results seem largely pre-cooked, then the whole enterprise of independent commissions will lose some credibility and questions will be raised by funders about whether such exercises are a sound way to expend scarce resources.

Fourth, while it is quite understandable that these projects have identified the UN as their prime target, it should be questioned when and where this is most appropriate. In most of these matters, it is the member states, not the UN secretariat, that are the key decision-makers and implementers. Even in the realm of UN reform, the member states are the final arbiters of most big-ticket items. Capitals have the keys to both financial and political capital. The UN, moreover, tends to be a place of grand visions and weak follow-through. By bringing their visions and ambitious action plans to the United Nations as their primary target, these commissions have tended to compound this gap between vision and practice in the world body.

Fifth, at the same time, this pattern tends to exacerbate the gap between US politics and global norm-building processes. On both sides of the split between the United States and other member states on global issues, the tendency is for the like-minded to talk to each other, reinforcing their perspectives and presumptions. When global commissions purporting to represent the range of relevant views chronically leave out certain perspectives – including those of US conservatives and legislators – it reinforces the impression that Americans are not a part of the global consensus, and that their views are not welcome in global gatherings.

So, yes, I do believe that these blue-ribbon initiatives have been influential on the whole. They have had, no doubt, more effect on the way we think about global issues and institutions than on specific policy choices. But to assert that they have been influential does not mean that their influence has always been constructive. That judgement may well depend on whether we make some mid-course corrections and begin to address the kinds of questions raised here. In another decade or two, historians hopefully can give us more authoritative answers. In the meantime, these speculations can serve as a starting point to such an inquiry.

Appendix

International Commission on Weapons of Mass Destruction

Ambassador Jayantha Dhanapala

Mandate

The twentieth century saw the discovery and use of weapons of mass destruction (WMD). Treaties were negotiated to ban some categories of these weapons, but the threat of their use with horrifying consequences to humankind remains. Political initiatives, though relatively successful in some areas, have nevertheless been unable to address the evolving threats to international peace and security in the area of WMD and materials and technology used for their production. Existing multilateral disarmament and non-proliferation treaties in the area of WMD have yet to become universal or enter into force. Furthermore, recent trends, fuelled in particular by fears of terrorism after the horrific attacks on the United States on September 11, 2001, point towards a new dark age for disarmament as WMD and the means to deliver them spread not just to more states but to terrorist groups and other so-called non-state actors.

The possible use of military action not only offers little hope to eliminate WMD threats, but it also creates its own dangers.

The twenty-first century must therefore see a new era free of WMD. An international commission of independent, eminent persons would be able to make creative and far-reaching recommendations for fresh initiatives towards this end. An international commission would provide an alternative and focused forum for examining on a prior basis issues regarding security in a WMD-free world. Such a commission should also suggest practical, constructive, and realistic steps in a manner that takes us closer, step-by-step, to that goal, including ways of dealing with stability and security in the transitional period. In considering the WMD threat, the international commission would also address the proliferation of WMD delivery systems.

The mandate of the international commission on WMD should explicitly extend to both disarmament and non-proliferation – one cannot be sacrificed for the other without losing credibility. It would also cover possible terrorist use of such weapons and specific multilateral, regional, plurilateral, or national strategies – including unilateral initiatives – to address such threats. The commission would further focus on identifying opportunities to promote multilateral cooperation, strengthen the rule of law and improve the efficiency and effectiveness of multilateral institutions to address these challenges.

The mandate of the commission would last for one year during which time it would hold four working sessions.

Status

The international commission on WMD would be an independent body. Ideally, the international commission would obtain essential political support from one or two governments that are internationally respected for their support of disarmament and non-proliferation efforts.

A private foundation or research institution could provide alternative support for the launching of the work of the commission. Joint support from a government and a private organization might be yet another possibility.

The final product

The commission would produce a report that could serve as both a call to action and a useful and authoritative instrument for governments and civil society alike to use in advocating greater progress on disarmament. The report would not only look into relevant issues with an investigative eye, but it should also pinpoint alternative courses of action in addressing problems arising from the existence of WMD and the related materials and technology that are used in their production. Alternative ways of addressing the ongoing crisis in multilateral disarmament policy should also be proposed. The report could be launched by the Secretary-General of the United Nations and presented to the General Assembly, thereby ensuring a wider debate on its content.

The commissioners

The commission would consist of no more than twelve individuals, in addition to two co-chairs from the North and South, respectively. Commissioners would be drawn from two distinct groups of individuals. The first group would be composed of experts with recognized expertise and knowledge on issues relating to weapons of mass destruction, related materials, and technology. The second group would include renowned personalities, recognized by their national or international political standing. Together, the commissioners should bring a range of professional expertise and political insight into the work of the commission. Commissioners should be appointed with due regard to equitable geographic, political, and gender balance. There should be no more than one member from any given country.

The advisory board

An advisory board of prominent political leaders and dignitaries, as well as senior officials from relevant international organizations (i.e. the International Atomic Energy Agency (IAEA), the Organisation for the Prohibition of Chemical Weapons (OPCW), the Preparatory Committee of the Comprehensive Nuclear-Test Ban Treaty Organization (PrepComCTBTO), and the World Health Organization (WHO)) would serve as the political and substantive point of reference for the commission, and would help to build broad political support for the work of the commission. The advisory board would also help to build the political momentum and public engagement required for effective follow-up on the recommendations of the commission. A chair to the advisory board would also be required. The advisory board would not be responsible for the contents of the final report, the responsibility for which would be entirely borne by the commission.

Secretariat

In order for the commission to carry out its work in a smooth and effective manner, it would require a secretariat to provide it with the necessary substantive, administrative, and organizational support. The secretariat would, inter alia, undertake the necessary fund-raising to support the activities of the commission, organize meetings and consultations, and assist in obtaining relevant background information, published studies, and bibliographies, as well as other such resources as the commissioners may require. The secretariat would also manage the publication and distribution of the report of the commission and of all the background research used in its work, and it would take the lead in the diplomatic efforts to engage governments and build political support for the debate.

The secretariat resources, human and otherwise, could be provided by an interested government or governments supporting the work of the commission, a private foundation or research institution, or by both a government and such a private organization. It would be essential to ensure the independence of the secretariat.

Research and consultation

The commission's research efforts should build upon and complement the many efforts already undertaken in the various areas of concern relating to WMD by research institutes, academia, individual governments, and relevant international organizations. The commission would further draw upon the relevant debate in the international community. In addition, papers and studies might be commissioned to provide commissioners with state-of-the-art research on new issues under consideration, including from relevant international organizations.

As an additional input to its work, the commission would hold a number of hearings in key regional centres in order to obtain a wide spectrum of views in different geographical areas.

Funding

Financial and political support for the work of the commission would be sought from a variety of sources, in particular private foundations and interested governments.

Proposed areas of study for the Commission

Nuclear

- Universality of the Non Proliferation Treaty (NPT) and involvement of three nuclear-weapon-capable states in the process of nuclear disarmament and non-proliferation.
- Implementation of the 13 steps of the FD of the 2000 NPT Review Conference (article VI); this would include, inter alia, the role of nu-

clear weapons in security policies, as well as confidence-building measures with regard to nuclear weapons, including the reduction of the operational status of nuclear weapons to avoid accidental or unauthorized use of nuclear weapons, increased transparency in nuclear arsenals.
- Measures to enhance the safety and security of nuclear material facilities.
- Strengthening and consolidation of existing nuclear-weapon-free zones, establishment of additional nuclear-weapon-free zones (NWFZs).
- Possibilities/ways to expedite the entry into force of the Comprehensive Test Ban Treaty (CTBT).
- Means to improve controls over weapons-grade fissile materials (plutonium and highly enriched uranium (HEU)) and other radioactive materials that could be used in "dirty" bombs.
- Political, legal, technological and institutional requisites of a nuclear weapons convention.

Chemical

- Strengthening the Chemical Weapons Convention (CWC) with a view to the fullest implementation of its provisions, taking also into account new advances in science and technology as well as new related verification techniques.
- Ways to effectively strengthen existing means to monitor global trade in precursor chemicals while at the same time ensuring economic and technological development and cooperation in chemical activities for peaceful purpose.
- Measures to enhance safety and security of precursors and facilities.

Biological

- Strengthening the Biological Weapons Convention (BWC), not least in the area of verification of compliance.
- Strengthening confidence-building measures, as agreed to at the Second BWC Review Conference and as amended at the Third Review Conference.
- Strengthening the Secretary-General's responsibilities under General Assembly resolution 42/37 C (1987) and Security Council resolution 620 (1988).
- Measures to enhance safety and security of biological agents/toxins and facilities.

WMD delivery systems

- Establishment of universal norms or instruments dealing with missile-related concerns.
- Consideration of missile-related confidence-building measures, dual-use technologies.

Outer space

- Strengthening of existing legal regime and addressing possible lacunae to prevent weaponization of outer space.

Potential for terrorism with WMD or related materials and technology

- Strengthening and full implementation of disarmament and non-proliferation treaties.
- Promoting the early conclusion of a treaty on the suppression of nuclear terrorism.
- Role of national authorities to ensure security of WMD components as well as the security of nuclear, biological, and chemical facilities.
- Preparation and enactment of domestic legislation consistent with commitments undertaken under relevant disarmament treaties; criminalization of illegal activities related to weapons of mass destruction; unauthorized use or transfer of materials and technologies by their nationals.
- Reinforcement of ethical norms and creation of corporate codes of conduct – through international and national scientific societies, institutions teaching sciences or engineering skills related to weapons technologies, and the Global Compact network – to prevent the involvement of defence scientists or technical experts in terrorist activities.
- Bilateral, regional, or sub-regional arrangements to verify that civilian nuclear, biological, or chemical installations are not being diverted for non-peaceful uses.
- Links between organized crime, proliferation of conventional arms, and terrorist access to WMD components.

Dynamic underlying disarmament and non-proliferation efforts

- Institutional and political bases of sustainable disarmament.
- Ways in which the "disarmament divide" – where higher compliance

standards apply to non-proliferation than to disarmament – can be bridged.

- Ways in which legitimate national security concerns can be met with minimum dislocation caused to economic and social potential and with minimum perceived threat posed to others.
- Potential of preparing and publishing "disarmament indices" – similar to the "human development indices" developed by the United Nations Development Programme (UNDP) – that can be used for comparable purposes in sustaining the process of "results-based disarmament".

Contributors

Prof. Dr. Ramesh Thakur is the Senior Vice-Rector of the United Nations University (UNU) and Assistant Secretary-General of the United Nations. Born in India, he was educated in India (University of Calcutta) and Canada (Queen's University). He has held full-time academic appointments in Fiji, New Zealand and Australia, as well as visiting appointments in other places. He was Professor of International Relations and Director of Asian Studies at the University of Otago in New Zealand, and Professor and Head of the Peace Research Centre at the Australian National University in Canberra. He was appointed Vice Rector (Peace and Governance) of UNU in 1998; a Commissioner on the International Commission on Intervention and State Sovereignty in 2001; Senior Advisor on Reforms and Principal Writer of the UN Secretary-General's second reform report in 2002; and Senior Vice Rector of UNU with the rank of Assistant Secretary-General in 2003.

Andrew F. Cooper is Associate Director of the Centre for International Governance Innovation (CIGI) and Professor in the Department of Political Science at the University of Waterloo, Canada. In 2000 he was a Fulbright Scholar at the Nitze School of Advanced International Studies, Johns Hopkins University, Washington, DC. He has authored/co-authored a number of articles on diplomatic innovation, comparative foreign policy, and governance in a wide number of journals including *International Organization*, *Journal of Democracy*, *Washington Quarterly*, *International Studies Perspectives*, *Political Science Quarterly*, and *Third World*

Quarterly. His most recent books are *Tests of Global Governance: Canadian Diplomacy and United Nations World Conferences* (Tokyo: United Nations University Press, 2004); and as co-editor with John English and Ramesh Thakur of *Enhancing Global Governance: Towards a New Diplomacy?* (Tokyo: United Nations University Press, 2002).

Ambassador Jayantha Dhanapala was former UN Under-Secretary-General for Disarmament Affairs 1998–2003 and the President of the 1995 NPT Review and Extension Conference. Ambassador Dhanapala joined the Sri Lanka Foreign Service in 1965 and in 1984 was appointed ambassador to the United Nations in Geneva. In 1987 he left the Foreign Service to head the United Nations Institute for Disarmament Research (UNIDIR). In 1992 he returned to the Foreign Service as Additional Foreign Secretary before taking up the position of Ambassador to the United States. He has also served as Commissioner in UNSCOM, the Head of the Special Group visiting the Presidential Sites in Iraq and a member of the 1996 Canberra Commission on the Elimination of Nuclear Weapons. He presently serves as a Commissioner on the Weapons of Mass Destruction Commission.

John English is Executive Director of the Centre for International Governance Innovation (CIGI) and Professor of History at the University of Waterloo. He has served as a Member of Parliament and was Parliamentary Secretary to the Minister of Intergovernmental Affairs and President of the Privy Council of Canada. He served as Chair of the House of Commons Committee on Sustainable Human Development and Vice-Chair of the Committee on Foreign Affairs and International Trade. He served as a Special Envoy for Landmines and for the Security Council Election. He is the past Chair of Canada's Museum of Civilization and War Museum and a former president of the Canadian Institute of International Affairs. He has written a biography of former Canadian Prime Minister Lester Pearson and is currently writing a biography of another Canadian Prime Minister, Pierre Elliott Trudeau.

Nicole Fritz is a lecturer in international and constitutional law at the University of Witwatersrand's School of Law. She clerked for Justice Richard J. Goldstone at South Africa's Constitutional Court and assisted him in his work as chairperson of the Independent International Commission on Kosovo.

Richard J. Goldstone was a justice of the Constitutional Court of South Africa From 1994–2003. He was the Chief Prosecutor of the United Nation's Criminal Tribunals for the former Yugoslavia and Rwanda from 1994–1996. In 2000 he chaired the Independent International Commission on Kosovo and in 2002/3 co-chaired the International Bar Association's Task Force on International terrorism. He is presently teaching in New York (NYU and Fordham Law Schools) and is a member of the Independent Inquiry Committee investigating allegations concerning the Iraq Oil for Food Programme.

Marianne Hanson is Senior Lecturer in International Relations and Director of the Rotary Centre for International Studies in peace and conflict resolution at the University of Queensland, Australia. Her research interests focus on international security, especially on issues of arms control and disarmament, the role of international institutions and the evolution of ideas and norms in security. She is the co-editor of *International Relations in the New Century: An Australian Perspective* (Melbourne: Oxford University Press, 2001).

Jorge Heine (PhD, Stanford) is ambassador of Chile to India (2003–) and served previously as ambassador to South Africa (1994–1999). A member of the Executive Committee of the International Political Science Association (IPSA) and of the International Board of Governors of the Center for International Governance (CIGI) in Waterloo, Canada, he has been a visiting fellow at St. Antony's College, Oxford, a research associate at The Wilson Center in Washington, DC and a consultant to the Ford Foundation and the United Nations. He is the author, co-author or editor of eight books and some fifty articles in journals and symposium volumes.

Sanjeev Khagram is a faculty member at the JFK School of Government at Harvard University where he co-leads the Transnational Dynamics and Architectures of Governance Initiative. He is the author of *Dams and Development: Transnational Struggle for Power and Water* (Ithaca, New York: Cornell University Press, 2004). From 1998–2000, he was Senior Policy Advisor at the World Commission on Dams.

W. Andy Knight is Professor of International Relations and McCalla Research Professor in the Department of Political Science at the University of Alberta. He is past Vice Chair of the Academic Council on the United Nations System and currently editor of Global Governance Journal. His recent books include *A Changing United Nations: Multilateral Evolution and the Quest for Global Governance* (London: Macmillan/Palgrave Press, 2000), as editor *Adapting the United Nations to a postmodern Era: Lessons Learned* (London: Macmillan/Palgrave Press, 2001) and as co-author *Building Sustainable Peace* (Edmonton/Tokyo: University of Alberta/United Nations University Press, 2004). He is director of a three-year research project on Children and Armed Conflict that is funded by the Social Sciences and Humanities Research Council of Canada.

Edward C. Luck is Director of the Center on International Organization and Professor of Practice in International and Public Affairs at Columbia University. A past President and CEO of the United Nations Association of the USA and one of the architects of the UN reform efforts from 1995–1997, he has published widely on UN affairs, US foreign policy, and a range of security and political issues. Among his publications are *Mixed Messages: American Politics and International Organization, 1919–1999* (Washington, DC: Brookings Institution Press for the Century Foundation, 1999), *Reforming the United Nations:*

Lessons from a History in Progress (New Haven, CT: ACUNS, 2003), and, with Michael Doyle as editors, *International Law and Organization: Closing the Compliance Gap* (Lanham, Maryland: Rowman & Littlefield, 2004).

S. Neil MacFarlane is Lester B. Pearson Professor of International Relations at the University of Oxford, and Professorial Fellow at St. Anne's College. His articles have appeared in numerous journals, including *World Politics*, *International Security*, *Survival*, *Security Studies*, *Third World Quarterly*, *International Affairs*, *Études Internationales*, *Internationale Politik und Gesellschaft*, *Security Dialogue*, *The International Journal*, and *Development and Security*. In 2002, he completed an Adelphi Paper for the International Institute for Strategic Studies on intervention in contemporary world politics, and (with Yuen Foong Khong) is completing a critical history of the concept of human security for the United Nations Intellectual History Project.

Jon Pedersen was trained as a social anthropologist and is currently Deputy Managing Director of Fafo Institute for Applied International Studies in Oslo, Norway. He has been working extensively in supplying social statistics and analysis in conjunction with the Middle East Peace Process and in transition, post-conflict and conflict countries and has also done research on the role of social science in peace processes and transitions.

Elizabeth Riddell-Dixon is a Professor of international relations at the University of Western Ontario. Her publications include *Canada and the Beijing Conference on Women: Governmental Politics and NGO Participation* (Vancouver: University of British Colombia Press, 2001), and as co-author *The State of the United Nations, 1993: North-South Perspectives* (Providence, RI: ACUNS, 1993), as well as articles in *Global Governance*, *The International Social Science Journal*, *Canadian Journal of Political Science*, *International Journal*, and *Journal of Comparative and Commonwealth Politics*. From 1998 to 2003, she was the Co-Director of the Summer Workshop Programme for the Academic Council on the United Nations System.

Heather A. Smith is an Associate Professor and Chair, International Studies Programme, University of Northern British Columbia. She has been a visiting professor in the Departamento Académico de Estudios Internacionales, Instituto Tecnológico Autónomo de Mexico (ITAM) in Mexico City. Her research interests focus on climate change policy and gender and foreign policy. Her most recent book is as co-editor, *Feminist Perspectives on Canadian Foreign Policy* (Toronto: Oxford University Press, 2003). She is currently a member of the International Studies Association Executive Council and Past President of the ISA-Canada Executive.

Jean-Philippe Thérien is a Professor in the Department of Political Science at the Université de Montréal, and Associate Academic Director of the Centre d'Études et de Recherches Internationales de l'Université de Montréal (CÉRIUM). His research focuses on North–South issues, development assistance and inter-American politics. His publications have appeared in several journals, including *American Political Science Review*, *Comparative Political Studies*, *Global Governance*, *International Organization*, and *Third World Quarterly*. He is co-editor of *Foreign Policy and Regionalism in the Americas* (Boulder, CO: Lynne Rienner, 1996).

Carolin J. Thielking is a doctoral candidate in International Relations at the University of Oxford. Her research focuses on human rights and humanitarian intervention. As a fellow of the Robert Bosch Foundation and the German National Academic Foundation Postgraduate Programme in International Affairs, she is currently pursuing a project on small arms control.

Jennifer Welsh is University Lecturer in International Relations at the University of Oxford, and a Fellow of Somerville College. She is a former Jean Monnet Fellow of the European University Institute in Florence, and was a Cadieux Research Fellow in the Policy Planning Staff of the Canadian Department of Foreign Affairs. She spent five years in the private sector – first as a consultant with the international firm, McKinsey and Company, and subsequently as a partner in d~Code, a research and strategy firm focused on the "Nexus Generation." Her most recent publications include *Humanitarian Intervention and International Relations* (Oxford: Oxford University Press, 2004) and *At Home in the World: Canada's Global Vision for the 21st Century* (Toronto: HarperCollins Canada, 2004).

Geoffrey Wiseman was an Australian diplomat, serving at embassies in Stockholm, Hanoi, and Brussels, and as private secretary to the Australian Foreign Minister. He also worked at the Ford Foundation in New York. He has a doctorate in International Relations from Oxford University, and currently teaches diplomacy and international security in the School of International Relations at the University of Southern California. He has written *Concepts of Non-Provocative Defence: Ideas and Practices in International Security* (New York: Palgrave, 2002) and shorter pieces on Asia-Pacific security, common security, and diplomatic culture.

Index

Abzug, Bella 255, 257
accountability 170, 187, 211, 212
Afghanistan 108; and ICISS report 213, 214; and responsibility to rebuild 210–11; Soviet invasion 30, 57; US intervention 9, 167, 175; and women's rights 256
Afheldt, Horst 51
Africa 158; conflicts and intervention 176
Africa Leadership Forum 66
African Union 216
agriculture 39; production issues 143, 150
AIDS/HIV issues 103
Al-Qaeda 213
Albanians 209
Algeria 258
Allende, Salvador 231
Allison, Roy 64
Almeida, Grace d' 169
Alternative Defence Commission 52
Alvear, Soledad 235
An American Legacy: *Building a Nuclear Free World* (Stimson Center) 123
American Nuclear Weapons Freeze Campaign 53, 63
American Progressive movement 78
Amin, Samir 35, 37
Angola 108, 211
Annan, Kofi (UN Secretary-General) 13, 19, 94, 113; and conflict prevention 284; and gender analysis 254; Global Compact proposal 113–15; and human rights violations 174; and humanitarian intervention 181, 223–4; and ICISS report 194–5, 199, 209, 213, 214; and Rwandan genocide 226–7
Antarctica 128
Anti-Terrorism Act (Canada) 214
Anti-Terrorism Crime and Security Act (UK) 214
Arabs/Arab studies 268
Arbatov, Georgi 14, 47, 54, 58–9
Arbour, Louise 256, 257
Argentina 145, 236, 237, 243; and women's rights 250, 258
armed interventions *see* military interventions
arms control: and Canberra Commission 124; and disarmament 56, 131; initiatives 131
arms exports 33
Armstrong, Neil 109
ASEAN *see* Association of Southeast Asian Nations
ASEAN Regional Forum (ARF) 56
Ashipala, Selma 249

Ashwari, Dr. Hanan 169
Asia 216, 224, 234, 258; Central 275; East/Southeast Asia 158
Asia-Pacific region 68; and Palme Commission ideas 51, 54–5
Asmal, Kader 149
Aspin, Les 137
Association of Southeast Asian Nations (ASEAN) 56
asylum seekers 214, 215
atrocities: and ICISS report 195; and international law 187, 190, 193; and justification for intervention 176, 188, 204, 205, 223; and national sovereignty 226
Australia 149; and common security concept 54–6, 63, 64, 68; and disarmament diplomacy 131–2; and East Timor intervention 230; foreign policies 126–8, 131, 138; and humanitarian intervention 228; security interests 130; and women's rights 250, 257
Australian Labor Party 54–5
authority: and interventions 190–1, 209, 217, 226, 271; national vs. international 190–1; and responsibility to protect 210; and UN 191–4, 227
Axworthy, Lloyd 15, 181, 199
Ayoob, Mohammed 186

Bahr, Egon 47, 51, 65
Balkans 56
Bank for Reconstruction and Development 12
Barnaby, Frank 52
Baxi, Upendra 116–17
BCR *see* Brandt Commission Research agency
Beijing Declaration and Platform for Action 254
Bellamy, Carol 114
Benedick, Richard 81
Bergsten, C. Fred 35, 36
Better World Fund 279
Bhopal disaster (India 1984) 80
big dam projects: decline in numbers 143–4; funding 143–4; institutional involvement 143, 145; opposition 144–6; political-economic factors 145; and sustainable development 142, 144, 147, 154, 160
Biological Weapons Convention (BWC) 292
Blair, Tony 200, 216
Blechman, Barry 53, 66
Blix Commission on Weapons of Mass Destruction 12
"Blue Ribbon Power: Independent Commissions and UN Reform" 279
Bolivia 145
Booth, Ken 52, 64, 67–8
borders: and intervention 192, 223, 225; security 62, 110; and sovereignty 187; trans-border issues 103, 250; and UN 191
Bosnia 20, 210
Bouteflika, President Abdelaziz (Algeria) 227
Boutros-Ghali, Boutros 101, 251, 259, 282, 283, 284
Brahimi Report on peacekeeping 13, 212
Brandt 21 Forum 19, 40
Brandt Commission 6, 11, 12–13, 14, 15, 16, 18, 19; composition 31–2; and development 62; funding 31; impact and influence 38–41; and international community 29–31; setting up and establishment 29–32; *see also* Independent Commission on International Development Issues
Brandt Commission Research agency (BCR) 40
Brandt Report (1980) 8, 10, 13, 22, 119; Bretton Woods paradigm/UN paradigm 28–9, 38, 42; content 32–5; effect on development 27–8; and global wealth redistribution 33, 34, 36; and Keynesianism 29, 37, 40; reactions to 35–7; and Right-Left spectrum 35–6; *see also North-South: A Program for Survival*
Brandt Report II (1983) 27, 35; *see also Common Crisis. North-South: Co-operation for World Recovery*
Brandt, Willy 10, 11, 14, 19, 32, 37, 39; and Commission on Global Governance 40, 101; and common security concept 51; and Palme Commission 58, 65
Brazil 17, 83, 149, 236, 237
Bretton Woods agreement 12; institutions 13, 28, 39; and Washington Consensus 39
Brezhnev, Leonid 32, 55

Britain: and common security concept 52, 64; and nuclear disarmament 52; and ozone depletion 80–1; peace movement 52; *see also* United Kingdom (UK)
Brundtland Commission (1987) 9, 10, 11, 15, 20, 22, 76–98, 156, 267, 273, 274; as commission model 199; critics/criticism 89; and development/environment issues 62; report 18, 76, 119; *see also Our Common Future*; sustainable development
Brundtland, Dr. Gro Harlem 10, 11, 12, 13, 18, 19, 20, 40, 48, 65, 66; biography 94–5; and UN system 256–7; on UNCED 82, 83
Budapest 169
Bull, Hedley 201–2
Burma 131
Bush, George W. 68
Business Charter for Sustainable Development (ICC) 90
Butler, General Lee 132, 138
Butler, Richard 138
Buzan, Barry 52, 64
BWC *see* Biological Weapons Convention

Cairo Conference on Population and Development *see* United Nations International Conference on Population and Development (ICPD) (Cairo 1994)
Cambodia 108, 229; 1990 peace plan 127
Campaign for Nuclear Disarmament (UK) 52
Canada 169; foreign policy 199; and human rights 257; human security concept 234–5; and humanitarian intervention 228; and ICISS 216, 274; and women's rights and status 250, 254, 257
Canada and the Nuclear Challenge (Canadian Parliamentary Report) 124
Canberra Commission on the Elimination of Nuclear Weapons (1996) 6, 9, 11, 12, 15, 16; and Australia's arms control diplomacy 130–2; domestic political considerations 125–6; and good international citizenship (CIC) 132–6; impact 135–6; international context 124–5; Keating/Evans initiative 16, 132, 138; report 17, 124, 133, 135–6; success elements 136–9; *see also* good international citizenship (GIC)
Cancùn Summit (2001) 19, 38–9
Cape Town, South Africa 150
capitalism 37, 79, 221
Caribbean countries 257–8
Carlsson, Ingvar 11, 14, 40, 101, 284
Carnegie Commission on Preventing Deadly Conflict 15, 20, 134, 202, 267, 272–4, 283–4; membership 273; reports 283–4
Carruthers, David 78, 89, 91
Carter, Jimmy 15, 82
Catholic Campaign for America 258
CBMs *see* confidence-building measures
CD *see* Conference on Disarmament
Central American Democratic Security Treaty (1995) 235
CFE *see* Conventional Forces in Europe
"The Changing Atmosphere: Implications for Global Security" conference (Toronto 1988) 83, 84
Chechnya 190, 204, 205, 206, 210, 227
Checkel, Jeffrey 58
Chemical Weapons Convention (CWC) (1993) 125, 128, 131, 292
Chernobyl (1986) disaster 80
Childers, Erskine 255, 285
Chile 145, 222, 237, 243
China 38, 55, 131, 149; and Kosovo stance 227; and military intervention 200, 204; nuclear tests 126; and UN peacekeeping operations 210
Chrétien, Jean (Canada) 19, 199, 216
civil society 258–60; concept 21, 116; global 102; organizations 106; *see also* good international citizenship (GIC) concept
Clark, David (UK) 216–17
Clifford, J. 268–9
climate change awareness 81
Clinton administration 137, 233
Cold War: ending 57–60, 100; and Palme Commission 69; revival 30; *see also* post-Cold War
Collins, Alan 58
Colombia 221, 233, 237, 242, 243
colonialism 29, 185; decolonization era 186
Commission on the Elimination of Nuclear Weapon *see* Canberra Commission
Commission on Global Governance (1995) 6, 9, 11, 13, 14, 18, 20, 21, 40, 99–122, 272, 279; character and make-up 100–2;

concepts and intellectual/policy context 102–17; funding/costs 101–2, 284; proposals 11–12; report 100, 104–5, 113–19; *see also Our Global Neighbourhood*
Commission on Human Security 18, 22
Commission on International Development (1969) 10, 27; *see also* Pearson Commission
Commission of Macroeconomics and Health 18, 272, 273
Commission on the Social Dimension of Globalization 10, 272
Committee on International Security and Arms Control 134
Common Crisis. North-South: Co-operation for World Recovery (Brandt Commission report) 19, 85
common security concept 21, 46, 50–1, 52, 67–9; and arms control 56; and non-offensive defence 50, 51, 52–7; transnational 59
Common Security Forum 66
Common Security (Palme Commission report 1982) 13, 15, 48, 85
Comprehensive Nuclear-Test Ban Treaty Organization (CTBTO) 290
Comprehensive Test Ban Treaty (CTBT) 125, 128, 292
Concepts of Security (UN Experts' report 1986) 62
Conference on the Changing Atmosphere (Toronto) 83
Conference on Disarmament (CD) 131
Conference on the Environment and Development (Rio de Janeiro 1992) 249; *see also* United Nations World Summit for Sustainable Development
Conference on Human Rights *see* United Nations World Conference on Human Rights (Vienna 1993)
Conference on International Economic Cooperation 30
confidence-building measures (CBMs) 46, 56
conflicts: African 176; and "CNN effect" 198–9, 221–2; effects on women and women's rights 247, 248; internal 221, 222–3; prevention and peacebuilding 188–9, 202–3, 284; and responsibility to rebuild 210–11; and root causes 267; and "Second Cold War" 49; *see also* Carnegie Commission; interventions; war
Congo, Democratic Republic of 215, 232
Contadora Group (1983) 234
A Continent Apart: Kosovo, Africa and Humanitarian Intervention (Jo'burg Seminar papers 2000) 176
Convention on the Elimination of all Forms of Discrimination Against Women (1979) 251
Conventional Forces in Europe (CFE) talks (1989) 59
Cooper, Andrew 129–30
Copenhagen Centre for Peace and Conflict Research 51; *see also* Copenhagen Peace Research Institute
Copenhagen Peace Research Institute (COPRI) 51, 64
Copenhagen Summit for Social Development (1995) 250
COPRI *see* Copenhagen Peace Research Institute
Cortright, David 53
Costa Rica 236, 237
Council on Foreign Relations: Palestinian project 275; report on the Ferghana Valley 274–5
Court of Criminal Justice 21
Cox, Robert 3
CTBT *see* Comprehensive Test Ban Treaty
CTBTO *see* Comprehensive Nuclear-Test Ban Treaty Organization
Cuba 38, 231, 236, 243
cultural issues 104; change 93; and globalization 109, 114, 115; influences 4, 107; rights/traditions 100, 249–51, 258
cultural relativism issue 249–50
Curitiba Declaration 145
CWC *see* Chemical Weapons Convention
Czech Republic 169

Dahlgren, Hans 65, 66
dams *see* big dam projects
Decade for Women (1976–1985) 247, 259
decision-making 34, 79, 154, 159; and globalization 104, 105; processes 160, 164; and sustainable development 142, 146; and UN 209; and women's rights/involvement 247, 257
Declaration on the Elimination of Violence against Women (1993) 252, 259

Declaration on Friendly Relations among States (UN 1970) 215
Declaration of Principles between Israel and PLO (1993) 271
defence spending 111
Demilitarization Fund proposal 111
democracy/democratization 107, 211, 233
den Uyl, Joop 47, 65
Denmark 51, 68, 228
developing states: and non-intervention 192; and poverty 86; and sovereignty 185; and UN 216
development: assistance and financing 33–4, 111, 131; and Bretton Woods paradigm/UN paradigm 28–9, 38, 42; diplomacy 6, 29, 38; and key symbols 267; limits to growth discourse 79; and security 42; *see also* sustainable development
Dhanapala, Jayantha 12, 194–5
diplomacy 5–6; Inter-American 234
disarmament: debates 37, 124, 132, 134, 136; efforts 293–4
discrimination 251, 253, 260; "People of Middle Eastern Aspect" (PMEAs) 206; in refugee camps 270
disease(s) 103, 105, 248
Disney organization 114
Doha Development Round (WTO) 16
domestic violence 249, 250
Dominican Republic 229, 231, 236
Domoto, Senator Akiko 169
Dörfer, Ingemar 52, 57, 65
Dow Chemical 114
Drago doctrine 231
drug trafficking 103, 105
Dunne, Tim 67–8

East Asia 39, 66, 158
East Timor conflict 176, 180, 194, 221, 226; and humanitarian intervention 233; and responsibility to rebuild 210–11; and unified command 212
East–West relations: confrontations/hostility 46, 49, 110; cooperation 58; equilibrium 30
economic issues: equality and women's rights 247; growth and development 92
Economic and Social Council (of the UN) (ECOSOC) 28
The Economist 30
Ecuador 258
education: female illiteracy 250; and women's rights 247, 250, 255, 256, 258
Egeland, Jan 270
Egypt 17
Elliott, Lorraine 77, 85, 91, 95
energy 37; global policy 34
English, Robert 58
ENGOs *see* environmental non-governmental organizations
environmental issues: and big dam projects 145; disasters 80; endangered species 103, 105; and GIC activism 131; and global governance 95, 103, 105; global warming 81; ozone depletion awareness 81; public awareness 80–1; and UNEP 92
environmental non-governmental organizations (ENGOs) 81, 90, 95
Estrada doctrine 231
ethnic cleansing 111, 188, 189, 193, 216, 221; and legitimacy of interventions 204–5, 209, 216
European battlefield nuclear-weapon-free zone proposal 50, 53, 65
European Socialists party 40
European Union (EU) 185, 215, 235; and women's rights and status 250, 254, 257
Evangelista, Mathew 58
Evans, Gareth 11, 14, 15, 54–5, 63, 65; and Canberra Commission 124–41; and good international citizenship concept 127–8; and ICISS 182, 199; and middle power leadership 129–30

Facing the Challenge (South Commission report) 16
Facing Nuclear Dangers (Tokyo Forum report) 124
Fafo (Institute for Applied Social Science, Norway) 8, 269–70, 271–2; and Middle East peace process 267–8
fairness, notion of 170, 172, 173
Falk, Richard 14, 15, 21, 102, 169
famine 103, 105
Farman, Joseph 81
Federation of American Scientists 126
feminism/feminists 255, 258
Ferm, Anders 62
Financing an Effective UN (Ogata, Volcker et al.) 282–3, 285

Finding Ways study 268
First International Conference of People Affected by Dams (Curitiba, Brazil 1997) 145
flood control 143
Florence 169
Focus on the Family (US) 258
Ford Foundation 279, 282, 283, 285
Forsberg, Randall 53
Foucault, Michel 117
Foundation for International Security 52
Founex Report (1971) 78
France 145, 169; nuclear tests 126, 137–8
Franck, Thomas 170, 172
Frank, Andre Gunder 35, 37
Freeze movement (US) 53; *see also* American Nuclear Weapons Freeze Campaign
Frei, Eduardo 31
From Protest to Policy: Beyond the Freeze to Common Security (Solo) 53
Fuerzas Armadas Revolucionarias de Colombia (FARC) 233
Fukuyama, Francis 3

G-77 *see* Group of Seventy-Seven
Gaddis, John Lewis 213
Galtung, Johan 35, 51, 65
Garcia-Robles, Alfonso 48
GATT *see* General Agreement on Tariffs and Trade
Gaviria, César 235
Gender Awareness Information and Networking System (GAINS) 253
gender concept 261; and analysis debates 248, 249, 250; and equality 255; within UN system 254
Gender Contact Group 249
General Agreement on Tariffs and Trade (GATT) 28, 36
genetic diversity preservation 103
genocide 180, 193, 221; 1948 convention 205
Georgia 211
German Social Democratic Party (SDP) 51, 62
Germany 145, 152, 169; and common security concept 65; and ozone depletion 80–1; and responsibility to protect concept 216; and sustainable development concept 78
GIC *see* good international citizenship
girl-children: and cross-border prostitution rackets 250; genital mutilation 250; and human rights 247
Gland Reference Group 146–7, 151, 157, 159
Global Compact recommendation 113–14
Global Development Network 266
Global Engagement: Cooperation and Security in the 21st Century (ed. Nolan) 53
global governance 21, 23, 95, 284–5; civic ethic/core values proposal 107; conceptualizing 102–8; and "conduct of conduct" 117; and democratization 107–8; and denuclearization programme 110; institutions 103–4; as inter-national governance 119; and multilateralism 118; and population growth 112; and resources 103, 105; roles and tasks 104–5; and state(s) 104; and world government/federalism 105; *see also* Commission on Global Governance
global interdependence 187
global military strategic terrain 110
global neighbourhood concept 109, 116
global politics 266–76; and ideas 266; and knowledge economy 267; research 267; systemic changes 102, 108–12
globalization: cultural and social effects 114; and "fragmagration" 109; and humanitarian intervention 233; and nation-state 203; and technology 109–10; *see also* transnational issues
"Globalization Debate of Prime Minister Guy Verhofstadt: the Belgian Initiative" 10
Goldstone, Justice Richard 169
Goldsworthy, David 128
good international citizenship (GIC) concept 124, 126–8, 138; and Canberra Commission 132–6; and element of active leadership 128–30
Gorbachev, Mikhail 19, 20; and Brundtland Commission 83; and common security concept 55, 58–60, 65; and ending of Cold War 58, 80; founding of Green Cross International 90; and Palme Commission 63, 64
Goulart, Joao 231
Graham, Bill 203

Grant, Bruce 54
Green Cross International 90
Green Revolution 247
Green, Rosario 235
Grenada 229
Grinevsky, Ambassador Oleg 139, 169
Gromyko, Andrei 48
Grotius, Hugo 206–7
Group of Seventy-Seven (G-77) 225, 254
Guatemala 210, 258, 270
Gulf states 258
gunboat diplomacy 6, 231, 233

Haas, Peter 76, 91, 92
Haiti 108, 226, 231, 232, 242
Hamburg, Dr. David 15, 283
Hamilton, Lee 15
Hammarskjöld, Dag 48
Hard Choices (Vance) 48
Harvard Nuclear Study Group 52
Hayden, Bill 54
Healey, Dennis 52
Heath, Edward 14, 31, 82
HI *see* Humanitarian Intervention
Higgott, Richard 14, 129–30
highly enriched uranium (HEU) 292
Holl, Jane 20
Holst, Johan Jørgen 51, 65
Holsti, Kal 5
Holy See 254, 258
Honduras 258
human rights 131; activists and military intervention 225; and Australian foreign policy 131; and big dam projects 145; civil-political 186; and genocide 180; and Global Compact 115; and international law 222; organizations 199; post-9/11 attacks 206; and sovereign equality 198; violations 174, 212, 221–2, 232
Human Rights Watch 223
humanitarian disasters 234
humanitarian interventions (HIs) 9–10, 195; alliances and regional organizations 230–1; and atrocities 188, 193; authority for 226; conditions and guidelines 229–31; and conflict prevention/peacebuilding 188–9, 207–8; criteria and principles 189–90, 192, 229–31; effectiveness and legitimacy 207–10; evolving debate 228–31; follow-up assistance and reconstruction 183, 184; and ICISS 180–97; and international law 228; justification and dilemmas 181; and Kosovo Commission's findings 175, 176; and Latin America 224–8, 231–8; lawfulness of 173, 174–6; proportionality rule 230; and "responsibility to protect" concept 181–2, 184, 186–7, 201, 206, 221–45; Rio Group discussion document 238–40; thresholds 230; *see also* military interventions
Hungary 80–1
Hussein, Saddam 205, 216
hydropower companies 160

IAEA *see* International Atomic Energy Agency
Iberoamerican Heads of State Summit (2000) 236
ICC *see* International Chamber of Commerce
ICISS *see* International Commission on Intervention and State Sovereignty
ICISS report 17, 181, 182–4, 190, 193, 194–5, 198–220, 224; on assumptions and controversies 203–11; on conflict prevention and peacebuilding 188–9; criteria and principles framework 189–90, 203, 209; international law and morality 206–7; intervention effectiveness 207–10; and operational challenges 211–12; post 9/11 impact 200; recommendations 193, 217; and "responsibility to protect" concept 181–2, 183, 198–220; and responsibility to rebuild 210–11; on right authority and due process 190–1; sovereignty and intervention 185–8, 200–3
ICOLD *see* International Commission on Large Dams
ICRC *see* International Committee of the Red Cross
ideas 4, 266–76; channelling and purpose 5–8; and global politics 266; and key symbols 267, 275; relabelling 53, 54, 56
Ideas-Institutional Nexus conference 255, 261
IDPs *see* Internally Displaced Persons
Ignatieff, Professor Michael 169

IGOs *see* international government organizations/intergovernmental organizations
ILO *see* International Labour Organization (of the UN)
IMEMO *see* Institute of the World Economy and International Relations (Russia)
IMF *see* International Monetary Fund
Independent Commission on Disarmament and Security Issues 40; Report (1982) 46; *see also* Palme Commission
Independent Commission on International Development Issues 11, 27, 47; *see also* Brandt Commission
Independent International Commission on Kosovo 6, 9, 11, 12, 13, 14, 15, 18, 20, 167–77, 224; composition 169, 171, 172; conclusions and recommendations 171, 172–3, 177; debate 22; establishment 168–9; fairness discourse 170–2, 177; framework of principles 174–5; funding 172; mandate and terms of reference 169; plenary meetings 169; reports 168, 170–3; and UN 13; *see also* humanitarian interventions
India 22, 55, 68, 145, 149; and intervention 186, 204; nuclear power status 110, 133, 138
indigenous peoples 145
Indonesia 83, 131
inequality, global 40–1
INF *see* intermediate-range nuclear forces
Informal Contact Group on Gender report 249
INGOs *see* international non-governmental organizations
Institute for Applied Social Science (Norway) *see* Fafo
Institute for International Economic Studies 272
Institute of the World Economy and International Relations (Russia) (IMEMO) 58
institutionalism, liberal 118
institutionalization 251–4
institutions 266–76
Inter-American Human Rights Court, Institute, and System 232
Inter-American Treaty for Peaceful Conflict Resolution 231–2
Inter-American Treaty of Reciprocal Assistance 231
intermediate-range nuclear forces (INF) 49, 57
Internally Displaced Persons (IDPs) 222
international aid 111
international arms trade 34, 110–11
International Atomic Energy Agency (IAEA) 290
International Bank for Reconstruction and Development 12
International Chamber of Commerce (ICC) 90, 91
International Commission on Intervention and State Sovereignty (ICISS) 1, 6, 10, 11, 15, 18, 19, 180–97, 272, 273; and 9/11 aftermath 213–15; composition 182; debate terms and contributions 184, 200; mandate and goals 182, 199; meetings/consultations/research 183, 199; principles and priorities 200; *see also* ICISS report
International Commission on Large Dams (ICOLD) 160
International Commission on Weapons of Mass Destruction 8, 288–94; advisory board 290; commissioners 290; funding 291; report 289; research and consultation 291; secretariat 290–1; status 289; study areas 291–4
international commissions 266–76; Australian involvement 15–16; blue ribbon panels 61, 67, 100–2, 115, 277, 282, 285, 286–7; Canadian contributions 15, 216, 274; catch phrases/key symbols 20–1, 267, 273; categories 17–19; composition and gender 31–2, 161–2; content and delivery 17–23; criteria for success 61–5, 67, 161–5, 273; final report and recommendations 164–5; funding and independence 67, 172; goals and justification 161–2; guiding principles 162; interactions and deliberations 164; knowledge generation 163; "ownership" 12–17; role of women 19–20; Soviet representation 14; stakeholders and non-state actors 6, 48, 92, 106, 113, 162–3, 177; structures and processes 163–4; and the US 14–15; *see also* named commissions

International Committee of the Red Cross (ICRC) 184, 242
international community: and Brandt Commission 29–31, 34; defence spending 34; development assistance 34; initiatives 172; and international law 167–8, 172, 176; new ethos 170; *see also* interventions
international corporate business 114–15; *see also* multinational corporations
International Criminal Court 21, 210, 254, 256
International Criminal Tribunals *see* International War Crimes Tribunals for Rwanda and the former Yugoslavia
International Financial Institutions (IFIs) 12
international government organizations/ intergovernmental organizations (IGOs) 104, 258
International Hydropower Association 160
international institutions 12, 34
International Labour Organization (of the UN) (ILO) 28
international law: and armed interventions 167–8, 172, 176, 180–1; and ethics intersection 193; and human rights 222; and humanitarian intervention 228; and International Criminal Court 21, 210; and morality 206–7; and principle of non-intervention 233
international leadership: and middle powers 129–30
International Monetary Fund (IMF) 28, 36, 88
international monetary system 34
international non-governmental organizations (INGOs) 145
international order 187
international organizations (IOs) 1, 5, 19; and big dam building 145; and commission panels 290, 291; and intervention 187, 202, 203, 204, 207, 210, 215; and Kosovo 171; and Latin America 223, 236; and multilateralism 119
International Peace Academy seminar (New York 2002) 194
international politics 23; and Canberra Commission 125, 129, 130, 139; and humanitarian intervention 230; and ICISS 203, 205, 217; and trade 30, 292
international relations: ideational turn 1–2, 3, 4, 6, 22, 23; scholars 52, 54
international security: and nuclear arms control 123; and Palme Commission's role 56
International Security journal 52
International Studies Perspectives 279
international terrorism 103, 105; 9/11 attacks 19, 67, 184, 200, 288; and post-9/11 counter-terrorist actions/ reactions 213–15; and weapons on mass destruction 288–94
International Union for the Conservation of Nature *see* IUCN
International Union for the Conservation of Nature (IUCN) 78, 146, 147
International War Crimes Tribunals for Rwanda and the former Yugoslavia 222, 254, 256
international women's movement 259
International Women's Rights Action Watch 260
International Women's Year (1975) 247, 259
intervention(s): assessment of evidence 205; criteria and principles 189–90, 192; debates 180; disparity of actions 176; and ethnic cleansing 204–5, 216; and human protection 190–1; legality of 174–6; and reconstruction 176; and right authority 209; right vs. responsibility 201; threshold for 204–6; and UN 199; *see also* humanitarian interventions; military interventions
IOs *see* international organizations
Iran 258; Islamist revolution (1979) 30; US hostage-rescue mission 38, 47
Iraq: and military intervention 9, 167, 175, 205; nuclear ability 133
Iraq war 19, 26, 216–17; and ICISS criteria 205; and responsibility to rebuild 210–11
Ireland 17
irrigation issues 143, 150
ISKAN 47, 59
Islamic states (fundamentalist) 249; and women's rights 250, 258
Ismail, Razali 277
Israel/Iraelis 213, 268, 269

Jackson, Robert 201–2
Japan 80–1, 169

Johannesburg 169, 176
Jordan 268, 269

Kaldor, Professor Mary 169
Kantian logic, and morality 207
Keating government 126
Keating, Paul 124, 131, 137
Keck, Margaret E. 59
Keohane, Robert 4
Keynesianism 2; and Brandt Report 29, 37, 40; "new deal" 13
Khalid, Mansour 82
Kikkink, Kathryn 59
King, Anthony 2
Kissinger, Henry 201–2
knowledge economy 267
Kokoshin, Andrei 59
Kónigswinter meeting (Germany 1990) 101
Korea 55, 68
Kortunov, Andrei 54
Koskenniemi, Martti 170
Kosovo: conflict 170, 180, 221, 226; and ethnic cleansing 204; and humanitarian intervention 224, 233; and ICISS criteria 205, 209; NATO intervention/bombing 167, 168, 171, 181, 188, 190, 192–3, 194, 200, 223, 235–6; and operational challenges 211–12; and responsibility to protect concept 206–7; responsibility to rebuild 210–11; status of "'conditional independence" 168, 173; and UN Security Council authority 227; *see also* Independent International Commission on Kosovo
Kreisky, Bruno 14, 47

Labour Party (UK) 52
labour practices 115
"Large Dams: Learning from the Past, Looking to the Future" workshop (Gland, Switzerland 1997) 146
Latin America 22, 66, 158; HI discussion summary 237–8; and humanitarian intervention concept 224–8, 231–8; non-intervention principle 231, 236; research agenda 238–40; and US interventionism 231, 233–4
leadership: directional 130, 137; and GIC objectives 129, 137; individual 255–7; international 129–30; and research 257; state 257–8
Learning to Manage Global Environmental Risks (Social Learning Group study) 80
Lebanon 268
legitimacy: political 271–2
Lesotho 145
liberalism 2, 28, 39, 118
Lindahl, Goran 149
Lipton, Michael 35, 37
Living with Nuclear Weapons (Harvard Nuclear Study Group) 52
Lodgaard, Sverre 51
López Portillo, José 38
Luck, Edward 61–5, 66, 67, 176

MacArthur Foundation 279
McDonalds organization 114
Macedonia 210
McNamara, Robert 11, 12, 15, 27, 31, 132
MacNeill, Jim 82–3, 84
Madrid Peace Conference (1991) 268
Mahathir Bin Mohamad, Dr. 16
Makinda, Samuel 22
Mali 270–1
Malnes, Raino 130, 137
Malta 258
Mangold, Peter 52
Mao Tse Tung 266, 275
Martin, Paul 19, 22
media: and "CNN effect" 198–9, 221–2
Mendelson, Sarah 58
MERCOSUR 232
Mexico 17, 39, 145, 236, 237
Middle East 56, 66, 158, 258; peace process 267, 268, 270
middle powers 17, 22; and active leadership 128–30
military interventions 167–79, 182, 188, 190; accountability mechanisms 212; and civil co-ordination 212; criteria and principles 189–90, 192–3, 208–10; and doctrine of self-defence 175; for human protection purposes 188, 190; justification 189–90; legality of 167–8, 174–6; operational challenges 211–12; "red light"/"green light" approach 192–3; and responsibility to rebuild 210–11; right authority and due process 190–1; and unified command 212; *see also* humanitarian interventions
Milosevic, Slobodan 222
Minow, Professor Martha 169

Mitra, Dr Amit 91
MNCs *see* multinational corporations
modernity 269
Møller, Bjørn 64
Montreal Protocol on Substances That Deplete the Ozone Layer 81–2
morality: and international law 206–7; and Kantian logic 207
Mozambique refugee camps 90
Mulroney, Brian (Canada) 84
multilateralism 118
multinational corporations (MNCs) 104, 114–15; standards and codes of conduct 115
Mutual Security: A New Approach to Soviet-American Relations (eds Smoke and Kortunov) 53–4
Myrdal, Alva 48

Nagpal, Tanvi 88, 91
NAM *see* Non-Aligned Movement
Nardin, Terry 207
National Association of People's Movements (India) 149
NATO (North Atlantic Treaty Organization) 47; and Afghanistan forces 214; and armed interventions 181; and INF deployment 57; Kosovo action 167–73, 181, 190, 229; legality of 174; military doctrine 62–3; and non-intervention 229; security policy 49–50
Neild, Robert 52
neo-liberalism 28, 39, 40
neo-realism 118
Netherlands 80–1, 228
networks/networking 266, 272
New Agenda Coalition (UN) 17, 134
New Cold War 80; *see also* "Second Cold War"
"New World Order" 94
New York 169
New Zealand 17; and common security concept 54–6, 63, 64; and humanitarian intervention 228
NGO Forum on Women (1995) 259
NGOs *see* non-governmental organizations
Nicaragua 30
NIEO (New International Economic Order) project 22, 28, 29–30, 39
Noel-Baker, Philip 47
Nolan, Janne E. 53
Non-Aligned Movement (NAM) 30, 38, 65, 225
non-governmental organizations (NGOs) 40, 61, 63, 64, 275; and big dam projects 144–5; and global governance 104, 106; and human rights 259; monitoring compliance of agreements 260; and UN system 259; and women's rights/status 246, 258–9
non-intervention principle 198; in Latin America 221–45; and NATO 229; and sovereignty 202
non-offensive defence concept 50, 52–7, 67, 68
non-state actors (NSAs) 106
North Africa 258
North Atlantic Treaty Organization *see* NATO
North Korea 56; nuclear power status 110, 133
North-South: A Program for Survival (Brandt Commission report) 13
North–South relations 27; and Brandt Report 33, 35; dichotomy 109; ideological shifts 39–40; interdependency 29, 42; political stalemate 39–41; and transfer of resources 33, 34, 36
Norway 17, 145, 152; and Middle East peace process 268, 270; and women's rights 250
Norwegian Church Aid 270–1
Nossal, Kim 129–30
NPTREC *see* Nuclear Non-Proliferation Treaty Review and Extension Conference
NSAs *see* non-state actors
nuclear arms control 291–2; and international security 123; Non Proliferation Treaty (NPT) 125, 291; weapons-grade fissile materials 292
nuclear disasters 80
nuclear forces 49
Nuclear Non-Proliferation Treaty Review and Extension Conference (NPTREC) 128
nuclear proliferation 110
nuclear testing 126, 133, 137–8
nuclear weapon states (NWS) 110, 135–6
nuclear weapons: disarmament/elimination 123, 125, 132, 136, 137; Non Proliferation

Treaty (NPT) 125, 291; regulation 123; studies 123–4
nuclear-weapon-free zones (NWFZs) 292
nuclearism resurgence 135
NWFZs *see* nuclear-weapon-free zones
Nye, Joseph 4
Nyerere, Julius 16

OAS *see* Organization of American States
OAU *see* Organization of African Unity
Obasanjo, Olusegun 47, 62, 66
Ogata, Sadako 20, 256, 257, 282
oil crises (1973/1979) 29, 30
Olusegun
O'Neill, Robert 135
OPCW *see* Organisation for the Prohibition of Chemical Weapons
OPEC (Organization of Petroleum-Exporting Countries) 29
Opertti, Didier (Uruguay) 235, 236
Organisation for the Prohibition of Chemical Weapons (OPCW) 290
Organization of African Unity (OAU) 230
Organization of American States (OAS) 223, 230, 231; Human Rights Commission 232
Organization of Petroleum-Exporting Countries 29
Ortner, S.B. 267
Our Common Future (Brundtland Commission report) 76, 78, 80, 82, 84, 94, 256; contents 85–8; radicalism 89
Our Global Neighbourhood (UN Global Governance Commission report) 9, 13, 14, 40, 100, 104, 119, 279; criticisms 115–17; impact of report 113–17
Owen, David 47, 61, 65, 66

Pact of San Jose (1969) 232
Pagnucco, Ron 53
Pakistan 68, 214; nuclear power status 110, 133, 138
Palestine/Palestinians 169, 213; refugees 268; and Taba negotiations (2000) 269; West Bank and Gaza 268, 269
Palme Commission 6, 9, 11, 12, 14, 15, 17–18, 19, 46–75; funding 48; influence on Gorbachev and Soviet Union 63, 64, 67; international policy context 49–60; and international security 51–7, 62; origins, membership, leadership 47–9; reports 8, 13, 17, 18, 119; success/failure assessment 60–7; *see also Common Security* (1982), *A World at Peace* (1989)
Palme, Olaf 11, 14, 31, 40, 46, 47, 48, 49, 65
Paraguay 145
Paris Conference (1975–1977) 38
Pastrana, President Andrés 233
Patkar, Medha 149
Paul VI, Pope 29
peace movements 49–50, 52
peace processes: as key symbols 267; Middle East 267, 268, 270
Peace Research Institute of Oslo (PRIO) 51
Pearson Commission 11, 12, 32, 33; report (1969) 10
Pearson, Lester 10, 15, 27
Pérez de Cuellar, Javier 82, 95
Pericaz, Deputy Minister (Brazil) 236
Persian Gulf 66
Persson, Goran 14, 168
Peru 233, 242
the Philippines 149
Pinochet, General Augusto 222
Plan of Action women's conference (Mexico City 1975) 252
Plan Colombia 233
Platform for Action women's conference (Beijing 1995) 249, 250, 252, 257, 258, 260, 261
Pol Pot 229
Poland 57
political legitimacy 271–2
political realism 6, 182, 183, 183–4
population growth 92, 112–13
pornography industry 250
post-Cold War: and nuclear weapon reduction 124, 133, 137; politics and diplomacy 126, 129–30; and security debates/issues 125, 130–2; systemic changes 102, 108–12
poverty: alleviation/elimination 114; and Brandt Report 37, 41–2; and developing states 86; as key symbol 267; in refugee camps 269; and women's rights 247, 250; and World Bank 90
Prager, Carol 115–16
Pratt, Cranford 35
Preventing Deadly Conflict (Carnegie Commission final report) 284
principle of non-intervention 221–45

principle of "right authority" 210
PRIO *see* Peace Research Institute of Oslo
Programme for Survival (Brandt) 85
Progressive Governance Summit (London 2003) 216
Pronk, Jan 101
protection *see* "responsibility to protect" concept
Puerto Rico 231

Qureshi, Moeen 283

Ramphal, Shridath "Sonny" 11, 40, 47–8, 62, 65, 66, 82, 101
rape, as tool of war 248
Reagan administration 49, 53, 63, 80; and SDI 80
Reagan, Ronald 30, 38–9, 49, 53, 64
REAL Women of Canada 258
Refugee Working Group 267–8, 269
refugees 214; and discrimination 270; and effects of war 248; Palestinian 267–8; study of Palestinian camps 268–70; and women's status 257
religion: organizations 271; rights 249–50
The Report of the Independent Inquiry into the Actions of the United Nations during the 1994 Genocide in Rwanda 170
Report of the Panel on United Nations Peace Operations 170
The Report of the Secretary-General Pursuant to General Assembly Resolution 53/35 (1998) 170
reproductive rights 250, 255, 258, 259
research/researchers 266
responsibility: and sovereignty 201; spectrum of 201–3; to rebuild 210–11
"responsibility to protect" concept 20, 181, 184, 185, 186–7; and conflict prevention 188–9; and humanitarian/military intervention 193, 206–7, 221–45; and ICISS report 198–220; and prevention/reconstruction 202–3, 210–11; and war on terrorism 214–15
Richardson, Elliot 285
Rieff, David 175
Rio Group 234, 235; document key subjects 238–40; Santiago Summit (2001) 242; Working Group 241–2
Rio Tinto Corporation 114
Risse-Kappen, Thomas 58
Roberts, Adam 52
Robinson, Mary 256, 257
Roman Catholicism 249; Holy See 254, 258
Rosenau, James 109
Rosenfeld, Stephen S. 53
Rothschild, Emma 62, 66
Ruggae, John 2, 4–5
Rupnik, Professor Jacques 169
Russia 83, 139, 169; and Chechnya 190, 204, 206, 213; and Kosovo stance 227; and regional security 56
Russo-Chinese-Indian borders 62
Rwandan genocide 20, 170, 176, 180–1, 194, 205, 208, 221; and HI guidelines 229, 232; Special Tribual for War Crimes 222; UN failure to act 226–7

Sachs, Jeffrey 18
Sachs, Wolfgang 76, 78, 89, 91, 92–3, 95
SADC *see* Southern African Development Community
Sahnoun, Mohamed 182, 199
Said, E. 268
Salim, Dr. Salim Ahmed (Tanzania) 48
Salim, Elim (Indonesia) 83
Samkange, Stanlake 183
Sandoz fire disaster (Switzerland 1984) 80
Santos, Brazil 90
Save the Narmada Movement (India) 149
SDI *see* Strategic Defence Initiative (US)
"Second Cold War", and armed conflicts 49
security issues 46, 234; collective 232; and development 42; multilateral agreements 132; preventive detention 206; regional dialogues 55–6; *see also* borders; common security; Palme Commission
Seers, Dudley 35, 37
Sen, Amartya 20
Serbia 209
Sierra Leone 176, 221, 226
Singer, Hans W. 35, 36, 37
Singh, Jasjit 22
Singh, Manmohan 16
SIPRI *see* Stockholm International Peace Research Institute
Slaughter, Anne-Marie 7
Smoke, Richard 53–4
Smouts, Marie-Claude 103
social democrats 37
Social Learning Group 80

social rights issue 249–50
social science: four types of products 267
Socialists International 47
Soedjatmoko 48, 62
solidarity (international) 33, 42, 184
Solo, Pam 53
Somalia 180, 214, 226
Sommer, Theo 169
South Africa 17, 149, 260; post-apartheid 56
South African Armed Forces 56
South Asia 158
South Commission (1987–1990) 16
South Korea 39
Southern Africa 66
Southern African Development Community (SADC) 216
Southern Alliance for Indigenous Resources 90
sovereignty: as changing concept 200–1, 204; and decolonization era 186; and global interdependence 187; and humanitarian interventions 181–2, 185–8; and Latin America 231; and military intervention 223; and non-intervention 186–7, 202; as responsibility 187–8; state/national/constitutional 185–6, 198
Soviet Union (USSR): border disputes 55; and common security concept 56–7, 64; ending of Cold War 56–60, 80; and Palme Commission 47, 57–60; and US 46, 49
Spain 145
Special Tribunal for War Crimes in the former Yugoslavia 222, 254
Srebrenica 180
START *see* Strategic Arms Reduction Treaty
State of the World Forum: The Commission on Globalization 21
Statement by International Civilian Leaders 123
Statement on Nuclear Weapons by International Generals and Admirals (1996) 123
state(s): and global governance 104; and international human rights 250; responsibilities 203–4, 226; sovereignty 185–8
Stewart, Frances 35
Stiglitz, Joseph 266
Stimson Centre (Washington) 66; Steering Committee reports 123, 126, 134
Stockholm 169
Stockholm Conference (1972) 78
Stockholm Initiative on Global Security and Governance (1991) 101
Stockholm International Peace Research Institute (SIPRI) 51, 52
Stoltenberg, Jens 270
Strange, Susan 35
Strategic Arms Reduction Treaty (START) II 125
Strategic Defence Initiative (SDI) 52, 57, 59, 60, 80
Strengthening Palestinian Public Institutions report 275
Strong, Maurice 19, 78, 79, 82, 83, 93
sub-Saharan Africa: economy 39
subsidiarity 108
Successor Vision study (Richardson et al.) 285
Sudan 258
Summits of the Americas (1994, 1998, 2001) 232, 234
sustainable development 20, 21, 65, 183, 203, 252, 256; and business/economic aspects 91; concept and definition 76–7, 79–82, 85–6, 95, 112, 256; and dam construction 142, 144, 147, 154, 160; and environmental discourse 78, 93–4; financing 88; and Global Compact 115; as key symbol 267; promotion/acceptance of concept 83–4, 87, 90, 92; radicalism of concept 89
Sweden 17, 145, 152; anti-Americanism 66; and Palm Report 51, 66
Switzerland 145, 149, 250
Syria 133

Taba negotiations (2000) 269
Taiwan 145
Tanzania 186
temporary international non-governmental organizations *see* TINGOs
terrorism *see* international terrorism
Thacher, Peter 78
Thailand 145; and East Timor intervention 230
Tham, Carl 169
Thatcher, Margaret 30, 84

think-tanks 266–76; authority and legitimacy 271; importance of networks 272; and key symbols 267; and policy agendas 274–5; and social policy 270; Stimston Centre, Washington 66
Third Industrial Revolution 221
Third World: and Brandt Report 33, 34, 37; and Palme Commission 65; and US 39; weapons imports 34, 110–11
Three Mile Island nuclear disaster (1979) 80
Tibet 210
Tinbergen, Jan 35
TINGOs (temporary international non-governmental organizations) 60–1, 65, 66, 68
Tokyo Forum 22, 124, 138; report on Reducing Nuclear Dangers 134, 138
Tolba, Mostafa 82
Toronto Conference: "The Changing Atmosphere ..." (1988) 83, 84
transarmament 51
transnational issues 102–3; groups and network analysis 68–9
Treaty of Westphalia (1648) 198, 223
Tucker, Robert 35

The UN in Its Second Half Century (Qureshi, Weizsäcker et al.) 283
UNA-USA *see* United Nations Association of the USA
UNCED *see* United Nations Conference on Environment and Development (1992)
UNCTAD *see* United Nations Conference on Trade and Development
UNDP *see* United Nations Development Programme
UNEP *see* United Nations Environment Programme
UNGA *see* United Nations General Assembly
UNHCE *see* United Nations Conference on the Human Environment
UNHCR *see* United Nations High Commissioner for Refugees
United Kingdom (UK) 64, 169; *see also* Britain
United Nations Association of the USA (UNA-USA) 277, 285
United Nations Charter 105, 106, 174, 180, 184, 191, 192–3, 216; and human rights 223, 259; and sovereignty 226; and the use of force 241–2, 243; and women's rights 246
United Nations Charter of Human Rights 223
United Nations Commission on Human Rights 253, 254; Special Rapporteur on Violence Against Women 253
United Nations Commission on Private Sector and Development 22
United Nations Commission on the Status of Women 246, 252, 253, 254
United Nations Commission on Sustainable Development 89
United Nations Committee on the Elimination of Discrimination against Women 253, 260
United Nations Conference on Environment and Development (1992) (UNCED) 79, 80, 81, 89, 91; Agenda 21 89–90
United Nations Conference on the Human Environment (UNCHE) 78; *see also* Stockholm Conference (1972)
United Nations Conference on Trade and Development (UNCTAD) 28, 29
United Nations Conferences on Disarmament, Geneva (1982) 13, 48
United Nations Development Fund for Women (UNIFEM) 253
United Nations Development Programme (UNDP) 28, 102–3, 294; Human Development Report (1993) 234
United Nations Division for the Advancement of Women (DAW) 252–3, 254
United Nations Earth Summit (Rio de Janeiro 1992) 90
United Nations Economic and Social Council 106, 252, 253, 254
United Nations Environment Programme (UNEP) 78, 92–3; Dams and Development Unit 159
United Nations Experts Group 62
United Nations Foundation 152, 279
United Nations Framework Convention on Climate Change (2002) 91
United Nations General Assembly (UNGA) 29, 78–9, 80, 106, 125, 133, 174, 191, 215; Emergency Special Session 193–4; and humanitarian intervention

199, 228–9; and Rio Group 235; and women's rights 247, 252
United Nations High Commissioner for Human Rights 242, 257
United Nations High Commissioner for Refugees (UNHCR) 184, 242
United Nations International Conference on Population and Development (ICPD) (Cairo 1994) 249, 250, 259
United Nations International Research and Training Institute for the Advancement of Women (INSTRAW) 253
United Nations Millennium Declaration 90
United Nations Millennium Summit (2000) 18, 41, 199, 223
United Nations New Agenda Coalition 134
United Nations Office of the Secretary-General 106
United Nations Organization (UN): authority of 191–4; budgetary process 106; criticisms 170–1; development and record 99–100; promotion of women's rights 246–65; proposed Forum of Civil Society 106; proposed People's Assembly 106; reforms/progress 105–6, 215–16; and state sovereignty 186–7, 223; volunteer force proposal 106
United Nations Peacekeeping Operations 13, 210
United Nations Reform Commissions 8, 277–87; assessment/lessons drawn 279–80, 282; caveats, worries, provocations 285–7; costs and funding 281, 282, 285–6; follow-ups 281; General Assembly Strengthening Working Group 277; panel composition 285; projects/examples 281, 282–5, 286; reform proposals 277–8; standards of success 278–9; studies and reports 279, 281, 282–3, 284, 285–6
United Nations Secretary-General and Secretariat 28, 191, 254; *see also* named Secretaries-General
United Nations Security Council 106, 171, 180–1, 186–7; and authorization for intervention 226; five permanent members (P-5) veto 227–8; and ICISS report 215–16; and military interventions 191–4, 205, 209, 215; and responsibility to protect 210; and use of veto 209–10, 215, 242
United Nations Special Session on Disarmament (UNSSOD) 13, 48, 62
United Nations Sub-Commission on Prevention of Discrimination and Protection of Minorities 253
United Nations World Conference on Human Rights (Vienna 1993) 249, 250, 259, 260; Vienna Declaration and Programme of Action 254
United Nations World Summit on Sustainable Development (UNWSSD) 91, 92, 250
United Nations – business collaboration 115
United States (US): and Canberra Commission report 139; and Cancùn Summit (2001) 38; common security discourse 53–4, 56, 63; foreign policy 274–5; and humanitarian intervention 228; and ICISS report 215–16; and international commissions 286; and international politics 139; and Korean Airlines incident 57, 80; Kosovo Commission 169; and national sovereignty 185; nuclearism resurgence 135; and Palme Commission 52, 54; post-September 2001 attacks 136, 206; resistance to Tokyo Forum 22; and Soviet Union 46, 49; and Third World 39; and thresholds for military intervention 205, 206; and women's rights 250; and World Commission on Dams 145, 149
Universal Declaration of Human Rights 191–2
UNOCAL 114
UNSSOD *see* United Nations Special Session on Disarmament
UNWSSD *see* United Nations World Summit for Sustainable Development
Urban, Jan 169
Urquhart, Brian 255, 285
Uruguay 236–7, 243
US National Academy of Sciences, Committee on International Security and Arms Control reports 123
USA PATRIOT Act 214
USSR 38; *see also* Soviet Union

Vance, Cyrus 15, 47, 48, 54, 64, 65, 283
Vayrynen, Raimo 17, 18, 66

Venezuela 236
Vienna Declaration and Programme of Action (1993) 254
Vietnam 56
Vietnam War 66
violence: against women 247, 251; culture 111–12; triggers 202
Volcker, Paul 282

Wallerstein, Immanuel 35
Ward, Barbara 35, 37
war(s): civilian casualties 223, 248; internal conflicts 221; just 206–7, 210; legality and justification 175–6, 190–1; and refugees 248; on terrorism 213; *see also* conflicts; humanitarian interventions; military interventions
Warsaw Pact 47, 49
Washington Post 53
water supplies 143; irrigation 143, 150
Waterman, Peter 116
WB *see* World Bank
WCD *see* World Commission on Dams/ World Conference on Dams
WCED *see* World Commission on Environment and Development
weapons: proliferation 103, 105; small arms proliferation 110–11
weapons of mass destruction (WMDs) 68, 110, 288–94; biological 292; chemical 292; delivery systems 293; disarmament/non-proliferation efforts 293–4; and international terrorism 288; nuclear 291–2; outer space 293; potential for terrorism 293
Weiss, Thomas W. 183, 199
Weizsäcker, Richard von 283
West Germany 51
Western Europe 52, 55, 63–5
Wheeler, Nicholas 64, 209, 229
WHO *see* World Health Organization
WMD *see* weapons of mass destruction
women: abortion 256; advancement and empowerment 253–4, 256; and cross-border prostitution rackets 250; and educational rights 247, 250, 255, 256, 258; and human rights 249–50; rape and sexual abuse 248, 254, 257; as refugees 248, 257; roles in international commissions 19–20, 32, 149, 151; and social services 251; social status 249; and UN system 255–6; *see also* women's rights
Women's Environment and Development Organization 255
women's rights: and cultural relativism 249–50; gender concept and analysis 248, 249; health care 251; ideas and conceptual shift 247–51; overview 246–7; precedence controversy 249–50; progress 261–2; promotion factors 255–61; and religion 249; reproductive rights 250, 255, 258, 259; UN integration with Human Rights 254; UN promotion 246–65; sexual rights 258; violations 249–50
Woods, Ngaire 2–3
A World at Peace (Palme Commission final report, 1989) 49
World Bank (WB) 28, 36, 88, 111, 275; and international commissions 12–13; as international think tank 31; Operation Evaluation Department 146; and sustainable development 90; and World Commission on Dams 146, 152, 156
World Charter for Nature 78
World Commission on Dams (WCD) 6, 12–13; activities/Work Programme 153–5, 156, 158; case studies 158; commissioners/secretariat composition 147, 148–51; conclusions 161–5; constituent structures 148–53; Forum 151–2, 155, 156, 157, 159; funding/ resources 152–3, 158, 160; genesis 142–6; guiding principles 147–8; post-commission follow-up 159; private sector participation 157, 160; purpose and nature 146–8; report 159–60; results and challenges 156–61; stakeholder representation/involvement 149–50, 153, 154, 157–8; time factor 158–9; *see also* Gland Reference Group
World Commission on Environment and Development (WCED) 10, 11, 13, 14, 15, 76–98, 156, 256, 272; origins and formation 78–85; reflections on 93–5; report 40; significance of 88–93; *see also* Brundtland Commission; *Our Common Future*
World Commission on the Social Dimension of Globalization 22; *see also* ILO Commission

World Conference on Dams (WCD) 12, 18, 20; *see also* World Commission on Dams (WCD)
World Conferences on Women: First (Mexico City 1975) 246, 247–8, 252, 260; Second (Copenhagen 1979) 247, 260; Third (Nairobi 1985) 247, 249, 261; Fourth (Beijing 1995) 247, 249, 254, 257, 259, 260–1
World Conservation Strategy 78
World Conservation Union *see* IUCN
World Court Project 125
World Development Fund 33
World Economic Forum (Davos 1999) 113–14
world economy stagnation 30
World Health Organization (WHO) 256–7, 290
World Summit on Sustainable Development (Johannesburg 2002) 90, 250
world trade 34
World Trade Organization (WTO) 16, 28
World Wildlife Fund (WWF) 78
Worlds in Collision (Booth and Dunne) 67–8
WSSD *see* World Summit on Social Development
WTO *see* World Trade Organization
WWF *see* World Wildlife Fund

Xinjiang 210

Yakovlev, Aleksandr 58
Yale University 283
Young, Iris Marion 175
Young, Oran 129–30
Yugoslavia 188, 222; *see also* Kosovo

Zedillo, Ernesto 22
Zimbabwe 90